Dilemmas of Intervention

Social Science for Stabilization and Reconstruction

Edited by Paul K. Davis

Contributors: Claude Berrebi, Christopher S. Chivvis, Paul K. Davis, Sarah Olmstead, Julie E. Taylor, Véronique Thelen, Stephen Watts, Elizabeth Wilke

Prepared for the Office of the Secretary of Defense

Approved for public release; distribution unlimited

NATIONAL DEFENSE RESEARCH INSTITUTE

The research described in this report was prepared for the Office of the Secretary of Defense (OSD). The research was conducted within the RAND National Defense Research Institute, a federally funded research and development center sponsored by OSD, the Joint Staff, the Unified Combatant Commands, the Navy, the Marine Corps, the defense agencies, and the defense Intelligence Community under Contract W74V8H-06-C-0002.

Library of Congress Cataloging-in-Publication Data

Dilemmas of intervention : social science for stabilization and reconstruction / edited by Paul K. Davis.
    p. cm.
    Includes bibliographical references.
    ISBN 978-0-8330-5249-0 (pbk. : alk. paper)
  1. Nation-building. 2. Peace-building. 3. Postwar reconstruction. I. Davis, Paul K., 1943–

    JZ6300.D54 2011
    327.1—dc23
                                                                      2011036807

Published 2011 by the RAND Corporation
1776 Main Street, P.O. Box 2138, Santa Monica, CA 90407-2138
1200 South Hayes Street, Arlington, VA 22202-5050
4570 Fifth Avenue, Suite 600, Pittsburgh, PA 15213-2665
RAND URL: http://www.rand.org/
To order RAND documents or to obtain additional information, contact
Distribution Services: Telephone: (310) 451-7002;
Fax: (310) 451-6915; Email: order@rand.org

Preface

Education

This monograph surveys and integrates scholarly social-science litera-ture relating to stabilization and reconstruction (S&R). Its intent is to inform analysis and decisionmaking within the Department of Defense and other government agencies concerned with international interven-tions in the wake of conflict. It is a follow-on to a prior RAND study reviewing and integrating work on terrorism and counterterrorism:

> Paul K. Davis and Kim Cragin, eds., *Social Science for Counter-terrorism: Putting the Pieces Together*, Santa Monica, Calif.: RAND Corporation, 2009.

The project was sponsored by the Modeling and Simulation Coor-dination Office of the Office of the Secretary of Defense (OSD), with oversight provided by James Bexfield, the Director of Planning and Analytical Support in OSD's Cost and Program Evaluation (CAPE) and the Irregular Warfare Modeling and Simulation Senior Advisory Group. Comments and questions are welcome and should be addressed to the editor and project leader, Paul K. Davis (Santa Monica, Califor-nia; pdavis@rand.org).

This research was conducted within the International Security and Defense Policy Center of the RAND National Defense Research Institute, a federally funded research and development center spon-sored by the Office of the Secretary of Defense, the Joint Staff, the Uni-fied Combatant Commands, the Navy, the Marine Corps, the defense agencies, and the defense Intelligence Community.

For more information on the RAND International Security and Defense Policy Center, see http://www.rand.org/nsrd/ndri/centers/isdp.html or contact the director (contact information is provided on the web page).

Contents

Figures

Tables

Summary

Paul K. Davis

Introduction

Objectives and Scope

Governments intervening in post-conflict states find themselves beset with numerous challenges and profound dilemmas: It is often unclear how best to proceed because measures that may improve conditions in one respect may undermine them in another. Our study was an integrative review of the scholarly social-science literature relevant to stabilization and reconstruction (S&R). We sought to inform strategic planning at the whole-of-government level. Thus, we deal not only with stability operations—i.e., operations to maintain or reestablish a safe and secure environment, provide essential governmental services, construct emergency infrastructure, and offer humanitarian relief—but also possible activities related to transition, reconstruction, and nation-building.

Our research drew from such subject areas as civil wars, conflict resolution, conflict prevention, developmental economics, political development and political economy, stability operations, peacekeeping, and intervention. This base reflected such disciplines as economics, political science, policy analysis, sociology, psychology, history, and anthropology. We also drew on practitioner-informed works by the U.S. Institute of Peace, the State Department's Office of the Coordinator for Reconstruction and Stabilization (S/CRS), foundations, RAND, and other civilian and military organizations.

Approach

We took a "system view," attempting to view the entire system rather than just one or another separate component. Figure S.1 is a top-level depiction of the problem space.* It asserts that S&R success depends on success in *each* of four component domains dealing, respectively, with security, political, social, and economic issues. We treat these as individually critical: Achieving some threshold level of success in each component is *necessary* for overall success. Although this concept is often mentioned informally, we build it into analysis. Just as a military commander knows that he *must* attend to logistics as well as to maneuver, so also intervenors must attend to all of the critical components indicated. Further, to understand a situation or draw conclusions from data, analysts need to address all of the critical components and their nonlinear interactions. More foreign aid to a post-conflict country, for example, should be *expected* to do no good if the security situation is sufficiently abysmal.

Figure S.1
The Four Top-Level Components and Their Interactions

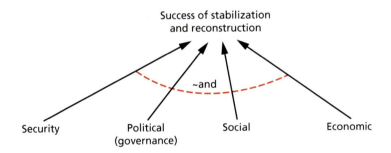

NOTE: The factors apply at a snapshot in time.
RAND *MG1119-S.1*

---

* Figure S.1 is a "factor tree" depicting the factors that contribute to a phenomenon at a given time. If one factor points to another, then more of the former will tend to increase the latter. The notation "~and" means that, to a first approximation, some threshold values of all of the factors are necessary for overall success. Such factor trees apply at a snapshot in time and do not show feedback effects and other cross-factor interactions over time. Thus, they tell only part of the story.

Figure S.1 provides a static view, but the S&R challenge is dynamic: Over time, "everything is connected to everything," as depicted in Figure S.2. This interconnectedness makes analytic work difficult, but recognizing it is essential to meaningful communication and good S&R planning. Separating the two perspectives (of Figures S.1 and S.2) allows us to modularize in functionally natural ways and to reason in causal terms at a given time, while recognizing that—over longer periods of time—interconnections are complex and the usual concept of causality is troublesome. Sometimes, interactions are more immediate.

A third element of our system approach is recognizing that the effects of an approach, or of individual factors, depend on the context, i.e., the situation or case. As an example, increasing intervenor troops to stabilize a chaotic situation (a first case) may initially be effective and greeted with enthusiasm, but—if foreign troops become associated with occupation rather than stabilization (a second case)—more of them may worsen a situation rather than improve it.

Alternative courses of action, then, need to be assessed as a function of case, perhaps as illustrated schematically by Table S.1, which imagines four factors. Each row would represent a different case. The table also recognizes (in the last column) that, in the realm of S&R,

Figure S.2
Over Time, Everything Affects Everything

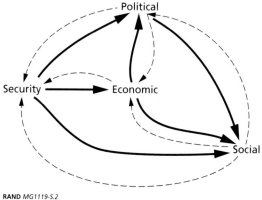

RAND *MG1119-S.2*

Table S.1
Notional Decision Aid for Choosing Strategy as Function of Case

Case	Factor 1	Factor 2	Factor 3	Factor 4	Approach	Hedges
...(many rows)						

choosing an approach is fraught with uncertainties. Thus, the approach should include hedging actions and monitoring to allow subsequent adaptations. This is consistent with the experience of practitioners.

Against this background, the next four sections discuss the four components of the S&R challenge. They are followed by some analytic observations and a short set of conclusions. The full monograph includes extensive references to the original literature.

Establishing Favorable Security Conditions

An Integrating Conceptual Model

Establishing security is a sine qua non for success in S&R: Without establishing a fair degree of security first, it is nearly impossible to proceed effectively on the other fronts. Subsequently, how quickly the quality of security improves further will depend in part on progress on the other component efforts. Although we focus primarily on what are nominally post-conflict interventions, some level of insurgency (resistance) may continue, and the level may escalate suddenly. Thus, dealing with and deterring increases of resistance is a major part of establishing security.

The scholarly literature on aspects of establishing security is fragmented, but we constructed a unifying conceptual model that draws on concepts implicit in the various literatures. Figure S.3 is a top-level view of the conceptual model in the form of a factor tree indicating, at a snapshot in time, what factors affect degree of security. The values of those factors can depend on previous values of the other factors.

Figure S.3
Factors Influencing Degree of Security

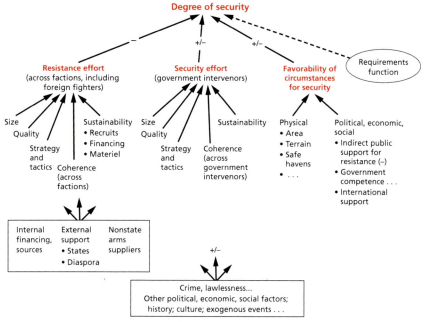

NOTE: The factors apply at a snapshot in time.
RAND *MG1119-S.3*

The issue highlighted at the top of Figure S.3 is the *degree* of security. This is shown as depending primarily on the resistance effort, the security effort, favorability of circumstances, and something we call the "requirements function." The resistance and security efforts depend on the size and quality of forces, their strategy and tactics (e.g., purely kinetic or population-centric), their coherence, and their sustainability. Favorability of circumstances relates to case. For example, an insurgency may be assisted by terrain that provides cover, or by the existence of sanctuary in neighboring countries. As indicated at the bottom left of the figure, both public support and external foreign support for the opposition are also important—not just by providing resources, but through mechanisms such as tolerating the opposition's presence rather than informing authorities or by arguing the case for the opposition internationally.

We highlight the requirements function because it is currently unclear how much security effort is "enough," even if we know how to characterize resistance and situation. This can be seen in today's operations in Afghanistan. Historical experience suggests the need for far more "boots on the ground" than exist currently. However, the new technology-intensive tactics may prove to be a big force multiplier. That history has not yet been written.

Finally, along the bottom of Figure S.3 are boxes indicating factors, such as the level of crime and lawlessness, that have cross-cutting effects on the factors in the tree. Some such effects may be positive or negative, as indicated by a + or − symbol.

Figure S.4 illustrates what an analytic formulation might look like if knowledge were better developed. Three curves are shown for substantially different levels of resistance, but sometimes with large

Figure S.4
Security Achieved as a Function of Effort and Resistance

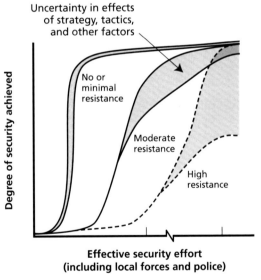

uncertainties (the gray areas), reflecting uncertainties in the requirements function for different strategies and tactics.

Figure S.5 addresses the key issue of whether the opposition
chooses to resist, i.e., to restart, or escalate, conflict. Figure S.5 reflects
both rational-choice modeling and recognition of other factors. If fully
rational, the opposition's leaders effectively consider the pros and cons
of the alternatives and their probabilities. They consider not just their
"best guesses" about what would happen, but also best-case and worst-
case variants. For example, they may see the most likely outcome of
cooperation (right side) as their participation in government and a
degree of rights and services. However, a darker possibility (risk) is that

Figure S.5
Factors Affecting the Decision to Renew Fighting

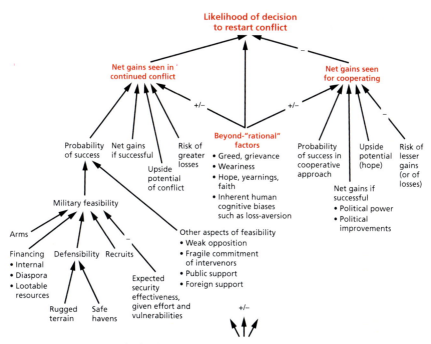

NOTE: The factors apply at a snapshot in time.
RAND *MG1119-S.5*

the government will renege and repress further opposition brutally once the opposition leaders come out of hiding and lay down arms. Looking to the option to restart conflict (left side), the opposition might expect a long struggle with no clear-cut victory or defeat, but might also see the alluring possibility of decisive victory at some point (upside potential). However, it might see the risk that, if war starts up again, the state would achieve a total victory, with no incentive for accommodation or inclusion; the opposition might be annihilated, not just defeated. Even a highly rational opposition has difficulties making choices given such uncertainties.

Reality is even more complicated because decisions are *not* fully rational, even though most of the literature uses a rational-choice model. The blood may be running so hot that any suggestion of compromise by either side's leadership will be unacceptable to its constituents. Conversely, if a leadership has the desire to fight on (or is more risk-taking in nature), the rank and file may be too war-weary to comply. Both practitioners and scholars refer to windows of opportunity and vulnerability.

Finally, *those making the decisions are often far more concerned with personal or in-group survival and power than with what might be best for the people at large.* Thus, even if "rational," leaders' actions may injure their country.

Clearly, the ability of outsiders to predict what the state or opposition will do in a given post-conflict situation will often be quite limited. Nonetheless, this model identifies the factors and considerations at work.

Measuring the Constructs of the Security Model

The scholarly literature does not define how to measure the constructs described above, but we have suggestions:

- Degree of security can probably be measured by using an index variable of the sort familiar to social scientists. Having a uniform standard would allow semi-quantitative discussion good enough for discussing alternative strategies.

- Security effort could be measured with "equivalent scores" reflecting number of personnel, equipment and modernization, quality, and combined-arms mix. Such scoring has long been used for good-enough calculations in force planning and operational planning.
- Resistance could be measured similarly, but would also need to reflect the differences between, e.g., active and passive support by the population.
- It might prove possible to classify situations and, for each such case, reflect the effects of modern technology and tactics as "multipliers" of the security and resistance efforts.

Establishing Favorable Political Conditions

General Observations

The second component of S&R noted in Figure S.1 is political, dealing with establishing effective governance in a country that is at peace with its neighbors and responsive to the concerns of its citizens. That might be accomplished in innumerable ways, but intervenors often plunge ahead in ways reflecting their own history and ways of doing things, which can be a poor fit for the country in question for reasons of history, culture, and circumstance.

What, then, are the bare essentials? The core requirements? The three most fundamental are that the government is

- *Stable*: Free of internal or external threats to the nation, its constitution, and its governmental system.
- *Functioning*: Able to take and implement effective decisions, providing core services to the nation's people.
- *Legitimate and Accountable*: Subject to censure or removal if officials violate established rules, laws, and rights; and legitimate internationally.

Figure S.6 summarizes these in the form of a corresponding factor tree identifying general factors contributing to the quality of gover-

Figure S.6
Factors Determining the Quality of Governance

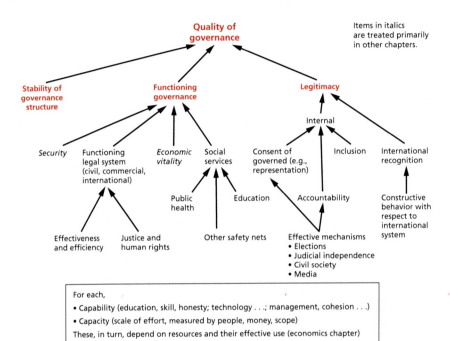

NOTES: The factors apply at a snapshot in time. Bulleted items are mere examples.
RAND *MG1119-S.6*

nance, independent of its precise form. As shown at the bottom, success depends also on capability, capacity, and implementation (e.g., including control of corruption, which can infect all aspects of S&R). Real-world governments may fall short in some factors but still be "adequate" in some sense. In principle, an autocratic government can be high-functioning even if it has little other political legitimacy. A democratic government may have high legitimacy but be dysfunctional.

A considerable degree of scholarly consensus exists on political goals to be emphasized (which relate closely to the factors in Figure S.1), particularly (1) dispersing benefits, (2) assuring that factions participate in governance and decisionmaking, (3) establishing barriers against excessive centralization and exclusion, and (4) creating self-enforcing mechanisms to assure accountability and responsiveness. However, identifying such general goals is one thing; choosing among *approaches* to governance is another, as is deciding on criteria of adequacy.

Attempting to actually create or enhance a government raises sensitive issues, such as (1) partitioning as an option for a post-conflict situation, (2) different regime types, (3) differing arrangements for power-sharing, (4) connecting the government to the people (i.e., establishing legitimacy), and (5) enforcement of state-society obligations. What is feasible and desirable depends on the situation, including the history of how the war came about in the first place, root problems, and the nature of leaders and parties, who often operate for selfish purposes. Such social-science emphasis on context dependence is sometimes disappointing to those looking for formulas, but the discussion has an important implication for intervenors:

> An early *priority* should be understanding: the country's human, economic, and cultural make-up; sources of contention; capacities and objectives of the factions; available state-building options; and an honest assessment of intervenors' commitment and capabilities.

This would be unexceptionable except that intervenors often do not build this base of information early, but rather proceed apace with insufficient knowledge.

Political Dilemmas

Pursuing broad goals is difficult because intervenors almost invariably encounter dilemmas. Not only do they find competing "theories" about how to proceed, they also find that any approach taken is likely to have significant side effects. Table S.2 describes three conflicting paradigms that have been used by U.S. policymakers over the past several decades—all of which are still in play. Controlled state-building sees economic development as the primary engine. Liberal-democratic state-building emphasizes inclusion and democratization. Decentralized S&R suggests minimalist objectives overall (primarily stabilization) and stresses "bottom-up" developments in which local communities and power holders set priorities, in which case governance is more distributed and local.

Table S.2
Conflicting Paradigms for Thinking About Governance Dilemmas

Paradigm	Priorities	Economic Concept	Political Concept	Security Concept
Controlled state-building	Economic growth, state capacity	Economics is engine of modernization.	Democratization is the long-term result of growth, but its success depends on preconditions.	A strong state must protect against violent challenges.
Liberal-democratic state-building	Political inclusion, equitable growth	Economic growth improves incentives for peace, but only if equitable and sustainable.	Democratization is crucial to achieving stability and movement toward sound state.	Security is achieved through political inclusion and military transparency.
Decentralized S&R	Minimalist objectives: absence of large-scale violence	Local communities, power-holders should set their own economic priorities.	Political inclusion and accountability are important, but may occur outside the formal state and differ between localities.	Stability is achieved when localities are secure from each other and able to maintain stability within their regions.

Upon reviewing these conflicting paradigms and a long list of common political dilemmas, we identified three composite dilemmas that are common in S&R:

- *Inclusion*: Should the approach emphasize short-term political order, which might translate into military solutions followed by autocracy and repression, or should it emphasize negotiated solutions that may be more inclusive and less repressive, but might also be fragile and even ineffective?
- *State Capacity*: Should the approach favor a strong and efficient central state, which will probably require high cost and extended commitments, or should it emphasize achieving more informal governance quickly and at lower cost, but with the resulting government quite possibly being unable to provide services effectively?

- *Transition*: Should the approach emphasize institutions and practices good for securing an end to war, or institutions better suited to the long term, with the dilemma being that power relationships created to promote an end to war tend to resist subsequent transitions?

The dilemmas are real and no formulaic solutions exist. Nonetheless, we can offer admonitions and suggestions, as summarized in Table S.3. If a relatively inclusive and legitimate state exists that external intervenors are willing to support, then one of the most important tools for stabilization is to reduce state vulnerability by reducing resources available to the opposition. This may require regional security arrangements, especially when neighboring states support insurgency or other mischief or are part of a solution. Other mechanisms include buyer cartels and neotrusteeships (i.e., governance that includes significant multilateral external control, as occurred in Bosnia and East

Table S.3
Dealing with Political Dilemmas

Admonition	Examples of Mechanisms for Intervenors to Use or Encourage
1. Reduce state vulnerability by reducing opposition's resources.	Regional security arrangements Buyers' cartels? Neotrusteeship?
2. Arrange for appropriate power balance.	Countervailing mechanisms, such as constitutional inclusiveness, peacekeepers, guarantees, costs
3. Shape negotiations and operations based on reality of power balances.	Avoiding incentives to change "facts on ground" Avoiding disconnects between *de jure* and actual practices unless means and will to enforce compliance exist
4. Protect vulnerable groups (moral imperative and pragmatic necessity).	Developing and using institutions Using carrots and sticks to influence competing factions
5. Plan for evolution of parties' bases of power.	Anticipation of transitions Incentives drawing people into formal institutions and rule of law
6. Work through or around governments.	Base strategy on circumstances, i.e., the governance quality and the governance capacity

Timor, among many other cases). These are especially useful when insurgents are using "lootable resources," such as oil or diamonds, to fund their activities.

Achieving an appropriate power balance is often difficult (as in today's Iraq), but mechanisms include constitutional guarantees, international peacekeepers, and carrots and sticks to influence leaders. Early on, power-balance issues can be crucial. The literature warns against creating incentives to change facts on the ground (e.g., seizures of territory) during negotiations. It also suggests that any incongruence between legal/constitutional dictates and those that actually apply on the ground will have to be enforced by external parties, which suggests that negotiators limit their aspirations in what will be enforceable later. Planning transitions is another aspect of S&R, since power bases change and incentives are needed to encourage leaders, and the people more generally, to join in developing institutions and activities under the rule of law.

Table S.4 suggests how strategy, including positive and negative inducements, might vary across cases differing in whether the external circumstances for negotiated peace are favorable (e.g., are third parties willing to provide guarantees; are neighboring countries supportive of or hostile to peace), whether the opposition is judged to be ultimately reconcilable, and whether the opposition enjoys broad popular support. Table S.4 lists eight cases, defined according to these factors in the leftmost four columns. In the more unfavorable cases (e.g., case 8), the strategy (column 5) should focus on *weakening the opponent*, as indicated in later columns by, e.g., cutting off resources and seeking to work with other regional states. It might also include (not shown) looking for ways to improve reconcilability (e.g., wait for a change of leaders or objective realities as seen by the opposition leader). In more favorable cases, some aspects of the intervenor's approach may be straightforward, but others less so. For example (cases 5 and 6, in which regional circumstances may not be favorable), it may be necessary to provide "physical" guarantees by maintaining international peacemakers or guaranteeing intervention to enforce the protections that are essential in enticing the opposition to pursue peace. We see Table S.4 as the sketch of a tentative framework for making distinctions and commu-

Table S.4
A First Attempt to Suggest Political Strategies by Case Characteristics

| Case | Favorable Environment | Reconcilable Opposition | Broad Support of Opposition | Strategy | Inducements | | | | | |
| | | | | | Positive | | | Resources | Negative | |
					Inclusion	Protections	Economic		Military	Faction Engineering
1	Yes	Yes	Yes	Find accommodative solution	Cooptation with soft guarantees					
2	Yes	Yes	No	Find solution; include reasonable incentives		Transparency; political mechanisms	Some side payments	Squeeze		
3	Yes	No	Yes	Weaken opposition; separate from its base				Cut off		
4	Yes	No	No	Weaken opposition				Cut off	Defeat via security cooperation	
5	No	Yes	Yes	Improve environment; find solution	Structural guarantees	Physical	Some side payments (not personal)	Cut off	Defeat	
6	No	Yes	No	Improve environment; find solution	Structural guarantees	Physical	Some side payments	Squeeze		
7	No	No	Yes	Improve environment; weaken opposition				Cut off		
8	No	No	No	Improve environment; weaken opposition				Cut off	Defeat via security cooperation	

nicating, although it will often be very difficult even to know which case applies. Is the opposition *really* irreconcilable as it claims? Are the promises of a neighboring state credible or mere deviousness? Such problems are visible today in Afghanistan and related negotiations with Pakistan and Iran. In any case, constructs such as a more fleshed-out version of Table S.4 could be helpful in guiding discussion, although they would at best sharpen issues rather than resolve them.

Looking back to Table S.3, its last item deals with another cross-cutting dilemma, whether to encourage and work through a centralized government or instead deal with decentralized elements of governance, including relatively informal versions where local customs and processes are a part of governance. Choices must be case-specific. In Afghanistan, for example, the central government has always been weak, with most governance being local and sometimes informal. Working with local leaders has many advantages, such as reduced costs and encouraging a bottom-up development of leaders and governance that can bring with it legitimacy. However, it is more difficult to deal with multiple leaderships; there are reasons for favoring a strong state, such as improving ability to defend against neighbors and economies of scale; and local governance may seem less desirable and benign if it comes with a tradition of discrimination or abuse of minorities or women, criminal control, or highly intolerant religious interpretations (as with the Taliban). Thus, the dilemma is nontrivial. Table S.5 summarizes some of the pros and cons of working through informal governance mechanisms.

Establishing Favorable Social Conditions

Initial Observations
The third component of our system structure deals with social matters. The social component is dismayingly broad and notoriously difficult to affect, especially for intervenors. Regrettably, we were unable in our study to deal in depth with such issues as the implications of tribal competition, corruption, or organized crime. Instead, we focused on the importang but more humble challenge of achieving *a degree* of trust

Table S.5
Working Through Informal Institutions of Governance

Strengths of Informal Institutions	Weaknesses of Informal Institutions	Challenges Faced by Foreigners
Adapted to local realities	Inefficiencies of scale	Variation between localities
Inexpensive, immediately available	Weaknesses in regulating inter-communal conflict	Visibility
Strong and resilient	Inequality	Training, experience of international personnel
Can be part of bottom-up legitimization of leaders and institutions	Degradation of traditional authority over years of fighting	Scale, personnel required for decentralized operations
		Potential incongruence with policy goals
		Potential incongruence with human rights standards

and cooperation among disputing factions in a culturally appropriate manner. As noted repeatedly in the scholarly literature, achieving a degree of trust and cooperation is *essential* for success (not just a nice-to-have objective pursued by idealists)—and can be feasible despite past history. A great deal is known from social science about how to proceed, and—significantly—about pitfalls and naivetés to avoid.

A starting point is recognizing the different types of trust, as summarized in Table S.6, which fall into two broad categories: "calculation-based trust" and "relationship-based trust." The former requires only that each party concludes that the other can be trusted on a specific matter because it is in its interests to cooperate. Relationship-based trust is different, and grows with improved understanding and the discovery of some common concerns and goals. Both kinds of trust improve over time with *positive* experiences and, of course, suffer from negative experiences.

Distrust is more than the lack of trust. Not trusting someone has a passive connotation. Active distrust is characterized by fear, skepticism, and vigilance. Even if the level of trust is low, if the more active sense of *dis*trust can be reduced, then dealings among people may include formal courtesies and arms-length interactions, whereas if the level of

Table S.6
Types of Trust

	Calculation-Based Trust	Relationship-Based Trust
Source of trust	Intendedly rational calculations of others' self-interest	Identification with others by relationship and association
	Experiential history of interactions	Some emotional attachment, even empathy
Actors' focus	Behavior control with incentives and enforcement mechanisms	Identifying common goals
		Building positive familiarities
	Information-gathering about motives and actions	Engaging in emotional reciprocity; encouraging empathy
Ways to develop	Education	Collaborative projects
	Clear, consistent communication	Emphasizing commonly held identities, values, and goals
	Credible commitments	Education about each others' histories, narratives, and travails (empathy-building)
	Repeated, equal-status interactions with appropriate incentive structures	

distrust is high, there may be active fear, paranoia, and the perceived need to attack preemptively.

Prescriptions for Trust-Building

Figure S.7 summarizes a great deal of social science on how to build degrees of trust and cooperation. Doing so includes orchestrating successful contacts and joint activities, building familiarity with each other's concerns and narratives, creating structural and other incentives for at least limited cooperation, and providing education that encourages understanding and toleration while undercutting hatred and negative stereotypes. Even modest progress on these matters can have large effects well before trust is deep and enduring. This said, much can go wrong with poorly designed efforts. Contact and the experience of trying to work together can, for example, *deepen* hostilities and reinforce prejudices.

Figure S.7
Factors Affecting Intergroup Trust and Cooperation

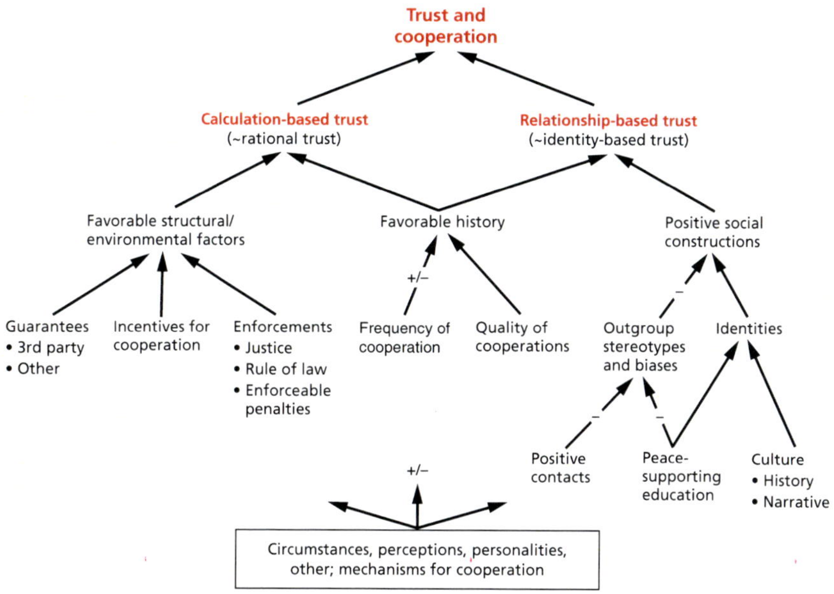

NOTE: The factors apply at a snapshot in time.
RAND *MG1119-S.7*

Establishing Favorable Economic Conditions

Why Post-Conflict Economics Is Different

The last of our four components (from Figure S.1) is economic. The economic dimensions of S&R are numerous, complex, and ridden with what are or often appear to be dilemmas. Figure S.8 is a general factor-tree depiction of what contributes to a healthy economy. As indicated at the bottom, economic health also depends on security, governance, and social conditions. This depiction could apply to either post-conflict or normal development settings, but with differences relating to the relative intensity of effort on different factors, the sequencing of those efforts, the type of aid employed, and the type of market system used. For a given country, some of the branches will be much more problematic than others. Thus, Figure S.8 is useful for seeing the whole, but not for deciding what approach to take.

Figure S.8
Factors Contributing to Economic Health

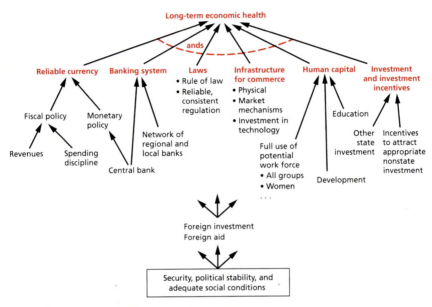

NOTE: The factors apply at a snapshot in time.
RAND *MG1119-S.8*

Indeed, perhaps the most important conclusion from our review is, bluntly,

> Economists seeking to advise in post-conflict circumstances must adjust their thinking substantially: The usual paradigms of "good economics" are counterproductive.

The differences between normal and post-conflict economics have been at the heart of bitter disagreements over the years between some development economists on the one hand and the World Bank and International Monetary Fund (IMF) on the other. Often, policies have included immediate and unremitting fiscal and monetary austerity—including not printing money, cutting public spending, setting high interest rates, and constraining credit—all of which can keep inflation down and decrease debt. For a post-conflict situation, however, intervenors must worry first about the short run; they want to see that people have incomes so that money can start flowing through the system. The actions may seem to be "political" and be perceived negatively by some, but the principle is that *the best economics in a post-conflict situation is heavily political and social*. Jump-starting the economy is the primary objective, although laying the foundations for sound longer-term economics is also essential. Table S.7 summarizes differences between economics for normal development and for post-conflict settings. Theory and data agree on these matters, and consensus is emerging among development economists even though battles continue more broadly. In recent times, even the World Bank and IMF have relaxed their stringent austerity policies in some post-conflict situations.

Economic Practices for the Post-Conflict Situation

Economic strategy must reflect country-specific circumstances and history, but the literature supports some overarching themes, which are meaningful because so much past practice has violated the corresponding principles:

Table S.7
Economic Planning in Normal Versus Post-Conflict Development

Economic Planning in Normal Development	Economic Planning in Post-Conflict Circumstances
Focus is on medium- and long-term goals.	Focus must often be on short-term (potentially distortionary) emergency programs.
Choices are largely merit-based, without regard to group affiliations.	Choices must often include preferential efforts to assist groups affected by conflict and by social inclusion policies.
Foreign assistance is low and stable.	Foreign assistance spikes immediately after conflict, varying thereafter.
Government institutions establish and carry out rule of law.	Foreign troops support or possibly replace weak or nonexistent government institutions (e.g. police, army, judiciary) to promote rule of law.
International community need not involve itself in the country's politics.	International involvement in country politics is often intrusive and intense.

Expectations. Expectations are a problem. Too often, those involved in S&R set high goals, not realizing that doing so undercuts political support and diminishes the government. The more realistic description for the short term would be *jump-starting*. What is needed most is to get the engine started and to establish attitudes of responsible local ownership.

Measures. An important element of action should be collecting and analyzing data to help assess whether progress is greater where jump-starting actions are employed. This can help both in management and in building support for the activities, individuals, and institutions responsible. When the actions are not making a positive difference, adaptations may be needed. Metrics are important, of course, but should be developed within a system framework because more narrow metrics will often have very troublesome side effects.

Simplicity and Flexibility. The need for "simplicity" is often mentioned, almost as a cliché. However, the admonition has substantial content. Strategy should not have too many components and, certainly, should not try to drive too many factors or be sensitive to intricate interconnections and subordinate controls. "Moving in the right direction" along several lines of effort and "doing essential coordination" conveys the idea. Complex orchestration, as is common and necessary for efficiency in modern commercial settings, is the opposite. Simplicity can also improve transparency and increase buy-in and support by local stakeholders. Finally, plans need to be flexible, so that if activities are not working (as will often be the case), this fact will be recognized and adaptations can be made. Measures to identify failure and enable smooth changes need to be planned and agreed on in advance. This is easier when plans are simple. Interestingly, these themes will all be familiar to military commanders who deal with analogous issues in their traditional domain.

Figure S.9 summarizes how priorities and intensity of effort might reasonably change between the short, mid, and long terms. We see this structuring of priorities over time as resolving some of the apparent dilemmas in the economic component of S&R: Some issues are not so much true dilemmas as conflicts of competing theories due to failures to distinguish sharply among time periods.

Figure S.9
Summary of Priorities Over Time

		Timing		
		Early	Mid-Term	Later
Intensity	High	Security Good use of post-conflict security aid	Human-capital development Revenue collection	Incentives to attract investment
	Medium	Physical infrastructure Education Rule of law	Rebuilding central bank	Network of regional banks
	Low	Full assessment of available workforce	Fiscal policy	Monetary policy

RAND *MG1119-S.9*

Special Issues of Foreign Aid

Special economic issues arise with respect to foreign aid because of numerous tensions:

- short-term versus longer-term objectives
- traditional versus more stabilization-specific objectives
- strengthening government by funneling aid through it and allowing the related buildup of patronage systems versus improving the efficiency of aid by delivering directly to the population
- strengthening central government and improving some kinds of efficiency by working through that central government versus emphasizing bottom-up developments at the local and province levels
- imposing conditionalities to improve national performance versus attending quickly to urgent needs.

Table S.8 is our effort to resolve the tensions. The conflict between short-term and long-term issues is less of a dilemma than a matter of diagnosing problems and recognizing what is feasible for the particular country at the particular time: It matters, for example, whether the

Table S.8
Reconciling Tensions

Tension	Resolution
Short term versus long term	Base relative emphasis on starting conditions.
Traditional versus stabilization-specific objectives	Improve the collaboration and the integration of the different development aid agencies.
Strengthening government from the bottom up by building patronage systems versus strengthening central government	Build the credibility and the legitimacy of the government, e.g., encourage concrete and observable actions.
Imposing conditionalities or not doing so in the interest of speed	Focus conditionalities on matters uniquely important to leaders, while not putting at risk matters important to the population at large, e.g., exclude conditionality on humanitarian activities. Include institution-building in the conditions.
Working through or around governments	Base strategy on circumstances, i.e., the governance quality and the governance capacity.

country has suffered grievous damage and whether it had or still has a substantial base of human capital.

The tension between traditional development and stabilization-specific objectives is sometimes very troublesome, but one element of mitigating the tensions is to improve the way in which different organs of government and different agencies relate to each other and to non-government organizations (NGOs). Military-style "command and control" is most unlikely, but much more coordination, collaboration, and even integration may be possible.

A fundamental issue—sometimes a dilemma and sometimes just a difficult issue to diagnose and deal with—is whether to support and strengthen the central government (a natural tendency for the United States and other developed-country intervenors) or to take the approach of strengthening governance from the bottom up by working through local leaders. Which approach is better will depend on the specific case, but a cross-cutting principle is that

> Whichever strategy is adopted, implementation should support leaders at all levels who actually provide services to their people.

It should help to strengthen their reputations and base of support and power and to improve the legitimacy of the governance system. Such leaders will use or build networks of people that they trust to get things done. Such leaders should be chosen by the people, however, not by the intervenor.

Interestingly, this approach might be seen as building "patronage networks" in a pejorative sense, with elements that might be seen as cronyism. However, it should also be seen positively as establishing patronage networks with bottom-up "emergence" of talented, dedicated, networked people strengthening the core of the nation. Intervenors should influence leaders to be inclusive as they build their networks.

Conditionalities are another common source of dispute. Concerns such as fears of corruption or exclusion lead donor countries to set requirements to assure that their assistance is well used. However, these conditionalities often have bad effects on the people. The primary admonition is that conditionalities should be focused on influencing leaders while not interfering with immediate humanitarian efforts. Conditions should often be tied to institution-building.

The last of Table S.8's issues has to do with the tension mentioned in earlier paragraphs, whether to work through the government or act more directly. We conclude that the issue is one of correct diagnosis, i.e., in identifying the relevant case. As indicated in Table S.9, very different approaches are suggested merely by recognizing the quality and capacity of the government. If both are lacking (case 1), direct delivery makes sense, especially for short-term humanitarian relief. At the other extreme (a government with relatively high quality and capacity, as in case 4), every effort should be made to work through the government rather than undercutting and delegitimizing it, and rather than setting up ad hoc processes without the benefit of local knowledge and expertise. For in-between cases, hybrid strategies are appropriate, along with adaptation. Intervenor resources may supplement government forces but be clearly in an assistance role. In the event of rank incompetence or total corruption, however, a more direct role is called for. This typol-

Table S.9
Relating Donor Strategy to Quality and Capacity of Governance

| | Circumstances | | Response | | |
| | | | Donor Strategy's Relative Emphasis | | |
Case	Governance Quality	Governance Capacity	Short-Term	Long-Term	Nature of Donor Actions
1	Low	Low	•••	•	Direct to people
2	High	Low	••	••	Direct to people; but government presence and guidance
3	Low	High	••	••	Through government if possible; direct if necessary
4	High	High	•	•••	Through government

NOTE: Number of bullets indicates weight of emphasis.

ogy is simple but nontrivial, because intuition is often wrong and pressures are often mischievous.

Analytic Observations

Most of our study was organized around the four components of S&R from Figure S.1, but in addressing those we reviewed a great deal of analytical literature and, in the course of doing so and making our own assessments, we reached a number of conclusions significant in their own right.

We drew heavily on the empirical literature. Empirical evidence, however, comes in many forms, such as case histories, more-than-anecdotal practitioner accounts, and statistical-empirical analysis. Each has strengths and weaknesses. We usually found case histories to be the most useful because they provide rich contextual information and identify "real" factors rather than the variables that happen to be convenient for data analysis. Ultimately, as illustrated in recent years by prominent researchers, there is great opportunity to combine case-history information and quantitative analysis in research, but that is quite demanding.

It is appropriate to comment specifically on statistical-empirical work because of a common misperception that it is more rigorous and policy-relevant than is the case. Some even equate it with "evidence-based research." In fact, we (and the strongest articles of the literature) are especially reluctant to draw policy conclusions from the past statistical-empirical work relating to S&R. The reasons are many. First, much of the work has been overly "macro" in nature and dependent on historical data that did not stem from the controlled experiments to which the methods apply. After a decade of study and counterstudy, it is clear that much of the analysis has been afflicted by hidden variables, endogeneity, "coding issues," and a sensitivity of results to the detailed form of equations used for the statistical analysis (the so-called "specification problem"). We find that very few results about the relative importance of factors have held up well across analyses. Where a factor has been shown to correlate with past results, the correlation has often not been truly causal. Further, where a factor has not correlated with past results, we find that has not necessarily meant much. For example, foreign aid has often not had hoped-for effects, but the aid may have been wasted because of poor security, governance, or implementation that precluded its usefulness. In summary, the rich back-and-forth in the quantitative-analysis literature has been very helpful and insightful in identifying factors, influences, and issues, but not very useful in assessing the relationships among factors or their strengths.

Despite these cautions, past "negative" empirical results from quantitative analysis (i.e., an instrument didn't seem to help) should be extremely sobering to those advocating the use of a particular instrument. If the instrument has not been effective previously, then why should it be more valuable this time? What will be different—and even if there are differences (and there always are), why should they be thought to be so important as to lead to different results? The salience of this admonition was illustrated in the Iraq war and its aftermath.

Illustrative Results

As noted above, many factors have been studied for their potential value in statistical prediction of war occurring or, given a cessation of war, of peace persisting. Most conclusions have proven soft after successive studies and critiques, but much has been learned. Table S.10 is our selected abstraction from the literature that illustrates some of the issues. Looking at the first row of the table, an early conclusion was that prospects for peace have been best when the previous war ended decisively, an intuitively sensible conclusion with troublesome policy implications. Further study, however, has shown that "decisiveness" is too aggregated. Some analyses indicate that when rebels have won decisively, prospects have been better than if the government won (perhaps because the governments in question had problems that persisted). Other studies find a different result (using a wider set of cases, including cases with fewer casualties and less destruction), so the only conclusion is probably that who wins matters. Significantly, analysis indicates that intervention by external peacekeepers can trump the sig-

Table S.10
What Affects Prospects for Enduring Peace? (illustrative)

Theory/Hypothesis	Statistical Evidence	Illustrative Complications
Decisive conclusion to war	Yes, but	Not necessary. Also, decisive for government or for rebels? Details matter. Further, interventions by an external power can trump this factor.
Mobilization along ethnic lines	Yes, perhaps, but	Ethnicity is probably not "root cause" but manufactured rallying point; does it matter?
Absolutist objectives	Yes, but	Factions routinely exaggerate their firmness or hide their real intentions, or both.
Intervention and guarantees by external power	Yes (about as strong as it gets), but	Not all guarantees are equally credible, nor all interventions equally well sustained.
Regime type/political institutions (degree of democratization)	Yes	Civil wars has been less likely with more democratic governments, but reoccurrence in a post-war environment has been more likely with a factionalized partial democracy
Cutting off opposition's resources	Yes, but	Constraints on government can also help.

NOTE: Bold indicates items with persuasive and policy-relevant significance.

nificance of the previous war's decisiveness. Such scientific back-and-forth is quite valuable for understanding factors and issues.

Looking to the second row, has ethnic hatred been a major factor? By and large, the conclusion from a combination of evidence is that ethnicity has not been a *root* cause, but rather a manufactured rallying point exploited by demagogues. Unfortunately, once a war has been fought with mobilization organized along ethnic lines, the ethnic factors become independently significant. The existence of absolutist objectives has also been studied and found significant. However, it should surprise few readers that factions are sometimes more willing to compromise than their rhetoric suggests and that, other times, peace-seeking language disguises more malevolent intentions. The last three items in Table S.10 (shown in bold) are those that we found had persuasive and policy-relevant significance. Intervention and guarantees by external powers have been correlated in the past with success, which makes sense from theoretical considerations. If a faction is contemplating a negotiated peace, it will be more willing to take risks if there is some *credible* guarantor to step in if necessary and use its influence more generally to protect the faction's interests. Continuing in the table, recent research provides strong evidence that, with a good specification, regime type is a strong statistical indicator of when civil wars occur. Again, that is consistent with theoretical considerations. It is also encouraging because regime type is something that can be influenced. However, another part of the conclusion is that partial, highly factionalized democracies—not uncommon in a post-conflict situation—are especially fragile. Finally, we mention cutting off the opposition's resources. If the intervenor supports the government (perhaps a newly formed government), then a major issue from the literature is that the opposition may well continue fighting if it has the resources to do so. Both logic and statistical data support the idea that cutting off such resources can be valuable.

Conclusions and Suggestions for Future Research

We conclude from our work that the "system view" is both necessary and helpful. The potential value of intervenor options depends on baseline values of the security, political, social, and economic components; on the direct ways in which the proposed options can affect them; and on indirect effects (sometimes called second- and third-order effects). Planners can benefit from having concepts of virtuous self-reinforcing loops, as in the illustrative influence diagram in Figure S.10, where progress in each component positively influences developments in another. In the particular example (only one of many that could be

Figure S.10
Virtuous, Reinforcing Cycles

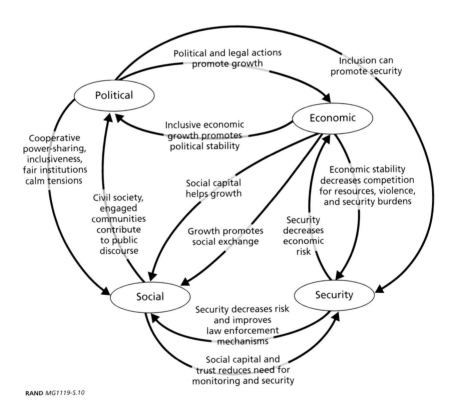

drawn), levels of self-reinforcing intergroup cooperation can help establish a norm of cooperation in political circles, which reduces the likelihood of stalemate, thereby increasing government effectiveness. That in turn reduces risk and increases cooperative behavior. Also, effective establishment of transitional justice can legitimize a new government (at the possible cost of exacerbating residual tensions with the society). Civil-society organizations can partner with government to provide human services guided by government to increase social capital via service delivery as well as perceptions of state capacity. Conversely, political corruption decreases trust in all levels of society, both horizontally and vertically. Political structures that encourage nepotism or favoritism create disincentives to cooperation, which in turn decrease economic opportunity, which creates more competition, and so forth.

Regrettably, the possibilities here work in both directions. Failure in one component can undercut progress in others. Side effects are common. Moreover, *most of the virtuous feedback effects do not occur automatically*, but must rather be planned for and enforced. That can be difficult to achieve when the parties in question (e.g., a government and a prime opposition party) are led by individuals or groups of individuals driven more by personal ambitions, greed, and power considerations than by concern for the people at large.

Analytically, we see much value in "influence-diagram" depictions for understanding potential effects and side effects, especially for reasoning and communication. Many authors over the years (primarily in other domains, including policy analysis and business planning) have reached similar conclusions. We emphasize that the greatest value is in "seeing" the relationships, not literally building computer models that generate "predicted" results over time. Such models could be quite valuable for exploratory analysis, which in the future could provide useful analytic insights about prospects for success and about possible side effects to plan against, but for now the more qualitative influence diagrams (and factor trees presented earlier) are the most useful.

Operations as Experiments

Because of the uncertainties and complications discussed above, those developing strategy for S&R will be well advised to think of the chosen strategy as an experiment, one that will probably have to be adapted to reinforce what is working and to find substitutes for what does not. This requires monitoring developments, which requires signposts of success or failure. Metrics can either help or hurt in this regard, depending on how well they are constructed and how well they reflect the idiosyncratic nature of the particular intervention. We believe that improved metrics can be constructed using the results of our survey and its system depictions (including competing influence diagrams that represent differences of expert opinion).

Intervernors are also likely to discover that the problems they are addressing are what theorists call "wicked" problems. At the outset, there is no unique solution to be found by merely applying an algorithm: Antagonists do not yet know what they will, in the end, find satisfactory; objective factors, such as the economy's development, are not yet realistically predictable; the quality and motives of emergent leaders are yet to be determined; and what intervenors and the world community will find it possible to sustain will be dictated by future and partially unpredictable events. When dealing with wicked problems, process is important so that, if the stars align themselves properly, an adequate solution can emerge in due course.

Suggestions for Research

Research in S&R will continue, and we offer some suggestions:

- Reject narrow approaches to "evidence-based research" that depend strictly on quantitative methods. A mix of methods is a stronger approach to using empirical information. Qualitative methods, particularly case studies and comparative case studies, are often more insightful.
- Within quantitative work, increase emphasis on "micro-level" quantitative analysis in a single country, so as to hold more contextual elements more or less constant.

- Disaggregate to recognize different phases or regions within a single country as substantially different cases.
- Commission experiments in operational theaters large enough to permit using different instruments in different areas or time periods; use people trained in quasi-experimental methods to design meaningful efforts.*
- Support further work with "agent-based rational-choice decisionmaking models" to anticipate (and in some cases even predict) the maneuverings of political factions competing for influence by forging alliances.
- Encourage quantitative analyses that are more theory-informed in a system-theory sense, rather than based on traditional linear regression and minor variants. Develop a new approach to metrics accordingly.
- Adapt the methods of multiresolution modeling and exploratory analysis to social-science analysis on S&R.

---

* Although adding complexity to their efforts, operational commanders could see this as a portfolio approach to managing risk, one offering an empirical basis for reinforcing successful approaches. Although we recommend such experiments, we caution against high expectations because data will often prove too sparse for the number of factors at play.

Acknowledgments

The book benefited greatly from suggestions from many people, including Charles Ries (who co-led the first phase of the project but took leave from RAND to be executive vice president of the Clinton-Bush Haiti Fund), Graciana del Castillo (Columbia University), John Herbst (then at the Department of State, now at National Defense University), Jack Goldstone (George Mason University), Michael Intrilligator (University of California, Los Angeles), Roger Myerson (University of Chicago), Roland Paris (Ottawa University), Nicholas Sambanis (Yale University), Tom Szayna (RAND), Barbara Walter (University of California, San Diego), Andreas Wimmer (University of California, Los Angeles), and Susan Woodward (City University of New York). Professor Goldstone and RAND colleague Kim Cragin reviewed the book as a whole; Professors Myerson, Sambanis, Walter, and Wimmer reviewed particular portions. James Dobbins provided numerous suggestions on the final manuscript, as did Charles Ries. Some of our DoD sponsors had comments that helped improve the monograph's clarity. This said, any residual problems are the responsibility of the authors.

CHAPTER ONE

Introduction

Paul K. Davis

Scope

This monograph deals with social science relating to the higher-level challenges affecting whole-of-government activities in post-conflict situations involving stability and reconstruction (S&R) operations.[1] Thus, we address issues from the early phases, in which establishing security is primary, to later phases, in which reconstruction and what some would call nation-building take place. We do this without prejudice as to how ambitious intervention operations should be.

The research base on which we drew included numerous subject areas, such as (1) civil wars, conflict resolution, and conflict prevention; (2) developmental economics; (3) political development and political economy; and (4) stability operations, peacekeeping, and intervention. The literature also reflected many disciplines, notably economics, political science, sociology, psychology, history, and peace and conflict studies. Although not highlighted in the book, our work was informed by the emerging science of complex adaptive systems and by past policy-analytic work using system dynamics and related methods. The sources of information included academia, think tanks, and governmental and international organizations.[2]

Background

As observed by Secretary of Defense Robert Gates in a pivotal *Foreign Affairs* article (Gates, 2009), the United States continued for years to put near-total emphasis on planning for possible future wars with advanced rogue states or future near-peer threats despite the nation being almost constantly embroiled in *actual* operations from 1990 onward, operations variously labeled as examples of traditional war, irregular warfare, hybrid warfare, complex operations, counterinsurgency, peace enforcement, and peacekeeping. It was only after major setbacks in Iraq in 2003 and 2004 that a shift in emphasis began that eventually put a good deal more effort into preparing for the demands of irregular operations and dealing with complex post-conflict situations. Operationally, the Army and Marine Corps substantially revamped counterinsurgency doctrine.[3] In strategic planning, Gates's demand for a rebalancing of efforts became the principal theme of the 2010 subsequent Quadrennial Defense Review (QDR) (Gates, 2010).

One aspect of the shift was a challenge posed to the analytic community, broadly construed: How should analysis be adapted to meet the needs of the here-and-now challenges? The Department of Defense's (DoD's) analytic toolkit had been honed during the Cold War and refined further in the 1990s, but its focus was almost exclusively on medium-sized or large "kinetic wars." Although many studies were accomplished on subjects such as military operations other than war (MOOTW), military operations in urban terrain (MOUT), and small-scale contingencies (SSCs), most of these were not especially "analytic" if by that one means characterized by theories, models, data, and experiments. The department established an analytic agenda of building analytic capabilities to fill the gaps while continuing to provide the basis for longer-term work with future wars in mind (Rumsfeld, 2006). An important aspect of the gap-filling work in that analytic agenda was to better understand lessons from the social sciences that should inform the work of analysts throughout the department. It was all too evident from the experience of here-and-now military challenges that many of the issues being faced were quintessentially human issues, rather than issues describable by physics and engineering.

An early step in DoD's effort was to commission an integrating review by RAND of the social science relevant to terrorism and counterterrorism (Davis and Cragin, 2009). The present monograph reports on a follow-on effort requested by DoD, a request made in the context of what was then called security, stabilization, transition, and reconstruction (SSTR)—i.e., whole-of-government activities related to everything from stabilization to reconstruction. The study was intended to serve multiple agencies of government, but it was also recognized that, in practice, military commanders find themselves involved in all aspects of post-conflict operations—sometimes as an enabler of activities by civilian government organizations and sometimes as temporary stand-ins for those or other organizations in a high-threat environment.[4] Social science has insights to offer for that larger context.

The questions posed at the project's outset asked, How are S&R operations affected by

1. levels of economic development or the dominant system of economic production?
2. the ethnic and cultural diversity of a population?
3. geographical and topographical factors?
4. historical legacies, such as a background in colonial rule, democracy, absence of strong governance, or rampant corruption?
5. social conditions?
6. special underlying levels of conflict in society?
7. possible exogenous factors?

The study, then, was to be more broadly strategic than narrowly military. Finally, we hoped to provide insights about potential levers of influence, i.e., to identify classes of actions that could be taken by the United States, other countries, and nongovernmental organizations, directly or indirectly, to advance U.S. interests and help stability operations to succeed.

Prior Work

In conducting our research we drew on prior efforts that have also taken a broad view.[5] In particular, the U.S. Institute of Peace has been a major contributor, providing a comprehensive reader (Crocker, Hampson, and Aall, 2007), a primer on international intervention that underscores the paramount importance of establishing security (Covey, Dziedzic, and Hawley, 2005), broad principles for stabilization and reconstruction (United States Institute of Peace and United States Army Peacekeeping and Stability Operations Institute, 2009), and a compendium of possible metrics (Agoglia, Dziedzic, and Sotirin, 2011). Other practitioners have provided overviews that explain motivations for international intervention and what is involved in states being able and willing to intervene constructively (Ghani and Lockhart, 2008).[6]

More generally, the literature is rich in information, ideas, and debate—as befits the term *social science*. A number of scholars are generally positive about the possibilities of S&R (Berdal and Economides, 2007; Call, 2008; Doyle and Sambanis, 2006; Fukuyama, 2004; Dobbins et al., 2003)—despite emphasizing its inherent complexity and difficulty. Others are more skeptical (e.g., Brownlee, 2007; Coyne, 2007; Englebert and Tull, 2008; Etzioni, 2010). Fukuyama (2004) provides a good theoretical overview of state-building broadly.[7] He explores strengthening state institutions with a focus on public administration. Others (Paris, 2004; Barnett, 2006) look at post-conflict stabilization from a perspective akin to political theory.

The growing literature on fragile and failed states is particularly relevant to this volume because such states have many of the same issues as post-conflict states—indeed, often *are* post-conflict states. Kaplan (2008) and Ghani and Lockhart (2008) offer overarching theories of why states fail in the first place, which are broadly relevant to post-conflict stabilization, including establishing security. Kaplan emphasizes economic forces. Ghani and Lockhart discuss those, but also the "weakness of the sovereign" in many failed states. Numerous studies examine the conditions and causes of violence and state collapse for particular regions, such as Africa (Lemarchand, 2009; Bates, 2008; Herbst, 2000).

Past RAND work on nation-building has been broad, and focused primarily on practical policy lessons (Dobbins et al., 2003, 2005, 2007, 2008a, 2008b). Some primary conclusions are as follows:

- Overall level of effort by the intervening powers, "measured in time, manpower and money" is the most important controllable factor in a post-conflict environment (Dobbins et al., 2003, p. xxv). Further, there is no "quick route" to lasting peace; stabilization takes time.
- Multilateral strategies of nation-building have advantages over lead-nation strategies. They can be more complex and time-consuming but tend to bring about more thorough transformations, with resulting higher levels of ultimate stability.
- Casualties fall as the number of troops dedicated to stabilization operations increases.

The first and third of these relate directly to establishing security. Other RAND authors have addressed, e.g., organization for stability operations (Bensahel, 2007), the military's role in economic development (Crane et al., 2009), and an approach to counterinsurgency (Gompert et al., 2008). All of these benefited heavily from practitioner experience.

Yet another aspect of prior work, although not nominally of the "scholarly variety," is important to note. That is the development of updated doctrine for counterinsurgency mentioned earlier (Department of the Army, 2007). The revised doctrine reflects not only enduring lessons from history and previous doctrinal efforts but also research by and advice from scholars, including anthropologists. The British government has also published good discussions of what it calls the "Comprehensive Approach" (Joint Doctrine and Concepts Centre, 2006) and principles (DFID, 2009).

Although the current volume was intended to draw primarily from the academic literature, the practitioner literature is important not only for the experience conveyed but also because in some cases the lessons from practice (sometimes surprisingly encouraging) have gone well beyond what scholarly theory currently deals with effectively. Indeed, academic research would benefit greatly by some changes in orientation and method, as discussed later. This will require more context specificity, more factors, and a system perspective.

Overarching Questions to Guide Research

When attempting to survey numerous vast literatures, it is essential to have some overarching questions to guide the search and prioritize the innumerable interesting topics. Based on an initial survey phase in 2009, which culminated in a workshop that gathered a number of prominent academic experts, we decided to focus on the following questions, issues, and dilemmas.

Generic Issues

1. *Typologies.* Are there qualitatively different types of S&R operations (perhaps defined in terms of causes, characteristics, and exogenous factors) that help assess feasibility and prospects? If so, what are reasonable objectives and likelihoods of success for the intervenor?
2. *Driving Factors.* For each member of the typology, what are the key factors, challenges, dilemmas, and resources?
3. *Monitoring.* For each type, what should be monitored to assess progress and prospects, and to trigger adaptivity?

The literature was especially helpful on the second item (driving factors). It was not as helpful regarding typologies. There is some recent work on metrics (Agoglia, Dziedzic, and Sotirin, 2011), but it is not yet mature, and much remains to be done. We only touch upon the subject here.

Recurring Dilemmas

Our initial research concluded that—looking across the vast literature—certain recurring dilemmas loom large. The term *dilemma* is appropriate, because those who seek to conduct a stability operation and associated nation-building find themselves having to make difficult choices that cannot be made on the basis of some simple calculation, but instead require best-guess judgments about which course of action is most likely to have the most favorable effects. The facts of the situation are often ambiguous or uncertain, the experts often disagree vehemently (even on-scene experts), and each course of action can be expected to have troublesome side effects. We concluded that we would take particular pains to address these issues as best we could, either by drawing directly from the scholarly literature or by attempting to resolve the conflicts through analysis and synthesis. The dilemmas we identified in the first phase of work (completed in September 2009) were as follows:

1. *Balance in Governance.* How can a balance be struck among government effectiveness, stability, responsiveness, and democratization (especially since institutions that strengthen progress toward one of these goals can weaken progress toward another)?
2. *Transition.* How can the transition be made from externally enforced arrangements to self-enforcing institutions?
3. *Balance in Instruments.* How can use of instruments of national power be properly balanced when intervenors' organs of power are imbalanced?
4. *Coherence in Command and Control.* How can coherence be achieved when intervenors and other participants have distinct interests and objectives?
5. *Short-Term Versus Long-Term.* How can effective short-term economic policies be pursued while also preparing for the longer term? When and how can the transition be made?
6. *Central Government.* Should intervenors push for a strong central government or a network of linked, locally responsive power centers?
7. *Freedom to Fail?* How should the importance of "local ownership" be balanced against the imperative of demonstrating concrete returns to peace or support for the legitimate government? How does this balance change over time? Under what circumstances might local actors' failures be acceptable, and when would they entail unacceptably harmful consequences?
8. *Reconciliation.* How and under what circumstances should former combatants be reintegrated?

9. *Tilting?* Where one group is stronger or more capable than others, is stability enhanced by strengthening the stronger group or putting limits on it?

10. *Patronage?* What is the balance of interests in the development of patronage networks? Do they support or undermine stability?

11. *Returns.* Is stability generally enhanced if refugees and the internally displaced are returned to their original residence or resettled?

12. *Corruption.* What kinds and levels of corruption, if any, are acceptable, and what kinds and levels of corruption will undermine stability operations?

As discussed in the latter portions of the book, we attempted to view some of these dilemmas in groups.

Approach: The Necessity of a System Perspective

After our initial survey, it was apparent that an integrative monograph would need to take a system perspective. Further, we would need to impose analytic constructs of system thinking that are seldom evident in the literatures on which we were drawing.

A System View and Analytic Hypotheses

Taking a system perspective is hardly controversial. It is almost a cliché that stability operations must take, to use terms from the 2010 Quadrennial Defense Review, a "whole-of-government approach" that addresses all of the "instruments of power."[8] We have organized the monograph accordingly so that all of the problem's dimensions are addressed to some extent. In addition, we found it difficult to make sense of the literature without a core hypothesis that will be used guardedly throughout the monograph:

> Assessing the potential successfulness of stability operations can best be addressed with a system formulation in which the system has four *critical components*: the quality of security, political, social, and economic conditions. If any of these components fail,

then—consistent with the adjective *critical*—we must expect the system as a whole to fail.

If this is true, then it follows that increasing the effort in any one critical component cannot compensate for failure in one or more of the others. For an intervenor to do more of what he knows how to do, and what he has the capacity to do, cannot fully compensate for abject failures in critical processes for which the intervenor lacks sufficient knowledge or capacity.

Further, under this hypothesis:

> The critical components are interrelated over time. Sequencing may be necessary because progress on one component may depend fundamentally on prior progress on another.

This hypothesis has important analytic implications for interpreting the scholarly literature, critiquing the knowledge base, constructing theory and models to help inform thinking about and conduct of stability operations, and conducting further empirical and theoretical research.[9] It means, for example, that the probability of success in a stabilization operation would be essentially zero if failure occurred in *any* of the critical components. In such cases, doubling or even tripling the effort on the other critical components might accomplish nothing.

To relate this to intuition, it is perhaps evident that sending in a small force of even very good soldiers will accomplish nothing to establish security in a large troubled area. How much is enough? Depending on circumstances, it might be modest (a thousand?) or enormous (hundreds of thousands?) in terms of boots on the ground. Where would the turning point be at which degree of security starts to build quickly with additional effort? Where would be the point of diminishing returns? Chapter Two discusses such issues.

As another example, if stability operations have failed in past cases even when vast sums of money have been poured into economic activities, it is not necessarily valid to conclude that such economic aid is wasteful or irrelevant: It may be that the failures occurred because of severe shortcomings (such as rampant and unrestrained corruption) on the political, social, or security dimensions or in the administration of the aid. This is not an idle speculation, but one that seems apt when we look at listings of failed instances of stability efforts. Moreover, it corresponds to the qualitative explanations given by many observers.

Another implication is that if our analytic hypothesis is correct, then *lack of correlation does not imply lack of causation*. That is, a factor may help "cause" something to happen in propitious cases, but the causality can only be seen in certain circumstances that are not well represented in the database. This is important for interpreting the literature, because so many of the research findings are otherwise paradoxical or implausible. For example, increasing the extent of foreign aid has not correlated well with success. That evidence should be (and is) troubling, but understanding the reasons for the lack of success may not be so straightforward.

Note that this analytic hypothesis also fits the frequently voiced view of experts on the scene in a failing operation that "we can do more, but the limiting factor is . . . and unless that turns around. . . ." In thinking about Afghanistan today, for example, it is commonly believed that the determining factor will be whether the Afghan government can achieve some minimal level of competence and deliver some minimal level of governance.[10]

Another recurrent analytic problem in interpreting the literature is that many researchers organize their analysis around convenient measurables, which sometimes correlate with results. That, however, may impede clear thinking about causation. If, for example, stabilization efforts tend to succeed if they follow long, drawn-out, and intensive conflict with a conclusive victor, one might infer that a would-be intervenor would be wise to let the protagonists fight themselves into exhaustion before intervening. That is almost surely true in some circumstances, but mistaking this for a general principle would be tragic if it meant failing to assist early in circumstances where early intervention could succeed.

Depicting System Relationships

Visual graphics are often helpful in communicating interrelationships and system concepts. Earlier RAND work, on the social science of counterterrorism, emphasized the value of simple depictions that seek only to identify the factors at work (doing so with hierarchical "factor trees") and some modest indication of how the factors interact in the simplest cases (Davis and Cragin, 2009; Davis, 2009). In the current work, however, it seemed crucial to include also simple depictions of dynamics, because affecting those dynamics is at the very heart of stabilization operations and related nation-building. Further, decades of experience in other domains tell us that some of the most serious strategic-level errors are made as the result of a failure to understanding the phasing of effects. Sometimes, for example, patience is called for because favorable developments are underway even if results are not yet visible. In other cases, alarmism is appropriate because of not-very-visible unfavorable developments that are underway and that will be quite troublesome unless stemmed early.

With this in mind, we use the following kinds of analytic representation in this monograph.

Factor Trees. Figure 1.1 shows a factor-tree depiction relating the four factors to success.[11] This example includes an explicit "and" relationship, although—as noted in the figure—this should be interpreted to mean that each factor's quality must be "good enough," as distinct from very high. That is, the quality of governance, for example, need not be up to Western standards to make stabilization feasible. Similarly for the others.

Figure 1.1
Factor Tree Depiction

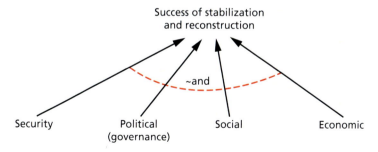

NOTE: The factors apply at a snapshot in time.
RAND MG1119-1.1

Simple Dynamics. Figure 1.2 shows dynamics and interrelationships of a different form. This might be seen as a variation of a simple causal-loop diagram as used in the system dynamics methods pioneered by Jay Forrester[12] or of influence-diagram techniques, which have been used for many years in diverse disciplines, including the study of managerial and other social problems in organizations.[13] We have used line thickness and dashes to indicate something about importance and sequencing, so that the picture conveys a story. Starting with a security effort, improved security enables improvements in the political, economic, and even social dimensions. Economic improvements reinforce political and social dimensions quickly. Thereafter, improvements in all of the dimensions feed back, reinforcing each other. To be sure, this story is what is *desired*, not necessarily what transpires. Further, the diagram can also be interpreted to mean that weakness in any dimension will weaken the others. This idealized image will not occur automatically. Indeed, political progress may not help the economy without sound policies being adopted; progress in health and education may not help security or politics if the health/education assistance is focused only in certain areas or serves only certain groups. More generally, vigilance is needed to ensure that political, economic, and social progress is fair and balanced and seen as aiding the legitimacy of the regime,

Figure 1.2
Time-Labeled Causal-Loop Diagram

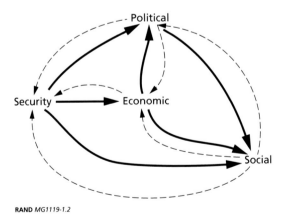

as well as increasingly effective. The primary point, then, is that the dimensions are tightly connected—for both good and ill. It usually makes sense to modularize as in Figure 1.1 and to treat the interactions of Figure 1.2 as occurring on longer time scales, although interactions can sometimes be more immediate.

Figure 1.3 provides an alternative depiction of dynamics. If relationships exist as in Figure 1.2, then the result over time might ideally be as in Figure 1.3 (ideal because, realistically, even in a good case there would be ups and downs rather than steady progress). Starting from a very low base in the immediate post-conflict environment, a combination of foreign and internal security forces are built up over time. Economic aid starts early, but is modest and of a humanitarian variety. Subsequently, it jump-starts a domestic economy, after which progress is slower. As security improves, the domestic economy begins to grow. That, in turn, enables gradual political and social improvements. Again, the purpose of the diagram is merely to create an image of what is being sought in a successful but not ideal intervention. Security, however, is a sine qua non for progress on the other dimensions.

Figure 1.3
An Idealized Future History for Stabilization and Reconstruction

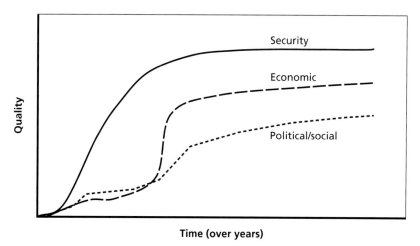

RAND *MG1119-1.3*

Case Dependence. A third element of our system approach is recognizing that how a course of action affects factors and what overall approach should be taken depends on case—i.e., context or situation. For example, increasing intervenor forces to stabilize a chaotic situation (one case) may be effective and appreciated, whereas doing so after those forces come to be seen as occupiers (a different case) could be counterproductive. An implication is that alternative courses of action need to be assessed as a function of case, as suggested schematically in Table 1.1. This notional decision aid imagines that "case" is determined by four factors. Each row in the table's body is a different case. For each, there is a suggestion approach (course of action) but also, as indicated in the last column, suggested hedges. An approach should include monitoring and hedges that will allow adaptations, which as operators can attest, will often be necessary.

Table 1.1
Notional Decision Aid for Choosing Strategy as Function of Case

Case	Factor 1	Factor 2	Factor 3	Factor 4	Approach	Hedges
...(many rows)						

Structure of This Monograph

Against this background, the remainder of the monograph is structured as follows. Chapter Two (Chivvis and Davis) surveys the literature relating to security and suggests a unifying conceptual model. Chapter Three (Taylor) surveys the literature on political issues, such as government and governance, noting the different approaches available for both. Chapter Four (Watts) takes a somewhat different view of political issues, noting the common dilemmas that make choices difficult; it goes on to suggest ways to deal with them. Chapter Five (Wilke, Davis, and Chivvis) addresses a major class of social issues, establishing a degree of trust and cooperation. Chapters Six and Seven deal with economics. Chapter Six (Berrebi and Olmstead) reviews and integrates the broad literature on post-conflict economics; Chapter Seven (Berrebi and Thelen) deals specifically with the special dilemmas that arise with respect to foreign aid. Chapter Eight (Davis) adds some final observations, in part about lessons learned regarding policy analysis and suggestions for future research. The monograph's executive summary is a summary of the whole.

The monograph's chapters overlap to some degree (as do their subjects!), and even have some differences of emphasis. This is deliberate. The intention was for the chapters to be readable individually and to reflect some differences in perspective for an inherently complex subject matter. That said, we have sought to use consistent concepts and terminology throughout, and to use similar methods where possible.

Endnotes

[1]   Part of S&R is stability operations, which include "operations to maintain or reestablish a safe and secure environment, provide essential governmental services, construct emergency infrastructure, and offer humanitarian relief" (Flournoy, 2009).

[2]   The research did not address such aspects of stability operations as military capabilities, doctrine, or intelligence collection. The research was also focused on the strategic rather than the tactical aspects of post-conflict operations—that is, concerned with objectives, criteria, and approaches rather than implementation.

[3]   The reworking of doctrine is associated with General James Petraeus (Army) and General James Mattis (Marine Corps). The material can be found in a published book (Department of the Army, 2007).

[4]   See Crane and Terrill (2003). We also benefited from a National Defense University briefing on the historical role of military forces in post-conflict operations (Moore, 2010).

[5]   Christopher Chivvis is responsible for some of the literature review discussed in this chapter.

[6]   A number of studies have described the historical experiences of Great Britain and others, although only some of that information is publicly available (Eaton et al., 2007).

7   We use *state-building* and *nation-building* interchangeably, although some authors use the former more narrowly, to address institutional and structural issues, but not broader economic, security, humanitarian, and other efforts included in the latter.

8   In acronym-speak, documents refer to taking a "WOG approach that considers all of the PMESII factors and applies all of the DIME or DIMEFIL instruments of power." WOG stands for "whole of government" (often interpreted even more broadly to include, e.g., other nations' governments, the United Nations, and non-governmental organizations such as the United Red Cross and Physicians Without Borders); PMESII stands for "political, military, economic, social, infrastructure, and information"; DIME stands for "diplomatic, information, military, and economic"; and DIMEFIL: stands for "diplomatic, information, military, economic, financial, intelligence and law enforcement." We shall not use these acronyms further.

9   For example, a conceptual model for estimating the likelihood of success might be expressed as the product of a threshold factor times a linear weighted sum of P, M, S, and E, measures of the political, military, social, and economic components of the problem. The threshold factor could be 0 unless each of the component measures exceeded a threshold, but 1 otherwise. This would be in contrast to the more usual linear form used in regression analysis, especially when data are sparse. Some recent papers, however, do consider nonlinear forms (e.g., Collier, Hoeffler, and Rohner, 2009; Goldstone et al., 2010).

10   This issue was discussed and debated heatedly by top U.S. policymakers in the 2009 strategy review regarding Afghanistan (Woodward, 2010). The same issues remain salient today.

11   The factor-tree methodology is described elsewhere (Davis, 2009; Davis and Cragin, 2009). A primer is in development and will likely be published by mid 2011, with examples from multiple applications.

12   This refers to methods pioneered by Jay Forrester at the Massachusetts Institute of Technology in the 1960s and early 1970s (Forrester, 1961, 1969, 1971). A good modern primer is available (Sterman, 2000). Many researchers use similar approaches that describe "system dynamics" but use different modeling methods and languages (Morgan and Henrion, 1990; Davis, 2006). In this book, then, "system dynamics" should be interpreted in the more general sense.

13   This type of "influence diagram" is different from that used in Bayesian analysis and decision-tree methods. Ours are more akin to those of System Dynamics, or certain kinds of cognitive, mental, or concept mapping. The U.S. Agency for International Development's (USAID's) Office of the Coordinator for Reconstruction and Stabilization (S/CRS) has found the influence diagrams helpful as a tool in interventions (personal discussions with T. Tjip Walker and Cynthia Irmer of S/CRS, and author discussions in early 2011 as part of a USAID effort pursuing the

techniques). RAND has used influence diagrams for years in various policy-analysis applications and in adversary modeling (e.g., Davis and Jenkins, 2002).

References

Agoglia, John, Michael Dziedzic, and Barbara Sotirin, eds., *Measuring Progress in Conflict Environments (MPICE): A Metrics Framework*, Washington, D.C.: U.S. Institute of Peace, 2011.

Barnett, Michael, "Building a Republican Peace: Stabilizing States After War," *International Security*, Vol. 30, 2006, pp. 87–112.

Bates, Robert H., "State Failure," *Annual Review of Political Science*, Vol. 11, 2008, pp. 1–12.

Bensahel, Nora, "Organizing for Nation Building," *Survival*, Vol. 49, 2007, pp. 43–75.

Berdal, Mats, and Spyros Economides, eds., *United Nations Interventionism: 1991–2004*, New York: Cambridge University Press, 2007.

Brownlee, Jason, "Can America Nation-Build?" *World Politics*, Vol. 59, 2007, pp. 314–340.

Call, Charles T., ed., *Building States to Build Peace*, Boulder, Colo.: Lynne Rienner, 2008.

Collier, Paul, Anke Hoeffler, and Dominic Rohner, "Beyond Greed and Grievance: Feasibility and Civil War," *Oxford Economic Papers*, Vol. 61, 2009, pp. 1–27.

Covey, Jock, Michael J. Dziedzic, and Leonard R. Hawley, eds., *The Quest for Viable Peace: International Intervention and Strategies for Conflict Transformation*, Washington, D.C.: U.S. Institute of Peace Press and Association of the U.S. Army, 2005.

Coyne, Christopher, "Deconstructing Reconstruction: The Overlooked Challenges of Military Occupation," *Economics of Peace and Security Journal*, Vol. 2, 2007, pp. 93–100.

Crane, Keith, Olga Oliker, Nora Bensahel, Derek Eaton, S. Jamie Gayton, Brooke Stearns Lawson, Jeffrey Martini, John L. Nasir, Sandra Reyna, Michelle Parker, Jerry M. Sollinger, and Kayla M. Williams, *Guidebook for Supporting Economic Development in Stability Operations*, Santa Monica, Calif.: RAND Corporation, 2009. As of April 8, 2011:
http://www.rand.org/pubs/technical_reports/TR633.html

Crane, Keith, and W. Andrew Terrill, *Reconstructing Iraq: Insights, Challenges, and Missions for Military Forces in a Post-Conflict Scenario*, U.S. Army Strategic Studies Institute, Carlisle, Pa.: U.S. Army War College, 2003.

Crocker, Chester A., Fen Osler Hampson, and Pamela Aall, eds., *Leashing the Dogs of War: Conflict Management in a Divided World*, Washington, D.C.: U.S. Institute of Peace, 2007.

Davis, Paul K., "A Qualitative Multiresolution Model for Counterterrorism," in Dawn A. Trevisani, ed., *Proceedings of Enabling Technologies for Modeling and Simulation Science X*, Proceedings of SPIE, Vol. 6227, 2006.

———, *Specifying the Content of Humble Social-Science Models*, Santa Monica, Calif.: RAND Corporation (reprint of an article from Proceedings of the Summer Computer Simulation Conference, Istanbul, Turkey, 2009), 2009. As of April 8, 2011:
http://www.rand.org/pubs/reprints/RP1408-1.html

Davis, Paul K., and Kim Cragin, eds., *Social Science for Counterterrorism: Putting the Pieces Together*, Santa Monica, Calif.: RAND Corporation, 2009. As of April 7, 2011:
http://www.rand.org/pubs/monographs/MG849.html

Davis, Paul K., and Brian Michael Jenkins, *Deterrence and Influence in Counterterrorism: A Component in the War on al Qaeda*, Santa Monica, Calif.: RAND Corporation, 2002. As of April 8, 2011:
http://www.rand.org/pubs/monograph_reports/MR1619.html

Department of the Army, *U.S. Army/Marine Counterinsurgency Field Manual*, Chicago: University of Chicago Press, 2007.

Department for International Development (UK), *Building the State and Securing the Peace*, London, 2009.

DFID—*See* Department for International Development (UK).

Dobbins, James, Seth G. Jones, Keith Crane, Christopher S. Chivvis, Andrew Radin, F. Stephen Larrabee, Nora Bensahel, Brooke Stearns Lawson, and Benjamin W. Goldsmith, *Europe's Role in Nation-Building: From the Balkans to the Congo*, Santa Monica, Calif.: RAND Corporation, 2008a. As of April 7, 2011:
http://www.rand.org/pubs/monographs/MG722.html

Dobbins, James, Seth G. Jones, Keith Crane, and Beth Cole DeGrasse, *The Beginner's Guide to Nation-Building*, Santa Monica, Calif.: RAND Corporation, 2007. As of April 7, 2011:
http://www.rand.org/pubs/monographs/MG557.html

Dobbins, James, Seth G. Jones, Keith Crane, Andrew Rathmell, Brett Steele, Richard Teltschik, and Anga R. Timilsina, *The UN's Role in Nation-Building: From the Congo to Iraq*, Santa Monica, Calif.: RAND Corporation, 2005. As of April 7, 2011:
http://www.rand.org/pubs/monographs/MG304.html

Dobbins, James, John G. McGinn, Keith Crane, Seth G. Jones, Rollie Lal, Andrew Rathmell, Rachel M. Swanger, and Anga R. Timilsina, *America's Role in Nation-Building: From Germany to Iraq*, Santa Monica, Calif.: RAND Corporation, 2003. As of April 7, 2011:
http://www.rand.org/pubs/monograph_reports/MR1753.html

Dobbins, James, Michele A. Poole, Austin Long, and Benjamin Runkle, *After the War: Nation-Building from FDR to George W. Bush*, Santa Monica, Calif.: RAND Corporation, 2008b. As of April 7, 2011:
http://www.rand.org/pubs/monographs/MG716.html

Doyle, Michael S., and Nicholas Sambanis, *Making War and Building Peace: United Nations Peace Operations*, Princeton, N.J.: Princeton University Press, 2006.

Eaton, Hugh, Greg Boehmer, Eric Rambo, Lana Oh, Jeremy Works, Michael Clarke, Warren Chin, Andrew Dorman, Stuart Griffin, David Ucko, Rod Thornton, David Whetham, Kimberly Holloman, Robert Tyler, Joanna Centola, Christine Balisle, and Angela D'Haene, *Network Centric Operations (NCO) Case Study: The British Approach to Low-Intensity Operations: Part I*, Washington, D.C.: Office of Force Transformation, Department of Defense, 2007.

Englebert, Pierre, and Denis M. Tull, "Post-Conflict Reconstruction in Africa: Flawed Ideas About Failed States," *International Security*, Vol. 32, 2008, pp. 106–139.

Etzioni, Amitai, "Bottom-Up Nation Building," *Policy Review*, December/January 2010, pp. 51–62.

Flournoy, Michele A., *Department of Defense Instruction Number 3000.5: Stability Operations*, Washington, D.C.: Department of Defense, 2009.

Forrester, Jay W., *Industrial Dynamics*, New York: Productivity Press, 1961.

———, *Urban Dynamics*, Cambridge, Mass.: Wright Allen Press, 1969.

———, *World Dynamics*, New York: Productivity Press, 1971.

Fukuyama, Francis, *Statebuilding: Governance and World Order in the 21st Century*, Ithaca, N.Y.: Cornell University Press, 2004.

Gates, Robert, "A Balanced Strategy: Reprogramming the Pentagon for a New Age," *Foreign Affairs*, January/February 2009.

———, *Report of the Quadrennial Defense Review*, Washington, D.C.: Department of Defense, 2010.

Ghani, Ashraf, and Claire Lockhart, *Fixing Failed States: A Framework for Rebuilding a Fractured World*, Oxford, UK: Oxford University Press, 2008.

Goldstone, Jack A., Robert H. Bates, David L. Epstein, Ted Robert Gurr, Michael B. Lustik, Monty G. Marshall, Jay Ulfelder, and Mark Woodward, "A Global Model for Forcasting Political Instability," *American Journal of Political Science*, Vol. 54, No. 1, January 2010, pp. 190–208.

Gompert, David C., John Gordon IV, Adam Grissom, David R. Frelinger, Seth G. Jones, Martin C. Libicki, Edward O'Connell, Brooke Stearns Lawson, and Robert E. Hunter, *War by Other Means—Building Complete and Balanced Capabilities for Counterinsurgency: RAND Counterinsurgency Study—Final Report*, Santa Monica, Calif.: RAND Corporation, 2008. As of April 7, 2011:
http://www.rand.org/pubs/monographs/MG595z2.html

Herbst, Jeffrey, *States and Power in Africa*, Princeton, N.J.: Princeton University Press, 2000.

Joint Doctrine and Concepts Centre, *The Comprehensive Approach (Joint Discussion Note 4/05)*, Shrivenham, UK, 2006.

Kaplan, Seth D., *Fixing Fragile States: A New Paradigm for Development*, New York: Praeger, 2008.

Lemarchand, René, *The Dynamics of Violence in Central Africa*, Philadelphia: University of Pennsylvania Press, 2009.

Moore, R. Scott, "Complex Operations: The Civ-Mil Dilemma," National Defense University, Center for Complex Operations, Washington, D.C., 2010.

Morgan, M. Granger, and Max Henrion, *Uncertainty: A Guide to Dealing with Uncertainty in Quantitative Risk and Policy Analysis*, Cambridge, UK: Cambridge University Press, 1990.

Paris, Roland, *At War's End: Building Peace After Civil Conflict*, New York: Cambridge University Press, 2004.

Rumsfeld, Donald, *Report of the Quadrennial Defense Review*, Washington, D.C.: Department of Defense, 2006.

Sterman, John D., *Business Dynamics: Systems Thinking and Modeling for a Complex World*, Boston: McGraw-Hill/Irwin, 2000.

United States Institute of Peace and United States Army Peacekeeping and Stability Operations Institute, *Guiding Principles for Stabilization and Reconstruction*, Washington, D.C., 2009.

Woodward, Bob, *Obama's Wars*, New York: Simon & Schuster, 2010.

CHAPTER TWO

Establishing Security

Christopher S. Chivvis and Paul K. Davis

Introduction

This chapter addresses the security component of stabilization and reconstruction (S&R). If security is achieved with the nation at peace with itself and its neighbors (even with imperfect governance), the mission will likely be regarded to have been at least partially successful (in the short run); if the country redescends into conflict, the intervention will almost always be judged to have been a failure. Thus, establishing self-sustaining security can be seen both as a requirement and as the most urgent objective in S&R. As discussed in Chapter One, the political, social, and economic problems are intertwined, and a measure of success is essential in all of them, but without security, progress on the other components is very difficult.[1]

The chapter proceeds as follows. The next section draws on the scholarly literature to identify issues, factors, and points of agreement and disagreement. The literature is quite fragmented, so we then present a conceptual model, our synthesis of how to understand "establishing security" analytically. The model draws from theory and empirical work, but reorganizes for policy-analytic purposes. Our intent was not to choose among competing mini-theories, but to sketch a more general structure incorporating the diverse contributions and adding missing elements. Subsequent sections discuss factors in that model one by one. We then discuss instruments for improving security in S&R operations and linkages to the political, social, and economic challenges. Finally, we give brief conclusions.

Several considerations affected our work. First, given the monograph's subject (S&R), we focus on *post-conflict* factors affecting whether war reoccurs. However, some level of resistance may persist after conflict nominally halts, and intervenors must worry about deterring or coping with escalating resistance. This is a theme within our conceptual model. We touch only lightly on root causes of initial conflict and the proximate causes of the original civil war. We do not deal explicitly with cases in which one side achieved a total victory, because that is seldom the circumstance of S&R. Further, we *assume* that intervenors have chosen to support the government or emerging government against an opposition faction or factions. We do not discuss the problem that sometimes arises of whether and how to "choose sides." As readers will appreciate, the government being helped may have serious shortcomings. We briefly discuss how its behavior affects the ability to create security, but it is for other chapters of this volume to discuss political and social issues and the mechanisms by which intervenors can influence governments constructively.

Overview of the Literature

As one article points out in its first line, "Over half of all civil wars that began between 1944 and 1997 were followed by at least one if not more episodes of civil war" (Quinn, Mason, and Gurses, 2007, p. 167). Understanding why is obviously important.[2]

Different Approaches to Theory

Researchers have taken diverse approaches in attempting to understand the factors affecting prospects for sustained peace or its converse, the restart of war. The diversity reflects disciplinary backgrounds, methodological preferences, organizational settings, and personalities. Differences even exist in how the researchers group factors. One categorization is as follows:

1. *Motivations* for fighting: factors affecting the desire of faction(s) to fight. For the opposition, these may include government

repression or incompetence, political exclusion, and historically based hatred. For the government, a motivation might be the opportunity to crush the opposition or fear that the opposition would undermine it if power-sharing occurred.

2. *Means*: factors affecting the ability of the opposition to mount and conduct a war. These include recruits and sustained resources, whether from internal or external sources.

3. *Circumstances*: factors affecting the propitiousness of fighting, such as weakness or strength of the government; external and internal support beyond the providing of resources covered under means; and the presence or absence of international intervention, including mediators and guarantors.

4. *Aspects of decisionmaking*: factors affecting decisions, which depend on the above factors but also on values, perceptions, fears, and other aspects of psychology.

This categorization borrows in part from, but inverts, one used in an influential book about the conditions for peace in a post-conflict environment (Walter, 2002). Walter grouped factors positively, in terms of whether the conditions are ripe for negotiations, whether the underlying issues are resolvable, and whether the parties can realistically make credible commitments to peace. At this point in our chapter on security issues, it seemed more appropriate to focus on the "negatives" that create security challenges.

Selected Empirical Findings

Researchers have generated a long list of discrete hypotheses, which their authors often champion as providing primary explanations or predictions. Disciplinary preferences stand out, with authors focusing variously on economic, historical, power-balance, political, and other factors. The results do not converge, and we ultimately concluded that much of the empirical-statistical work was far more useful for the authors having suggested factors than for any conclusions about the quantitative significance of those factors (see also Chapter Eight).[3] Nonetheless, a few findings are more robust than others.

Table 2.1 lists *selected* factors frequently discussed in the literature, notes the class of factor they fall in and whether they have statistical support, and mentions why—in virtually all cases—interpretation is ambiguous (often with conflicting results). The citations shown are to recommended entry points to the literature.[4] The notation in the second column is that a + or − indicates whether the factor in question is hypothesized as increasing or decreasing, respectively, prospects for continued peace in a post-conflict setting. Our summary is cryptic to minimize digression from the main themes of the chapter.

Those doing statistical-empirical analysis have suggested a much longer list of what we consider "other" considerations that can affect decisions to cooperate or fight. We summarize many of these in Table 2.2, again cryptically, along with illustrative citations to relevant literature.

Another class of empirical findings that can be mentioned here relates to metrics. We do not address metrics in any detail in this study, but substantial efforts have been made to construct metrics of fragility and metrics to aid in S&R. In this chapter we can merely point to some references.[5]

Specific Insights from the Counterinsurgency Literature About Providing Security

The preceding material stems primarily from the civil-war and peace-and-conflict literatures. The counterinsurgency (COIN) literature also has insights specifically relevant to establishing security (Paul, Clarke, and Grill, 2010; Connable and Libiki, 2010; Cornish, 2009; Kilkullen, 2009; Marston and Malkasian, 2008; Department of the Army, 2007; Gallula, 2006; Hoffman, 2006; Long, 2006; Kilcullen, 2005; Schindler, 2004; Metz, 2003). It tends consistently to emphasize the need for (1) good local intelligence, (2) focusing on the political dimension of the effort (including the need for a population-centric approach), (3) close civilian-military cooperation and doctrine, and (4) training that reflects the previous three items. Such considerations are incorporated into the counterinsurgency field manual (Department of the Army, 2007). Empirical support for some of these hypotheses can be seen in two recent studies (Paul et al., 2010; Connable and Libicki, 2010), as well as older literature.

Table 2.1
Selected Factors Studied in the Literature Relating to the Prospects for Sustained Peace

Factor	Hypothesized Effect on the Prospects for Continued Peace	Type of Factor	Statistical-Empirical Support	Discussion
Residual hostility	–	Motivations	Yes[a]	
Residual government capacity	+	Means	Yes[a]	
Intervention and guarantees by intervenors	+	Means, circumstances	Yes,[a,b] strongly supported, although…	Intervenor forces can outstay welcome. UN peacekeepers have been better accepted.
Relatively more democratic regime type and political institutions	+	Motivations	Mixed[c]	Democratization correlates with absence of civil war, but in post-conflict settings, factionalized partial democracies have been more unstable. See Chapters Three and Six for discussion of related dilemmas.
Feasibility of going back to war, i.e., resources	–	Means, circumstances	Yes[d]	See Chapter Six.
Economic well-being and access to political participation	+	Motivations	Yes,[e] but…	Interpretations are complex. Poverty, for example, is not necessarily a direct determinant but is correlated with poor governance.
Decisive victories	+	Means	Yes,[f] but…	Less aggregated analysis indicates that such decisiveness is not necessary, that whether rebels or government wins matters, and that which is "better" depends on details. Further, intervention for peacekeeping can compensate for indecisive victory.

Table 2.1—Continued

Factor	Hypothesized Effect on the Prospects for Continued Peace	Type of Factor	Statistical-Empirical Support	Discussion
Absolutist objectives; indivisibility of stakes	−	Motivations	No, yes, not really[g] but....	True almost by definition, but stated objectives may be misleading and create difficulties in bargaining and signaling.
Ethnic or other identity tensions	−	Motivations	No, but...[h]	Ethnic divisions are less "root causes" than something to be inflamed and exploited; subsequently, they can become "causes" of hatred and fear.

[a] Doyle and Sambanis (2006) and Sambanis (2005).

[b] Walter (2002); Doyle and Sambanis (2006); Quinn, Mason, and Gurses (2007); Kreutz (2010a).

[c] Goldstone et al. (2010).

[d] Collier, Hoeffler, and Rohner (2009) and references therein. These authors focus on what they call "feasibility."

[e] Walter (2004) and, for more discussion of economic effects but with a different interpretation, Collier, Hoeffler, and Rohner (2009) and references therein. Fearon and Laitin (2003) note the correlation between poverty and governance.

[f] Walter (2002); Quinn, Mason, and Gurses (2007); and Kreutz (2010a). Doyle and Sambanis (2006) note that intervention and peacemaking has trumped results of the prior conflict.

[g] Walter (2002) for discussion of ambiguities.

[h] This topic has been debated for some years.[6]

Table 2.2
Other Factors Discussed in the Empirical Literature

Issue	Comments	Examples
Availability of weapons	Necessary for fighting, which suggests value of the disarming, demobilization and reintegration process (DDR).	Knight and Ozerdem, 2004, pp. 499–516 Muggah, 2006, pp. 190–205
Availability of recruits	Necessary for fighting; affected by perceived prospects and economic conditions.	Collier, Hoeffler, and Söderbom, 2008 Collier, Hoeffler, and Rohner, 2009 Miguel, Satyanath, and Sergenti 2004
Lootable resources	Source of funding for fighting and incentive for greed-based actions; "lootability" often corresponds to state weakness. Resources, however, can also be used productively and need not be lootable.	Chapter Six Lujala, 2010, and citations to earlier literature
Diasporas	Can be source of funding for fighting, but also positive factor in S&R.	Doyle and Sambanis, 2006 Hedges, 1999 Collier, Hoeffler, and Söderbom, 2008
Defensability (e.g., rugged terrain or sanctuary in neighboring country)	Can prolong conflict, as in Democratic Republic of Congo.	Prunier, 2009 Lemarchand, 2009
Reactions to intervention	Intervention often triggers insurgencies; the problem can be mitigated by, e.g., an official settlement, an emphasis on maintaining order, and reconstruction of indigenous security forces.	Bensahel, 2006
Duration of the preceding war	1. Statistically, recurrence of war is less likely after long wars. 2. If war does restart, the chances are higher that it will do so quickly.	1. Hartzell et al., 2001; Walter, 2002; Fortna, 2004; Doyle and Sambanis, 2006 2. Collier and Hoeffler, 2004

One reason for failure in COIN is said to be excessive mechanization, which makes the selective application of force very difficult (Lyall and Wilson, 2009). The claim is that large numbers of light, highly mobile ground forces are the most appropriate for COIN. The claim is arguably a misstatement in that the availability of mechanized equipment is less the villain than the concept of operations and training (in principle, mechanized units can dismount and can be no less population-hostile than light infantry).

Most of the literature agrees on the population-centric approach, on the grounds that the cooperation of the population is crucial to insurgent success and that providing security for the population is the number-one priority. This makes COIN a highly political activity, as well as a very local activity. Much of the debate over counterinsurgency has focused on what influences the population's cooperation (e.g., Kilcullen, 2009; Long, 2006; Leites and Wolf, 1970; Sunderland, 1964). Some argue that the deciding factors are material and include safety, access to economic goods, and the degree of predictability that cooperation can bring (Kilcullen, 2009). That said, ideological and emotional factors are also likely to have an impact on the extent to which the population will cooperate with military actions by rebel forces (Long, 2006). Clearly, if the population shares the same ideology and aims as the rebel group, it will be more inclined to cooperate. Whether ideal or material factors dominate is unclear, but it is likely that the population will base any reasoned decisions on the marginal utility of each. If rebel groups are unable to provide any human security, then ideological affinities may not matter much at all.

Much less is written about the negative tactical components of a population-centric approach. Collective punishment is typically not an option for the United States and its NATO allies, even though adversaries often use intimidation tactics to maintain public "support" (as with the Taliban currently). There are, however, some articles on the related "cost theory" of counterinsurgency, essentially the theory that increasing the costs of cooperating with an insurgency is the surest means to victory (see Long, 2006, which reviews RAND studies during the Vietnam war). Some heterodox scholars have argued recently that Russia has had some success in the North Caucasus with random bombings of Chechen villages (Lyall and Wilson, 2009).

Edelstein (2009) identifies two dilemmas that peacekeepers face in attempting to provide security. The *duration dilemma* refers to the trade-offs between effective long-term peacemaking and peacekeepers outlasting their welcome. The *size-of-force dilemma* is related: Although larger forces may be more effective at their task, they may increase nationalist resentment. This dilemma was also reflected in the 2009 review of strategy for Afghanistan. Secretary Gates was especially concerned about the problems of an excessive "footprint" but was later convinced that how the occupying forces operate and what they accomplish are more important than the size of the footprint per se (see Tyson, 2009).

On a related point, Berdal (2009) emphasizes that planning must adapt to context and that providing security requires legitimacy for both the intervening force and the government being established. Although he presumably has in mind continuing security issues rather than initial stabilization, Berdal argues that it is more useful to conceive of "eliciting" security than imposing it.

A Unifying Conceptual Model

As the preceding overview of the literature indicates, the causes of violence in a post-conflict situation are multiple, complex, and variable. Many factors have been studied, but in a fragmented way. In what follows, we present a unifying conceptual model for establishing security. It systematizes the main insights from this literature but uses a causal representation suitable for discussion and assessment of policy and strategy.[7] This structuring is different from the categorization used earlier in referring to the empirical literature. We begin with an overview of the model and its motivation. We then discuss the model's elements in more detail, one by one, citing relevant literature.

Overview

The model focuses on describing factors that determine *degree of security*, a characterization of the overall level of security in a particular post-conflict system. Degree of security will be a function of time. With future research it could presumably be defined as an index variable on a scale of, say, 0 to 10, corresponding to a range from very insecure to very secure, as depicted schematically in Figure 2.1. Its value would be a function of overall levels of violence, both political and criminal in nature. Standardization of such an index would be quite useful for communication and analysis.

Given the status of current social science, we aspire only to identify and organize the factors determining degree of security, without purporting to predict results. Figure 2.2 is a pictorial synthesis in the form of a factor tree. It applies at a snapshot in time. The value of a given factor at a specific time, however, can depend not only on subordinate factors in the same branch of the tree but also on earlier values of factors elsewhere in the tree. This is necessary because, as emphasized in the literature (e.g., Quinn, Mason, and Gurses, 2007), developments have "path dependence," i.e., history matters.

Figure 2.2 depicts degree of security as resulting from two or three primary factors, depending on whether some resistance continues even in the nominally post-conflict environment. Those factors are the resistance effort (a function of motivations and means), the security effort, and the favorability of circumstances for establishing security. Degree of security also depends on what we call the "requirements function," which is not a factor like the other elements in the figure but rather describes how the factors interact to produce degree of security. It is

Figure 2.1
Increasing Degree of Security

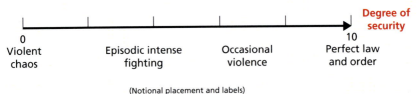

(Notional placement and labels)

Figure 2.2
Overview of a Conceptual Model

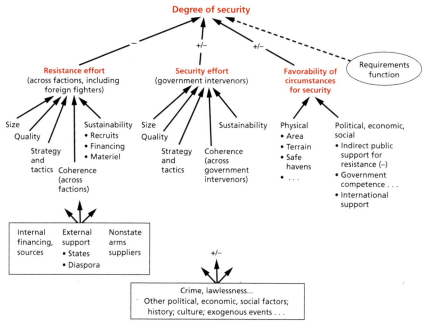

NOTE: The factors apply at a snapshot in time.

RAND MG1119-2.2

unusual to show such a function in factor-tree diagrams, but we wish to dramatize the fact that there is much uncertainty about how big the security effort must be.

Whether there is significant resistance is a major factor in Figure 2.2. That depends on decisions. Figure 2.3 decribes factors affecting the parties' decisions on whether to restart or reescalate conflict, rather than cooperate. It reflects our desire to have a causal model rather than a risk-factor model as found in the statistical-empirical literature. Thus, whereas researchers examining data on past postwar developments look for what they call "determinants," such as past history, resources for conflict, ethnic divisions, and the way in which the previous conflict stopped, we see it as more useful to highlight the role of decisions (see also Quinn, Mason, and Gurses, 2007, p. 173; Kreutz,

Figure 2.3
Factors Affecting the Decision to Renew Major Fighting

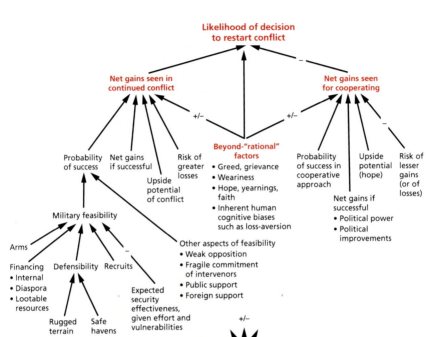

NOTE: The factors apply at a snapshot in time.

2010b). The various determinants examined in the statistical-empirical literature can be factors affecting the decisions, either explicitly or implicitly. Note that Figure 2.3 includes factors favoring both the restart of war and the commitment to peace.

If we understood and could measure degree of security, security effort, resistance, and favorability of circumstances, we could aspire to decision aids something like what is shown in Figure 2.4, which illustrates schematically how much security could be achieved as a function of the security effort (defined here as the maximum effort achieved after a buildup that might take many months or even years). The postulated relationship is that the security effort required grows substan-

Figure 2.4
What We Would Like to Have: Notional Security "Requirement Curves"

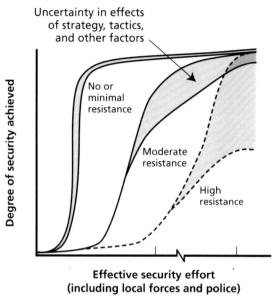

RAND MG1119-2.4

tially with resistance level and is quite uncertain unless resistance is minimal. This would be especially true if the index measuring degree of security reflected antigovernment subversive elements that might be continuing without much visible violence. Consider the size of the internal-security apparatus routinely present, and presumably required, in countries such as the former Soviet Union, East Germany, Iran, or Saddam Hussein's Iraq. These were in addition to regular security forces, such as armies.

We also need to touch on dynamics. If we use *security effort* to mean the maximum level of effort achieved after a buildup, and S(t) to indicate the time-dependent level, then for simplicity, assume a buildup as shown in the top portion of Figure 2.5. Initially, S(t) grows entirely because of the deployment of foreign forces (assuming that the country's internal security apparatus has collapsed). Over time, local forces begin to replace the foreign forces while maintaining the total

Figure 2.5
Notional Security-Effort Dynamics

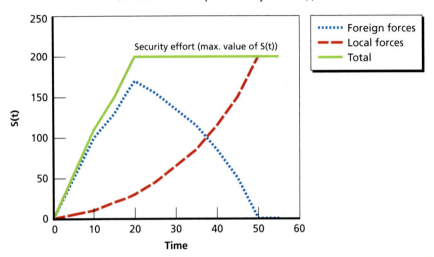

a. Notional buildup of security effort S(t)

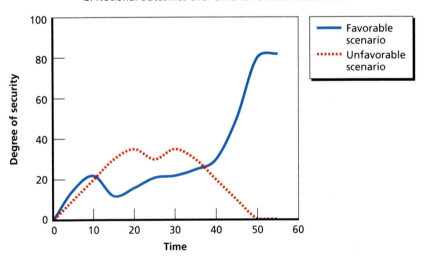

b. Notional outcomes over time for different scenarios

level of effort. The intent, of course, is that degree of security should improve steadily until reaching some acceptable level. Progress, however, is often nonlinear: Even in good cases, progress may be in fits and starts, and the entire effort may fail—perhaps because the security effort was too small. The bottom portion of Figure 2.5 illustrates nonlinearity for good and bad scenarios. In the favorable scenario, security becomes "self-sustaining" after about 40 time periods. Thereafter (not shown), it might be sustained with a decreasing effort. In the unfavorable case, the initial effort is promising, but the later effort fails.

Let us now discuss the elements separately: the security effort, resistance effort, favorability of circumstances, and the requirements function. Except that we treat the security effort first, discussion will follow the factor-tree depiction of Figure 2.2 from left to right.

Security Effort

As its name suggests, security effort is a measure of the total effort going into creating security. We have in mind the maximum level of effort over time, as in the top portion of Figure 2.5. It reflects the capability and capacity of all security organizations in the system, foreign and local, military and law enforcement. It incorporates qualitative as well as quantitative dimensions. The *effective* level of effort, after all, depends not just on the number of personnel involved but also on their quality, the strategy and tactics used, the coherence of efforts (e.g., across foreign and local forces), and their sustainability. The scale of the security effort might be large, but effectiveness low because of poor training, command incompetence, and other factors. As illustrated in the top portion of Figure 2.5, the standard expectation would be that local forces increasingly substitute for foreign forces and then take over. One result of successful stabilization, then, will be a state capable of securing itself with minimal or no external assistance. Success should also mean declining violence and declining levels of effort required for the same degree of security. How long achieving this success takes depends in part on how rapidly domestic forces can be recruited, equipped, and trained. That, in turn, depends on political, economic, and social developments discussed in other chapters of this volume.

Measuring Security Effort. It is beyond the scope of this chapter to define security effort more precisely, but we suggest an approach akin to that used successfully for many years in approximating force balances.[8] The basic unit of measure might be something akin to "equivalent brigades." A standard U.S. Army brigade suitable for a given type of post-conflict operation might be given a score of 1, and all other units being used in stability operations would be scored on a relative basis. A unit might have a lower score, due to its being, for example, small, poorly equipped, or being poorly trained and commanded (often the case for local forces, as in Afghanistan). The overall score of the security effort might be enhanced by multipliers reflecting, e.g., air supremacy, routine armed surveillance, and command and control. It might be discounted by multipliers reflecting combined-arms imbalances, such as inadequate mobility, the complete absence of armor, or a severe shortage of infantry (Allen, 1992). The effectiveness of such a force would depend on circumstances and the requirements function, as discussed below. Although this approach may seem complicated and subjective, experience indicates that it can be far simpler (and even more credible to military "operators" and force planners, if not to simulation modelers) than methods that are more data-intensive or based more on computer models. This approach does not, however, substitute for more in-depth analysis, such as those conducted by operations planners.

Resistance Effort

Assuming conflict (we discuss the decision about that below), understanding the resistance effort (left branch of Figure 2.2) is even more challenging than understanding the security effort. The resistance effort would also depend on scale (e.g., number of people involved in insurgency or other subversive activities), quality, strategy and tactics, coherence, and sustainability. However, because resistance can take many forms and be either potential or actual, measuring it will require research to define new methods. We speculate that it may be most useful to characterize the resistance effort with an index variable of the sort commonly used by social scientists, perhaps on a scale of 0 to 10 with 10 being very high resistance (Figure 2.6), to attach a magnitude as well, and to use terms such as *low, moderate,* and *high* as shorthand

Figure 2.6
A Scale of Resistance

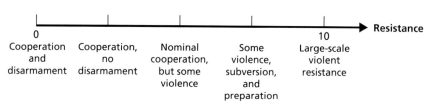

(Notional placement and labels)

NOTE: Index addresses character of violence; scale would be addressed separately.
RAND *MG1119-2.6*

in depictions such as in Figure 2.4. The effectiveness of the opposition's resistance effort will depend on the security effort, the circumstances, and the requirements function, as discussed below.

One reason for an index scale would be to recognize that actors have more than the binary choice of deciding whether to fight or cooperate. As in Figure 2.6, they have a spectrum of possibilities, ranging from cooperation and disarmament through conflict via proxies to direct violent confrontation. The overt level of resistance will change as the political, military, and economic situations ebb and flow. This is a familiar phenomenon in the continuing struggle between Israel and Palestinians.

As mentioned above, there is both a *potential* for violent resistance and a *realization* of violence. An opposition faction may decide to cooperate temporarily while retaining the capability to take resistance actions later if necessary, and perhaps making plans for subsequent insurgency. Or it may effectively decide to allow its capabilities to wane. What we are calling *resistance effort*, then, is probably a function of both exhibited violence and the level of other subversive activities. Again, refining this concept is a subject for future research, but the need is evident from history and other aspects of the research literature.

Favorability of Circumstances

A major factor determining what degree of security can be achieved is the favorability of circumstances for the security effort (third branch of Figure 2.2). That depends on different types of subordinate factors. Some are physical (e.g., whether the opposition has mountains, forests, or otherwise remote and difficult-to-access areas in which to hide; whether the country's infrastructure makes government access more or less difficult; and whether safe havens exist, as in a neighboring country).

Other factors are political, economic, and social. Perhaps the biggest is whether the opposition enjoys a significant degree of popular support, which can drastically affect the opposition's ability to operate (i.e., do locals report their presence to authorities or do they allow them to use their homes for safety, help them obtain intelligence, and facilitate their obtaining necessary material?). This will depend on such matters as whether the governance system is competent and providing services, or the opposite. The effectiveness of the resistance effort will also depend in some instances on international support, which might involve intelligence, special weapons, military advisors, international criticisms of government security efforts (whether or not justified), and sanctuary.

Underlying some of these factors are various aspects of history. Every conflict has a unique history that shapes the post-conflict environment. Sometimes factors from the prewar era will have a significant impact on stabilization. More often than not, war changes societies, and the history most important to the post-conflict environment will be the immediate experience of the war. Bosnia is a case in point. Before the war, Bosnia's ethnic groups were intermixed and highly tolerant (much more so than was often reported in the early years of the Bosnian difficulties). After the war, ethnic relations were polarized on a geographical, political, social, and emotional level. The failure to recognize the full impact of the war hampered postwar stabilization efforts (Woodward, 1999; Ramet, 2005; Chivvis, 2010).

Some starting points will be more propitious than others. Starting points where indigenous security forces are well on their way to providing security for the population, or where the population is prepared to acquiesce to the new post-conflict reality, will obviously be easiest. Starting points where the foreign forces are required to provide most or all of the security from the start and where there are groups of the population that are not prepared to acquiesce to the post-conflict arrangement (e.g., Iraq for several years after the 2003 invasion) will be the most challenging.

Some factors, such as geography and topography, will ordinarily remain stable. Others may change due to "exogenous" developments, such as the policies and stability of neighboring states or the moral and political support in foreign capitals for S&R activities. Still other factors will change "endogenously" as the result of, e.g., economic growth and political maturation.

The Decision to Seek Peace or Reinitiate Conflict

As discussed above, a key issue is the decision about whether to restart (or escalate) conflict rather than cooperate.[9] Figure 2.3 describes the decision as the result of three kinds of factors. The left and right branches correspond to a kind of rational-choice model in which the factions address the pros and cons of either resisting to various degrees (restarting conflict) or cooperating in stabilization. The central branch adds recognition that human decisions are not, in fact, well described by rational-analytic models. Nor are decisions based exclusively on the so-called expected values of options as assumed in much of the S&R-relevant literature. Instead, people think about upside potential ("it is at least possible that we could achieve a glorious victory") and about downside risks ("but if we lose next time, it could mean our annihilation"). Since people do not get to relive their lives many times, it is understandable that they do not necessarily make decisions based on the expected value.

Beyond-Rational Considerations. A number of phenomena undercut rationality, whether by individuals or groups:

Perceptions. Even when attempting rational decisions by examining pros and cons, perceptions of reality can be quite wrong—especially in post-conflict societies, where fears are intense and easily manipulated.

Information. In many instances, the pros and cons cannot be evaluated for simple lack of information (What is the adversary thinking? Is he planning treachery? How big is his army, really?). The lack of information or ability to process was at the heart of what is called, in economics and other social sciences, *bounded rationality* (the basis for a Nobel Prize by Herbert Simon; for his speech reviewing the matter, see Simon, 1992).

Cognitive Biases. According to the accumulated research of psychologists over decades, it is unnatural and difficult for people to make entirely rational risk-benefit calculations. Most relevant, perhaps, is that people often have a decided bias toward avoiding options that involve losses (even if, in doing so, they run risks of much bigger losses). This phenomenon is discussed under the rubric of prospect theory (which resulted in a Nobel Prize for Daniel Kahneman; for his acceptance speech, see Kahneman, 2002) and has been explored quite recently in the context of recurrence of war in post-conflict situations (Kreutz, 2010b). There are benefits to some of the cognitive biases, which probably explains why they are wired into our minds. In many instances, more intuitive or "naturalistic" decisionmaking is superior to what happens when people attempt to do rational-analytic decisionmaking without sufficient information or imagination. The styles of decisionmaking are reviewed and compared in Davis, Kulick, and Egner (2005).

One aspect of the cognitive bias issue is that when people balance an option's likely outcomes, best-case outcomes (upside potential), and downside risks, they often tend—depending on their situation—to be "unreasonably" risk-avoidant or "unreasonably" risk-taking. This has been examined in connection with deterrence in counterterrorism and counterinsurgency and crisis decisionmaking, among other places (Davis, 1994; National Academy of Sciences, 1996; Davis, 2010).

Other Factors. The economic and structural factors emphasized by some researchers (e.g., Collier, Hoeffler, and Rohner, 2009) can be seen as natural contributors to the rational-analytic portions of the model. Some of the factors emphasized by others (e.g., Sambanis, 2004, 2005; Goldstone et al., 2010; Quinn, Mason, and Gurnes, 2007; Kreutz, 2010a, 2010b) arguably manifest themselves at least in part through the beyond-rational factors, as do behavioral factors discussed extensively in the Vietnam war social-science literature (Long, 2006).[10]

Our conceptual model of the decision rejects the temptation to choose one of the rival "theories" of the literature (e.g., those that focus on greed, grievance, motivation, or feasibility rather than political factors, or vice versa). The intent is to move toward a comprehensive theory within which one can discuss all considerations and—for a given context—narrow down. For example, in a given country at a given time and circumstance, the economic factors and a rational-actor model might drive decisions on resistance (assuming account is taken of misperceptions, uncertainty, and the like). In other cases and times, the beyond-rational factors would dominate.

The Requirements Function

The rightmost part of the factor tree in Figure 2.2 shows the requirements function. This is not a factor in the usual sense, but rather the function that dictates what degree of security is achieved for a given resistance effort, security effort, and set of circumstances. In combat modeling, a simplistic requirements function for an attacker has often been said to be as follows: If the defender has well-prepared defenses in favorable terrain, then if the attacker has a force ratio much higher than 3:1, the attacker will prevail; if the force ratio is significantly smaller than 3:1, the defense will prevail; and if the force ratio is around 3:1, results are highly uncertain. For establishing security, a historically derived rule of thumb has been that the ratio of "boots on the ground" to population must be at least 1:40 for a significant counterinsurgency (Quinlivan, 1995–1996)—implying the need for far more than the troop levels in Afghanistan currently. It can be argued that this rule does not apply if the stabilization force has air supremacy, reconnaissance strike capability, extensive use of special operations forces, and world-class command and control. Perhaps such advantages will buy a factor of two or more in effectiveness. Others shake their heads skeptically, noting that technology-oriented people often claim great results from their innovations, but that history has not been kind on the matter: Having many boots on the ground is essential. Truth on this and related matters is yet to be determined.

A better requirements function would probably depend on a much more fine-grained approach. After all, not all of a country needs to be stabilized at the same time, some regions pose less difficulty than others because of terrain and local sentiments, and the actual troop requirements depend on the missions to be performed—all of which suggest use of tools translating missions to tasks and force requirements, which depend on military doctrine rather than the more coarse-grained social-science literature.[11] Whether such refinements would change the conclusions, and whether doctrine-based calculations can keep up with changes in technology and tactics, is unclear. Our bottom line here is that even if one understands the security effort, resistance effort, and circumstances, there are big uncertainties in requirements.

The Security Dilemma

The preceding section dealt largely with how a decision to cooperate or fight might be made. It focused on high-level concepts, such as risk. To fully understand the issues, however, a much deeper look is needed, and social science has a good deal to offer.

An appropriate starting point for discussion is a particularly well-studied element of political science called the security dilemma, depicted simply in Figure 2.7 as though there are only two actors, such as the government and the main opposition faction. The security dilemma strongly affects perceptions, fear, and behavior.

The security dilemma describes the perspective of an actor (a person, group, or state) who, facing an inherently insecure environment, seeks to increase its own security but, in doing so, decreases the perceived security of other actors in the system; the actor thereby inadvertently decreases both its own security and the system's overall level

Figure 2.7
Security Dilemma with Two Actors, A and B

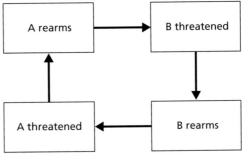

RAND MG1119-2.7

of security (Jervis, 1978; Posen, 1993; Walter and Snyder, 1999; Rose, 2000; Walter, 2002; Byman, 2002). The vicious circle of the security dilemma is active in both wartime and post-conflict situations. It can apply between rival opposition factions and between such a faction and the government. It exists at the level of large groups and at the individual level. Individuals, for example, might purchase small arms and form groups for self-protection, but this will threaten former adversaries who will do likewise, leading to increased tensions and pressures to break the peace preemptively. Increasing the degree of post-conflict security requires reversing this vicious circle (Walters, 2002).

One implication is that where credible commitments to the peace are lacking, one of the main roles of international forces is to provide that credibility and thus reduce fears and facilitate cooperation. Increasing the strength of a state's military, however, can increase the security dilemma's intensity if rebels are not included in the government and thus have reason to fear the government will renege on its peace promises (Collier and Hoeffler, 2006; 2007). Such issues are discussed further in later chapters.

The ferocity of the vicious cycle may reflect psychological, ideational, and cultural matters, as well as reality. Weapon technology that is offensive in nature can also increase fear, as do certain political geographies that create incentives for pre-emptive strikes (Posen, 1993; Rose, 2000). If the past war was irregular or involved atrocities, historical baggage can be expected to exacerbate fear and distrust (Kalyvas, 2006). This is one reason that the trust-building measures discussed in Chapter Four can have such an important impact.

The security dilemma need not be acute at the outset of an episode, but it may develop subsequently (e.g., the security dilemma was hardly acute among Shia, Sunni, and Kurdish factions in Iraq before the 2003 invasion, when Saddam was firmly in control, but became a reality subsequently).

Still another phenomenon can be understood in security-dilemma terms. Common crime, even of a serious nature, should be distinguished analytically from politically motivated violence, granted that the two can overlap in some situations. Nevertheless, "petty" and random violence can still increase fear. The need for protection from random violence can increase the tendency to gather small arms and take other measures that inherently, if unintentionally, increase offensive capabilities of one group over another. Moreover, common crime can have broader implications if it is interpreted through a meta-narrative of ethnic violence. For example, if random local violence results in the death of an individual from one ethnic group at the hands of another, even if the violence was criminal or personal and not political in nature, the crime can easily take on political meaning and thereby tend to undermine security (Kalyvas, 2006). Random violence of a local or criminal nature, therefore, even if not linked to political aims, can still increase the overall demand for security by intensifying fears and hence the security dilemma. This is why effective police forces and rule of law have positive impacts on security far beyond their ability to eliminate insurgents.

To overcome the security dilemma, people's behavior and expectations must change. Trust between former and potential future adversaries must grow. This is why such acts as public displays of disarmament are important and also why inflammatory rhetoric, even if otherwise innocuous, can be dangerous. Notably, where adversarial groups are not unified internally and leaders are forced to struggle for power within their own groups, the tendency toward inflammatory rhetoric increases, as was the case in Bosnia, where nationalist leaders were often pushed to maximalist positions in order to gain power within their own groups, and in the process efforts to build trust between ethnic groups were hampered.

Time is also likely to be a factor. On the simplest level, one of the main forces intensifying fear will be the memory of the war. As that memory fades, so will the intensity of the security dilemma. Conscious efforts on the part of group leaders to keep the memory of the war alive will, of course, work against this effect. Building trust takes time and repeated interactions to rebuild social capital destroyed by the war. The longer security lasts, the more fears can be expected to diminish.

To summarize some primary points here:

- People arm themselves and prepare to fight because they fear the state, other groups, or both. The security dilemma, then, is multisided.

- The state must be strong enough to prevent groups from being harmed by other states, *but* its own actions and structure must be sufficiently restrained, and the state must be sufficiently accountable, so that groups do not fear being targeted or excluded by the state (see also Wiatrowski and Goldstone, 2010).
- Security forces that are dominated by one ethnic group, or that are themselves corrupt and dangerous to civilians, worsen the dilemma and reinforce resistance rather than stabilization.

The implications of these issues include the need to create inclusive and accountable governance and to pursue trust-building among others. Such issues are discussed in other chapters of this volume, particularly Chapters Three and Five.

Improving the Security Effort

Security Forces

Let us now return to the security effort itself, and discuss briefly some of the ways in which it can be improved, focusing on points not made earlier.

Foreign Forces. We assume that in most S&R operations initial security will be provided in part or fully by foreign forces, with local forces replacing them over time (Figure 2.5). The level of foreign troops needed is a complex issue, as discussed earlier, but several points are important:

- Ideally, the character of foreign forces should be quite different from those optimized for mechanized warfare (Binnendijk and Johnson, 2004).
- When the foreign forces come from multiple countries, successful stabilization operations may depend significantly on the congruence of the interests in the international community (Pei and Kasper, 2003).
- Their perceived legitimacy is crucial and will depend on the country's history, the identity of the foreign forces, and their professionalism and training (including cultural training). In the past,

UN forces, although often less capable, have enjoyed greater legitimacy than coalitions of western forces.

- The acceptance of foreign forces wanes over time, making it even more important that handover is seen to be occurring, and does.

Building Local Forces. Building local security forces is a well-known challenge with details beyond the scope of this chapter. Some key points relating to security force assistance (SFA), security sector reform (SSR), and other processes are as follows:

- Developing local professional military forces can be an important part of the S&R process, since military service to the nation is an age-old form of building consensus across groups (Krebs, 2004).
- More security forces, however, may either improve or worsen stability, depending on details. Professionalism and coherence matter.
- As discussed above in connection with the security dilemma, security forces dominated by one faction (e.g., a particular ethnic group) can exacerbate insecurities and raise resistance.

The starting point will vary across countries. Often, it will be poor because civil wars tend to occur in underdeveloped countries with poor, incohesive, factionalized militaries. Security forces may have a deservedly bad reputation and no legitimacy. Other societies have a long tradition of professional militaries, in which case rebuilding domestic capacity is easier.

Linkages to Political, Social, and Economic Issues

The degree of security will be intimately intertwined with processes taking place in the political, social, and economic spheres. The interactions can be mutually reinforcing, but can also conflict (Dobbins et al., 2007; Brinkerhoff, 2005; Doyle and Sambanis, 2006). The political, social, and economic components of S&R are discussed in other chapters of this volume, but some particular issues linked to security are worth noting here.

Disarmament, Demobilization, and Reconstruction (DDR). DDR is often an important part of S&R affecting degree of security. Getting DDR right can reduce security requirements and also have direct benefits for recovery and the pace with which the state can have self-sustaining security and stability (Colletta and Muggha, 2009). The pace and quality of DDR, however, depend on available resources, the state of the local economy, and characteristics of the individual combatants. Disarmament of soldiers can generate economic growth if the process diverts national resources from production of military goods toward production of nonmilitary goods and services. The effect will be diminished if labor is abundant, as is the case in many countries where S&R operations are apt to take place. Also, if the economy is stagnant or the combatants are excluded from employment, reintegration is liable to falter and the possibilities of insurgency or renewed insurgency will increase.

Some scholars (e.g., Humphreys and Weinstein, 2007) are skeptical about the returns on investment in DDR to date, but lackluster results do not necessarily imply that DDR is worthless, but rather that it could be done better. The same authors find that, as expected, past participation in abusive military factions creates difficulties for combatant reintegration, and that wealthier, better educated, and younger combatants tend to be more difficult to reintegrate.

Fiscal and Economic Resources. Economic conditions affect not only the feasibility of fighting but also the state's ability to pay for security in peacetime. Poor countries find it difficult to generate the income necessary to pay military and other security services well enough to attract talented recruits and supply them with the training and equipment needed to carry out their basic functions professionally. This can also affect side-taking. In Afghanistan, for example, there was a period in which the Taliban paid better than did the Afghan National Army. In the immediate post-conflict period, much of the funding for security forces may come from the international donor community, but only sustained economic growth will generate the tax revenue needed for the state to afford the security it needs over the long run.

Political and Social Context. Establishing effective local security forces that overcome the security dilemma and generate self-sustaining peace is not merely a technical matter of training and resources. It also depends on *esprit de corps* and dedication to service to the nation, however defined in the imagination of the people (Rubin, 2008). This requires not only a certain state legitimacy but also military and political leaders capable of drawing on their legitimacy to inspire service and loyalty to military institutions. Lacking this, the pace at which security forces are built is apt to fall.

The ability of a state's institutions to pass necessary reform legislation and to achieve effective civilian control will also depend on its unity. If the state lacks executive authority, building high-quality, professionalized security forces will be difficult. Unfortunately, divided authority is a common feature of the political landscape in post-conflict situations. The arrangements that exist may have the benefit of increasing the chances that peace will hold but the disadvantage of reducing the government's ability to govern effectively and support its own security forces. The Dayton Peace Accords that ended Bosnia's civil war are a case in point: The compromises inherent in them have made post-war politics and reform in Bosnia extremely onerous.

The very process of security-sector reform will also be influenced by the politics of the peace process. In a post-conflict situation, access to military resources is a crucial object of political action. In a fragmented post-war situation with various political forces, actors may seek control over parts of the armed services to ensure their physical security, bolster their political strength, and, in some cases, increase their ability to extract rents (usually illegally) from the land. All of this works against desirable versions of security-sector reform (Rubin, 2008).

Some Important Dynamics. We have noted repeatedly the interconnections among S&R components, shown in Figure 1.2 of Chapter One. Both the complicated influences and the ambiguity of effects need to be reflected in serious thinking about security in an S&R context. Perhaps the most important points are these:

- Because of the security-dilemma issues, increased security effort may either improve or worsen stability. How the internal security effort is approached is crucial.

- Developing security forces is inherently political and social, and is strongly linked to political legitimacy (Papagianni, 2008, pp. 49–71; Kratochwil, 2006; Lipset, 1959), which is further discussed in Chapters Three, Six, and Seven.

Conclusions: Security and Self-Sustaining Peace

If security is to become self-sustaining, both the propensity for violence and the degree of fear (often fear of the state's security forces) must decline to a point at which people no longer arm or otherwise prepare themselves excessively for fighting—allowing the state to have more or less a monopoly on the legitimate use of violence, as defined in the classic work of Max Weber (1946). A virtuous cycle may ensue.

At any time, however, events can impede or reverse this virtuous cycle—developments in any or all of the security, political, social, or economic components. Thus, even though establishing security is widely accepted as primary in the hierarchy of needs in post-conflict stabilization, it does not follow that higher degrees of security are in themselves sufficient for post-conflict S&R. Understanding the interrelationships (in Figure 1.2) is a core challenge for S&R.

Endnotes

[1] Many references exist on this, but see, e.g., Dobbins et al., 2007; Caplan, 2005; Rotberg, 2004; Schwartz, 2005; and Chesterman, 2004.

[2] The literature on post-conflict stability is relatively small, so we also drew on literatures dealing with nation-building, fragile states, counterinsurgency (COIN), and civil wars. The civil-war literature tends to be concerned with causes of violence. The COIN literature deals more with lessons learned and the effectiveness of different strategies for fighting insurgencies. The methods used by researchers include statistical regression, game theory, theoretical economics, econometrics, and historical case studies, each with its own advantages and disadvantages. As should be expected for a field at this stage of development, much of the literature entangles theory building and theory testing.

[3] Much of the quantitative analysis has worked with highly aggregated, heterogeneous historical data from different conflicts in different parts of the world and dif-

ferent contexts. The resulting analysis suffers from hidden-variable problems, endogeneity, and weaknesses in the underlying, mostly linear models used. The work has been interesting and productive, but, as a prominent contributor noted in a review of an earlier draft of this manuscript, "The problem is that the more careful social scientists are about making causal arguments, the less they have to say about the very complex questions that this manuscript addresses." See also Chapter Eight.

4   The literature is large. Pioneering work on economic factors in civil wars began only in the last decade (Collier and Hoeffler, 2000, 2004; Fearon and Laitin, 2003; Humphreys 2005; Lujala et al., 2005). It helped dispel the impression that post–Cold War outbreaks of violence in Africa, the Balkans, Latin America, and elsewhere were wholly irrational and incomprehensible to the "civilized" western world. Originally cast in terms of whether greed or grievance dominated motivations, later work emphasizes feasibility:

> The feasibility hypothesis proposes that where rebellion is feasible it will occur: motivation is indeterminate, being supplied by whatever agenda happens to be adopted by the first social entrepreneur to occupy the viable niche, or itself endogenous to the opportunities thereby opened for illegal income. (Collier, Hoeffler, and Rohner, 2009)

Political factors were often given short shrift in the early work, but recent work by prominent authors, while not disputing that economic factors play a role, concludes that regime type has been the strongest statistical indicator of whether civil war will occur (Goldstone et al., 2010). The authors note (p. 205):

> We view the model as, not as one of instability, but rather one of resilience. If the factors associated with stability are in place—high income, low discrimination, few conflicts in the neighborhood, and most important, a noncontested or unified political regime—the model suggests that the polity will remain stable.

5   The Governance and Social Development Resource Centre (GSDRC) of the United Kingdom and Australia has a website with numerous materials relating to state fragility (GSDRC, 2006). See also Agoglia, Dziedzic, and Sotirin (2011) for a compendium on measuring progress in conflict environments.

6   It is easy to believe that many wars are driven by ethnic hatreds, but evidence is limited (Fearon and Laitin, 1996; Fearon and Laitin, 2003; Collier and Hoeffler, 2004). Recent articles argue that a correlation does exist if proper measures of ethnic factionalism are used (Cederman and Girardin, 2007; Montalvo and Reynal-Querol, 2005). Ultimately, it seems that ethnicity plays a role primarily because it defines a ready-made social network for the formation of subnational groups (Esteban and Ray, 2008; Habyarimana et al., 2007; Alesina and La Ferrara, 2005)—something easily exploited by leaders seeking to create resonant themes around which to gather supporters. That said, after a struggle is organized around ethnicity,

ethnic tension may be so high as to be a risk factor in itself (see also Gurr, 2000; Horowitz, 1985).

The case of the Balkans illustrates the issues. In the early 1990s, some argued that continued conflict was inevitable because of ancient ethnic hatreds (Kaplan, 1993), an argument contributing to the reluctance of European and U.S. leaders to intervene. Other observers insisted that Bosnia's ethnic groups had lived peacefully together for decades and even intermarried (Malcolm, 1994; Posen, 1993). They argued that the real force behind the violence was the aggressive power-building of Milosevic and other nationalist leaders, who used ethnic rhetoric to divide Yugoslavia along ethnic lines. Still others pointed to how criminal activities were furthered by ethnic politics (Mueller, 2000).

[7]   A "causal representation" shows factors causing effects. It does *not*, however, imply the ability to predict results with any confidence. In the S&R domain, prediction is difficult because of uncertainties in the factors' values, the functions that connect them, and complex dynamics over time. Factor trees and influence diagrams, however, can still be very useful, e.g., in suggesting how to influence events positively or negatively.

[8]   The older methods used terms such as *armored division equivalents* (Kugler, 2006), *WEI-WUV scoring* (Mako, 1983), and *situational scoring* (Allen, 1992, 1995). Despite inherent mathematical limitations and criticisms, the methods proved valuable over decades, especially when situationally adjusted for terrain and combined-arms mix (Allen, 1992), as in the RAND Strategy Assessment System. These older methods were used in war games, higher-level campaign analyses, balance assessments, and other applications within the United States and NATO, and they were sometimes more insightful than results from big-model exercises. For such methods to work well, however, a good deal of class knowledge is needed, along with structured methods for estimating scores that draw on both experienced military officers and analysts, as well as history (Dupuy, 1987).

[9]   Significantly, conflict may be started not by one of the previous antagonists, but by a spin-off faction that will not accept the peace to which the original faction had agreed (Kreutz, 2010a, 2010b).

[10]   As one example, rebellion against tyranny often has emotional components not captured by a *stable* utility function. Although rational-analytic methods could be used to infer a "revealed" utility function, such utility functions are not stable over time (e.g., between periods of revolutionary zeal and periods of physical and moral exhaustion) and are therefore dubious concepts.

[11]   One such computerized tool, the Stability Operations Army Force Estimator (SAFE), was developed by colleague Tom Szayna and collaborators for the U.S. Army. It draws directly on Army doctrine. Only a short description exists in the open literature (Army Science Board, 2006).

References

Agoglia, John, Michael Dziedzic, and Barbara Sotirin, eds., *Measuring Progress in Conflict Environments (MPICE): A Metrics Framework*, Washington D.C.: U.S. Institute for Peace, 2011.

Alesina, Alberto, and Eliana La Ferrara, "Ethnic Diversity and Economic Performance," *Journal of Economic Literature*, Vol. 43, No. 3, September 2005, pp. 762–800.

Allen, Patrick D., *Situational Force Scoring: Accounting for Combined Arms Effects in Aggregate Combat Models*, Santa Monica, Calif.: RAND Corporation, 1992. As of April 7, 2011:
http://www.rand.org/pubs/notes/N3423.html

———, "The Need to Represent a Wide Range of Battle Types in Air-Ground Combat Models," *Military Operations Research Journal*, Vol. 1, No. 3, 1995, pp. 19–26.

Army Science Board, *Enhancements to the Modular Force Support Brigades*, report of the FY 2006 Summer Study, 2006, pp. 33–37.

Barnett, Michael, "Building a Republican Peace: Stabilizing States After War," *International Security*, No. 30, Vol. 4, 2006, pp. 87–112.

Barron, Patrick, Kai Kaiser, and Menno Pradhan, "Local Conflict in Indonesia: Measuring Incidence and Identifying Patterns," *World Bank Policy Research Paper*, No. 3384, 2004.

Bates, Robert H., *When Things Fall Apart: State Failure in Late Century Africa*, Cambridge, Mass.: Harvard University Press, 2008.

Bellamy, Alex J., "Security Sector Reform: Prospects and Problems," *Global Change, Peace and Security*, Vol. 15, No. 2, 2003, pp. 101–119.

Bensahel, Nora, "Preventing Insurgencies After Major Combat," *Defence Studies*, Vol. 6, No. 3, 2006, pp. 278–291.

Berdal, Mats, "Beyond Greed and Grievance—and Not Too Soon…" *Review of International Studies*, Vol. 31, 2005, pp. 687–698.

———, *Building Peace After War*, Adelphi Paper 407, London: International Institute of Strategic Studies, 2009.

Berdal, Mats, and Spyros Economides, eds., *United Nations Interventionism: 1991–2004*, New York: Cambridge University Press, 2007.

Berger, Mark T., and Douglas A. Borer, "The Long War: Insurgency, Counterinsrgency and Collapsing States," *Third World Quarterly*, Vol. 28, No. 2, 2007, pp. 197–215.

Binnendijk, Hans, and Stuart E. Johnson, eds., *Transformation for Stabilization and Reconstruction Operations*, Washington, D.C.: National Defense University Press, 2004.

Blattman, Christopher, and Edward Miguel, "Civil War," National Bureau of Economic Research, Cambridge, Mass., NBER Working Paper 14801, March 2009.

Brinkerhoff, Derick W., "Rebuilding Governance in Failed States and Post-Conflict Societies: Core Concepts and Cross-Cutting Themes," *Public Administration and Development*, Vol. 25, 2005, pp. 3–14.

Brown, Michael E., "The Causes of Internal Conflict," in Michael E. Brown, Owen R. Coté, Sean M. Lynn-Jones, and Steven E. Miller, eds., *Nationalism and Ethnic Conflict: International Security Reader*, Cambridge, Mass.: MIT Press, 1997.

Brownlee, Jason, "Can America Nation-Build?" *World Politics*, Vol. 59, January 2007, pp. 314–340.

Bryden, Alan, and Heiner Hänggi, eds., *Security Governance in Post-Conflict Peacebuilding*, Brunswick, N.J.: Transaction, 2005.

Buhaug, Halvard, and Scott Gates, "The Geography of Civil War," *Journal of Peace Research*, Vol. 39, No. 4, 2002, pp. 417–433.

Byman, Daniel, *Keeping the Peace: Lasting Solutions to Ethnic Conflicts*, Baltimore, Md.: Johns Hopkins University Press, 2002.

Byman, Daniel, and Taylor Seybolt, "Humanitarian Intervention and Communal Civil Wars," *Security Studies*, Vol. 13, No. 1, Autumn 2003, pp. 33–78.

Call, Charles T., ed., *Building States to Build Peace*, Boulder, Colo.: Lynne Rienner, 2008.

Call, Chuck, "Police Reform, Human Rights, and Democratization in Post-Conflict Settings: Lessons from El Salvador," Department of Political Science, Stanford University, no date. As of April 8, 2011:
http://www.iadb.org/document.cfm?id=362102

Caplan, Richard D., *International Governance of War-Torn Territories: Rule and Reconstruction*, Oxford, UK: Oxford University Press, 2005.

Cederman, Lars-Erik, and Luc Girardin, "Beyond Fractionalization: Mapping Ethnicity onto Nationalist Insurgencies," *American Political Science Review*, Vol. 101, No. 1, February 2007, pp. 173–193.

Chanaa, Jane, *Security Sector Reform: Issues, Challenges, and Prospects*, Oxford, UK: International Institute for Strategic Studies, Adelphi Paper No. 344, 2002.

Chesterman, Simon, *You, the People: The United Nations, Transitional Administration, and State-Building*, London: Oxford University Press, 2004.

————, "Ownership in Theory and in Practice: Transfer of Authority in UN State-Building Operations," *Journal of Intervention and Statebuilding*, Vol. 1, No. 1, March 2007, pp. 3–26.

Chivvis, Christopher, "Back to the Brink in Bosnia?" *Survival*, Vol. 52, No. 1, February–March 2010, pp. 97–110.

Colleta, Nat, Marcus Kostner, and Ingo Wiederhofer, "Case Studies in War-to-Peace Transition," World Bank Discussion Paper No. 331, Washington, D.C., 1996.

Colletta, Nat, Markus Kostner, and Ingo Wiederhofer," Disarmament, Demobilization, and Reintegration: Lessons and Liabilities in Reconstruction," in Robert I. Rotberg, ed., *When States Fail: Causes and Consequences*, Princeton, N.J.: Princeton University Press, 2004, pp. 170–181.

Colletta, Nat, and Robert Muggah, "Rethinking Post-War Security Promotion," *Journal of Security Sector Management*, Vol. 7, No. 1, 2009.

Collier, Paul, *The Bottom Billion*, New York: Oxford University Press, 2007.

————, *Wars, Guns, and Votes: Democracy in Dangerous Places*, New York: Harper Collins, 2009.

Collier, Paul, V. L. Elliott, Håvard Hegre, Anke Hoeffler, Marta Reynal-Querol, and Nicholas Sambanis, *Breaking the Conflict Trap: Civil War and Policy Development*, Washington, D.C.: The World Bank and Oxford University Press, 2003.

Collier, Paul, and Anke Hoeffler, "Greed and Grievance in Civil War," Washington, D.C.: World Bank Development Research Group, Policy Research Working Paper 2355, 2000.

————, "Greed and Grievance in Civil War," *Oxford Economic Papers*, Vol. 56, No. 4, 2004, pp. 563–595.

————, "Military Expenditures in Post-Conflict Societies," *Economics of Governance*, Vol. 71, 2006, pp. 89–107.

————, "Unintended Consequences: Does Aid Promote Arms Races?" *Oxford Bulletin of Economics and Statistics*, Vol. 69, 2007, pp. 1–28

Collier, Paul, Anke Hoeffler, and Dominik Rohner, "Beyond Greed and Grievance: Feasibility and Civil War," *Oxford Economic Papers*, Vol. 61, No. 1, 2009, pp. 1–27.

Collier, Paul, Anke Hoeffler, and Mans Söderbom, "Post-Conflict Risks," *Journal of Peace Research*, Vol. 45, No. 4, July 2008, pp. 461–478.

Collier, John, and Nicholas Sambanis, eds., *Understanding Civil War: Evidence and Analysis*, two volumes, Washington D.C.: World Bank, 2005.

Connable, Ben, and Martin Libicki, *How Insurgencies End*, Santa Monica, Calif.: RAND Corporation, 2010. As of April 7, 2011:
http://www.rand.org/pubs/monographs/MG965.html

Contemporary Security Policy, Special Issue: Inconspicuous Disarmament: The Politics of Destroying Surplus Small Arms and Ammunition, Vol. 29, No. 1, 2008.

Cooper, Neil, and Michael Pugh, "Security Sector Transformation in Post-Conflict Societies," draft paper for Centre for Defence Studies, King's College, London, 2002.

Cornish, Paul, "The United States and Counterinsurgency: 'Political First, Political Last, Political Always,'" *International Affairs*, Vol. 85, No. 1, 2009, pp. 61–79.

Coyne, Christopher, "Deconstructing Reconstruction: The Overlooked Challenges of Military Occupation," *Economics of Peace and Security Journal*, Vol. 2, No. 6, 2007, pp. 93–100.

Cramer, Christopher, "Does Inequality Cause Conflict?" *Journal of International Development*, Vol. 15, 2003, pp. 397–412.

Crocker, Chester A., Fen Osler Hampson, and Pamela R. Aall, *Grasping the Nettle: Analyzing Cases of Intractable Conflict*, Washington, D.C.: U.S. Institute of Peace, 2005.

Davis, Paul K., "Improving Deterrence in the Post–Cold War Era," in Paul K. Davis, ed., *New Challenges in Defense Planning: Rethinking How Much Is Enough*, Santa Monica, Calif.: RAND Corporation, 1994. As of April 7, 2011:
http://www.rand.org/pubs/monograph_reports/MR400.html

———, *Simple Models to Explore Deterrence and More General Influence in the War with al Qaeda*, Santa Monica, Calif.: RAND Corporation, 2010. As of April 7, 2011:
http://www.rand.org/pubs/occasional_papers/OP296.html

Davis, Paul K., and Kim Cragin, eds., *Social Science for Counterterrorism: Putting the Pieces Together*, Santa Monica, Calif.: RAND Corporation, 2009. As of April 7, 2011:
http://www.rand.org/pubs/monographs/MG849.html

Davis, Paul K., Jonathan Kulick, and Michael Egner, *Implications of Modern Decision Science for Military Decision Support Systems*, Santa Monica, Calif.: RAND Corporation, 2005. As of April 7, 2011:
http://www.rand.org/pubs/monographs/MG360.html

Department of the Army, *U.S. Army/Marine Corps Counterinsurgency Field Manual*, Chicago: University of Chicago Press, 2007.

Do, Quy-Toan, and Lakshmi Iyer, "Poverty, Social Divisions and Conflict in Nepal," unpublished working paper, Harvard Business School, 2007. As of April 8, 2011:
http://hbswk.hbs.edu/item/5669.html

Dobbins, James, Seth G. Jones, Keith Crane, and Beth Cole DeGrasse, *The Beginner's Guide to Nation-Building*, Santa Monica, Calif.: RAND Corporation, 2007. As of April 7, 2011:
http://www.rand.org/pubs/monographs/MG557.html

Doyle, Michael W., and Nicholas Sambanis, *Making War and Building Peace*, Princeton, N.J.: Princeton University Press, 2006.

———, "The UN Record on Peacekeeping Operations," *International Journal*, Summer 2007, pp. 495–518.

Dupuy, Trevor N., *Understanding War*, New York: Paragon House, 1986.

———, *Understanding War: History and Theory of Combat*, New York: Paragon House, 1987.

Economides, Spyros, and Paul Taylor, "Former Yugoslavia," in Mats R. Berdal and Spyros Economides, eds., *United Nations Interventionism*, New York: Cambridge University Press, 2007, pp. 65–107.

Edelstein, David M., "Occupational Hazards: Why Military Occupations Succeed or Fail," *International Security*, Vol. 29, No. 1, Summer 2004, pp. 49–91.

———, "Foreign Militaries, Sustainable Institutions," in Roland Paris and Timothy Sisk, eds., *Dilemmas of Statebuilding*, New York: Routledge, 2009.

Elbadawi, Ibrahim, Havard Hegre, and Gary J. Milante, "The Aftermath of Civil War," *Journal of Peace Research*, Vol. 45, 2008, pp. 451–460.

Englebert, Pierre, and Denis M. Tull, "Post-Conflict Reconstruction in Africa: Flawed Ideas About Failed States" *International Security*, Vol. 32, No. 4, Spring 2008, pp. 106–139.

Esteban, Joan, and Debraj Ray, "On the Salience of Ethnic Conflict," *American Economic Review*, Vol. 98, No. 5, 2008, pp. 2185–2202.

Etzioni, Amitai, "Bottom-Up Nation Building" *Policy Review*, December 2009–January 2010, pp. 51–62.

Fearon, James D., "Primary Commodity Exports and Civil War," *Journal of Conflict Resolution*, Vol. 49, No. 4, 2005, pp. 483–507.

Fearon, James D., and David D. Laitin, "Explaining Interethnic Cooperation", *American Political Science Review*, Vol. 90, No. 4, 1996, pp. 715–735.

———, "Ethnicity, Insurgency and Civil War," *American Political Science Review*, Vol. 97, 2003, pp. 75–90.

Feil, Scott, "Building Better Foundations: Security in Post-Conflict Reconstruction," *Washington Quarterly*, Vol. 25, No. 4, Autumn 2002, pp. 97–109.

Fortna, Virginia Page, "Does Peacekeeping Keep Peace? International Intervention and the Duration of Peace After Civil War," *International Studies Quarterly*, Vol. 48, No. 2, 2004, pp. 269–292.

———, *Does Peacekeeping Work? Shaping Belligerents' Choices After Civil War*, Princeton, N.J.: Princeton University Press, 2008.

Fukuyama, Francis, *Statebuilding: Governance and World Order in the 21st Century*, Ithaca, N.Y.: Cornell University Press, 2004

Gagnon, V. P., "Ethnic Nationalism and International Conflict: The Case of Serbia," *International Security*, Vol. 19, No. 3, Winter 1994–1995, pp. 130–166.

Gallula, David, *Pacification in Algeria: 1956–1958*, Santa Monica, Calif.: RAND Corporation, 2006 (1963). As of April 8, 2011:
http://www.rand.org/pubs/monographs/MG478-1.html

Gates, Scott, "Recruitment and Allegiance: The Microfoundations of Rebellion," *Journal of Conflict Resolution*, Vol. 46, No. 1, 2002, pp. 111–130.

Ghani, Ashraf, and Clare Lockhart, *Fixing Failed States: A Framework for Rebuilding A Fractured World,* New York: Oxford University Press, 2008.

Gleditsch, Kristian Skrede, "Transnational Dimensions of Civil War," *Journal of Peace Research*, Vol. 44, No. 3, 2007, pp. 293–309.

Goldstone, Jack A., Robert H. Bates, David L. Epstein, Ted Robert Gurr, Michael B. Lustik, Monty G. Marshall, Jay Ulfelder, and Mark Woodward, "A Global Model for Forcasting Political Instability," *American Journal of Political Science*, Vol. 54, No. 1, January 2010, pp. 190–208.

Goode, Steven M., "A Historical Basis for Force Requirements in Counterinsurgency," *Parameters*, Winter 2009–2010, pp. 45–57.

Governance and Social Development Resource Centre, "Fragile States," 2006. As of April 8, 2011:
http://www.gsdrc.org/index.cfm?objectid=
4D340CFC-14C2-620A-27176CB3C957CE79

GSDRC—*See* Governance and Social Development Resource Centre.

Gurr, Ted Robert, *People Versus States: Minorities at Risk in the New Century*, Washington, D.C.: U.S. Institute of Peace Press, 2000.

Gutiérrez Sanín, Francisco, "Telling the Difference: Guerrillas and Paramilitaries in the Colombian War," *Politics and Society*, Vol. 36, No. 3, 2008, pp. 3–34.

Habyarimana, James, Macartan Humphreys, Daniel N. Posner, and Jeremy M. Weinstein, "Why Does Ethnic Diversity Undermine Public Goods Provision?" *American Political Science Review*, Vol. 101, No. 4, 2007, pp. 709–725.

Hartzell, Caroline, Matthew Hoddie, and Donald Rothchild, "Stabilizing the Peace After Civil War: An Investigation of Some Key Variables," *International Organization*, Vol. 55, No. 1, Winter 2001, pp. 183–208.

Hedges, Chris, "Kosovo's Next Masters?" *Foreign Affairs*, Vol. 78, No. 3, May–June 1999, pp. 24–42.

Hegre, Håvard, and Nicholas Sambanis, "Sensitivity Analysis of Empirical Results on Civil War Onset," *Journal of Conflict Resolution*, Vol. 50, 2006, pp. 508–535.

Herbst, Jeffrey, "Responding to State Failure in Africa," *International Security*, Vol. 21, No. 3, Winter 1996–1997, pp. 120–144.

———, *States and Power in Africa*, Princeton, N.J.: Princeton University Press, 2000.

Hoffman, Bruce, "Insurgency and Counterinsurgency in Iraq," *Studies in Conflict and Terrorism*, Vol. 29, No. 2, 2006, pp. 103–121.

Horowitz, D., *Ethnic Groups in Conflict*, Berkeley: University of California Press, 1985.

Howard, Lise Morjé, *UN Peacekeeping in Civil Wars*, New York: Cambridge University Press, 2008.

Humphreys, Macartan, "Natural Resources, Conflict, and Conflict Resolution: Uncovering the Mechanisms," *Journal of Conflict Resolution*, Vol. 49, No. 4, 2005, pp. 508–537.

Humphreys, Macartan, and Jeremy Weinstein, "Demobilization and Reintegration," *Journal of Conflict Resolution*, Vol. 51, No. 4, August 2007, pp. 531–567.

Huntington, Samuel, *Political Order in Changing Societies*, New Haven, Conn.: Yale University Press, 1968.

Jackson, Brian A., "Organizational Decisionmaking by Terrorist Groups," in Davis and Cragin, (2009).

Jervis, Robert, "Cooperation Under the Security Dilemma," *World Politics*, Vol. 30, No. 2, 1978, pp. 167–214.

Journal of International Affairs, Vol. 58, No. 1, Special Issue on State Building, Fall 2004.

Journal of Peace Research, "The Aftermath of Civil War," special issue, Vol. 45, No. 4, July 2008.

Kahneman, Daniel, "Maps of Bounded Rationality: A Perspective on Intuitive Judgment and Choice," Nobel Prize Lecture, 2002. As of April 7, 2011: http://nobelprize.org/nobel_prizes/economics/laureates/2002/kahneman-lecture.html

Kalyvas, Stathis N., *The Logic of Violence in Civil War*, New York: Cambridge University Press, 2006.

———, "Promises and Pitfalls of an Emerging Research Program: The Microdynamics of Civil War," in Stathis N. Kalyvas, Ian Shapiro, and Tarek Masoud, eds., *Order, Conflict, and Violence*, Cambridge, UK: Cambridge University Press, 2008.

Kalyvas, Stathis, and Matthew Adam Kocher, "Ethnic Cleavages and Irregular War: Iraq and Vietnam," *Politics and Society*, Vol. 35, No. 2, June 2007.

Kaplan, Robert D., *Balkan Ghosts: A Journey Through History*, New York: St. Martin's Press, 1993.

Kaplan, Seth D., *Fixing Fragile States: A New Paradigm for Development*, Westport, Conn.: Praeger, 2008.

Kaufman, Stuart J., *Modern Hatreds: The Symbolic Politics of Ethnic War*, Ithaca, N.Y.: Cornell University Press, 2001.

Kaufmann, Chaim, "Possible and Impossible Solutions to Ethnic Civil Wars," *International Security*, Vol. 20, No. 4, Spring 1996, pp. 136–175.

Kilcullen, David, "Countering Global Insurgency," *Journal of Strategic Studies*, Vol. 28, No. 5, 2005, pp. 597–617.

———, *The Accidental Guerrilla: Fighting Small Wars in the Midst of a Big One*, New York: Oxford University Press, 2009.

Knight, Mark, and Alpaslan Ozerdem, "Guns, Camps, and Cash: Disarmament, Demobilization, and Reinsertion of Former Combatants in Transitions from War to Peace," *Journal of Peace Research*, Vol. 41, No. 4, July 2004, pp. 499–516.

Krasner, Stephen D., and Carlos Pascual, "Addressing State Failure," *Foreign Affairs*, Vol. 84, No. 4, 2005, pp. 153–163.

Kratochwil, Friedrich, "On Legitimacy," *International Relations*, Vol. 20, No. 3, 2006, pp. 302–308.

Krause, Keith, and Oliver Jutersonke, "Peace, Security and Development in Post-Conflict Environments," *Security Dialogue*, Vol. 36, 2005, pp. 447–462.

Krebs, Ronald R., "A School for the Nation? How Military Service Does Not Build Nations, and How It Might," *International Security*, Vol. 28, No. 4, Spring 2004, pp. 85–124.

Kreutz, Joakim, "How and When Armed Conflicts End: Introducing the UCDP Conflict Termination Dataset," *Journal of Peace Research*, Vol. 47, No. 2, 2010a, pp. 243–250.

———, "Navigating the Fog of Peace," working paper for the SGIR 7th Pan-European International Relations Conference, Stockholm, September 9–11, 2010b.

Kugler, Richard, *Policy Analysis in National Security Affairs: New Methods for a New Era*, Washington, D.C.: National Defense University Press, 2006.

Lake, David, and Donald Rothchild, "Containing Fear: The Origins and Management of Ethnic Conflict," *International Security*, Vol. 21, No. 2, Autumn 1996, pp. 41–75.

Leites, Nathan Constantin, and Charles Wolf, *Rebellion and Authority: An Analytic Essay on Insurgent Conflicts*, Santa Monica, Calif.: RAND Corporation, 1970. As of April 7, 2011:
http://www.rand.org/pubs/reports/R0462.html

Lemarchand, René, *The Dynamics of Violence in Central Africa*, Philadelphia: University of Pennsylvania Press, 2009.

Licklider, Roy, and Pierre M. Atlas, "Conflict Among Former Allies After Civil War Settlement: Sudan, Zimbabwe, Chad, and Lebanon," *Journal of Peace Research*, Vol. 35, No. 1, 1999, pp. 35–54.

Liddell Hart, B. H., *Strategy*, 2nd revised edition, New York: Penguin, 1991 (1967).

Lipset, Seymour Martin, "Some Social Requisites of Democracy: Economic Development and Political Legitimacy," *American Political Science Review*, Vol. 53, 1959, No. 1, pp. 69–105.

Long, Austin, *On "Other War": Lessons from Five Decades of RAND Counterinsurgency Research*, Santa Monica, Calif.: RAND Corporation, 2006. As of April 7, 2011:
http://www.rand.org/pubs/monographs/MG482.html

Lujala, Päivi, "The Spoils of Nature: Armed Civil Conflict and Rebel Access to Natural Resources," *Journal of Peace Research*, Vol. 47, No. 1, 2010, pp. 15–28.

Lujala, Päivi, Nils Petter Gleditsch and Elisabeth Gilmore, "A Diamond Curse? Civil War and a Lootable Resource," *Journal of Conflict Resolution*, Vol. 49, No. 4, 2005, pp. 538–562.

Lyall, Jason, and Isaiah Wilson III, "Rage Against the Machines: Explaining Outcomes in Counterinsurgency Wars," *International Organization*, Vol. 63, Winter 2009, pp. 67–106.

MacDonald, Paul K., "Useful Fiction or Miracle Maker: The Competing Epistemological Foundations of Rational Choice Theory," *American Political Science Review*, Vol. 97, No. 4, 2003, pp. 551–565.

Mako, William, *U.S. Ground Forces and the Defense of Central Europe*, Washington, D.C.: Brookings, 1983.

Mako, William P., *U.S. Ground Forces and the Defense of Europe*, Washington, D.C.: Brookings, 2003.

Malcolm, Noel, *Bosnia: A Short History*, New York: NYU Press, 1994.

Mao Tse-Tung, *On Guerilla War*, New York: Praeger, 1961.

Marston, Daniel, and Carter Malkasian, eds., *Counterinsurgency in Modern Warfare*, Oxford, UK: Osprey Publishing, 2008.

McDonough, David, "From Guerillas to Government: Post-Conflict Stability in Liberia, Uganda and Rwanda," *Third World Quarterly*, Vol. 29, No. 2, 2008, pp. 357–374.

Metz, Steven, "Insurgency and Counterinsurgency in Iraq," *Washington Quarterly*, Vol. 27, No. 1, 2003, pp. 25–36.

Miguel, Edward, Shanker Satyanath, and Ernest Sergenti, "Economic Shocks and Civil Conflict: An Instrumental Variables Approach," *Journal of Political Economy*, Vol. 112, No. 4, 2004.

Montalvo, José G., and Marta Reynal-Querol, "Ethnic Polarization, Potential Conflict, and Civil Wars," *The American Economic Review*, Vol. 95, No. 3, June 2005, pp. 796–816.

Mueller, John, "The Banality of Ethnic War," *International Security*, Vol. 25, No. 1, Summer 2000, pp. 42–70.

Muggah, Robert, "Emerging from the Shadow of War: A Critical Perspective on DDR and Weapons Reduction in the Post-Conflict Period," *Contemporary Security Policy*, Vol. 27, No. 1, April 2006, pp. 190–205.

National Academy of Sciences, *Post–Cold War Conflict Deterrence*, Washington, D.C.: National Academy Press, 1996.

Papagianni, Katia, "Participation and State Legitimation," in C. T. Call with V. Wyeth, eds., *Building States to Build Peace*, Boulder, Colo.: Lynne Rienner, 2008, pp. 49–71.

Paris, Roland, "Human Security: Paradigm Shift or Hot Air?" *International Security*, Vol. 26, No. 2, Fall 2001, pp. 87–102.

———, *At War's End: Building Peace After Civil Conflict*, New York: Cambridge University Press, 2004.

Paul, Christopher, Colin C. Clarke, and Beth Grill, *Victory Has a Thousand Fathers: Sources of Success in Counterinsurgency*, Santa Monica, Calif.: RAND Corporation, 2010. As of April 7, 2011:
http://www.rand.org/pubs/monographs/MG964.html

Pei, Minxin, and Sara Kasper, "Lessons from the Past: The American Record on Nation-Building," Carnegie Endowment Policy Brief, No. 24, 2003.

Perwita, Anak Agung Banyu, "Security Sector Reform in Indonesia: The Case of Indonesia's Defence White Paper 2003," *Journal of Security Sector Management*, Vol. 2, No. 4, December 2004.

Posen, Barry, "The Security Dilemma and Ethnic Conflict," *Survival*, Vol. 35, No. 1, Winter 1993, pp. 27–47.

Prunier, Gérard, *Africa's World War: Congo, the Rwandan Genocide, and the Making of a Continental Catastrophe*, New York: Oxford University Press, 2009.

Quinlivan, James, "Force Requirements in Stability Operations," *Parameters*, Vol. 23, 1995–1996, pp. 59–69.

Quinn, J. Michael, T. David Mason, and Mehmet Gurses, "Sustaining the Peace: Determinants of Civil War Recurrence," *International Interactions*, Vol. 33, 2007, pp. 167–193.

Raleigh, Clionadh, and Håvard Hegre, "Population Size, Concentration, and Civil War: A Geographically Disaggregated Analysis," *Political Geography*, Vol. 28, No. 4, 2009, pp. 224–238.

Ramet, Sabrina P., *Thinking About Yugoslavia: Scholarly Debates About the Yugoslav Breakup and the Wars in Bosnia and Kosovo*, New York: Cambridge University Press, 2005.

Rose, William, "The Security Dilemma and Ethnic Conflict," *Security Studies*, Vol. 9, No. 4, Summer 2000, pp. 1–51.

Ross, Michael L., "What Do We Know About Natural Resources and Civil War?" *Journal of Peace Research*, Vol. 41, No. 3, 2004, pp. 337–356.

Ross, Michael, "A Closer Look at Oil, Diamonds, and Civil War," *Annual Review of Political Science,* Vol. 9, 2006, pp. 265–300.

Rostow, W. W., "The Take-Off into Self-Sustained Growth," *Economic Journal*, Vol. 66, No. 261, 1956, pp. 25–48.

Rotberg, Robert I., ed., *When States Fail: Causes and Consequences*, Princeton, N.J.: Princeton University Press, 2004.

Rubin, Barnett R., "The Politics of Security in Post-Conflict Statebuilding," in Charles T. Call, ed., *Building States to Build Peace*, Boulder, Colo.: Lynne Rienner, 2008, pp. 25–48.

Sambanis, Nicholas, "Using Case Studies to Expand Economic Models of Civil War," *Perspectives on Politics*, Vol. 2, No. 2, 2004, pp. 259–279.

———, "Poverty and the Organization of Political Violence," in Susan M. Collins and Carol Graham, eds., *Brookings Trade Forum, 2004*, Washington, D.C.: Brookings Institution, 2005, pp. 165–211.

Schindler, John, "Defeating Balkan Insurgency: The Austro-Hungarian Army in Bosnia-Hercegovina, 1878–1882," *Journal of Strategic Studies*, Vol. 27, No. 3, 2004, pp. 528–552.

Schwartz, Rolf, "Post-Conflict Peacebuilding: The Challenges of Security, Welfare and Representation," *Security Dialogue*, Vol. 36, No.4, 2005, pp. 429–446.

Simon, Herbert, "Rational Decision-Making in Business Organizations," in Assar Lindbeck, ed., *Nobel Lectures, Economics, 1969–1980*, Singapore: World Scientific Publishing Company, 1992.

Snyder, Richard, "Does Lootable Wealth Breed Disorder? A Political Economy of Extraction Framework," *Comparative Political Studies*, Vol. 39, No. 8, 2006, pp. 943–968.

Stewart, Frances, ed., *Horizontal Inequalities and Conflict: Understanding Group Violence in Multiethnic Societies*, London: Palgrave, 2008.

Sunderland, Riley, *Winning the Hearts and Minds of the People: Malaya, 1948– 1960*, Santa Monica, Calif.: RAND Corporation, 1964. As of April 7, 2011: http://www.rand.org/pubs/research_memoranda/RM4174.html

Tadjbaksh, Shahrbanou, "Human Security: Concepts and Implications: With an Application to Post-Intervention Challenges in Afghanistan," CERI Working Paper No. 117-118, September 2005.

Tyson, Ann Scott, "Gates May Be Open to Troop Increase," *Washington Post*, September 4, 2009. As of April 7, 2011: http://www.washingtonpost.com/wp-dyn/content/article/2009/09/03/AR2009090302744.html

United Nations, "Disarmament, Demobilization, and Reintegration of Ex-Combatants in a Peacekeeping Environment: Principles and Guidelines," UN Department of Peacekeeping Operations/Lessons Learned Unit, 1999.

Uvin, Peter, "Ethnicity and Power in Burundi and Rwanda: Different Paths to Mass Violence," *Comparative Politics*, Vol. 31, No. 3, April 1999, pp. 253–271.

Walter, Barbara F., *Committing to Peace: The Successful Settlement of Civil Wars*, Princeton, N.J.: Princeton University Press, 2002.

———, "Does Conflict Beget Conflict: Explaining Recurring Civil War," *Journal of Peace Research*, Vol. 41, No. 3, 2004, pp. 371–388.

Walter, Barbara F., and Jack Snyder, eds., *Civil Wars, Insecurity and Intervention*, New York: Columbia University Press, 1999.

Weber, Max, "Politics as Vocation," in H. H. Gerth and C. Wright Mills, translators and eds., *From Max Weber: Essays in Sociology*, New York: Oxford University Press, 1946 (1918), pp. 77–128.

Weinstein, Jeremy M., *Inside Rebellion: The Politics of Insurgent Violence*, New York: Cambridge University Press, 2007.

Wiatrowski, Michael D., and Jack A. Goldstone, "The Ballot and the Badge: Democratic Policing," *Journal of Democracy*, Vol. 21, No. 2, 2010, pp. 79–92.

Wood, Elisabeth Jean, "Civil Wars: What We Don't Know," *Global Governance*, Vol. 9, 2003, pp. 247–260.

Woodward, Susan, "Bosnia and Herzegovina," in Barbara F. Walter and Jack Snyder, eds., *Civil Wars, Insecurity, and Intervention*, New York: Columbia University Press, 1999, pp. 73–115.

CHAPTER THREE

Establishing Favorable Political Conditions

Julie E. Taylor

Creating Governing Institutions That Maintain Peace and Stability

General Observations

An important objective of stabilization and reconstruction (S&R) is to support the formation of an effective government that is responsive to the concerns of its citizens. Generically, a government is a system of social control for establishing and enforcing laws. A country's government usually has national, regional, and local layers. Huge variations exist across countries with regard to what functions are performed by which layer(s) of government. Governments also vary in terms of their structure, character, and basis of legitimacy. And, of course, they vary in their competence. Modern country-level governments (national governments) are typically expected to provide security from both external and internal threats to the nation and to provide national-level order, a system of national-level justice, and mechanisms to promote commerce (e.g., physical infrastructure, a currency, and relevant laws). They may or may not have a strong role in related functions at the regional and local levels. They may also have important roles in providing or contributing to social welfare, education, health, and even religion.

Any intervening authority, in seeking to affect such functioning of governance, is likely to be affected and even constrained by its own history and values, as well as by international standards, such as the UN Charter on Human Rights. This said, while military interventions are sometimes launched with lofty goals, their concern is peace, rather than social justice. That is, the top priority is to "leave a country at peace with itself and its neighbors" (Dobbins et al., 2007, p. xxxiv). That said, major issues remain about the form and shape of governments, how quickly proximate and higher-order goals can be achieved, what should happen when progress on one set of goals (be they objectives concerning rights, development, or security) impedes progress on another set of goals, and so on. These issues often loom large in post-conflict nation-building. This chapter surveys scholarly thinking on major, continuing issues, and points out matters of agreement, matters of disagreement, and dilemmas.

Distinguishing What Is Optimal from What Is Feasible

There is a tendency for intervening countries to try and remake host nations in their own image. Having been well served by the laws and institutions underpinning their own political and economic systems, intervening powers may assume that transplanting those institutions will likewise provide others with "that which they hold dear—domestic peace, the blessing of democratic politics, and the rich fruits of developed economies" (Etzioni, 2004, p. 1). Given that laws and institutions often evolve from a nation's normative values, intervening countries may not only perceive them to be the most beneficial choices, but also the most ethical. For example, the United States, because of its traditions, values, and experience, tends to go into post-conflict situations with the assumption that the national-level government should be relatively strong and cohesive, as well as at least reasonably democratic in terms of owing its legitimacy to the consent of the governed, promoting human rights (including protections of women and minorities), and holding officials accountable though electoral competition. These assumptions motivated much of the U.S. agenda in post-invasion Iraq and Afghanistan, but setbacks have caused the United States and its coalition partners to take a much closer look at the viability of their post-conflict aspirations.

There is now a movement afoot to scale back missions from what is optimal, in the eyes of the intervening party, to what is feasible given the limitations of a post-war environment (Etzioni, 2004, p. 1). In a looking-back-for-lessons essay, George McCall emphasizes that the implicit assumptions made by Americans in post-conflict nation-building are often seriously mismatched with reality, even to the extent of misunderstanding the direction of causality (McCall, 2009). For example, although most democracies have strong civil societies, increasing "social capital" may not improve democracy at all (McCall, 2009), and as Amaney Jamal points out in her study of Palestinian political parties, in a fragile and violent environment, civil society can be used to support authoritarian tendencies as well (Jamal, 2007). According to another study, the rich associational life in Germany's Weimar Republic helped the Nazis capture public support, thus contributing to their rapid rise to power (Berman, 1997). Investing in civil society sounds good on paper, but like many intuitive prescriptions for post-conflict states, the benefits may be realized only after a certain level of government control, institutionalization, or development has been achieved. Since these are the factors that post-conflict countries typically lack, well-intended policies can result in unintended or deleterious consequences.

In keeping with the push to limit the aims of S&R, there are also calls to proceed cautiously with policies that, though they might improve a population's general welfare in the long term, risk provoking hostilities during implementation. Support for girls' education in Afghanistan is one such example. Education, it was thought, would not only improve conditions for Afghan women who had suffered under the Taliban but would also benefit all of Afghan society: Numerous studies have shown that women's education levels are associated with economic growth, democracy, lower levels of intrastate conflict, and better health (Aslam, 2010, p. 2; Fish, 2002, p. 5; Melander, 2005, p. 695).[1]

Yet, despite considerable efforts and expenditures by the international community, improving girls' education in regions beyond Kabul has proven difficult. Many traditional Afghans consider it a stain on their honor to have female family members seen by men who are not immediate relatives. Most of the new girls' schools cannot accommodate traditional standards of modesty: Many are housed in tents that are open to outside viewing and, due to the dearth of qualified teachers, are staffed, at least partially, by male instructors and administrators. The Taliban have used the schools' challenge to traditional gender roles as the basis for attacks against teachers and students. The violence underscores the government's failure to protect its citizens, further eroding its popular support. If the Taliban are able to successfully exploit the issue of girls' education, and they are ultimately returned to power, then rather than liberating women from their inferior social status, girls' schools may be partially responsible for returning them to the confines of their homes and stripping them of their rights. Fearing such unintended consequences, planners are rethinking the efficacy of leading nation-building efforts with such culturally transformative policies and are emphasizing the need for policies to have strong local support (as has been the case in the well-known, but recently controversial school-building of Greg Mortenson, many for girls [Mortenson and Relin, 2006]). Recalibrating the strategy does not mean abandoning well-intended, long-term goals or violating U.S. sensibilities; rather, it involves adapting expectations and timelines to what can realistically be achieved (Ottoway, 2003, p. 316). Alternative strategies might include (1) greater investment in teacher training to ensure that before girls' education is introduced in rural areas, female teachers are available; (2) building school facilities that can accommodate the modesty requirements of Pardah; and (3) enhancing the value of girls' education by developing local female employment opportunities that are clearly linked to educational achievement. These approaches would slow the creation of educational opportunities for girls and women, but those opportunities created would likely be more sustainable.

Dilemma. Extending this particular discussion, the subject of women's rights poses a major dilemma for the United States and its UN partners in Afghanistan and elsewhere. As of summer 2010, President Hamid Karzai continues to favor reconciliation with the Taliban. Such a compromise might be welcome for providing peace if it included not supporting al Qaeda operations. Yet, as a condition for their participation in a coalition government, Taliban leaders would surely demand the reimposition of their strict interpretation of Islamic Law. How could Western leaders agree to a settlement that continued abject subjugation of women? Would reintegration—an alternative "compromise" strategy that aims to isolate Taliban leaders while reaching out to low- and mid-level fighters—likewise risk a precipitous reversal in the fortunes of Afghan women, or would the impact be less severe? In the shadow of the impending drawdown, a public debate about the impact of withdrawal rages on. Some critics argue that the status of women should not be used as a justification for a continued U.S. occupation—something they perceive to be a greater violation of Afghan liberty and a cause of continued conflict and suffering (Gopal, 2010; Nordland, 2010; Rothkopf, 2010). Others acknowledge that improving the treatment of Afghan women and girls will be difficult but believe that doing so is a matter of universal human rights, and that universal rights are rendered meaningless if applied selectively (Hudson and Leidel, 2010). Unfortunately, the academic literature has not caught up with current events, providing no significant guidance for U.S. leaders who grapple with trying to sort out the nation's strategic and ethical priorities in Afghanistan.

Core Requirements and Recurring Issues

The academic literatures on nation-building, democratization, and peacemaking are filled with recommendations for institution-building, but between the opposing predictions and findings, the varied quality of evidence, and the sheer number of related studies, it is easy to become overwhelmed. The purpose of this chapter is to systematically lay out the various arguments applicable to the political objectives of S&R, to indicate which are theoretical and which are supported by evidence, and to highlight where there is an emerging expert consensus and where the most important points of disagreement exist.

As a starting point we might ask, What features are most fundamental when contemplating post-conflict political development? Arguably, the three most fundamental are that the government is

1. *Stable*: Free of internal or external threats to the nation, its constitution, and governmental system.
2. *Functioning*: Able to make and implement effective decisions and provide core services to the nation's people.
3. *Accountable*: Subject to censure or removal if officials violate established rules, laws, and rights.

These three features of quality governance are mutually reinforcing and, to a limited extent, mutually dependent. If progress lags along one dimension, it will often hamper progress on the others—for instance, poor government service provision can undermine stability, or instability can hurt efforts to provide services. In some cases, wealthy governments, such as those in the United Arab Emirates and Singapore, have been able to overcome a developmental lag in one area by overcompensating in another. Both governments are less accountable to their citizens than most counties with commensurate gross domestic product per capita levels, yet they provide extensive government services, thereby dampening demands for public accountability. Governments in countries emerging from war, however, not only lack the ability to compensate for their shortcomings, their capabilities are typically depleted to an extent that precludes progress along any of these dimensions without outside assistance. Therefore, even though S&R aims to move governments along all three paths, a stable, functioning, and accountable government is an ambitious ideal to strive for, well beyond the likely measure of operational success.

Figure 3.1 sketches a factor tree for governance consistent with the above core attributes. It is a general factor tree based on the factors discussed in the literature as contributing to the quality of governance, but without prejudice as to the relative significance of the many branches or how or at what level the various functions of government should be accomplished. The factors, then, may be general, but what approach is taken to governance, and what the balance among factors must be, is another matter. The rest of the chapter is organized around those matters. The next section examines the merits of stabilizing states emerging from conflict by partitioning them into separate independent entities. The chapter then discusses the important issue of what type of regime should be contemplated. The section after that explores the types of conflict-mitigating, power-sharing, and integrative political mechanisms that are often a part of negotiated settlements. The chapter concludes with a discussion of ways to build strong state-society relations by encouraging greater transparency, civic participation, and government accountability.

Figure 3.1
Factors Determining the Quality of Governance

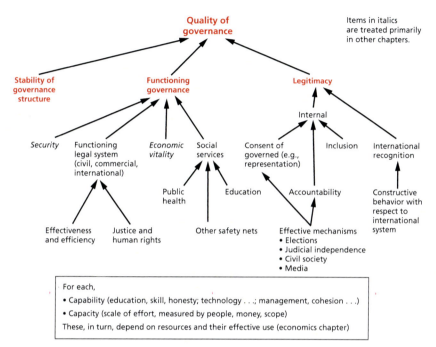

NOTES: The factors apply at a snapshot in time. Bulleted items are mere examples.
RAND MG1119-3.1

Territorial Partition

Before examining suggestions for establishing effective governing institutions and practices, it is helpful to first consider an option that could
potentially reduce the need for S&R operations, or at least minimize
their scope and duration. In the case of deeply entrenched and protracted struggles—many of which have an ethnic or sectarian basis—
several scholars have suggest that partitioning the country and providing former combatants control over their own territory and resources
is the best—and sometimes the only—path to peace (Horowitz, 1985;
Kaufmann, 1996, 1998; Mearshimer and Van Evera, 1995). Proponents argue that establishing a border between protagonists limits their
interaction and, in turn, their opportunities for conflict (Rothchild

and Roeder, 2005, p. 11). Partitioning territories aims to resolve the two central grievances that combatants fight over: inequality and insecurity. First, if participants agree to the division, once they establish self-governance, the inequitable distribution of power and resources becomes a moot point. Second, when they locate to defensible enclaves, contending groups should feel more secure. Governance may also improve. Because partition creates unified governments (within each of the partitioned territories), it is assumed that they will be able to make and implement decisions more easily than if rivals entered into a power-sharing arrangement, in which governance could become paralyzed by the divisive issues that drove the earlier conflict. Statistical studies have found support for a relationship between partition and stability: Research by Sambanis (2000) and Fortna (2004) indicates that after civil wars, states that are partitioned experience fewer incidents of violence than those which result in power-sharing governments.

Yet, even if the resulting regimes had all of the stabilizing features that partition proponents attribute to them, in many cases the costs of partition may not be worth the rewards. Though there are numerous precedents for partition—Ireland (1920), India and Pakistan (1947), Germany (1945), Korea (1953), Pakistan and Bangladesh (1971), Cyprus (1974), and Yugoslavia (1995)—it is a solution that is often politically and ethically problematic for the international community to support: No matter how calm and organized population transfers may be, in many cases, partition can constitute a form of ethnic cleansing[2]—a practice that violates international law (Kumar, 1997; Paris, 2004). In situations where mass migration is forced and chaotic, the human and material toll can be enormous. Page Fortna (2004) points out that Pakistan and India currently enjoy a cold peace, yet she overlooks that to get to this point, nearly 2 million people lost their lives and 12.5 million were displaced (Ahmed, 2002). Likewise, Sambanis and Schulhofer-Wohl (2009) note that, while plausible, the idea that policing a partition line is easier where populations are separated rather than intermixed has apparently not been satisfactorily tested, due to the limited number of cases and the influence of confounding factors, such as international pressure (pp. 116–117).

Another problem with partition is that it can set a dangerous precedent that leads to further disintegration. Once partition begins, the question becomes: At what level of aggregation should the divisions stop? In the case of Yugoslavia, many argued that partition into separate republics would create a number of weak and nonviable states. However, once partition began, division along ethnic lines quickly evolved from a limited solution to ethnic conflict to a "right" that could not be denied to other groups. Further territorial division resulted, and an even more dependent and fragile entity emerged, the Kosovo Autonomous Region, in 1999. Unable to defend itself against Serbia, its hostile neighbor, Kosovo continues to rely on NATO troops.

Due to such costs, even advocates of partition agree that it should be considered only under specific circumstances. If divisions have not yet devolved into violence, groups may be able to amicably divide their territory and have a "Velvet Divorce," as was the case with Czechoslovakia in 1993. The risks of partition are also more palatable when combatant groups are already concentrated into distinctive territories and dislocations can be minimized (Sisk, 1996; Johnson, 2008). And finally, if groups cannot live together under any circumstances, then—despite its steep costs—separation or even formal partition may be preferable to the destruction and possible genocide wrought by interminable conflict (Horowitz, 1985; Kaufmann, 1998). In such an extreme case, it is important that the population transfer be handled by a trusted third party, to ensure that it unfolds peaceably, and that supervision continues for a period afterward, to keep formerly civil conflicts from evolving into international wars or border clashes. Essentially, enforcement of the partition agreement and directing population transfers is a type of stability operation, but it involves a more modest set of objectives than those operations that seek to reconstruct and stabilize war-torn societies.

Regime Types

If partition does not occur and a more intensive stabilization operation is in order, one of the most crucial tasks is creating governing institutions that can maintain security and provide citizens with their basic needs. For most of the 1990s, there was little debate among nation-builders over which regime type could best achieve these goals. The collapse of the Soviet Union and its communist-totalitarian satellites was held up as proof of democracy's superiority. Indeed, it seemed that liberal democracy no longer had any plausible ideological competitors and that history was unfolding in a way that recognized this (Fuku-yama, 1992). The enthusiasm was sometimes excessive, for, as some scholars (Paris, 2004) note, democracy was soon touted as the curative for a host of societal ills, ranging from poverty to gender inequality, international wars to domestic conflicts. Further, the duration and dif-ficulty of democratic transitions, even under the best conditions—let alone in a post-conflict environment—was often underestimated.

A number of individual country case studies and broader statis-tical studies using cross-national, time-series data have indeed shown that democracy tends to promote development and economic growth (Jackman, 1973; Bollen, 1979; Burkhart and Lewis-Beck, 1994; Prze-worski et al., 2000) and that democracies seldom fight each other (Bueno de Mesquita and Lalman, 1992; Chan, 1984; Doyle 1986; Maoz and Abdolali, 1989; Morgan and Schwebach, 1992; Rummel, 1997; Russett, 1993; Weede, 1992; Bueno de Mesquita et al., 1999), yet democracy's relationship to civil violence remains widely debated. In the early 1990s, a string of post-conflict democratization success stories (El Salvador, Mozambique, Namibia) lent support to the pro-democracy camp, but by the mid 1990s, the horror stories of failed nation-building experiences in Angola, Liberia, Somalia, and Bosnia undermined confidence in the democratic cure-all—or, at least, in the feasibility of racing toward alleged democracy being always wise. Democracy, especially power-sharing democracy, still dominates rec-ommendations for post-conflict regime formation, but emerging con-cerns about the governing capacity of post-conflict democracies have caused state-building scholars to consider less democratic options and to rethink how to better sequence liberalization. The following subsec-tions, then, compare different regime types and how they may or may not be consistent with longer-term goals.

Autocracies

For obvious reasons, experts resist publicly extolling the "virtues of authoritarianism" (Halperin, Siegle, and Weinstein, 2004, p. 1), but objective assessments suggest that autocracy can have its virtues as well as its vices. It is often assumed that authoritarian regimes are inherently unstable because the succession process is often muddy (Olson, 1993), their societies lack social trust (Halperin, Siegle, and Weinstein, 2004, p. 104), and, in the long run, state oppression and exclusion may trigger a popular insurrection (Hafez, 2004). However, for those very reasons, autocrats sometimes use complex and adaptable strategies to support their rule, using oppression only sparingly as a method of control. Autocrats win support by distributing resources through broad patronage networks (Diaz-Cayeros, Magaloni, and Weingast, 2003) and by building robust security sectors that can effectively deter rebellious behavior, often simply by the threat of reprisals (Bellin, 2004). According to a long series of studies, these pragmatic policies have paid off: Consolidated authoritarian regimes[3] are found to be as stable as established democracies (DeNardo, 1985; Francisco, 1995; Muller and Weede, 1990; Hegre et al., 2001). While it may come as no surprise that soft authoritarian regimes with high levels of economic development, such as those in Singapore and Malaysia, remain firmly ensconced in power, even harsh dictatorships in poor countries can last a long time: Cameroon's Paul Biya has remained in power for 27 years, while Hosni Mubarak was Egypt's president for 29 years.

Arguments highlighting the merits of post-conflict autocracies come primarily from the democratization and economic development literatures. It is posited that dictatorships—because they are less beholden to popular support—are in a better position to initiate major policy changes and stave off crises than democracies, where the electoral cycle makes politicians beholden to particularistic concerns (Maravall, 1994). Not only are autocrats thought by some to be more effective "universal agents" (Bhagwati, 1993), but also their strong security apparatuses can put down threats before they grow into bigger challenges. In contrast, democracies are good at promising perks in exchange for cooperation, but due to their labored and inclusive decisionmaking, they are less credible when it comes to enacting punishments.

Cautions. Though superficially compelling, the argument for ensconcing autocratic regimes in war-torn countries is difficult to support even if one puts aside idealism. In the first place, it appears that the relationship between autocracy and stability is largely an artifact of oil wealth (Marshall, 2008, p. 11). Though most authoritarian regimes are poor, many autocratic, oil-producing states are highly stable due to the public support engendered by their provision of financial resources and public services (Ross, 2001; Smith, 2004). Second, even if authoritarian regimes were largely "stable," if a large portion of a county's population is repressed and excluded, it can hardly be thought of as peaceful (Doyle and Sambanis, 2006, p. 73). Third, nation-building does not operate in a vacuum, and if the preexisting government was an irredeemably weakened authoritarian regime that monopolized power and excluded or oppressed its rivals, replacing it with a similar system of government would not be palatable to either the population or the international community. And finally, the case for supporting authoritarian regimes is further eroded by the fact that the very things that reportedly make consolidated autocracies stable are hard to come by in a post-conflict environment. To maintain their position without resorting to violence, autocrats need substantial resources for funding the security sector and appeasing supporters. When resources are depleted—as is usually the case after prolonged conflicts—the government often turns to preying on the resources of the poor and marginalized. Bates (2008b) discovered that civil wars in Africa were usually preceded by periods of state predation that prompted victims to seek protection from anti-government forces. This in turn provoked repressive measures by the government and set in motion a downward security spiral. Several studies have shown that repression by states with weak institutions—as is often the case after conflict—reignites civil wars (Hegre et al., 2001; Lichbach, 1995; Moore, 1998). Financial resource depletion also undermines a government's capacity to maintain elite support and to crack down effectively on dissent—two factors that Lucan Way (2005) claims contributed to the "color revolutions" that challenged authoritarian regimes in the former Soviet republics. In sum, consolidated autocracies can in principle be stable, but without the capacity to build strong institutions and support networks, post-conflict autocracies typically remain weak, unconsolidated, and unstable.

What all of this means is that *the intervening authority needs to set up a local government if it is not to stay forever, and popular consent and representative forms offer the only means likely to be acceptable to the local population and the international community.**

Democracies

Democracy has several properties that improve citizens' welfare, but here we limit our discussion to how it can help promote peace and manage some of the challenges that post-conflict governments confront. In many respects, democracy appears well suited for states emerging from war. There is an emerging scholarly consensus that consolidated democracies[4]—like established autocracies—are highly stable (Gurr, 1993; Hegre et al., 2001; Quinn, Mason, and Gurses, 2007; Rummel, 1997). However, quite the opposite is true for the type of fledgling democracies that often emerge from peace negotiations (Doyle and Sambanis, 2006; Gurr, 1993; Hegre et al., 2001; Mansfield and Snyder, 2005). Hegre et al. (2001, p. 38) found that "intermediate" democracies were four times more prone to civil war than consolidated democracies, and regime type proved significant even when controlling for the destabilization caused by regime change. A possible, yet insufficiently tested, explanation is that, due to institutional weakness, unconsolidated democracies lack the capacity and checks on power that in a developed democracy discourage groups from resorting to "politics by other means" (Huntington, 1968). Moreover, while democratic openness and competition encourage dissent, unconsolidated democracies lack well-established rules or institutions for resolving conflicts and are more apt to resort to repression if challengers get out of hand (Haggard and Kaufmann, 1995). The resulting loss of legitimacy can create a security spiral that devolves into conflict. And finally, democracies established in the aftermath of war face low odds of survival because

---

* Kuwait is the exception that proves the rule, the one case in which a preexisting nondemocratic regime had not been discredited by the conflict and could be reinstalled with no effort to reform or democratize it in the process.

they also feature many of the economic characteristics that undermine democratic development and stability—namely, poverty, high inflation rates, low levels of social development (Przeworski et al., 2000), and low government revenues (Bates, 2008a, 2008b).

The fragility of unconsolidated democracies has prompted several scholars to argue in favor of delaying electoral competition until the conflict-mitigating aspects of a durable democracy (moderate parties, the rule of law, a monopoly on the legitimate use of force, an active civil society, cross-cutting cleavages, electoral rules that promote inclusion, etc.) are put in place (Brancati and Snyder, 2010; Kumar and Ottaway, 1998; Mansfield and Snyder, 2005; Paris, 2004; Zakaria, 2003). As Thomas Carothers (2007, p. 13) summarizes, advocates of sequencing believe that "Pursuing a sequential path promises to rationalize and defang democratic change by putting the potentially volatile, unpredictable actions of newly empowered masses and emergent elected leaders into a sturdy cage built of laws and institutions." During the transition phase, either an intervening power, the appointed authority, or some sort of "peacekeeping agency" (Paris, 2004, p. 206) would be responsible for shepherding the needed reforms and would step aside once these democratic preconditions have been met.

Cautionaries About Sequencing. While on the surface the argument for sequencing sounds reasonable, implementation could be fraught with obstacles. First, we live in a globalized world, and the desire for elections and self-determination is found in many countries, even among people who have never lived in a democracy. Elections are not only a policy suggested by nation-builders; citizens also clamor for a political voice and expect to be consulted on any issues that affect their future. In Iraq in 2004, Ayatollah Sistani—who until that time was not a known democrat—encouraged demonstrations and demanded that the United States stop dragging its feet on promised elections. Despite widespread violence on election day, Iraqis turned out in droves to exercise their hard-won right to vote (Toensing, 2005, p. 8). Given the popularity of elections, it is hard to conceive why citizens—who likely suffered under the preceding conflict and lost trust in political elites— would willingly submit to a paternalistic, "transitional" authority, even if those in charge were their own countrymen. Second, if the authority was indigenous, it would likely be autocratic (something that the advocates of sequencing avoid saying). It is not clear what would motivate autocrats to limit their own power by establishing the rule of law and then, at a propitious moment of their choosing, surrender it completely (Carothers, 2007, pp. 16–18). Third, from the perspective of intervening powers, postponing a country's elections and taking full responsibility for the transitional period is a commitment that few are willing or able to take, and even if they are, their commitment may quickly erode as costs mount. Fourth, the premise of the sequencing argument is that aspects of the regime type cause the instability associated with post-conflict democratization. Rather, as Mason et al. (2007) points out, the instability of post-conflict democracies is likely an artifact of the preceding struggle.

While victors can impose democracies, such as the United States did in Japan and Germany, more often post-conflict democracies emerge as a result of inconclusive and protracted struggles. Because no side can gain a monopoly on power, they seek out a "second-best solution" (Waterbury, 1994, p. 34) that can regulate, and perhaps resolve, the dispute (Olson, 1993; Przeworski, 1991; Rustow, 1970). There are several reasons why, regardless of regime type, such governments would be unstable. Studies show, first, that young regimes are more prone to conflict than older ones and, second, that recent war experience raises the likelihood of renewed violence (Doyle and Sambanis, 2006; Mason et al., 2007). And finally, post-conflict democracies are typically formed by rivals with power parity—if one side had been substantially stronger, the conflict would have ended in a decisive victory. Ironically, although parity makes democracy possible, it also makes it fragile. Any change to the status quo that is perceived as benefiting one side could change its opponent's strategic calculus, suddenly raising the appeal of a return to combat (a theme featured in the discussion of security in Chapter Two of this volume).

While democracy is by no means a perfect solution, for combatants involved in an interminable struggle, electoral competition provides a mechanism for managing and transforming disputes (Harris and Reilly, 1998; Przeworski, 1991). Opponents compete for essentially the same prize they vied for on the battlefield—political power—however, they win by gaining public support, not obliterating their enemies. Being cut out of power is usually what causes groups to reignite conflict, but it is argued that democracy lengthens the time horizons of rivals, counteracting the zero-sum mentality that perpetuated the earlier conflict. According to proponents, in democracies rival factions are willing to accept short-term losses without resorting to violence, because (1) elections hold out the possibility that their fortunes can change and they could be in a stronger position to "advance their interests in the future" (Przeworski, 1991), and (2) they realize that the costs of suppressing rivals exceeds the costs of regulated competition and constrained power (Diamond, 1994, p. 3). Institutional constraints on power—checks and balances, constitutional limitations, etc.—assure electoral losers that winners will not be able to rule arbitrarily once in office.

Democracy is also said to promote "good governance." By way of elections, "rulers are held accountable for their actions in the public realm by citizens, acting indirectly through the competition and cooperation of their elected representatives" (Schmitter and Karl, 1991, p. 76). In this way, elections can act as a vetting process that, theoretically, can weed out inferior candidates. Competition for votes is a self-enforcing mechanism of accountability: Political elites have a strong incentive to respond to the public interest in order to gain and maintain power (Ferejohn, 1999, p. 131). In fact, simply the threat of removal, or of reduced power, has been shown to make incumbents more responsive to their constituents' welfare (Posner, 1975; Trounstine, 2008). Effective and responsive governments can address problems before they evolve into destabilizing crises on which potential spoilers can capitalize. For example, many predicted widespread social protests in countries hit hard by the economic downturn in 2008–2009, but, with a few notable exceptions, they either did not materialize or were calm expressions of public dissatisfaction. In the few countries where destabilizing mass protests emerged—Moldova, Georgia, and Ukraine—governance had already been immobilized by political power struggles (Onuch, 2009).

Cautions About Transitions to Democracy. The argument that peaceful transitions from conflict to democracy can be brought about through a convergence of interests and institutional engineering is widely accepted in both practitioner and academic circles (Ghani and Lockhart, 2008; Harris and Reilly, 1998; Reilly, 2001). Although there are critics (Collier et al., 2003; Haggard and Kaufman, 1995), they have not presented a revision of the essential logic. Instead they contend that the incentives and punishments generated by electoral competition alone are not enough to entice and sustain the cooperation of combatants or to promote good governance. Critics of the institutional-engineering approach to post-conflict democratization seek to extend self-enforcing incentives beyond the electoral realm. They claim that to persuade combatants to cooperate,

1. Benefits should accrue immediately.
2. Benefits need to be sustained.
3. Benefits should be guaranteed.

And, to persuade former combatants to continue working within the newly established political order,

1. Punishments for reneging need to be assured (even if outside enforcement is necessary).
2. Punishments need to be costly.
3. The benefits of returning to violence should be reduced.

The prescriptions for strengthening the conflict-mitigating effects of democracy are found in the growing literature on post-conflict power-sharing governments and accountability in state-society relations. They will be discussed in turn below.

Power-Sharing Mechanisms

Even though only 20 percent of civil war settlements result in some form of negotiated power-sharing pact (Walter, 1997, p. 335), they merit being explored here in greater detail because they also often involve third-party interventions. According to Sisk (1996, p. 5), power-sharing does not involve a specific formula, but rather includes a lengthy menu of incentive structures that aim to build peace by

1. off-setting the costs and risks of demobilization
2. guaranteeing participants a role in decisionmaking
3. dissuading defection
4. integrating ascriptive identities into larger political groups that cross-cut traditional cleavages.

What follows examines some of the institutional means of fostering shared government and, when possible, will highlight the mechanisms suggested for particular scenarios. However, at this generalized level, little can be said about which institutional arrangements best fit a specific context. Such an assessment should ideally involve an assessment of the war's outcome and the issues that combatants fought over, the war's toll on financial and physical resources, the population's level of heterogeneity, and the willingness of third parties to enforce and support political agreements. That said, a clear understanding of the logic behind power-sharing governments, assorted institutional options, and critiques of those options is also helpful to planners of S&R.

The Logic of Power-Sharing

At minimum, negotiated agreements need to provide the most threatening potential spoilers some piece of the political pie (Diamond, 1994; Lijphart, 1977; Nordlinger, 1972). To be enticing, the size of the piece should be commensurate with the participants' capacity to follow through on their threats. Some conflicts end in power-sharing agreements in which the clearly dominant power offers the weaker one limited concessions and a highly circumscribed and subordinated decisionmaking role in exchange for an early truce. For more intractable conflicts, involving rivals with commensurate odds of victory, encouraging disarmament will likely require considerable perks for each side and result in a virtual balance of power within the government. It is these wars that tend to involve third-party interventions. Suggested mechanisms for forging a power-sharing democracy include oversized cabinets encompassing all major parties; "consensus-oriented decision rules" (Harris and Reilly, 1998, p. 145); proportional representation multiparty systems; and low participation thresholds (Lijphart, 1994, p. 199). In contrast to mechanisms that promote peace through "inclusion," some power-sharing mechanisms create offsetting benefits by partitioning power: Federalism grants regional groups greater control over subnational affairs, and bicameralism gives them a voice on national issues, even if their population constitutes a national minority (Harris and Reilly, 1998, p. 221).

Proponents contend that power-sharing arrangements reassure parties that elections will not be zero-sum contests that result in "one man, one vote, one time." Mechanisms such as federalism, bicameralism, the separation of powers, judicial review, and rigid constitutions serve to decentralize political authority and prevent incumbents from amassing the power to exclude rivals (Hartzell and Hoddie, 2003; Lijphart, 1994, 1999). Opponents are willing to agree to consensus policymaking, decentralized authority, and checks on power because these restrictions also constrain their opponents. Hartzell and Hoddie (2003) add that protagonists are further reassured when they share power on multiple dimensions. Their study found that as the dimensions of power-sharing increased, so too did the stability of the power-sharing arrangement. The authors attribute this outcome to a "cumulative effect on the actor's sense of security, with the mutual dimensions having the potential to become reinforcing" (p. 321). If implementation of one dimension of the power-sharing agreement fails, Hartzell and Hoddie argue that the overall agreement is less likely to collapse as long as progress on other dimensions continues (2003, p. 321).

Power-sharing can extend beyond territorial and political dimensions to an apportionment of economic and military power. It is feared that if incumbents obtained full control over a state's financial resources, they could use the resources to rearm and attack their rivals or, perhaps economically marginalize them and provoke retaliation (Mason et al., 2007, p. 10). To avoid a return to armed conflict, groups may seek to "have the state displace or place limits on market competition, directing the flow of resources through economic public choice policies and/or administrative allocations to assist economically disadvantaged groups" (Hartzell, 2006, p. 46). Economic power-sharing can be pivotal to regime stability if the conflict originated from perceived economic inequities (Esman, 1987). If the basis of the conflict was insecurity, shared control over the military takes on greater significance. Governments need to have a monopoly on the use of force to be seen as legitimate, but after a war, protagonists hesitate to disarm for fear that they will be left defenseless as the national army evolves into the personal militia of incumbents. Military power-sharing attempts to alleviate these fears by (1) initiating security-sector reforms that keep the military out of politics (Ball, 2000), (2) disarming and demobilizing former combatants, and (3) reintegrating those forces into the national army (Hartzell and Hoddie, 2003). Walter (1997, p. 362) points out that in a post-conflict environment—where the stakes of disarmament are high and trust is at a low—building confidence may depend on allowing rivals to maintain their arms temporarily or on incorporating them into the national armed forces without forced disarmament.

Glassmeyer and Sambanis (2008) find that rebel integration into the military is not strongly associated with peace, most likely due to the poor implementation of the power-sharing agreement. In a combined test of overlapping power-sharing agreements, other authors found that relatively lower-cost power-sharing provisions pertaining to military or territorial autonomy reinforce post-conflict peace, whereas high-cost political-sharing agreements are often destabilizing (Derouen, Karl, and Wallensteen, 2009).

Critiques of Power-Sharing

Four major objections have been raised about the ability of power-sharing regimes to promote peace and stability. The first is that the "stickiness" of power-sharing pacts is undemocratic. Critics point out the inherent incompatibility between the "certainty" underpinning a power-sharing agreement and the "uncertainty" that is the hallmark of healthy democracy (Barry, 1975; Lustick, 1979; Przeworski, 1991). Grand coalitions and strict seat allocations in legislatures essentially dissolve the opposition and do not allow for the reins of power to change hands—regardless of whether a party's popularity wanes or the electorate's make-up evolves. The result is rule by an elite oligarchy (Rothchild and Roeder, 2005, p. 36), and if elites become ensconced and a political system cannot evolve, then new spoilers will arise who feel that their interests are being ignored.

The second objection is that the "stickiness" and inclusiveness of power-sharing agreements undermines government effectiveness and promotes legislative atrophy, ultimately making the government unworkable (Lijphart, 2002, p. 41; Rothchild and Roeder, 2005, p. 36). Several studies have shown that, as a general rule, the more veto players there are in a decisionmaking system, the harder it is to pass policy changes, and, for those that do pass, the narrower they will be (Cox and McCubbins, 2001; Tsebelis, 1995). Legislative atrophy can in turn lead to conflict if groups resort to extra-constitutional methods to fulfill unmet needs (Rothchild and Roeder, 2005).

Third, power-sharing mechanisms have been accused of politicizing ascriptive identities, thereby creating deeper social cleavages. Since power-sharing agreements usually evolve from protracted wars, and many of these tend to be ethnic conflicts, the post-war allocation of seats and resources tends to, likewise, run along ethnic lines (Lijphart, 2002, p. 45). Ethnic identity becomes reified as the only issue that matters, making problems that were already the source of past violence increasingly combustible (Sisk, 1996, p. 39).

And finally, critics argue that even the sizable benefits of shared rule are insufficient to maintain peace in precarious post-conflict democracies. Given that the cost of disarmament could be complete annihilation, the risks are too high for protagonists to be wooed by carrots or by the assurances of their adversary (Walter, 1997, p. 335). Critics who fault power-sharing regimes for their weak enforcement capacity contend that the type of credible commitment needed to prevent reneging can only be provided by external forces that have a clear self-interest in peace and are therefore willing to make a sizable and costly commitment of manpower and resources (Walter, 2002; Zartman, 1995, p. 272). According to Regan (1996, p. 341), only third parties can make the costs of reneging prohibitive. Statistical studies have supported the argument that power-sharing regimes are more peaceful when third parties intervene (Walter, 1997; Doyle and Sambanis, 2006). And yet, critics question how in the long run it will be possible for independent, self-enforcing institutions to develop under the restrictions of power-sharing agreements and dependency on foreign powers. Bosnia provides one of the best examples of power-sharing institutions being sustained while foreign intervention winds down, yet given the continued weakness of its institutions, it is still too early to declare the process a success.

Even if all of these criticisms were to hold true, however, they would not invalidate the argument that power-sharing mitigates conflict. As Horowitz (1991, p. 472) points out, power-sharing could very well be more successful than it appears because it is mainly applied in difficult circumstances, such as when states are ethically divided or protagonists are evenly matched. Both situations present acute challenges for any state trying to consolidate and rebuild, regardless of whether they adopt power-sharing mechanisms. Under such precarious circumstances, the choice set is limited: Allowing challengers to fight to the finish would decimate the society, and no side can win decisively enough to set up its own government. Thus, even though the stability of shared governments is questionable, it is often the best option available.

Federalism

Since the end of the Cold War, most state failures and civil conflicts have been blamed on ethnic strife. Seeking a way to manage these violent conflicts, nation-builders have increasingly promoted federalism because it reportedly offers a way to maintain a unified and viable state, while simultaneously satisfying (at least in part) minority yearnings for autonomy and enfranchisement (Brinkerhoff, Johnson, and Hill, 2009, p. 8). Federalism involves different models for mixing a central (and to various degrees, shared) government with self-government. Power devolves from the central government to the various subnational units, and each level has jurisdiction over different issues, with the central government typically retaining control over national policy and security concerns (Monteux, 2006). Decentralization is not always limited to political issues. In fiscal federalism, subnational units can acquire the power to collect revenue or make fiscal decisions. The opposite of federalism would be a wholly unified state, in which decisions on all matters came from the top echelons of the government without any differentiation in policies across regions. While federalism usually involves granting semi-autonomy to subnational regions, when ethnic groups are not geographically concentrated they may adopt a form of multicultural federalism that grants ethnic/sectarian groups autonomy over certain issues, as is done in Canada and Switzerland (Tremblay, 2005).

Arguments in favor of post-conflict federalism emphasize its effect on peace, democracy, and policymaking. Constitutional provisions allow minorities to protect and further their own interests, while restrictions on the central government help reduce fears of being exploited by the majority (Lijphart, 2002, p. 52). In a cross-national study as well as case studies comparing federal India with unitary Bangladesh, Pippa Norris finds support for the claim that federal systems are "associated with stronger democratic performance" than unitary states (2008, p. 184). Federalism, proponents contend, enhances democracy because it promotes inclusion by creating more points of entry into the government system. It also improves representation by creating electoral incentives for national politicians to respond to subnational concerns in their quest to win or retain office. Both inclusion and representatives help improve minorities' sense of security and, in doing so, are said to indirectly enhance stability (Norris, 2008, pp. 159–161). With respect to policymaking, supporters of federalism claim that the centralized decisionmaking of unitary governments produces cookie-cutter regulations and policies that do not fit local circumstances and, therefore, can potentially provoke hostilities. In contrast, federalism encourages subnational representatives to formulate more-efficient policies that are tailored to address their local constituency's concerns (Keman, 2000).

Skeptics, however, claim that federalism has the exact opposite effect: In their eyes, federalism is destabilizing, undemocratic, and ineffective. According to Hale (2004), districting based on ethnic identity discourages compromise and consensus and instead encourages local politicians to "play the ethnic card"—fomenting xenophobia and feelings of superiority in order to win support. If left to fester, these feelings can trigger demands for succession (Simeon and Conway, 2001). Critics contend that as minorities' commitment to the state diminishes, it will prompt the state to impose control, perhaps triggering a destabilizing security spiral. Federalism can also be destabilizing because regions of the state and levels of government can develop at different rates, causing problematic disparities. Successful nation-building efforts need to be both bottom-up and top-down, but if the governance, security, and development capacity of local communities surpasses that of the central government, federal divisions can become a centrifugal force that fosters disintegration. Some scholars suggest that federalism is not sustainable in many parts of the world because it is the natural tendency of central governments to resist power devolution and the diminishment of their sovereignty (de Figueiredo, Rui, and Weingast, 2005, p. 104; Horowitz, 1991, pp. 452–453). What is feasible also depends on prior experience and current expectations; it is difficult to *impose* wholly unfamiliar arrangements (e.g., federalism) on societies.

Some critics consider federalism undemocratic because citizens are not treated equally. It can result in different conditions, opportunities, treatment, and rights across subnational units. Before 1971, for instance, Pakistan was divided into two provinces with equal seats in the legislature, even though the Bengali population of Eastern Pakistan was much larger than the Mahajir-dominated population in the West. As a result, the power of the Eastern vote was diluted, contributing to Western dominance over Pakistani politics and the military. The imbalance culminated in a civil war that split East from West Pakistan, creating the independent country of Bangladesh. Additionally, it is suggested that the multiple levels of bureaucracy in a federal arrangement muddy accountability by making it less clear who is responsible for policies and problems (Norris, 2008, p. 162).

With regard to government effectiveness, other scholars add that the duplication of administrative functions and bureaucracy under federal governments makes transactions inefficient and more complex (Ranson and Stuart, 1994). In addition to eroding efficiency, federalism is also accused of hindering decisiveness because—as mentioned in the power-sharing section—as the number of decisionmakers in a government grows, more interests must be accommodated, thus making it harder to legislate and govern.

It is difficult to test predictions of federalism's conflict-mitigating effects because, according to Lake and Rothchild (2005, p. 114), other than Bosnia and Iraq, there have been no attempts since World War II to establish decentralized postwar governments. The notable absence of decentralized governments is perhaps a sign that "warring parties may know something that policy enthusiasts in the West have yet to learn (Lake and Rothchild, 2005, p. 112). Even in the absence of a civil war, Lake and Rothchild find that decentralized arrangements are not as long-lasting as unified states and that they tend to evolve toward greater centralization (p. 114). Another study finds that when ethnic groups are intermingled, rather than geographically concentrated, federalism does not appear to help manage ethnic conflict (Mozaffar and Scarritt, 1999). Hence, there currently is not a clear case for the benefits of federalism in a post-conflict context. However, most experts claim that this is due to the inherent instability of the circumstances that necessitate any type of power-sharing arrangement and that federalism remains one of the best ways to facilitate agreement among former combatants.

Governing Institutions

As stated previously, the goal for state-builders in post-conflict environments is to foster stable, functioning, and accountable governments. For power-sharing governments, that specifically means selecting an executive configuration (presidential or parliamentary, see Table 3.1) and an electoral system (plurality/majoritarian or proportional representation, see Table 3.2) that both (1) promote inclusion of potential spoilers, representation of minority interests, moderation, and the ability to identify and punish errant representatives and (2) discourage deadlocks and the concentration of power. Meeting these objectives is a tall order for state-builders, made all the more difficult by the fact that progress on one front can lead to setbacks on others.

Consociationalism. In the quest to engineer governments that can manage conflicts in deeply divided societies, a general consensus has emerged based on a theory termed *consociationalism*. According to the consociational argument, institutions that bring elites from each group together for consultation and consensus-building, and that create barriers to keep power from becoming concentrated in the hands of one party, are the keys to stability in divided societies. The theory is most

Table 3.1
Prototypical Executive Configurations

Executive Configuration	Description
Presidential	Characterized by a separation of executive and legislative authority. The legislature makes laws, while the president "presides" over their execution. The president and legislators are elected separately, from different constituencies, and neither branch can unseat the other.[a] Both branches check the other's actions: Presidents can veto legislation, and legislators can override vetoes.
Parliamentary	Executive and legislative authority is fused. Members of the executive cabinet are drawn from the legislature and are responsible for both introducing and executing legislation. To remain in power, the prime minister and cabinet must enjoy the support of the legislature. When the legislature lacks confidence in the government (expressed through a no-confidence vote), cabinet members must resign. Likewise, it is the prerogative of the prime minister to dissolve parliament and call new elections.

[a.] The exception is the rare occasion of presidential impeachment.

Table 3.2
Classifications of Electoral Systems

Electoral System	Description
Plurality-majority	"Winner-take-all" systems. By garnering either a plurality or majority of the vote within a given district, the victor gains all of the available seats.
Semi-proportional	Translates votes in a manner that falls somewhere between plurality–majority and proportional representation systems.
Proportional representation	Aims to make a party's share of parliamentary seats proportional to the percentage of votes it received.

closely associated with the work of Arend Lijphart (e.g., Lijphart, 1977), who described consociational governments as having specific attributes:

- A *coalition cabinet* that shares executive power among parties. Rather than adopting a minimum winning governing coalition, the aim is to have oversized coalitions that include more parties than are needed to win office.

- A *balance of power* between the executive and legislature. Though presidential systems are based on a separation of powers, Lijphardt's other specifications make it clear that he prefers a parliamentary system. Hence, he suggests procedural methods for balancing that weaken both legislators' ability to vote out the cabinet, and the prime minister's ability to call new elections.
- *Decentralized and federal representation* so that minority and local interests can be addressed.
- *Bicameralism*, with each house composed of members representing different (typically regional and national) interests.
- *Proportional representation* that allows minorities to gain representation (Lijphart, 1999, pp. 42–45).

Consociationalism is often contrasted with majoritarianism, which Lijphardt and others criticize for allotting seats only to the largest parties, thereby disenfranchising large portions of the population. In addition to the consociational literature, a prominent argument found in democratic development studies argues that parliamentary regimes are more stable than presidential systems because, due to the separation of powers, the executive and legislative branches can be controlled by different parties, a condition that may in turn produce legislative deadlocks. Instability may ensue if actors attempt to settle the impasse through unconstitutional means (Linz, 1978; Linz and Stepan, 1996). Indeed, there is considerable evidence that parliamentary governments have historically lasted longer than presidential regimes (Cheibub and Limongi, 2002; Harris and Reilly, 1998; Przeworski et al., 2000). Prescriptions based on both arguments are commonly featured within the practitioner literature for state-building and S&R (Brahimi, 2007; Sisk, 1996).

Recent critiques of the consociational and democratic development literatures point out, however, that many of the mechanisms they support often do not produce the assumed results (inclusion, compromise, stability, etc); conversely, those mechanisms they reject often perform better than expected. For instance, in an article that contradicts much of the conventional wisdom concerning institutional and electoral engineering, Cheibub and Limongi (2002, pp. 175–176) find that

Parliamentary systems do not operate under a "majoritarian imperative"; deadlock is not as frequent as supposed under presidentialism and is not absent from parlimentarism; coalition governments are not foreign to presidential systems and emerge for the same reasons as they do in parliamentary systems; decision-making is not always centralized under parliamentarism and is not always decentralized under presidentialism.

In a different study, Reilly (2005, pp. 165–166) finds that the assumed connections among proportional representation electoral systems, inclusive executives, and stability are not borne out in practice. Although proportional representation systems typically lead to inclusive executives, and most stable, ethnically divided democracies have inclusive executives, the majority of stable, ethnically divided democracies do not have proportional representation electoral systems. Possible explanations are that proportional representation systems may help fractured societies initiate democratization, but they can be destabilizing during the consolidation phase because they make room for extremist parties that can undermine functional governance by entrenching the "perception that all politics must be ethnic politics" (Reilly and Reynolds, 1999, p. 31). Barkan (1995) shows that, in countries where ethnic groups are geographically concentrated, contrary to common expectations, first-past-the-post voting in single member districts can often represent minorities better than a proportional representation system. The list of critiques is too lengthy to adequately summarize here, and to do so would obscure what may be the most important takeaway for practitioners. The point of these works is not to say that there is a better institutional formula for achieving inclusive, moderate, and stable governments; rather, they challenge the notion that sustainable governance can be achieved by adopting a one-size-fits-all model. Contrasting the successful, multistaged development of South Africa's constitution, which was constructed by an interim government of National Unity, with the "messy" constitutional processes in Iraq and Afghanistan that involved much foreign meddling, Lakhdar Brahimi (2007, p. 9), former UN Special Representative to Afghanistan and Iraq, argues,

The tendency to prescribe universal constitutional advice, and broad rules and regulations that do not fit the country context and are not underpinned by broad, inclusive and participatory inputs from national populations must be resisted. The historic, cultural, institutional, ethnic and linguistic differences among countries cannot be ignored. Generic constitutional provisions cannot be indiscriminately applied to highly individualized contexts. Ignoring these basic principles leads to problems of substance and process at both the micro and macro levels.

Once state-builders have an in-depth understanding of a country's history, the balance of power among elites, demographic factors, and attitudes toward leadership and fairness, they can select among a wide variety of options for forming a government that displays the qualities mentioned above: inclusivity, accountability, moderation, and the ability to avoid deadlocks and high concentrations of power. The options for building such a government go well beyond the choice of executive type and electoral system. They include open and closed party candidate lists; transferable votes; rules for introducing, vetoing, and overriding legislation; electoral inclusion thresholds; gerrymandering; term limits; and a host of other factors. Hence state-builders have many tools at their disposal for constructing governments that meet a country's specific needs and for offsetting any potential drawbacks.

Connecting the Government and the Governed

Thus far, the focus of this chapter has been on the formation of stable governments that keep potential spoilers engaged by offering them a place at the table and reducing the threat of incumbents accumulating unchecked power. This section shifts the focus from balancing relationships within the government to stabilizing the relationship between the government and the governed. This relationship is crucial to future stability—regardless of relations within the government, if citizens believe their needs are not being met or that the government has violated "norms of fairness," they may withdraw their consent to be governed and cease their compliance (Levi, 1997, p. 35), signaling a loss of state control and legitimacy that can lead to a popular revolt or reignite previous conflicts (Brinton, 1938, p. 209; Goldstone, 2001, p. 150). Public disapproval of the government can be expressed through what the economist Alfred O. Hirschman (1970) termed "voice" (attempts to repair relations by expressing dissatisfaction) or by "exit" (withdrawing from the relationship). (Warning signs of exit include refugees, brain drain, "desertion of the intellectuals,"[5] tax evasion, expansion of the informal economy, employing private militias, and desertion.) To stabilize governments and discourage exit, it is crucial that citizens have the ability to voice their concerns and that there are incentives in place that encourage political leaders to hear them and respond. These conditions are achieved by establishing a self-enforcing bargain between citizens and their government in which each is better off cooperating than if they acted alone.

The Modern Social Contract

The bargain that establishes social order is based on Jean Jacques Rousseau's concept of the "social contract": essentially, a mutually agreed upon exchange whereby the population gives up some of its freedom for government-provided security, while the government allows limits to its power in exchange for popular acceptance of its authority, i.e., legitimacy (Bendix, 1977, p. 167). The foundation of this bargain has grown considerably since Rousseau's time; in addition to security, it now covers a host of obligations that the government needs to meet if it is to receive legitimacy and compliance. These include the provision of civil rights, a system of justice, essential services, and a functioning economic system (Ghani and Lockhart, 2008; USIP, 2009). Even though the bargain is theoretically mutually agreed upon and makes state-society relations better in the long-term, it is an abstraction that depends on the actions of individual politicians, citizens, and groups whose personal or immediate circumstances are often better served by complete rejection (exiting) or by "cheating"—trying to obtain the agreement's benefits without paying the costs. To deter cheating and exiting, it is incumbent on state-builders to establish self-enforcing incentive structures that make the actions of citizens and politicians transparent and that consistently hold them accountable. These concepts will be explored in greater detail below.

The discussion of fostering stable relations between governments and citizens proceeds below by, first, exploring the mutual obligations between the government and the governed; second, addressing the methods used by both sides to try to renege on their obligations without losing the benefits of the original bargain; and, third, concluding with an examination of what is needed to ensure that each side is accountable and upholds their side of the bargain.

Before beginning this discussion, a minor caveat is in order. Scholarly and practitioner literatures typically group several of the obligations and incentive structures mentioned below under the heading of "the rule of law." Indeed, the rule of law can encompass issues as varied as civil rights, judicial reform, transparency, and police training. To avoid ambiguity, the term has been used here sparingly, and instead the discussion focuses on the specific aspects of the rule of law that are central to the government-governed relationship.

State-Society Obligations

The obligations that form the basis for state-society relations in most stable democracies, and which are a primary objective of state-builders, are listed in Table 3.3. This can be seen as describing the de facto social contract in a different way, one that shows indirectly related topics rather than *direct* exchanges. For example, governments derive legitimacy not just from accepting constraints on their authority but also from providing security, public services, and a judicial system. Likewise, by paying taxes, citizens underwrite much of what the state provides, not simply public services.

Although not discussed here at length, corruption is a very important problem in many states relevant to this book. It exists everywhere to some degree and in significant measure in many countries as part of the ordinary routine, yet substantial corruption represents a serious failure of the state and corrodes everything. As stated in a USAID document devoted to the subject:

Table 3.3
Duties and Obligations Exchanged in the Modern Social Contract

States		Citizens	
Provide or Relinquish	Receive	Provide or Relinquish	Receive
Authority	Legitimacy	Consent	Rights and protections
Justice system	Compliance	Freedom	Recourse and justice
Security	Conscripts	Conscripts	Security
Essential services and a functioning economic system	Revenue	Taxes	Essential services

No problem does more to alienate citizens from their political leaders and institutions, and to undermine political stability and economic development, than endemic corruption among the government, political party leaders, judges, and bureaucrats. (USAID, 2002)

Constrained Authority and Legitimacy. Popular expectations for state-society relations vary according to a country's culture and political legacy. Yet, in nearly all societies—even most modern monarchies—leaders claim to rule at the behest of the people, asserting that it is from popular consent (often loosely defined) that they derive their legitimacy (Dogan, 2009). Citizens do not, however, give their consent freely. Fearing predation if leaders exercise unfettered power, citizens demand that governments be bound by laws that provide clear rights to individuals and corporate entities in exchange for their acceptance of state authority. Therefore, crafting constitutions that clearly stipulate duties and protections and contain self-binding mechanisms is not a recommended priority for state-builders simply because establishing human rights is a laudable goal; without an unambiguous statement of what states give up and what citizens receive, popular legitimation can also be withheld, and the entire state-building venture can be over before it has begun. Not only will state-building flounder, but, according to Mati Dogan (2009, p. 196), "Less legitimacy translates into more coercion," presenting the prospect of greater oppression, civil violence, or both. By agreeing to submit to the rule of law and make their behavior predictable, governments receive voluntary cooperation from citizens. This exchange leads to an environment that typically encourages private investment, reduces the cost of enforcing compliance, and bolsters international legitimacy (Ghani and Lockhardt, 2008, p. 126). A virtuous cycle of legitimacy takes shape as each consequence of adhering to the rule of law in turn legitimates the state and its legal foundation. This process of legitimation is what the Organisation for Economic Co-operation and Development has termed *process legitimacy*: legitimacy derived from abiding by and maintaining the constitutional rule of law (OECD, 2008, p. 2).

According to the logic of the social contract, those in power, and those they govern, abide by the law because doing so makes them better off than when they breach it (Weinstein, 2005, p. 8; Maravall and Przeworski, 2003, p. 3). Yet in states emerging from conflict, or those in which a low-level conflict continues, both the state and society are weak and may not have the capacity to maintain their respective side of the bargain. For example, even though national political leaders may act to fulfill their obligations, they may not be able to guarantee that provincial representatives will do the same. Also, if a government's reach is limited, citizens may feel they have no choice but to collaborate with rebels who either coerce their loyalty or win it by providing benefits (Kalyvas, 1999; Wood, 2010). Hence, in fragile states the purported benefits of the social contract may not be forthcoming, despite the best of intentions. In addition, civil conflicts typically sow distrust between states and citizens, whereby sides may be unwilling to entrust their future to a risky relationship of mutual dependence. This lack of trust can cause an intractable coordination problem: While the social contract can serve the interests of both sides, fearing the vulnerability of cooperating when the other side reneges keeps both sides from submitting to the law. Due to the reluctance created by post-conflict uncertainty, third-party supervision and enforcement may be necessary to encourage submission, to nurture cooperation-supporting social norms, and to provide side benefits to sweeten the deal, at least until a moderate level of government capability and social trust is restored.

The causal relationship between third-party participation and popular submission is often too obscure to see, but it is readily apparent in situations that involve repatriation. For instance, the United Nations Transitional Authority in Cambodia (UNTAC) guaranteed the safe return of refugees and provided money to buy land and establish homesteads. Without UNTAC supervision, it is unlikely that so many refugees would have returned, especially if doing so had required them to entrust their safety to the former combatants who had caused them to flee. Although the government of Cambodia still acts with impunity at times, the contribution of international aid to the national budget and the presence of international development agencies are thought to have a constraining effect on government actions. As with the power-sharing agreements discussed earlier, the greater the size and certainty of both benefits and punishments, the more likely it is that governments and citizens will submit to being bound by the law.

System of Justice and Compliance. A social contract is rendered meaningless without institutions that are adequately empowered to enforce the law. A functioning system of justice requires a uniform and rational framework of laws, judicial infrastructure, regulatory agencies, and well-trained officers, judges, and administrators. To be seen as credible, such a system should provide equal access to justice and equal accountability before the law. Furthermore, there is a general consensus in the literature that the rule of law cannot be achieved without judicial independence, especially in the case of constitutional courts. The judiciary is considered independent when it is politically insulated from the other branches of government and from private or partisan interests (Ferejohn, 1998–1999; Helmke and Rosenbluth, 2009). Independence also means that judicial decisions are not influenced by individual judges' personal interests (Stepenson, 2001). And, finally, the presence of a rule-of-law culture in which the public believes that laws are legitimate and that the courts are fair and effective arbiters for meting out justice helps the establishment of a functioning, independent legal system (USIP, 2009, pp. 7–65). Dobbins et al. point out that "Without a widely shared cultural commitment to the idea of rule of law, courts are just buildings, judges just employees, and constitutions just pieces of paper" (2007, p. 88).

Both states and citizens have much to gain from a functioning and independent justice system. National governments impose their authority and maintain public order through such institutions as courts, police, and regulatory agencies. Although limited coercion—or the threat of it—also contributes to public compliance, independent courts can compel compliance in a less costly manner because they are seen as protectors of the public interest. By performing a constitutional review of the legislative and executive branches, independent courts enforce laws passed by the legislative body and prevent either of the two branches from encroaching into the other's jurisdiction (Ely, 1980). In addition to maintaining law and order, an independent judiciary also functions to create an environment conducive to business activity and investment by delineating and protecting contract and property rights (Brunetti, Kisunko, and Weder, 1997; Feld and Voigt, 2003). Systems of justice provide citizens with access to recourse and redress, thereby discouraging the pursuit of justice by extralegal means. They also protect individuals and groups from arbitrary state action and prevent the infringement of their civil and political liberties (Heller, 2000).

In post-conflict societies, establishing such an independent judicial system is fraught with difficulties. War-torn states often lack competent individuals to staff the judiciary, either because they had a negligible or corrupt legal system to begin with or because educated citizens fled the fighting and/or pursued better opportunities abroad. In the most extreme case of human resource depletion, the Khmer Rouge, who ruled Cambodia from 1975–1979, killed most of the country's educated population. The Vietnamese-backed regime that followed provided few opportunities for legal training. As a result, a 2004 UN report found that Cambodia had only 200 judges and 275 lawyers (McGrew, 2009, p. 275).

Another obstacle to judicial independence is the natural reluctance of politicians to empower any institution that infringes on their authority. Leaders have some incentive to at least initiate judicial reforms, since doing so bestows upon them kudos for engaging in good governance. Moreover, international financial institutions are more than willing to provide funding to enact such reforms. However, those same institutions have proved very lax at monitoring implementation of judicial reforms. Ruling politicians shirk from engaging in *meaningful* implementation, since the newly empowered courts may later challenge their actions (Finkel, 2008). Independent courts may also threaten those in power because they can function as focal points around which civil society can mobilize against the ruling body, as has happened in Egypt (Moustafa, 2007) and, most notably, in Pakistan, where nationwide protests against the dismissal of judges forced General Pervez Musharraf to resign the presidency (Perlez, 2009). Since leaders view judicial reform as a threat, to promote independent judiciaries, state-builders must think of incentives that can offset politicians' concerns.

While several scholars and policymakers have hinted at the problems involved with meaningful implementation, very few have proposed concrete solutions. Of those few, Ginsberg (2003) finds that if electoral uncertainty exists at the time of drafting, constitutions tend to support stronger and more independent courts. He also finds that once promulgated, constitutions are more successfully implemented if there is a diffuse political environment that provides the court more potential allies (parties, nongovernmental organizations, etc.) if it decides to rule against an institution of the state. By examining judicial reform efforts in Latin America, Finkel (2008, p. 31) provides a nuanced explanation for this pattern. She finds that when a ruling party's political future is in doubt, it is more willing to pay the costs of empowering the court while the party is in office in order to gain the long-term goal of reducing the risks should it become the opposition. Helmke and Rosenbluth (2009) cite a similar phenomenon in South Korea, where exiting authoritarian leaders faced an uncertain electoral future and suddenly, while still in power, began to work on establishing independent constitutional courts. These studies provide important insights for state-builders as to the conditions needed to establish independent courts and the rule of law:

- Pluralist systems produce more potential for judicial reform than political systems with centralized power.
- Having multiple strong parties and civic organizations can protect courts that act independently.

- Although it is tempting to make strict power-sharing agreements, electoral uncertainty is not just necessary for a functioning democracy, it is an important impetus for judicial reform.

Security and Conscripts. While countries differ significantly in terms of the mutual expectations for governments and citizens, one commonly held expectation is that governments are responsible for security. Security provision is the linchpin for all aspects of state-building. Governments are difficult to form without ceasefires and peace agreements. Social and economic development needs the certainty of a peaceful environment to thrive. And, government legitimacy depends on popular acceptance of the state's monopoly on the use of force. Since Chapter Two treats security issues in more detail, this section will address just one element of security provision that bears on state-society relations—military conscription. A person's willingness to die for his or her country indicates a strong identification with the nation, as well as support for the ruling establishment (or at least the system that brought it into power). Both beliefs boost prospects for state-building. Conscription may not be a popular policy, but when citizens believe that their government is legitimate and acting in their interest, they will comply (Levi, 1997). Mass desertion or draft dodging signals that citizens do not believe the government has the right to impose its authority over them. In the 1980s, Afghan rejection of the Soviet-installed Babrak Karmal regime was readily apparent as thousands of young men fled the country to escape serving in the Soviet-controlled army. If the state cannot provide security, citizens will turn to those who can, thereby weakening the state and empowering its enemies (Kalyvas, 1999).

Conscription is more than a measure of government support—it can also be an avenue for building social cohesion and national identity in fractured states. Even though all-volunteer armies tend to have higher-quality troops, drafting soldiers into an organization in which they need to cooperate with individuals they previously fought against has the possible benefits of reducing social tensions and keeping potential recruits for rebel organizations gainfully employed and under state control.

Provision of Goods and Services and Taxes. It is widely recognized that, in addition to security, providing essential services is a critical need in post-conflict peacebuilding (Dobbins et al., 2003). As discussed in Chapters Six and Seven, assistance should initially take the form of emergency humanitarian relief, but the focus should later shift to strengthening governmental and societal capacity to provide for the nation's needs. This includes laying the foundation for a functioning economic system, an educational system, an effective civil service to administer government programs, and a system of health services and sanitation.

Providing essential services does much more than ingratiate governments with their publics: It enhances their legitimacy and, in turn, contributes to greater security (OECD, 2008, p. 2). Unmet expectations or the unequal distribution of resources can cause social fragmentation and lead to conflict. Collier (2000) argues that failure to provide services can also be an indirect cause of instability. He suggests that when governments cannot provide employment opportunities or assistance to the population, the price of labor plummets, easing insurgent recruitment (for a different analysis, see discussion of work by Berman and Felter in Chapter Six).

Pressure for the provision of essential services creates a revenue imperative that links states and societies in a mutually beneficial relationship conducive to state-building and stability. When individuals and businesses are required to pay taxes, they develop a stake in the "performance and accountability of state institutions" (OECD, 2008, p. 3). The small breakaway territory of Somaliland is an example of the impact that these dynamics can have on state formation. Taxes from businesses make up most of that state's revenue, and, as a result, authorities have adopted business-friendly economic policies, limited commercial risk, and controlled state coercion and corruption (Reno, 2006, p. 170). Consequently, business leaders and tribal elders remain supportive of the political order.

There also seems to be mounting support for the theory that taxation is causally linked to representation. According to the general argument, government dependency on tax revenue allows the public to make demands on the government, which typically translate into civil rights, the rule of law, and political representation (Bräutigam, Fjeld-stad, and Moore, 2008, p. 10). Michael Ross (2001) tested numerous versions of the "taxation leads to representation" argument and found that "higher taxes relative to government services tend to make states more democratic." Other studies have shown that states with plenti-ful natural resources that do not need to tax their societies—such as the Gulf oil monarchies—are less democratic (Fish, 2002; Ross, 2001; Tsui, 2005).[6]

The connections between government service provision, legiti-macy, and taxation have important implications for state-building. First, if officials are to gain public trust, they should carefully ana-lyze the source of previous conflicts before deciding how resources should be distributed or extracted. For example, while the civil war in Sri Lanka ran along ethnic lines, the government's policy of granting 1,000 houses to each ethnic group did not result in "horizontal equity"; rather, it perpetuated the real reason for the war, resource inequality (Anand, 2005, p. 12). Second, while building the state's revenue col-lection capability is important, in order for revenue imperatives to pro-duce legitimacy and representation dividends it is also important to support civic and business associations to strengthen their voice and leverage vis-à-vis the government (Englebert and Tull, 2008, p. 139). Third, prolonged large-scale assistance can ostensibly have antidemo-cratic properties. It dampens the government's dependence on its citi-zens, weakening the public's ability to hold their leaders accountable. In contrast, International Monetary Fund and World Bank stabiliza-tion and structural adjustment programs—which are often criticized as being antidemocratic because they dictate terms to fiscally weak governments—can foster accountability and representation by forcing governments to balance their budgets and improve revenue streams (Ross, 2004, pp. 247–248).

Cheating and Bias

Despite the fact that governments and citizens can often improve their lot by cooperating with each other within the confines of mutual obli-gations and duties, each side would be even better off—in a narrow sense—if it could make all the gains of a social contract without paying the costs. Without transparency and accountability, the chances of being caught for transgressions are low, and governments and citizens will try to gain an advantage and avoid meeting their obligations by cheating or biasing the system. Citizens cheat by evading taxes and circumventing laws—actions that may or may not indicate disapproval with the government (however, as mentioned above, when cheating takes place on a large scale, it may signal mass rejection of the governing system). To deter the public from cheating, states need to maintain social control through effective policing and oversight agencies; yet, if left unchecked, government authorities can abuse this power and deny citizens their civil liberties. Politicians are not only tempted to overreach their authority—the imperatives of electoral competition and their desire to remain in power often compel them to establish biased political arrangements that reduce uncertainty about their future (Trounstine, 2008, p. 21). According to Trounstine (p. 32), types of biasing and the mechanisms employed might include

- *Information Bias*: state control over the media or voluntary associations to limit the information available to citizens
- *Vote Bias*: poll taxes, registration laws, vote fraud, or vote buying (patronage distribution) to advantage incumbents and raise the costs of entry for new political actors
- *Seat Bias*: gerrymandering, malapportionment of representatives, or raising the number of government appointed seats to exaggerate the number of seats won by incumbents beyond voter preferences.

Hence, to deter citizens from cheating, governments from abusing their policing and oversight authority, and political leaders from biasing the system, societies need third-party institutions whose purpose is to monitor both citizens and government actors and report on their actions. Such institutions include an independent judiciary (discussed above), legislative oversight committees, and a free press. "Together they provide more reason for faith that commitments will be kept or, at least, that transgressions will be discovered and punished" (Levi, 1997, p. 23). Third-party organizations are insufficient, however, to promote transparency and accountability. In addition, mobilizing organizations, such as political parties and civil society organizations, are needed to promote civic participation and ensure that citizens remain vigilant in the struggle to articulate and protect their interests.

Improving Accountability and Mobilization

Media. There is near-universal recognition by practitioners that a free media plays an important role in post-conflict peacebuilding and is a crucial check on government authority (Brinkerhoff, Johnson, and Hill, 2009, p. 37; Dobbins et al., 2007, pp. 202–207; USIP, 2009, pp. 103 and 127). The media can act as a *watchdog* that promotes transparency and accountability by exposing abuses of power, as a *civic forum* that can inform voters and promote peaceful exchange among rivals, and as an *agenda-setter* that strengthens government responsiveness to social issues (Norris, 2008, p. 189). The media's independent impact on governance issues is also well documented: In the Watergate scandal, reporting by the *Washington Post* set into motion a series of disclosures that led to President Nixon's resignation, and studies in India show that the government is more responsive to social needs in areas where newspaper circulation and electoral accountability is highest (Besley and Burgess, 2002). Given the argument's intuitive sense and the strength of supporting evidence, state-builders should be encouraged to promote a free press in tandem with other governance initiatives.

Cautions. And yet, while there is considerable evidence that a free press is correlated with these peace- and democracy-supporting functions, there is no clear consensus as to the direction of the relationship or whether a similar correlation can be found in countries emerging from war. It may be that established democracies have the civil rights protections and social values that allow the press to function in a manner that reinforces peace and good governance. In less liberal media environments, the press's impact may be muted, and some studies have found that the media can exacerbate tensions in post-conflict situations. Ethnic divisions were solidified and mobilized by media sources prior to conflicts in Georgia and Rwanda (Ellis, 2006; Toupouria, 2000).

To safeguard against the media undermining peacebuilding efforts, Frohardt and Temin (2003) suggest a number of interventions.

To discourage partisanship, donor funding can be used to incentivize diversification of outlet ownership and of the journalist corps. To improve journalists' professionalism and capacity, media-support organizations, such as Internews and the Center for International Media Assistance, can provide material assistance and training workshops. Bringing journalists together can create an *esprit de corps*, and this professional solidarity can enforce standards of rigor and objectivity that supersede other personal group allegiances. To create a healthy legal environment for a free press, legislation to protect journalists and media outlets from government interference, as well as to protect individuals from media defamation or falsehoods, should be enacted. And, finally, the media need to be consistently monitored for early warning signs of impending conflict, such as hate speech and fearmongering, so that actions can be taken early on to mitigate building tensions (Frohardt and Temin, 2003, pp. 15–16).

Civil Society Organizations and Political Parties. While the press can expose transgressions and highlight problems, it does not directly hold the government accountable. That responsibility falls to civic organizations and political parties, which mobilize citizens and articulate their interests so that they can use mechanisms of accountability—typically elections, but also demonstrations, boycotts, and strikes—to their advantage. Independently, citizens can have little effect on bringing about change, and, as a result, they may have a propensity to politically disengage. Civil society organizations and political parties encourage engagement by acting as collective forums that offer citizens an opportunity to amplify their voices. They can also mobilize citizens by providing selective incentives (examples can range from camaraderie to low-rate insurance) that offset the costs of civic action and by instilling values that encourage political participation.

Civic organizations may be a necessary condition for accountable government, but, as is the case with a free press, the direction of the relationship remains unclear, especially in fragile societies. Most of the assumptions about the role of civil society are based on examinations of democracies (Putnam, 1993; Verba, Schlozman, and Brady, 1995), where parties and associations are autonomous from the government and "channels of political participation are guaranteed" (Jamal, 2007,

p. 7). Yet in less liberal or underdeveloped societies, the opportunities to link citizens to governments are shaped by the existing political system. If, for example, a society has strong patron-client networks, organizations will tend to reinforce those patterns. Rather than mobilize collective action or hold politicians accountable, civic organizations in clientelist societies tend to reinforce politicians' superior position by encouraging members to seek private benefits (jobs, housing, etc.) through informal channels. These organizations work within the system to make their members materially "better off," but in doing so they maintain their subordinate relationship to the government. If, however, civic organizations and opposition parties are denied both formal and informal mechanisms for pressuring the government, they may seek to overthrow the system (Jamal, 2007, p. 9). In both cases, civic organizations and parties serve to mobilize citizens but do not foster democratic values or accountability. Given that mobilizing organizations tend to reinforce the political systems they operate within, bottom-up approaches to democracy promotion and state-building are unlikely to work unless a political structure is already in place that has accessible channels for political participation and accountability.

Conclusion

This survey of the literature on governance and political development reveals that no factor is more important to the success of S&R than an understanding of the domestic context. Without it, one cannot not know the potential costs of partition, a country's capacity to man judicial institutions and enact the rule of law, or other information essential to making state-building choices. This conclusion may seem evasive, but it is fundamental; further, it has important concrete implications for action. In dealing with a stabilization and reconstruction challenge, substantial resources should be committed early to acquiring (1) an understanding of the country's human, economic, and cultural make-up; (2) a history of the sources of contention behind the conflict; (3) an understanding of the capacities and objectives of combatant groups; (4) expertise on state-building options for the particular country; and

(5) a realistic assessment of the nation-builder's own commitment and capabilities. In combination, this information defines the choice set within which nation-builders must operate if they are to be successful.

Although no generic formulas exist for creating a functioning and thriving political system, both because of contextual differences and the numerous institutional combinations that can combine for success, there is a broad consensus on a framework of political goals for post-conflict state-building. These political goals include

1. the dispersal of benefits
2. shared decisionmaking
3. barriers to overcentralization and exclusion
4. a self-enforcing system of accountability and responsiveness.

To dissuade former or potential combatants from returning to conflict, the benefits of peace must outweigh the benefits of war. Even if the costs of returning to conflict are raised, forming a sustainable government will likely require benefits to former and potential combatants. Benefits that address the original source of conflict will probably be the most persuasive. These may include positions of power, independent access to resources, some form of autonomy, veto power, or certain rights.

Shared decisionmaking is more than just a perk for ceasing hostilities. A broad consensus is often needed in post-conflict decisionmaking because the peace is so fragile that even the slightest increase in perceived threat can tip the balance in favor of conflict. Though shared decisionmaking is often recommended, the level and definition vary significantly among scholars and cases, ranging from parties having a voice in the decisionmaking process to strict consensus rules that force mutual agreement. Shared decisionmaking can be fostered by way of coalition cabinets that share executive powers, seat quotas, high vote thresholds, veto powers, and a wide assortment of procedural rules.

General consensus also exists among scholars that combatants are unlikely to surrender their weapons unless there are structures in place to protect them from exclusion and retribution. Separation of powers, proportional representation, federalism, and independent judiciaries all help reassure groups that are out of, or exiting, positions of power. Even if former combatants face setbacks in political competitions, these barriers help assure them that prospects for making future gains will remain open.

Finally, nearly all state-building experts agree on the political goal of establishing a system of accountability that binds citizens and the state (the reason that democracy is so frequently assumed to be the best form of government). Unlike other regime types, democracy is based on a self-enforcement mechanism that allows citizens to hold leaders accountable if they do not respond to their interests. Some democratic institutions, of course, enhance accountability more than others. For example, open-list electoral ballots allow voters to hold individual politicians accountable for their actions, whereas closed-list ballots restrict accountability to the party level. Fear of removal creates a strong incentive for better governance, but another reason that open-list ballots improve responsiveness is that by reflecting citizens' opinions about specific lawmakers they provide more accurate information about how voters want to be governed. Fiscal federalism is also thought to improve accountability. The control over government revenues that comes with fiscal federalism helps local politicians spread patronage and enact policies that serve their constituencies, both of which help them get reelected. When local governments have the power to tax, and corporations and individuals have the freedom to move, politicians want to ensure that sources of revenue do not leave their district. Competition among districts prompts politicians to enact reforms and provide incentives to attract tax dollars (Weingast, 1995). A system of accountability is especially important for post-conflict state-building because, without accountability, post-conflict regimes are susceptible to evolving into static oligarchies that may operate according to nominally democratic rules but in reality serve the interests of power-brokers instead of citizens.

Endnotes

[1]   As with studies on civil society, the direction of the causal relationship between these outcomes and women's education levels is a subject of considerable debate.

[2]   In 1993, a United Nations panel of experts defined ethnic cleansing to be the "planned and deliberate removal from a specific territory, [of] persons of a particular ethnic group by force or intimidation, in order to render the area ethnically homogeneous" (Carmichael, 2002, p. 2).

[3]   In consolidated authoritarian regimes, governing authority is concentrated in the hands of an individual or a small group of people who exercise power with few institutional constraints. The distribution of power is uncontested by prominent elite groups in the society (e.g., the business class, military, religious establishment, etc.), even though this is often the result of coercion or suppression.

[4]   We use the minimalist definition of *consolidated democracy* employed by Linz and Stepan (1996, p. 14): A consolidated democracy is "a political regime in which democracy as a complex system of institutions, rules, and patterned incentives and disincentives has become, in a phrase, 'the only game in town.'" When a democracy is consolidated, the population believes that elected officials are legitimate, and citizens engage the political system.

[5]   In his seminal work, *The Anatomy of Revolution* (1938), Crane Brinton articulates his concept of "the desertion of the intellectuals." Intellectuals often play the role of a society's moral compass. Brinton found that just prior to revolutions in Britain, America, Russia, and France, intellectuals—feeling socially alienated due to government actions—began to declare the government immoral and undeserving of the public's assent. Many of them sought refuge abroad. Scholars note similar patterns in revolutionary movements in China (Meisner, 1999), Iran (Boroujerdi, 1996), and Romania (Siani-Davies, 2005).

[6]   Bellin (2004) notes that oil-rich states are also more authoritarian because they can afford strong coercive apparatuses.

References

Abdellatif, Omayma, and Marina Ottaway, *Women in Islamist Movements: Toward an Islamist Model of Women's Activism*, Washington, D.C.: Carnegie Endowment, Carnegie Papers No. 2, July 2007.

Ackerman, Bruce, *The Future of Liberal Revolution*, New Haven, Conn.: Yale University Press, 1992.

Ahmed, Ishtiaq, "The 1947 Partition of India: A Paradigm for Pathological Politics in India and Pakistan," *Asian Ethnicity*, Vol. 13, No. 1, 2002, pp. 9–28.

Anand, P. B., *Getting Infrastructure Priorities Right in Post-Conflict Reconstruction*, Helsinki: World Institute for Development Economics Research, Research Paper No. 2005/42, June 2005.

Andeweg, Rudy B., "Consociational Democracy," *Annual Review of Political Science*, Vol. 3, 2000, pp. 509–536.

Aslam, Monazza, *Economic Returns to Education and the Link Between Education and Employment—A Gendered Perspective*, New York: United Nations Commission on the Status of Women, March 2010, pp. 1–9. As of April 8, 2011: http://www.un.org/womenwatch/daw/beijing15/ipanel_education/ Education%20Panel%20-%20Aslam,%20Monazza%20cover%20page.pdf

Azam, Jean-Paul, and Alice Mesnard, "Civil War and the Social Contract, *Public Choice*, Vol. 115, Nos. 3–4, 2003, pp. 455–457.

Ball, Nicole, "Towards a Conceptual Framework for Security Sector Reform," Center for International Development and Conflict Management, University of Maryland, paper prepared for the Roundtable on Security Sector Reform, Pearson Peacekeeping Centre, November 30–December 1, 2000.

Barkan, Joel D., "Elections in Agrarian Societies," *Journal of Democracy*, Vol. 6, No. 4, 1995, pp. 106–116.

Barry, Brian, "The Consociational Model and Its Dangers," *European Journal of Political Research*, Vol. 3, No. 4, 1975, pp. 393–411.

Bates, Robert H., "State Failure," *Annual Review of Political Science*, Vol. 11, June 2008a, pp. 1–12.

Bates, Robert, *When Things Fell Apart: State Failure in Late Century Africa*, New York: Cambridge University Press, 2008b.

Bellin, Eva, "The Robustness of Authoritarianism in the Middle East: Exceptionalism in Comparative Perspective," *Comparative Politics*, Vol. 36, No. 2, 2004, pp. 139–157.

Bendix, Reinhard, *Nation-Building and Citizenship*, 3rd edition, Berkeley and Los Angeles: University of California Press, 1977.

Benomar, Jamal, "Constitution-Making After Conflict: Lessons from Iraq," *Journal of Democracy*, Vol. 15, No. 2, 2004, pp. 81–95.

Besley, Timothy, and Robin Burgess, "The Political Economy of Government Responsiveness: Theory and Evidence from India," *Quarterly Journal of Economics*, Vol. 117, No. 4, 2002.

Berman, Sheri, "Civil Society and the Collapse of the Weimar Republic," *World Politics*, Vol. 49, No. 3, 1997, pp. 401–429.

Bhagwati, Jagdish, "Democracy and Development," in Larry Diamond and Marc F. Plattner, eds., *Capitalism, Socialism, and Democracy Revisited*, Baltimore, Md.: Johns Hopkins University Press, 1993, pp. 35–37.

Bollen, Kenneth, "Political Democracy and the Timing of Development," *American Sociology Review*, Vol. 44, 1979, pp. 57–87.

Boroujerdi, Mehrzad, *Iranian Intellectuals and the West: The Tormented Triumph of Nativism*, Syracuse, N.Y.: Syracuse University Press, 1996.

Brahimi, Lakhdar, "State Building in Crisis and Post-Conflict Countries," presented at the 7th Global Forum on Reinventing Government, June 26–29, 2007, Vienna, Austria. As of April 8, 2011: http://unpan1.un.org/intradoc/groups/public/documents/un/unpan026896.pdf

Brancati, Dawn, and Jack Snyder, *Time to Kill: The Impact of Election Timing on Post-Conflict Stability*, draft paper, St. Louis, Mo.: Washington University, Center in Political Economy Seminar, Spring 2010.

Bräutigam, Deborah, Odd-Helge Fjeldstad, and Mick Moore, *Taxation and State-Building in Developing Countries: Capacity and Consent*, New York: Cambridge University Press, 2008.

Brinkerhoff, Derick W., "Rebuilding Governance in Failed States and Post-Conflict Societies: Core Concepts and Cross-Cutting Themes," *Public Administration and Development*, Vol. 25, 2005, pp. 3–14.

Brinkerhoff, Derick W., Ronald W. Johnson, and Richard Hill, *Guide to Rebuilding Governance in Stability Operations: A Role for the Military?* Research Triangle Park, N.C.: RTI International, Strategic Studies Institute, June 2009, pp. 1–77.

Brinton, Crane, *Anatomy of a Revolution*, New York: Vintage Books, 1965 (1938).

Brunetti, Aymo, Gregory Kisunko, and Beatrice Weder, *Credibility of Rules and Economic Growth—Evidence from a World Wide Private Sector Survey*, Washington, D.C.: World Bank, background paper for the *World Development Report 1997*, 1997.

Bueno de Mesquita, Bruce, and David Lalman, *War and Reason*, New Haven, Conn.: Yale University Press, 1992.

Bueno de Mesquita, Bruce, James D. Morrow, Randolph M. Siverson, and Alastair Smith, "An Institutional Explanation of the Democratic Peace," *American Political Science Review*, Vol. 93, No. 4, 1999, pp. 791–807.

Burkhart, Ross E., and Michael S. Lewis-Beck, "Comparative Democracy: The Economic Development Thesis," *American Political Science Review*, Vol. 88, No. 4, 1994, pp. 903–910.

Carmichael, Cathie, *Ethnic Cleansing in the Balkans: Nationalism and the Destruction of Tradition*, London: Routledge, 2002.

Carothers, Thomas, "The 'Sequencing' Fallacy," *Journal of Democracy*, Vol. 18, No. 1, 2007, pp. 12–27.

Chan, Steve, "Mirror, Mirror on the Wall . . . Are the Freer Countries More Pacific?" *Journal of Conflict Resolution*, Vol. 28, No. 4, 1984, pp. 617–648.

Cheibub, José, and Fernando Limongi, "Democratic Institutions and Regime Survival: Parliamentary and Presidential Democracies Reconsidered," *Annual Review of Political Science*, Vol. 5, 2002, pp. 151–179.

Collier, Paul, "Rebellion as a Quasi-Criminal Activity," *Journal of Conflict Resolution*, Vol. 44, No. 6, 2000, pp. 839–853.

Collier, Paul, V. L. Elliot, Havard Hegré, Anke Hoeffler, Marta Reynal-Querol, and Nicholas Sambanis, *Breaking the Conflict Trap: Civil War and Development Policy*, World Bank and Oxford University Press, World Bank Policy Research Reports, 2003.

Cox, Gary W., and Mathew McCubbins, "The Institutional Determinants of Economic Policy Outcomes," in Stephen Haggard and Matthew D. McCubbins, eds., *Presidents and Parliaments*, New York: Cambridge University Press, 2001, pp. 21–63.

de Figueiredo, Jr., Rui J. P., and Barry R. Weingast, "Self-Enforcing Federalism," *Journal of Law, Economics, and Organization*, Vol. 21, 2005, pp. 103–135.

DeNardo, James, *Power in Numbers*, Princeton, N.J.: Princeton University Press, 1985.

Department of the Army, *Fiscal Year 2011 Budget Estimates, Volume 1: Operation and Maintenance*, February 2010. As of April 8, 2011:
http://asafm.army.mil/Documents/OfficeDocuments/Budget/BudgetMaterials/FY11/opmaint/oma-v1.pdf

Derouen, J. R., Jenna Lea Karl, and Peter Wallensteen, "The Duration of Civil War Peace Agreements," *Conflict Management and Peace Science*, Vol. 26, No. 4, 2009, pp. 367–387.

Diamond, Larry, "Introduction: Political Culture and Democracy," in Larry Diamond, ed., *Political Culture and Democracy in Developing Countries*, Boulder, Colo.: Lynne Rienner, 1994.

Diaz-Cayeros, Alberto, Beatriz Magaloni, and Barry R. Weingast, "Tragic Brilliance: Equilibrium Hegemony and Democratization in Mexico," working paper, April 2003.

Dobbins, James, Seth G. Jones, Keith Crane, and Beth Cole DeGrasse, *The Beginner's Guide to Nation-Building*, Santa Monica, Calif.: RAND Corporation, 2007. As of April 8, 2011:
http://www.rand.org/pubs/monographs/MG557.html

Dobbins, James, John G. McGinn, Keith Crane, Seth Jones, Rollie Lal, Andrew Rathmell, Rachel Swanger, and Anga Timilsina, *America's Role in Nation-Building: From Germany to Iraq*, Santa Monica, California: RAND Corporation, 2003. As of April 18, 2011:
http://www.rand.org/pubs/monograph_reports/MR1753.html

Dogan, Mattei, "Political Legitimacy: New Criteria and Anachronistic Theories," *International Social Science Journal*, Vol. 196, 2009, pp. 195–210.

Doyle, Michael W., "Liberalism and World Politics," *The American Political Science Review*, Vol. 80, No. 4, 1986, pp. 1151–1169.

Doyle, Michael W., and Nicholas Sambanis, *Making War and Building Peace*, Princeton, N.J.: Princeton University Press, 2006.

Ellis, Donald G., *Transforming Conflict: Communication and Ethnopolitical Conflict*, Lanham, Md.: Rowman & Littlefield Publishers, 2006.

Ely, J. H., *Democracy and Distrust: A Theory of Judicial Review*. Cambridge, Mass.: Harvard University Press, 1980.

Englebert, Pierre, and Denis M. Tull, "Postconflict Reconstruction in Africa: Flawed Ideas About Failed States," *International Security*, Vol. 32, No. 4, 2008, pp. 106–139.

Esman, Milton J., "Ethnic Politics and Economic Power," *Comparative Politics*, Vol. 19, No.4, 1987, pp. 395–418.

Etzioni, Amita, "A Self-Restrained Approach to Nation-Building by Foreign Powers," *International Affairs*, Vol. 80, No. 1, 2004, pp. 1–17.

Fearon, James, and David Laitin, "Ethnicity, Insurgency and Civil War," *American Political Science Review*, Vol. 97, 2003, pp. 715–735.

Feld, Lars P., and Stefan Voigt, "Economic Growth and Judicial Independence: Cross Country Evidence Using a New Set of Indicators," *European Journal of Political Economy*, Vol. 193, 2003, pp. 497–527.

Ferejohn, John, "Independent Judges, Dependent Judiciary: Explaining Judicial Independence," *Southern California Law Review*, Vol. 72, 1998–1999, pp. 353–384.

Ferejohn, John, "Accountability and Authority: Toward a Theory of Political Accountability," in Adam Przeworski, Susan Carol Stokes, and Bernard Manin, eds., *Democracy, Accountability, and Representation*, New York: Cambridge University Press, 1999, pp. 131–153.

Finkel, Jodi S., *Judicial Reform as Political Insurance: Argentina, Peru and Mexico in the 1990s*, Notre Dame, Ind.: University of Notre Dame Press, 2008.

Fish, M. Steven, "Islam and Authoritarianism," *World Politics*, Vol. 55, No. 1, 2002, pp. 4–37

Fjelde, Hanne, and Indra de Soysa, *Bullying or Buying? "State Extractive Capacity, Public Spending and Civil Peace 1961–2001,"* paper presented at the Annual Meeting of the International Studies Association 48th Annual Convention, Chicago, February 2007.

Fortna, Page, *Peace Time: Cease-Fire Agreements and the Durability of Peace*, Princeton, N.J.: Princeton University Press, 2004.

Fortna, Page, and Reyko Huang, "Democratization After Civil War," working paper, November 2009. As of April 8, 2011:
http://www.columbia.edu/~vpf4/research.htm

Francisco, Ronald A., "The Relationship Between Coercion and Protest: An Empirical Evaluation in Three Coercive States," *Journal of Conflict Resolution*, Vol. 39, No. 2, 1995, pp. 263–282.

Frohardt, Mark, and Jonathan Temin, *Use and Abuse of the Media in Vulnerable Societies*, Washington, D.C.: U.S. Institute for Peace, 2003.

Fukuyama, Francis, *The End of History and the Last Man*, New York: Free Press, 1992.

———, "How Academia Failed the Nation," *SAISphere*, Winter 2004a.

———, *State-Building: Governance and World Order in the 21st Century*, Ithaca, N.Y.: Cornell University Press, 2004b.

Ghani, Ashraf, and Clare Lockhart, *Fixing Failed States: A Framework for Rebuilding a Fractured World*, New York: Oxford University Press, 2008.

Ginsberg, Tom, *Judicial Review in New Democracies: Constitutional Courts in Asian Cases*, New York: Cambridge University Press, 2003.

Glassmyer, Katherine, and Nicholas Sambanis, "Rebel-Military Integration and Civil War Termination," *Journal of Peace Research*, Vol. 45, No. 3, 2008, pp. 303–320.

Goldstone, Jack A., "Toward a Fourth Generation of Revolutionary Theory," *Annual Review of Political Science*, Vol. 4, 2001, pp. 139–187.

Goldstone, Jack, Robert Bates, Ted Gurr, and Monty Marshall, *A Global Forecasting Model of Political Instability*, State Failure Task Force, McLean, Va.: SAIC, 2005.

Gopal, Priyamvada, "Burqas and Bikinis," *The Guardian*, August 3, 2010. As of April 8, 2011:
http://www.guardian.co.uk/commentisfree/2010/aug/03/burkas-bikinis-reality-afghan-lives

Gurr, Ted Robert, *Minorities at Risk: A Global View of Ethnopolitical Conflicts*, Washington, D.C.: U.S. Institute of Peace, 1993.

Hafez, Mohammed M., "From Marginalization to Massacres: A Political Process Explanation of GIA Violence in Algeria," in Quintan Wiktorowicz, ed., *Islamic Activism: A Social Movement Theory Approach*, Bloomington, Ind.: Indiana University Press, 2004, pp. 37–60.

Haggard, Stephan, and Robert R. Kaufmann, *The Political Economy of Democratic Transitions*, Princeton, N.J.: Princeton University Press, 1995.

Hale, Henry, "Divided We Stand: Institutional Sources of Ethno-Federal State Survival and Collapse," *World Politics*, Vol. 56, 2004, pp. 165–193.

Halperin, Morton, Joseph Siegle, and Michael Weinstein, *The Democracy Advantage: How Democracies Promote Prosperity and Peace*, London and New York: Routledge, 2004.

Harris, Peter, and Ben Reilly, eds., *Democracy and Deep-Rooted Conflict: Options for Negotiators*, Stockholm: International Institute for Democracy and Electoral Assistance, 1998.

Hartzell, Caroline A., "Structuring the Peace: Negotiated Settlements and the Construction of Conflict Management Institutions," in T. David Mason and James D. Meernik, eds., *Conflict Prevention and Peacebuilding in Post-War Societies: Sustaining the Peace*, New York: Routledge, 2006.

Hartzell, Caroline, and Matthew Hoddie, "Institutionalizing Peace: Power Sharing and Post-Civil War Conflict Management," *American Journal of Political Science*, Vol. 47, No. 2, 2003, pp. 318–332.

Hegre, Håvard, Tanja Ellingsen, Scott Gates, and Nils Petter Gleditsch, "Toward a Democratic Civil Peace? Democracy, Political Change, and Civil War, 1816–1992," *American Political Science Review*, Vol. 95, 2001, pp. 33–48.

Heller, Patrick, "Degrees of Democracy," *World Politics*, Vol. 52, 2000, pp. 484–519.

Helmke, Gretchen, and Frances Rosenbluth, "Regimes and the Rule of Law: Judicial Independence in Comparative Perspective," *Annual Review of Political Science*, Vol. 12, 2009, pp. 345–366.

Hirschman, Alfred O., *Exit, Voice, and Loyalty: Responses to Declines in Firms, Organizations and States*, Cambridge, Mass.: Harvard University Press, 1970.

Horowitz, Donald L., *Ethnic Groups in Conflict*, Berkeley: University of California Press, 1985.

———, "Making Moderation Pay: The Comparative Politics of Ethnic Conflict Management," in Joseph V. Montville, ed., *Conflict and Peacemaking in Multiethnic Societies*, New York: Lexington Books, 1991, pp. 451–475.

Hudson, Valerie M., and Patricia Leidel, "Betrayed," *Foreign Policy*, May 10, 2010.

Huntington, Samuel, *Political Order in Changing Societies*, New Haven, Conn.: Yale University Press, 1968.

Jackman, Robert W., "On the Relations of Economic Development to Democratic Performance," *American Journal of Political Science*, Vol. 17, 1973, pp. 611–621.

Jamal, Amaney, *Barriers to Democracy: The Other Side of Social Capital in Palestine and the Arab World*, Princeton, N.J.: Princeton University Press, 2007.

Johnson, Carter, "Partitioning to Peace: Sovereignty, Demography, and Ethnic Civil Wars," *International Security*, Vol. 32, No. 4, 2008, pp. 140–170.

Kalyvas, Stathis, "Wanton and Senseless? The Logic of Massacres in Algeria," *Rationality and Society*, Vol. 11, No. 3, 1999, pp. 243–285.

Kaufmann, Chaim, "Possible and Impossible Solutions to Ethnic Civil Wars," *International Security*, Vol. 20, No. 4, 1996, pp. 136–175.

———, "When All Else Fails," *International Security*, Vol. 23, No. 2, 1998, pp. 120–156.

Keman, H., "Federalism and Policy Performance. A Conceptual and Empirical Inquiry," in U. Wachendorfer-Schmidt, ed., *Federalism and Political Performance*, London: Routledge, 2000, pp. 196–227.

Kumar, Radha, "The Troubled History of Partition," *Foreign Affairs*, Vol. 76, No. 1, 1997, pp. 22–35.

Kumar, Krishna, and Marinna Ottaway, "General Conclusions and Priorities," in Krishna Kumar, ed., *Post-Conflict Elections, Democratization & International Assistance*, Boulder, Colo.; Lynne Rienner, 1998, pp. 229–237.

Lake, David A., and Donald Rothchild, "Territorial Decentralization and Civil War Settlements," in Philip G. Roeder and Donald Rothchild, eds., *Sustainable Peace: Power and Democracy After Civil Wars*, Ithaca, N.Y.: Cornell University Press, 2005.

Levi, Margaret, *Consent, Dissent, and Patriotism*, New York: Cambridge University Press, 1997.

Lichbach, Mark I., *The Rebel's Dilemma*, Ann Arbor: University of Michigan Press, 1995.

Licklider, Roy, "The Consequences of Negotiated Settlements in Civil Wars, 1945–1993," *American Political Science Review*, Vol. 89, 1995, pp. 681–690.

Lijphart, Arend, "Consociational Democracy," *World Politics*, Vol. 21, No. 2, 1976, pp. 207–225.

———, *Democracy in Plural Societies*, New Haven, Conn.: Yale University Press, 1977.

———, *Electoral Systems and Party Systems: A Study of Twenty-Seven Democracies, 1945–1990*, Oxford, UK: Oxford University Press, 1994.

———, *Patterns of Democracy: Government Forms and Performance in Thirty-Six Countries*, New Haven, Conn.: Yale University Press, 1999.

————, "The Wave of Power-Sharing Democracy," in Andrew Reynolds, ed., *The Architecture of Democracy: Consociational Design, Conflict Management, and Democracy*, New York: Oxford University Press, 2002.

Linz, Juan, *The Breakdown of Democratic Regimes: Crisis, Breakdown, and Reequalibration*, Baltimore, Md.: Johns Hopkins University Press, 1978.

Linz, Juan J., and Alfred Stepan, "Toward Consolidated Democracies," *Journal of Democracy*, Vol. 7, No. 2, 1996, pp. 14–33.

Lustick, Ian, "Stability in Divided Societies: Consociationalism v. Control," *World Politics*, Vol. 31, 1979, pp. 325–344.

Luttwak, Edward, "Give War a Chance," *Foreign Affairs*, Vol. 78, No. 4, 1999, pp. 36–44.

MacDonald, Mott, *Provision of Infrastructure in Post Conflict Situations*, London: Department for International Development, 2005.

Mansfield, Edward D., and Jack Snyder, *Electing to Fight: Why Emerging Democracies Go to War*, Cambridge, Mass.: MIT Press, 2005.

Maoz, Zeev, and Nasrin Abdolali, "Regime Types and International Conflict, 1816–1976," *Journal of Conflict Resolution*, Vol. 33, No. 1, 1989, pp. 3–35.

Maravall, José María, "The Myth of the Authoritarian Advantage," *Journal of Democracy*, Vol. 5, No. 4, 1994, pp. 17–30.

Maravall, José María, and Adam Przeworski, "Introduction," in Maravall and Przeworski, eds., *Democracy and the Rule of Law*, Cambridge, UK: Cambridge University Press, 2003.

Marshall, Monty, "Fragility, Instability, and the Failure of States: Assessing the Sources of Systemic Risk," New York: Council of Foreign Affairs, working paper, 2008, pp. 1–29. As of April 8, 2011:
http://www.cfr.org/publication/17638

Marshall, Monty G., and Benjamin R. Cole, *Global Report 2009: Conflict, Governance, and State Fragility*, Vienna, Va.: Center for Systemic Peace, 2009.

Mason, David T., Martha Crenshaw, Cynthia McClintock, and Barbara Walter, *How Political Violence Ends: Paths to Conflict Decentralization and Termination*, APSA Task Force on Political Violence and Terrorism, Group 3, American Political Science Association Conference, 2007.

McCall, George J., "Lessons About Nation-Building and Civil Society," *International Social Science Journal*, Vol. 192, 2009.

McGrew, Laura, "Re-Establishing Legitimacy Through the Extraordinary Chambers in the Courts of Cambodia," in Joakim Öjendal and Mona Lilja, *Beyond Democracy in Cambodia: Political Reconstruction in a Post-Conflict Society*, Copenhagen: NIAS Press, 2009, pp. 250–296.

Mearsheimer, John J., and Stephen Van Evera, "When Peace Means War," *New Republic*, December 18, 1995, pp. 16–18.

Meisner, Maurice, *Mao's China and After: A History of the People's Republic*, Third Ed., New York: Free Press, 1999.

Melander, Erik, "Gender Equality and Intrastate Armed Conflict," *International Studies Quarterly*, Vol. 49, 2005, pp. 695–714.

Monteux, Camille A., "Decentralization: The New Delusion of Ethnic Conflict Regulation?" *International Journal on Multicultural Societies*, Vol. 8, No. 2, 2006, pp. 161–182.

Moore, William, "Repression and Dissent: Substitution, Context, and Timing," *American Journal of Political Science*, Vol. 42, No. 30, 1998, pp. 851–873.

Morgan, T. Clifton, and Valerie L. Schwebach, "Take Two Democracies and Call Me in the Morning. A Prescription for Peace?" *International Interactions: Empirical and Theoretical Research in International Relations*, Vol. 17, No. 4, 1992, pp. 305–320.

Mortenson, Greg, and David Oliver Relin, *Three Cups of Tea: One Man's Mission to Promote Peace . . . One School at a Time*, New York: Viking, 2006.

Moustafa, Tamir, *The Struggle for Constitutional Power: Law, Politics, and Economic Development in Egypt*, New York: Cambridge University Press, 2007.

Mozaffar, Shaheen, and James R. Scarritt, "Why Territorial Autonomy Is Not a Viable Option for Managing Conflict in African Plural Societies," *Nationalism and Ethnic Politics*, Vol. 5, Nos. 3–4, 1999, pp. 230–253.

Muller, Edward, and Erich Weede, "Cross-National Variations in Political Violence: A Rational Action Approach," *Journal of Conflict Resolution*, Vol. 34, No. 4, 1990, pp. 624–651.

Nordland, Rod, "Portrait of Pain Ignites Debate Over Afghan War," *New York Times*, August 5, 2010.

Nordlinger, Eric A., *Conflict Regulation in Divided Societies*, Cambridge, Mass.: Center for International Affairs, Harvard University, 1972.

Norris, Pippa, *Driving Democracy: Do Power Sharing Arrangements Work?* New York: Cambridge University Press, 2008.

———, ed., *Public Sentinel: News Media and Governance Reform*, Washington, D.C.: World Bank, 2009, pp. 221–242.

O'Donnell, Guillermo, and Philippe C. Schmitter, *Transitions from Authoritarian Rule: Tentative Conclusions about Uncertain Democracies*, Baltimore, Md.: Johns Hopkins University Press, 1986.

OECD—*See* Organisation for Economic Co-operation and Development.

Olson, Mancur, "Dictatorship, Democracy, and Development," *American Political Science Review*, Vol. 87, 1993, pp. 567–576.

Onuch, Olga, "Crisis-Related Social Mobilization in Transition States," Development and Transition, United Nations Development Programme and the London School of Economics, No. 13, 2009. As of May 3, 2010: http://www.developmentandtransition.net/index.cfm?module=ActiveWeb&page=WebPage&DocumentID=731

Organisation for Economic Co-operation and Development, *State Building in Situations of Fragility—Initial Findings*, August, 2008. As of May 9, 2011: http://www.oecd.org/dataoecd/55/30/42546515.pdf

Ottaway, M. "Promoting Democracy After Conflict: The Difficult Choices," *International Studies Perspectives*, Vol. 4, 2003, pp. 314–322.

Paris, Roland, *At War's End: Building Peace After Civil Conflict*, New York: Cambridge University Press, 2004.

Perlez, Jane, "Pakistan Leader Backs Down and Reinstates Top Judge," *New York Times*, March 15, 2009.

Posner, Richard A., "The Social Costs of Monopoly and Regulation," *Journal of Political Economy*, Vol. 83, No. 4, 1975, pp. 807–827.

Przeworski, Adam, *Democracy and the Market: Political and Economic Reforms in Eastern Europe and Latin America*, New York: Cambridge University Press, 1991.

Przeworski, Adam, Michael E. Alvarez, José Antonio Cheibub, and Fernando Limongi, *Democracy and Development*, New York: Cambridge University Press, 2000.

Putnam, Robert D., *Making Democracy Work: Civic Traditions in Modern Italy*, Princeton N.J.: Princeton University Press, 1993.

Quinn, J. Michael, T. David Mason, and Mehmet Gurses, "Sustaining the Peace: Determinants of Civil War Recurrence," *International Interactions*, Vol. 33, No. 2, 2007, pp. 262–298.

Ranson, Stuart, and John Stuart, *Management of the Public Domain*, Basingstoke, UK: Macmillan, 1994.

Regan, Patrick M., "Conditions of Successful Third-Party Intervention in Intrastate Conflicts," *Journal of Conflict Resolution*, Vol. 40, No. 2, 1996, pp. 336–359.

———, *Civil Wars and Foreign: Outside Interventions and Intrastate Conflict*, Ann Arbor: University of Michigan Press, 2000.

Reilly, Benjamin, *Democracy in Divided Societies: Electoral Engineering for Conflict Management*, New York: Cambridge University Press, 2001.

————, "Does the Choice of Electoral System Promote Democracy? The Gap Between Theory and Practice," in P. G. Roeder and D. Rothchild, eds., *Sustainable Peace: Democracy and Power-Dividing Institutions After Civil Wars*, Ithaca, N.Y.: Cornell University Press, 2005.

Reilly, Patrick, and Andrew Reynolds, *Electoral Systems and Conflict in Divided Societies*, Committee on International Conflict Resolution, Commission on Behavioral and Social Sciences and Education, National Research Council, Washington D.C.: National Academy Press, 1999.

Reno, William, "Somalia: State Failure and Self-Determination in the Shadow of the Global Economy," in Valpy Fitzgerald, Frances Stewart, and Rajesh Venugopal, eds., *Globalization, Self-Determination and Global Conflict*, New York: Palgrave, 2006, pp. 147–178.

Reynolds, Andrew, ed., *The Architecture of Democracy: Consociational Design, Conflict Management, and Democracy*, New York: Oxford University Press, 2002.

Ross, Michael, "Does Oil Hinder Democracy?" *World Politics*, Vol. 53, No. 3, 2001, pp. 325–361.

————, "Does Taxation Lead to Representation?" *British Journal of Political Science*, Vol. 34, No. 2, 2004, pp. 229–249.

Rothchild, Donald, and Philip G. Roeder, "The Dilemma of Power Sharing After Civil Wars," in Philip G. Roeder and Donald Rothchild, eds., *Sustainable Peace: Democracy and Power-Dividing Institutions After Civil Wars*, Ithaca, N.Y.: Cornell University Press, 2005.

Rothkopf, David, "Women, Islam, Afghanistan, President Obama, and Andrew Sullivan," *Foreign Policy*, August 5, 2010.

Rummel, R. J., *Power Kills: Democracy as a Method of Non-Violence*, New Brunswick, N.J.: Transaction, 1997.

Russett, Bruce, *Grasping the Democratic Peace: Principles for a Post–Cold War World*, Princeton, N.J.: Princeton University Press, 1993.

Rustow, Dankwart, "Transitions to Democracy: Toward a Dynamic Model," *Comparative Politics*, Vol. 2, No. 3, 1970, pp. 337–363.

Sambanis, Nicholas, "Partition as a Solution to Ethnic War," *World Politics*, Vol. 52, No. 4, 2000, pp. 437–483.

Sambanis, Nicholas, and Jonah Schulhofer-Wohl, "What's in a Line: Is Partition a Solution to Civil War?" *International Security*, Vol. 34, No. 2, 2009, pp. 82–118.

Schmitter, Philippe C., and Terry Lynn Karl, "What Democracy Is . . . and Is Not?" *Journal of Democracy*, Vol. 2, No. 3, 1991, pp. 75–88.

Siani-Davies, Peter, *The Romanian Revolution of December 1989*, Ithaca, N.Y.: Cornell University Press, 2005.

Sisk, Timothy D., *Power Sharing and International Mediation in Ethnic Conflicts*, Washington, D.C.: U.S. Institute of Peace, 1996.

Simeon, Richard, and Daniel-Patrick Conway, "Federalism and the Managements of Conflict in Multinational Societies," in Alain-G. Gagon and James Tully, eds., *Multinational Democracies*, New York: Cambridge University Press, 2001, pp. 338–365.

Smith, Benjamin, "Oil Wealth and Regime Survival in the Developing World, 1960–1999," *American Journal of Political Science*, Vol. 48, No. 2, 2004, pp. 232–246.

Stepenson, Matthew, "Legal Institutions of the Market Economy," *Judicial Independence: What It Is, How It Can Be Measured, Why It Occurs*, Washington, D.C.: World Bank Group, 2001.

Toensing, Chris, "Iraqi Elections," *Middle East Report*, No. 234, 2005, pp. 8–9.

Toft, Monica Duffy, *Securing the Peace: The Durable Settlement of Civil Wars*, Princeton, N.J.: Princeton University Press, 2010.

Topouria, Giorgo, "Media and Civil Conflicts in Georgia," in Alan Davis, ed., *Regional Media in Conflict*, London: Institute for War and Peace Reporting, 2000.

Tremblay, Reeta Chowdhari, "Afghanistan: Multicultural Federalism as a Means to Achieve Democracy, Representation and Stability," in Sidney John Roderick Noel, ed., *From Power Sharing to Democracy: Post-Conflict Institutions in Ethnically Divided Societies*, Quebec, Canada: McGill-Queens University Press, 2005, pp. 198–214.

Trounstine, Jessica, *Political Monopolies in American Cities: The Rise and Fall of Bosses and Reformers*, Chicago: University of Chicago Press, 2008.

Tsebelis, George, "Decision Making in Political Systems: Veto Players in Presidentialism, Parliamentarism, Multicameralism, and Multipartyism," *British Journal of Political Science*, Vol. 25, 1995, pp. 289–326.

Tsui, Kevin K., *More Oil, Less Democracy? Theory and Evidence from Crude Oil Discoveries*, Job Market Paper, University of Chicago, November 11, 2005. As of April 8, 2011:
http://economics.uchicago.edu/download/tsui_applwksp_120505.pdf

Van de Walle, Nicolas, *Africa and the Politics of Permanent Economic Crisis, 1979–1999*, Cambridge, UK: Cambridge University Press, 2002.

Vaux, Tony, and Emma Visman, *Service Delivery in Countries Emerging from Conflict*, report for the UK Department for International Development, January 2005.

Verba, Sydney, Kay Lehman Schlozman, and Henry Brady, *Voice, and Equality: Civic Voluntarism in American Politics*, Cambridge, Mass.: Harvard University Press, 1995.

Walter, Barbara, "The Critical Barrier to Civil War Settlement," *International Organization*, Vol. 51, No. 3, 1997, pp. 335–364.

———, *Committing to Peace: The Successful Settlement of Civil War*, Princeton, N.J.: Princeton University Press, 2002.

———, "Does Conflict Beget Conflict? Explaining Recurring Civil War," *Journal of Peace Research*, Vol. 41, No. 3, 2004, pp. 371–388.

———,"Reputation and War: An Experimental Approach," American Political Science Association, Chicago, August 2007.

Waterbury, John, "Democracy Without Democrats? The Potential for Political Liberalization in the Middle East," in Ghassan Salamé, ed., *Democracy Without Democrats? The Renewal of Politics in the Muslim World*, New York: I.B. Tauris, 1994, pp. 23–47.

Watts, Stephen, *Enforcing Democracy? Assessing the Relationship Between Peace Operations and Post-Conflict Democratization*, New York: Columbia University International Politics Seminar, March 5, 2009.

Way, Lucan, "Authoritarian State Building and the Sources of Regime Competitiveness in the Fourth Wave: The Cases of Belarus, Moldova, Russia, and Ukraine," *World Politics*, Vol. 57, 2005, pp. 231–261.

Weede, Erich, "Some Simple Calculations on Democracy and War Involvement," *Journal of Peace Research*, Vol. 29, No. 4, 1992, pp. 377–383.

Weingast, Barry R., "The Economic Role of Political Institutions: Federalism, Markets, and Economic Development," *Journal of Law, Economics, and Organization*, Vol. 11, 1995, pp. 1–31.

———, "Self-Enforcing Constitutions: With an Application to Democratic Stability in America's First Century," Stanford University, November 2005. As of April 8, 2011:
http://politicalscience.stanford.edu/faculty/documents/
weingast-self-enforcing%20constitutions.pdf

Weinstein, Jeremy N., "Autonomous Recovery and International Intervention in Comparative Perspective," Stanford University, Center for Global Development, Working Paper No. 57, 2005. As of April 8, 2011:
http://www.stanford.edu/~jweinst/files/AutonomousRecovery_2005.pdf

Wibbles, Erik, *Federalism and the Market: Intergovernmental Conflict and Economic Reform in the Developing World*, New York: Cambridge University Press, 2005.

Wood, Reed M., "Rebel Capability and Strategic Violence Against Civilians," *Journal of Peace Research*, Vol. 47, No. 5, 2010, pp. 601–614.

U.S. Agency for International Development, *Foreign Aid and the National Interest: Promoting Freedom, Security, and Opportunity*, Washington, D.C., 2002.

———, *USAID Anticorruption Strategy*, PD-ACA-57, Washington, D.C., 2005.

USAID—*See* U.S. Agency for International Development.

U.S. Institute of Peace, *Guiding Principles for Stabilization and Reconstruction*, Washington, D.C., 2009.

United Nations 7th Global Forum on Reinventing Government: Building Trust in Government, *Workshop VII Final Report: Governance Challenges in Crisis and Post-Conflict Countries*, Vienna, Austria, June 2007.

USIP—*See* U.S. Institute of Peace.

Zakaria, Fareed, *The Future of Freedom: Illiberal Democracy at Home and Abroad*, New York: Norton, 2003.

Zartman, I. William, "Putting Things Back Together," in William Zartman, ed., *Collapsed States: The Disintegration and Restoration of Legitimate Authority*, Boulder, Colo.: Lynne Rienner, 1995, pp. 267–273.

CHAPTER FOUR

Political Dilemmas of Stabilization and Reconstruction

Stephen Watts

Introduction

Purpose

This chapter builds on the previous one, by Julie Taylor, about establishing favorable political conditions in stabilization and reconstruction (S&R). This chapter is a much-elaborated discussion of a few selected political *dilemmas* that routinely arise. Also, it takes the next step of suggesting ways to resolve, or at least mitigate, those dilemmas.

Overview

The U.S.-led interventions in Afghanistan and Iraq have profoundly influenced policy debates over when interventions should occur and what constitute appropriate ends and means. The international orthodoxy for repairing weak and failed states that prevailed in the wake of the Cold War called for transforming civil wars into nonviolent political conflicts through the creation of strong and inclusive formal governmental institutions, above all democratic ones, capable of redressing the grievances of formerly oppressed populations. Although this orthodoxy had its critics, and many argued that the international community's commitment to democracy promotion was more rhetorical than real, it nonetheless shaped international actions in countries as diverse as El Salvador, Cambodia, Mozambique, Bosnia, Sierra Leone, and Timor-Leste.[1] Disappointments from many of these operations have combined with the criticism of U.S. policies in Afghanistan and Iraq to fuel a new approach to interventions. This new approach emphasizes modest ends: a minimal conception of S&R focused more on stabilization (the end of large-scale violence) than on democratic transformation. Stabilization is to be accomplished primarily through the establishment of effective local governance—security above all, but the intent is also to provide such public services as education and public health.

The specifics of these policy debates have changed over time, but they ultimately have revolved around three central dilemmas (the third stemming from the first two):

1. *Inclusion.* Is it better for the government to co-opt challengers to the current regime and risk divisiveness within the government, or to exclude them and risk escalating spirals of violence?
2. *State Capacity.* Is S&R better served by strengthening the state and extending its powers further into aspects of social relations, or by relying on indirect and decentralized forms of governance?
3. *Transition.* Should intervenors pay the costs and accept the risks up-front for a form of government that will address the "root causes" of violence and be sustainable in the long term? Or should they accept a more easily achievable form of government in the short run for the sake of immediate peace, while hoping that gradual evolution to better institutions is possible with time (or even that gradualism would make that evolution more feasible)?

These three dilemmas have prompted furious debate for decades. No solution can fully resolve them, but we may hope to identify ways of navigating them. This chapter first grounds the contemporary policy debate in a historical context. It then examines the three dilemmas in turn, demonstrating that they are "true" dilemmas in the sense that they inevitably impose painful choices on would-be state-builders. The chapter concludes by proposing a few rules of thumb for coping with these dilemmas.

Debating Stabilization and Reconstruction

The challenges posed by instability and violence in weakly governed regions are not new; they are recognizable in policy debates since the era of decolonization, if not before. In many cases, instability prompts little response from foreign governments, but the external repercussions of "internal conflict" are sometimes enough to trigger military intervention. During the Cold War, the United States feared Soviet exploitation of instability. Since the end of the Cold War, civil wars have commonly resulted in spillover violence, massive refugee flows, economic disruptions, transnational crime, pandemic disease, and—of particular concern since 2001—transnational terrorism (Collier et al., 2003).

Although any attempt to group diverse policy positions into a smaller number of "camps" risks simplifying—and even mischaracterizing—specific arguments, it is useful to discern schools of thought on military interventions that have been dominant in different periods of American foreign policy over the past several decades. Three approaches in particular stand out: "controlled state-building," "liberal democratic state-building," and "decentralized S&R" (summarized in Table 4.1).

Controlled State-Building

During the early years of the Cold War, American policymakers focused on Europe and Northeast Asia (particularly Japan) and on deterring cross-border aggression. With such exceptions as Greece and the Philippines, where American military forces were not a principal actor, the United States did not focus on "internal wars" until the 1960s.[2]

The rise of American involvement in counterinsurgency from the 1960s onward coincided with the development of "modernization theory" in the American social-science community (Shafer, 1988). Classic works by Walt Rostow (Rostow, 1960) and Samuel Huntington (Huntington, 1968) provided much of the intellectual background for U.S. counterinsurgency policy.[3]

Modernization theory emphasizes the reciprocal relationships among economic, political, and cultural development. According to

Table 4.1
Summary of Stabilization Paradigms

Paradigm	Priorities	Economic Concept	Political Concept	Security Concept
Controlled state-building	Economic growth, state capacity	Economics is engine of modernization.	Democratization is the long-term result of growth, but its success depends on preconditions.	A strong state must protect against violent challenges.
Liberal-democratic state-building	Political inclusion, equitable growth	Economic growth improves incentives for peace, but only if equitable and sustainable.	Democratization is crucial to achieving stability and movement toward sound state.	Security is achieved through political inclusion and military transparency.
Decentralized S&R	Minimalist objectives: absence of large-scale violence	Local communities, power-holders should set their own economic priorities.	Political inclusion and accountability are important, but may occur outside the formal state and differ between localities.	Stability is achieved when localities are secure from each other and able to maintain stability within their regions.

the version of modernization theory popular in the 1960s, economic growth propelled changes in the other spheres. In the process of modernization, economic growth (and the related processes of industrialization and urbanization) began to break down traditional authority structures and economic relationships founded on small rural communities and extended kinship groupings, such as clans and tribes. Ideally these traditional forms of social order would be replaced by functioning markets and strong state institutions, substituting institutionalized social support networks appropriate to the scale of modern economies for the outmoded social protections offered by kinship.

Unfortunately, political modernization often did not keep pace with changes in the economy, leading to violence and instability, as in Iran. Two factors in particular prevented smooth transitions. First, economic development frequently disrupted traditional communities without providing enough economic surplus to alleviate discontent. Economic growth, in other words, failed to keep pace with the demands of a population that was fast losing its traditional sources of livelihood and protection in the event of adversity. Second, a powerful state with functioning political institutions often did not develop quickly enough to respond effectively to the political demands of the mobilized population. Without a strong state capable of responding to political demands in productive ways, the population was likely to be mobilized to violence and the overthrow of the regime.

Modernization theory suggested two policy responses to violence and the threat of Communist insurgency. First, rapid economic development—best accomplished through capitalist market structures—was critical. Second, state institutions must be strengthened before they could effectively accommodate popular political demands (see especially Huntington, 1968). Taken together, these two requirements implied a process of "controlled state-building," in which market-based economic development and the forging of a strong state apparatus must *precede* democratization. Although democracy was the long-term goal espoused by American policymakers, in the short-to-medium term they were typically willing to manage the process of modernization in such a way as to exclude political organizations and demands that they viewed as threatening to the modernization process and to postpone liberalization in the face of violent challenges to the state (Kirkpatrick, 1979).

In practice, however, the United States found it difficult to manage political change as prescribed by modernization theorists. First, local rulers proved adept at resisting demands for political reforms, thereby hindering the economic growth and partial political accommodation that was intended to substitute for raw repression in the management of political violence. Where rulers were indeed committed to reform, such as with Ramon Magsaysay in the Philippines, there was seldom need for substantial U.S. assistance, and where rulers were not committed to reform (as in South Vietnam), no amount of U.S. assistance appeared to help (Blaufarb, 1977). Second, by the 1980s American domestic political opposition made it difficult to continue military support for autocrats without insisting on democratic reforms, as in the case of congressional opposition to military aid for El Salvador (Peceny, 1995).

Liberal Democratic State-Building

The "third wave" of democratic revolutions from 1964–1990 combined with the end of the Cold War to produce a radically altered strategic landscape and perspectives on military intervention.[4] The primary factor prompting U.S. concern in the immediate post–Cold War era shifted from the threat of Communist subversion to what is known among social scientists as the "security externalities" of domestic instability: the costs—such as refugee flows, the spread of disease, the expansion of transnational organized crime, and terrorism—that are shifted from the failing state onto its neighbors and the international community more generally.

This period has often been characterized (fairly or not) as an era of "democratic triumphalism," typified by such works as Frances Fukuyama's *The End of History and the Last Man* (1992). Liberal democratic institutions were prescribed by many social scientists as the solution for problems ranging from economic stagnation to famines, corruption, the violation of human rights, and especially war (see Halperin, Siegle, and Weinstein, 2005, for an overview of these arguments).

Liberal democracy played a critical role in social-science theorizing about strategies for restoring peace to weak and failed states rent by violence. Ideally, the transition from civil war to democracy substitutes electoral competition for contests of destruction.[5] According to this line of thinking, civil wars and insurgencies are motivated by inequitable access to political power and the distribution of resources that flows from control of the state (e.g., UNDP, 2009, p. 3). Autocratic regimes spark rebellions because they use state resources to benefit a narrow portion of the population at the expense of other groups. Democratic competition for office should allow groups to press their demands on the state through peaceful channels rather than having to bear the devastations of war. Thus, the parties to conflict should be able to agree on a settlement that offers credible promises of political inclusion to all of the warring parties. Political inclusion played a major role in ending many of the civil wars that came to an end in conjunction with the end of the Cold War, such as those in El Salvador, Mozambique, and Nicaragua.

Obviously, military potential and electoral potential are not identical, so the agreement of militarily powerful but politically weak factions may have to be "bought" through disproportionate concessions, such as those made to the Revolutionary United Front in Sierra Leone. Similarly, minority groups might be permanently excluded from power in a purely majoritarian democracy, so some form of credible protections would have to be offered to these groups to convince them to accept democratic governance. An extreme example is the radical devolution of power to the "entity" level of government in Bosnia that was necessary to secure the acquiescence of the Bosnian Serbs to the Dayton Accords. A more moderate example is visible in post-Franco Spain, where federalism was used to assuage regional minorities' fears. Both of these challenges can, at least in theory, be resolved through power-sharing institutions that guarantee all parties to a conflict a reasonable opportunity to participate in future governance. Such systems of power-sharing should be easily recognizable to American observers; the U.S. Constitution is itself an elaborate system of checks and balances designed to prevent any one faction from gaining absolute control of government.

The belief that democracy could help to bring peace to war-torn societies—the liberal democratic state-building model—pervaded official thinking and became the basis for peacekeeping doctrine in the 1990s (see, for instance, Boutros-Ghali, 1992). The United States espoused a grand strategy of "democratic enlargement" to replace containment in the wake of the Cold War. The European Union also increased its support for democracy promotion in this period, providing slightly more funding for such initiatives than the United States (Carothers, 2004, p. 260). Then–Secretary-General of the United Nations Boutros Boutros-Ghali made democracy promotion a centerpiece of UN strategy with his *An Agenda for Democratization* (1996)—a commitment carried forward by his successor, Kofi Annan. Elections were a cornerstone of international peacebuilding efforts in El Salvador, Nicaragua, Cambodia, Namibia, Mozambique, Angola, Bosnia, Kosovo, Liberia, Sierra Leone, Timor-Leste, and elsewhere.

Much of the public rhetoric at the height of "democratic triumphalism" obscured the fact that many public officials and academics were much more sober in their assessments of what democracy could realistically accomplish in post-conflict environments. Even proponents of democracy were divided as to the pace at which democratization could realistically occur, the problems that democracy could be expected to ameliorate in the near-to-medium term, and the likely congruence of local practices with international human rights standards. Critics of democratization policies went a step further, making two claims in particular. First, democratization in such settings was highly unlikely to succeed and could even exacerbate intercommunal tensions. Second, even if democratization might ultimately be the best means to resolve the root causes of conflict, outsiders could do relatively little to facilitate the transition through any means short of enormous and lengthy military occupations.[6] Such acknowledgements of the limitations of democracy promotion in weak and failed states increased sharply as a result of the 2003 U.S. invasion of Iraq.

Decentralized Stabilization and Reconstruction

The limitations and outright failures of U.S. policy in Afghanistan and Iraq prompted a new wave of scholarship on the appropriate ends and means of military intervention. As with any attempt to characterize a strand of thinking, generalizations are difficult. Its proponents frequently disagree on specifics, and they are usually the first to emphasize that no uniform strategy can be applied across different contexts. Nonetheless, a number of commonalities are clear. Proponents of the new strategic thinking have focused on much more limited aims than those that prevailed in the 1990s. In particular, its advocates support stabilization (the absence of large-scale violence) over more transformative S&R agendas, such as democratization or the redress of grievances. To the extent that justice or political representation features in decentralized S&R strategies, the focus is on limiting government abuses of the population rather than righting broader wrongs. Many thinkers in this camp emphasize traditional conceptions of authority and legitimacy: Where restoration of political life before the start of large-scale violence is possible, the status quo ante is often the goal. (Of course, in many developing societies—especially countries such as Afghanistan and Somalia—the status quo ante was itself characterized by an extremely weak state; see, for instance, Clapham, 2004; Clunan and Trinkunas, 2010; and Herbst, 2000). The primary tool of stabilization is effective local governance, particularly the provision of security and other public services. While a strong central state might be desirable in the longer term, short-term expansive central state-building efforts are typically considered disastrous by proponents of this approach.[7] We may therefore refer to proponents of this line of thinking as proponents of "decentralized stabilization and reconstruction."

Because American soldiers have had to bear the price of policy shortcomings in Afghanistan and Iraq, it is unsurprising that the advocates of this approach include many from the U.S. military or associated with it.[8] Perhaps more surprising, many aspects of U.S. military thinking parallel debates within the development community and the evolution of academic debates on the causes of and policy prescriptions for insurgencies and civil wars. The academic political science literature has increasingly turned from state-level determinants of civil wars to local dynamics, a reorientation perhaps best captured by Stathis Kalyvas (2006). Moreover, the reaction against transformative agendas in Iraq combined with a pessimism born of the shortcomings of many peace operations to strengthen the social-science scholarship on the limitations and perverse outcomes of democracy promotion in deeply divided societies. Increasingly scholars have emphasized the need for indigenously initiated alternatives.[9]

Dimensions of the Debate

Despite varied strategic circumstances over the decades, debates over the ends and means of interventions consistently return to a few recurring questions. Two in particular stand out: (1) Is it better to co-opt challengers to the state and form an inclusive government, or is it better to form a cohesive but narrower ruling coalition? (2) Is it better for foreign intervenors to assist local actors in building a strong state, capable of providing a high level of public goods (such as security and state services), or is it better to rely on a wider range of actors both within and outside of the state to provide more decentralized—and typically more traditional or informal—governance? The answers to these two questions shape the strategies that the United States and other foreign actors will pursue, as shown in Figure 4.1.

The "controlled state-building" paradigm dominant in the 1960s emphasizes strong central states but with lower levels of political inclusion (at least in the short-to-medium term). The "liberal democratic state-building" perspective that guided the peace operations of the 1990s and early 2000s seeks to promote a strong state, but one bound by liberal institutions of political inclusion and participation. And the "decentralized S&R" strategies coming to the fore in many of today's policy debates emphasize meeting the needs of the entire population, but doing so through more informal and localized institutions of governance. The fourth logical possibility (narrow inclusion combined with decentralized governance) corresponds to the historical practice of feudalism. Although it is a path to state-building that was practiced with great frequency throughout the centuries, it is hard to identify a single international intervention in the post-colonial era that has adopted such an approach. It is therefore not included as an international S&R strategy.

Any attempt to narrow debates to a few critical questions and schools of thought sacrifices nuance. The horizontal and vertical axes in Figure 4.1 thus represent degrees of difference, not clear black-and-white distinctions. Proponents of controlled state-building often favor

Figure 4.1
International Strategies of Stabilization

		Governance	
		Less Centralized	More Centralized
Political Inclusion	Narrow	–	Controlled state-building
	Broad	Decentralized S&R	Liberal democratic state-building

RAND *MG1119-4.1*

political inclusion of moderate opponents of a regime, liberal democratic state-builders have commonly also advocated decentralization
of formal governmental institutions (while still attempting to build a
modern, Weberian state), and many advocates of decentralized S&R
support creation of a strong state security sector. Nonetheless, this
summary helps focus attention on the critical dilemmas, which are
discussed more fully below.

Dilemmas of Intervention

The ebb and flow of policy debates about ends and means for S&R are
shaped, naturally, by recent events. Problems encountered in Afghanistan and Iraq have prompted useful introspection and reassessment,
but it remains unclear what balance should be struck between the cooptation or exclusion of regime challengers (often called "spoilers")
(Stedman, 1996). Nor has social-science research established the optimal mix of formal governmental institutions and decentralized societal
mechanisms of governance. Rather, these debates reflect underlying
dilemmas.

This section outlines the logic of the dilemmas of inclusion and
state capacity. Interestingly, many advocates of both controlled state-
building and decentralized S&R profess to support a liberal, institutionalized political order as their eventual end goal. In many ways,
however, the early actions of intervenors commit them to particular
compromises and institutions from which it is difficult to evolve. The
challenges to gradual transition, then, constitute a third dilemma.

When posed starkly, all of these are truly dilemmas, posing a
choice between two comparably unpalatable alternatives. There is heu-
ristic value in stating them so bluntly so as to recognize the critical
choices and inevitable trade-offs inherent in S&R operations. Nonetheless, this is only a starting point for analysis, since there may be
policy prescriptions that would at least mitigate the negative effects or
improve the positive payoffs of the choices made. Some such possibilities are discussed later in this chapter. What follows elaborates on the
dilemmas themselves.

The Dilemmas of Inclusion

The principal dividing line of the policy debates over the civil wars of the 1990s was between those who advocated negotiated solutions and those who said it was necessary to allow the military victor to impose a new political order (or to "give war a chance" in Luttwak's [1999] provocative formulation). The turn to counterinsurgency in the 2000s has changed the stakes and some of the dynamics of the debate, but the underlying issues remain the same. The debate revolves around a central dilemma:

> **The Inclusion Dilemma.** Military victory appears to be associated with more durable post-conflict political orders, but these orders tend to be autocratic and repressive. Negotiated solutions tend to generate more fragile political orders, but they tend to be more politically inclusive—sometimes even democratic—and less repressive. The inclusion dilemma, therefore, apparently presents intervenors with a stark choice between either helping to broker a negotiated and more politically inclusive—but also highly fragile—end to a war or allowing one side to impose a relatively more stable—but also more autocratic and repressive—political order.

Analytically, war termination and political inclusion can be understood as two distinct processes, albeit closely interlinked. Civil wars or insurgencies erupt when factions capable of large-scale violence disagree on the appropriate political order for their state. These conflicts end when the parties reach agreement about the relative costs of fighting and benefits of a particular post-conflict political order.[10] Outside intervenors can influence the local parties' calculations—for instance, by decreasing the odds of victory (e.g., by intervening against one of the parties) or by making a political settlement more attractive (e.g., by providing economic aid or security guarantees to any party that agrees to the settlement). But even when a country like the United States intervenes, results from the battlefield still affect the ensuing political order. Before committing to an intervention and a particular S&R strategy, therefore, it is critical to understand the interrelationship between military outcomes and political inclusion.

Military Victory and the Benefits of Political Exclusion. The so-called realist perspective emphasizes that state-making has historically been a product of war-making (Tilly, 1999; Weinstein, 2005). While the humanitarian impulse may be to end a war as quickly as possible, some scholars argue that humanitarianism is in fact poorly served by such an approach. Ironically, the powerful states that now intervene elsewhere and seek to impose negotiated solutions ended their own internal struggles with clear-cut winners, as occurred in the American Civil War.

The process of waging war and the fact of decisive defeat facilitate the construction of stable regimes in a number of ways. First, according to this perspective, war-making is a form of state-making. To defeat opponents throughout the territory of a country, a faction leader must build relatively broad bases of support and develop a strong organizational structure—in other words, the foundations of a cohesive state.[11] Yoweri Museveni and his victorious National Resistance Movement (NRM), for instance, led Uganda from the depths of its conflicts in the 1960s and 1980s (when the country's name was almost synonymous with violent atrocities) to become one of the foremost examples of post-conflict recovery (Weinstein, 2005). Second, because a single faction or united coalition has triumphed, it can govern in a relatively coherent and decisive manner, rather than being incessantly forced to "buy off" opposition and make unsustainable compromises. Here it is possible to contrast the divergent post-conflict trajectories of Croatia, which defeated Serbian paramilitaries and has become a prosperous and democratic state, with Bosnia, which was forced to accept a military stalemate and has been mired in political near-paralysis since. Third, because opposing forces have been decisively defeated, the balance of power and the costs of renewed conflict are clear; a group that has suffered the consequences of military defeat is unlikely to seek renewed conflict—at least, not soon (Werner and Yuen, 2005).

Although there is significant debate (discussed below and in Chapter Two of this volume), a number of statistical studies of civil wars over the past century have seemed to support the idea that war-making and decisive defeat of rivals is an essential aspect of state-making. They have concluded that negotiated settlements are much more likely to degenerate into renewed fighting than are civil wars that end in military victory (Licklider, 1995; Toft, 2010; Werner and Yuen, 2005); indeed, Fortna (2004, p. 273) writes, "That peace is more stable after decisive military victories than after wars that end in a tie is perhaps the most consistent finding of the literature on the durability of peace after both civil and interstate conflict." From these studies, by themselves, the policy implication might seem clear: To end a war quickly, intervene decisively in favor of one of the protagonists, typically the government (Regan, 1996).

Critics of such an approach, however, point to problems with this argument: (1) the difficulty of achieving decisive military defeat, (2) the potential of external intervenors to decisively change the dynamics of post-conflict stabilization, and (3) the costs of military victory and political exclusion. *Nor is the statistical evidence in favor of military victory as robust as its proponents claim*; recent scholars have found significant shortcomings in the claimed relationship between military victory and durable peace (Doyle and Sambanis, 2006, p. 104). Consequently, proponents of political inclusion argue for negotiated settlements to civil wars and power-sharing arrangements that transform violent conflicts into peaceful political contestation.[12]

The first problem encountered by the "give war a chance" camp is the difficulty of achieving decisive military victory. The average duration of civil wars has increased from approximately *two* years in 1946 to *fifteen* years in 1999 (Fearon and Laitin, 2003, p. 68). Toft (2010, p. 8) argues that "the combination of the proliferation of weak states, refinements in insurgency strategy, and the wide distribution of small arms has made it relatively more difficult for even well-supplied and well-led combatants to achieve victory." As a war continues, the devastation mounts, destroying physical infrastructure, contributing to declines in public health that endure for years after the conflict, and causing the educated elite to flee and settle in more-developed countries. The overall process is a case of "development in reverse," leaving the country permanently weakened and thus at higher risk of renewed conflict—a phenomenon a World Bank report referred to as the "conflict trap" (Collier et al., 2003). Decisive victory has been elusive in countries ranging from Somalia to Afghanistan to the Democratic Republic of Congo. Even when it is achieved, as it apparently has been in Sri Lanka, the costs of decades of conflict can be enormous.

Second, while negotiated settlements themselves may be highly fragile, the presence of external intervenors can radically improve their chances of enduring (Doyle and Sambanis, 2000, 2006; Fortna, 2004, 2008; Walter, 1999, 2002).

Third, military victory is frequently purchased at the price of violent repression and sometimes even genocide. While Licklider (1995) finds that negotiated settlements are less stable than military victories, he also finds that one-fifth of identity (e.g., ethnic or sectarian) conflicts ending in military victory precipitate genocides, while not a single case of negotiated settlement has done so. Moreover, military victories are much more likely to result in authoritarian governments than are negotiated settlements (Gurses and Mason, 2008; Watts, 2009). Authoritarianism, in turn, is generally associated with a violent repression and even genocide (Rummel, 1995), particularly in the aftermath of civil war or other violent conflict (Harff, 2003). The atrocities of the victorious Khmer Rouge in Cambodia or the Indonesian military in East Timor are but two examples.

Finally, beyond the realities "on the ground," there are the realities of American domestic politics. At least under some circumstances, large parts of the American public (and European publics) have been unwilling to see unrestrained warfare take its course in countries ranging from Somalia to Bosnia and elsewhere. The intensity of this humanitarian sentiment and the extent to which government decisionmakers should be guided by these considerations is open to debate. At a minimum, however, public opinion poses a constraint on the most nakedly realpolitik options.

Negotiating Political Inclusion. Critics of the "give war a chance" school commonly claim that there is no such thing as a purely military victory. Even if a party (or coalition of parties) is capable of winning on the battlefield, it typically sows the seeds of its eventual downfall. The personalities and skills of the successful warlord are seldom the same as those of the gifted political leader. Asking a militia commander to submit to the rule of law "may be like asking a champion swimmer to empty the pool" (Collier et al., 2003, p. 82). Moreover, in the absence of an organized and powerful opposition, rulers seldom if ever feel compelled to offer meaningful opportunities for political participation to those outside of their support base (Olson, 1993; Przeworski, 1991; Rustow, 1970). Consequently, military victory in a civil war—whether on the part of the government or insurgents—typically results in the political exclusion of large parts of a country's population. Such exclusion, in turn, sets the stage for future conflict (see, for instance, Gurr, 2000, 2002).

Proponents of political inclusion argue that durable peace requires giving all major actors a stake in continued peaceful relations. If all actors are given access to an equitable proportion of both political and economic assets, then they all have an interest in retaining the system. Negotiated settlements based on political inclusion should make it possible both to end wars more quickly and to create the foundations for a more stable peace in the long term.

Two challenges to this approach immediately arise. First, it is difficult to determine what an "equitable proportion" of a state's assets are, and even more difficult to arrange the compromise in such a manner as to permit effective government. Second, even if a suitable compromise could be found, it is difficult to ensure that all parties to an agreement will stick to it in the future, especially if incentives for abiding by the compromise change over time.

Peace treaties for civil wars distribute control or influence over the state's institutions in a manner acceptable to all factions (see also discussion in Chapter Three). To induce the warring parties to accept the compromise, control or influence may be distributed in proportion to their fighting strength at the time of the peace treaty. Unfortunately, such a power-sharing framework is problematic for two reasons. First, unless the factions' fighting strength and electoral strength are equal, a compromise that is acceptable to the parties' wartime leadership will effectively underrepresent much of the population. Their political marginalization sets the stage for future conflict. Second, the guarantees and protections needed to induce all of the parties to sign a power-sharing agreement are frequently so extreme as to make effective governance extraordinarily difficult. Systems of mutual vetoes paralyze decisionmaking, and both budgets and staffing of the civil service become bloated by earmarking. In practice, it is extremely difficult to find a formula that divides power acceptably while still making effective government possible over time. In part for these reasons, power-sharing regimes formed in the wake of civil wars have a dismal historical record (Rothchild and Roeder, 2005).

A second problem with using political inclusion to bring civil wars and insurgencies to an end concerns the "time-inconsistency" problem (see especially Fearon, 1998; Walter, 2002). Przeworski (1991, p. 25) summarizes the problem succinctly when he writes that "The central difficulty of political power in any form is that it gives rise to increasing returns to scale." Once one party (or coalition of parties) obtains the upper hand in a post-conflict government, it is then in a position to use its control of state institutions to add to its power. Ultimately the governing party (or parties) may become powerful enough to repress all rivals. At this point the factions are unlikely to feel constrained to honor an agreement made under duress years ago. Thus, peace agreements signed at one point in time become unenforceable later. Recognizing this risk, warring factions either will not sign a peace deal or, if they do, will secretly retain the means of returning to war to protect themselves (a point discussed also in Chapter Two).

So long as a power-sharing agreement remains an oligopolistic balance of power among the wartime-era factions, it is extremely difficult to resolve these tensions. When "political inclusion" means the inclusion of only well-organized, well-armed factions who obtained their position by force of arms, then these groups have little incentive to normalize (demilitarize) politics. The public as a whole suffers from the political deadlock and inefficiencies of power-sharing, but the political elite may fare quite well. They typically collect "rents" from their control of the state and commonly maintain control of the illicit economies that sprang up during the course of the war, all the while justifying the political instability and economic stagnation in the name of protecting their constituent subpopulations from the possibility of renewed warfare. Such dynamics have been clearly visible in Bosnia, where stories abound of political leaders preventing the implementation of aid programs so as to keep voters radicalized.

The typical policy prescription for escaping this impasse is to institute mechanisms of popular accountability, as discussed in Chapter Three—that is, to empower the public to insist on improved performance from office holders and sanction failure by removing underperforming officials from office. Such a perspective is common in the development community and among multilateral organizations such as the United Nations Development Programme (UNDP): "By promoting inclusive participation of all members of society, including disadvantaged and marginalized groups, and by helping to build up responsive governing institutions and respect for human rights, it is possible to mitigate conflict and promote peace" (UNDP, 2009, p. xi). To introduce formal institutions of popular accountability to a system of broad political inclusion, however, is to create a form of democratic governance. And here we stumble on all of the problems inherent in ambitious projects of democratization in post-conflict environments.

After the initial period of "democratic triumphalism" following the fall of the Berlin Wall, observers are now much more measured in their assessments of when and how democratic institutions can contribute positively to a country's development. Many have warned about the limited ability of foreigners to introduce and support systems of democratic governance elsewhere and the often-dismal record of past efforts (Carothers, 2004, pp. 60, 232; Ottaway, 2000; Pei and Kasper, 2003; Whitehead, 1986; Zuercher, 2006; but see Dunning, 2004; Goldsmith, 2001; and Van de Walle, 2005, for contending views). Even with democratic institutions in place, the evidence is mixed as to how much they contribute to the quality of a government's performance or its responsiveness to its population. Thomas Carothers (2002), for instance, warns about two common and enduring patterns of low-quality democracy, what he labels "feckless pluralism" (where parties alternate in power, but no party seems capable of effective or responsive rule) and "dominant-power" quasi-democracy (in which a single party is capable of ruling indefinitely without facing effective electoral challengers). Perhaps most damning for the notion of democratic conflict resolution, many scholars caution that *mature* democracies are the most stable and peaceful type of regime, but states that are *in the process of democratizing* may be the most unstable and prone to violence (see Bates, 2008, pp. 8–9; Goldstone et al., 2005; Hegre et al., 2001; Mansfield and Snyder, 2002; Snyder, 2000). Those who fear the destabilizing consequences of democratization tend to recommend an extended period of state capacity-building and gradual liberalization before democratization is attempted (see, for instance, Zakaria, 2003; but see Chapter Three of this volume for skeptical comments). With such proposals the policy debate has come full circle, with at least some observers returning from the liberal state-building of the 1990s to the controlled state-building of Samuel Huntington's *Political Order in Changing Societies* (1968) and other classics of the 1960s.

Assessing the Inclusion Debate. Although idealism and dogmatism undoubtedly played their roles, much of the international community's incorporation of democratic elements into their strategies for stabilization derived from more sober considerations—in particular, frustrations with the limitations of both elite-based power-sharing and the type of state-building associated with military victories. Decisive victories might lay the foundations for a strong state, but they are difficult to achieve in the contemporary era—Sri Lanka is one of the very few recent cases. Even if one faction emerges victorious, the state-building that occurs is likely to be autocratic, repressive, and possibly even genocidal. To cite even a relatively mild example, the score-settling that followed the Greek civil war distorted politics in that country for three generations. Repressive governance, in turn, is associated with refugee flows, the radicalization of oppressed minorities and diasporas, and many of the other "security externalities" that the international community has sought to limit in the past two decades. When diplomats turned to more inclusive S&R strategies, however, such as power-sharing arrangements, they found them typically difficult to broker, ineffectual, inflexible, and fragile. Efforts to make power-sharing more effective by incorporating formal mechanisms of popular accountability foundered on the well-known limitations of democracy promotion in weak and divided states.

Clearly the debate is too blunt, at least in the condensed form in which it has been presented here. It is worth noting that even proponents of state-making through military victory, such as Jeremy Weinstein (2005), offer numerous caveats and insist that it is an approach advisable in only some circumstances. Similarly, most advocates of democratic conflict resolution have been chastened by the disappointments of the past two decades and offer more limited and more nuanced support for the concept than they once did. Moreover, when American decisionmakers consider how best to stabilize a war-torn region, geopolitical considerations of national interest affect support for policy options based on *who* is to be included or excluded—whether they are Communists (during the Cold War), close allies of al Qaeda (in the present era), or some other grouping that has objectives inimical to those of American foreign policy. In the final section, such factors will be explicitly taken into consideration as various policy prescriptions are developed. Before turning to this discussion, however, it is important to understand the other dimensions of the contemporary debate.

The Dilemma of State Capacity

Despite differences of opinion about the appropriate degree of political inclusion and democratization in a strategy of stabilization, would-be stabilizers throughout most of the past two decades have almost universally agreed that establishing a strong, capable state is the best way to restore peace and promote development in war-torn and chaotic countries (Barakat, 2004, p. 16; Doyle and Sambanis, 2000, p. 680; Fukuyama, 2004; Zuercher, 2006, p. 1). Typical of this approach is the guidance issued by the World Bank (2005, p. v): "Erosion of state capacity or accountability eventually results in failure to mediate competing interests, generate economic growth or provide services in an inclusive and accountable way, creating the space for political instability or conflict." From this perspective, the policy prescription is obvious: "A long-term focus on state capacity and accountability is critical in all fragile state contexts if these countries are ever to find a durable exit from crisis" (World Bank, 2005, p. 3).

Recently, however, many scholars and practitioners have pushed back against the strong-state orthodoxy. Even in many middle-income countries of Latin America the reach of the state is limited, and institutions of informal governance can be as effective, or even more so in some circumstances, in mediating disputes and delivering public services (Helmke and Levitsky, 2006). In low-income and extremely impoverished countries, the state may be little more than an abstraction for most of the territory beyond the capital city. In large reaches of Africa and in parts of Asia, such as Afghanistan, the state has never approached the ideal of the Western state system (Clapham, 2004; Ellis, 2005; Englebert and Tull, 2008; Herbst, 1996, 2000; Jones, 2009). Consequently, an increasingly intense debate has arisen between those who believe in a strong state as the means to long-term stability and development and those who believe that social structures and informal institutions must realistically play a much greater role in the governance of many sectors in the less developed countries of the world.

The debate, in fact, reflects an underlying dilemma:

> **The Dilemma of State Capacity.** Stated starkly, the dilemma of state capacity suggests that intervenors may be able to create a strong central state capable of efficient service provision and defeating violent challenges to its authority, but typically only at tremendous cost and a lengthy foreign commitment. Alternatively, intervenors can create more informal governance more quickly and at much lower cost—but with corresponding weaknesses in the state's ability to provide the services that both its population and foreign powers would prefer.

Where the central state is weak—whether due to lack of resources, runaway corruption, a historical tradition of weak central government, or some combination of factors—the external powers conducting a stability operation have two basic options. They can attempt to strengthen the central state, or they can work around it, by seeking to provide services through nongovernmental organizations or empowering informal institutions of governance, such as tribes (see also related discussion in Chapter Seven). The former approach may be prohibitively lengthy and expensive, and, in some regions without any history of strong state institutions, it may simply be infeasible. Moreover, by attempting to create such a state apparatus, foreigners may provoke a violent reaction from the local population—what David Kilcullen (2009, p. 38) describes in terms of "an immune response in which the body rejects the intrusion of a foreign object." On the other hand, without effective central state institutions, the partner state may be unable to foster economic development, enforce the rule of law throughout its territory, or mediate potentially violent disputes between local factions. Peace based on such foundations is likely to be quite precarious. Even if peace endures, it is not clear that the state will be able to resolve the underlying issues—such as refugee flows or the presence of violent transnational networks—that precipitated foreign intervention in the first place.

The remainder of the section on the dilemma of state capacity begins with some definitions, follows with a review of the strengths and weaknesses of governance mechanisms, and ends with conclusions about the debate.

The Nature and Scope of Governance. State capacity may be defined as the ability of the state to provide such public goods as security, infrastructure, and welfare services. More specifically, as former Colombian Minister for Economic Development Mauricio Cardenas observed in a recent paper (2010, p. 2), "much of the literature in the social sciences uses the term to mean the professionalization of the state bureaucracy, its ability to protect property rights and make credible commitments to private investors, as well as its ability to raise revenue from the society."

State capacity, however, is only one element of the broader concept of governance. Traditionally *government* refers to the formulation and execution of the policies of the state. *Governance*, on the other hand, has a much broader scope. The United Nations Development Programme recently defined it to mean

> the exercise of political, economic, and administrative authority in the management of a country's affairs at all levels. Governance is a neutral concept comprising the complex mechanisms, processes, relationships and institutions through which citizens and groups articulate their interests, exercise their rights and obligations and mediate their differences. (UNDP, 2009, p. 2)

The concept of governance thus includes both formal and informal institutions.

Informal institutions in turn may be defined as "socially shared rules, usually unwritten, that are created, communicated, and enforced outside officially sanctioned channels" (Helmke and Levitsky, 2006, p. 5). Informal institutions of governance may include tribal courts or councils of elders, patronage networks or "political machines," networks of merchants self-organized to enforce private contracts, and "informal police," such as tribal militias or vigilante gangs. Informal institutions are ubiquitous in all societies. In countries where stability operations typically occur, however, these institutions differ in degree and often in kind from those found in most developed societies. Because the formal state is usually much weaker in developing societies, informal institutions necessarily have a more pervasive role in regulating social behavior. While informal institutions may be effective in regulating social behavior, however, they may not conform to international principles of human and civil rights. And while states can be pressured to accept such standards, autonomous social networks are difficult to regulate.

Informal institutions depend on three requirements to function effectively (Dixit, 2004; Engerman and Sokoloff, 2008, p. 129; Haggard, MacIntyre, and Tiede, 2008, p. 220; Helmke and Levitsky, 2006; Lyon and Porter, 2009). First, they require a commonly understood (although usually unwritten) code of conduct. Informal institutions typically arise within ethnic groups or co-religionists because they can "draw on a reservoir of common cultural material—language, experience, understanding about modes of interaction—that makes it easier for community members to communicate and work together" (Habyarimana et al., 2007, p. 711). Second, they depend on a mechanism for obtaining reliable information about the actions (and especially transgressions) of others within the network. In the absence of more formalized institutions of monitoring (such as government regulators or a well-developed and free media), information is normally obtained through face-to-face relationships and the development of long-standing relationships and reputations within a given community, whether it be an extended family, a rural village, a network of traders, a secret religious society, or some other grouping. Finally, informal institutions require an enforcement mechanism to punish those who violate the commonly understood rules. Enforcement mechanisms vary considerably. They may be violent, as in the case of Russian organized criminal gangs who enforce order within a given locality or economic sector (see, for instance, Volkov, 2000), or militias formed from tribes or secret societies, such as the Arbakai of Afghanistan or the Kamajors of Sierra Leone, or private police forces hired by merchants to ensure the safety and reliability of markets in places such as Nigeria and Somalia (Lyon and Porter, 2009; Mubarak, 1996). But often enforcement mechanisms are much subtler: the loss of reputation or social shaming and stigmatizing, either of which can carry serious material as well as social consequences in societies based on community and trust (Helmke and Levitsky, 2006; Lyon and Porter, 2009, p. 906).

Strengths of Informal Institutions. The preceding discussion has already indicated many of the strengths of informal institutions. Unlike many grandiose state-building projects, informal institutions are closely adapted to local realities because they evolve from the fabric of everyday interactions (Scott, 1998). Drawing on existing networks and practices, they are inexpensive and immediately available; they do not require extensive training, new facilities, or salaried employees. They are usually strong and resilient: Whereas state institutions may be an abstraction for much of the population, neighbors and families are real and present, and religious or other norms are internalized. Where states fail, informal institutions typically take over the functions of governance.

States impose a more or less uniform set of institutions across often highly diverse societies, resulting in inevitable disjunctions between the formal rules of the state and the informal practices of many subpopulations (Scott, 1969, p. 1143). In practice, office holders often accommodate various social actors, adapting formal institutions of the state to local contexts through informal bargains (Helmke and Levitsky, 2006; Migdal, Kohli, and Shue, 1994; Migdal, 1994). Foreign state-builders operate at an enormous disadvantage by often being only dimly aware of the nuances of such informal institutions. Moreover, foreign intervenors in the contemporary era operate on relatively short timelines, while the process of accommodation between state and society typically unfolds over a much longer period. Intervenors such as the United States also lack the ruthlessness for imposing change demonstrated by historical empires. Consequently, in the short term, informal institutions of governance will almost inevitably be better adapted to local realities than would newly rebuilt formal state institutions.

Second, informal institutions already rooted in local society are inexpensive and immediately available. In contrast, Western court systems, for instance, require substantial investment over years. Lawyers, judges, and clerks must be trained, an extensive legal system must be developed, records must be kept, and so on. Such systems are beyond the reach of many developing countries, let alone post-conflict societies (Haggard, MacIntyre, and Tiede, 2008, pp. 215–216; Samuels, 2006, p. 18).[13]

Third, informal institutions are commonly both strong and resilient. They have undertaken a great many functions of governance at which the state has failed or for which the state's capabilities need to be supplemented. The networks of personal relationships on which informal institutions are based are often "held to form the critical 'primary environment' by which an individual is related to the larger society" (Friedkin, 2004, p. 416; see also Scott, 1969, pp. 1146–1146; Scott, 1962, p. 94).

Informal institutions play a ubiquitous role in the governance of most developing countries. In Nigeria, informal merchant networks supply more than 60 million city-dwellers with food from more than 60 million countryside producers, despite doing so with "no recourse to legal systems, a corrupt and ineffective police force, minimal banking infrastructure, poor communications, and a highly degraded transport infrastructure" (Lyon and Porter, 2009, p. 903). This vast market relies on trust, reputation, informal systems of credit, and private police forces hired by the merchants to monitor marketplaces. Similar systems are responsible for maintaining a functioning economy in large parts of Somalia despite the utter collapse of the state—and indeed, in the better-run Somali localities, the economy is performing better than it did under the Barre regime (Mubarak, 1996). Informal institutions play a vital role in mediating disputes in countries where the judicial system is so weak, corrupt, or inaccessible that it does not play a significant role in many communities (Barfield, Nojumi, and Thier, 2006; Decker, Sage, and Stefanova, 2005; Samuels, 2006, p. 18; Widner, 2001). They also provide protection and policing functions for the local community through such institutions as blood feuds, militias organized along tribal or religious lines, and organized criminal "gangs" that enforce a form of order (while commonly demanding payment in return).

Weaknesses of Informal Institutions. Informal institutions also have significant limitations. Relying on them to provide most governance functions certainly saves a stabilization operation from the hubris of ambitious state-building; it entails serious liabilities as well.

First, as already noted, informal institutions commonly operate on a much smaller scale than the institutions of a modern state. In his study of "informal economics," Avinash Dixit (2004, p. 12) writes that for informal institutions to work, "the society needs good information networks and credible multilateral punishment strategies. . . . However, the quality of information and the credibility of punishment both degrade as the size of such a group increases." Restricting economic and political activity to smaller networks can mean foregoing economies of scale. As Bardhan (2000, pp. 219–220) argues, "A major problem of 'collectivist' systems of enforcement is that the boundaries of the collectivity within which rewards and punishment are practiced may not be the most efficient ones and they may inhibit potentially profitable transactions with people outside the collectivity." Where informal institutions depend on community ties such as those of a rural village or kinship structures, relying on them for governance often implies a radical geographic decentralization (localization) of power. In such systems, the tendency is to over-invest in highly localized infrastructure and under-invest in larger regional or national projects with substantial economies of scale (e.g., highway networks or power grids) (Cheema and Rondinelli, 2006, p. 8). A loss of efficiency may seem like a small price to pay for obtaining some form of governance for an otherwise chaotic country. Multiplied by innumerable transactions, however, and recognizing the value of transportation and communication in any modernization effort, the overall result is a substantial impediment to economic growth. Even as he extols the various informal institutions that have continued to provide governance and a functioning economy in post-Barre Somalia, for instance, Jamil Mubarak (1996) makes clear that significant and sustainable economic development will require the formation of much stronger state institutions.

A second problem of informal governance concerns the regulation of intercommunal relations. While communities have normative codes, information, and enforcement mechanisms for punishing transgressors *within* the community, few of these mechanisms are available to regulate conflicts *between* communities. Without a centralized state capable of resolving disputes and enforcing judgments between different communities, severe crises can escalate, potentially requiring resort to so-called self-help mechanisms, such as blood feuds and tribal militias (Bates, 2001). Where informal governance based on narrow community bonds is combined with centralized government and democratic elections, the result can be electoral mobilization on the basis of narrow identities. Such mobilization can either trigger or exacerbate divisive, even violent, politics (see, for instance, Belloni, 2008, p. 193; Doherty, 2001). Of course, social networks also exist that bridge the divides between different communities, but such bridging social networks are often too weak to regulate intercommunal tensions effectively once strong central government institutions have broken down and civil war erupts.[14] In the absence of a strong central government and other bridging mechanisms, a stabilization strategy that focuses on local, informal governance institutions (such as tribal militias) may result in only a decentralized and highly fragile balance of power that requires the indefinite deployment of foreign troops to prevent collapse (see, for instance, Dorronsoro, 2009, on Afghanistan).

Third, structures of informal governance are often (although not necessarily) highly inequitable. Patron-client relationships, for instance, are a common form of informal governance in which a powerful patron provides for the needs of his clients in return for the clients' loyalty. The clients' basic needs are met—and may even be provided for more effectively than under formal but dysfunctional institutions of government—but the resulting social structure is highly unequal (see especially Scott, 1962). Redressing every social injustice neither can nor should be the aim of a stability operation. Where inequalities generate intense discontent, however, and that discontent threatens to become violent (or perpetuate violence), then social injustices are indeed the concern of a stability operation. In the case of Sierra Leone, for instance, high levels of corruption among the country's "Big Men" (patrons) fueled the anger of young men throughout the country, providing a ready source of recruits for the various militias as the state weakened (Malan, Rakate, and McIntyre, 2002, Chapter 1). In such circumstances, where traditional authorities are viewed with considerable resentment by portions of the population, the restoration of traditional authorities may arguably lay the groundwork for renewed violence (Fanthorpe, 2006).

Finally, it may not be possible to restore informal institutions of governance on the basis of traditional authorities because the traditional authorities were themselves weakened or destroyed during the course of war. Stathis Kalyvas, for instance, dissects how traditional patterns of alliance and conflict (social "cleavages") radically realign in periods of civil violence:

> War may generate new local cleavages because power shifts at the local level upset delicate arrangements. . . . One of the most potent cleavages produced by civil wars is generational: rebels (but also incumbents) often recruit young people who then proceed to repress their village's elders. The war may also lower the cost of opportunistic behavior, triggering tens of local cleavages. When local cleavages subvert central ones, factional conflicts emerge within supposedly unified political camps. (2003, pp. 480–481)

Restoring "traditional authorities" as a means of restoring (informal) governance is frequently impossible, either because the traditional authority-holders have been killed, or because the very nature of "traditional authority" is what was at stake in a civil war and attempts at restoring it would immediately reignite the conflict. In Afghanistan, for instance, observers have frequently questioned the reliability of agreements brokered with tribal elders, because "it is not clear that the elders, whatever their intentions, will be able to command the loyalties of their own members. After 30 years of incessant warfare, many of the traditional societal networks in this country have been weakened or destroyed" (Filkins, 2010; on a related process in Pakistan's tribal belt, see Markey, 2008, p. 6). Similarly, critics of international peacebuilding efforts in Mozambique charged that foreign officials and aid workers sought to reinstate a form of "traditional authority" that was in fact highly contested during that country's civil war. Mozambique's then–Prime Minister, Pascoal Mocumbi, condemned such efforts in a revealing statement: "all those who demand a law on traditional authority are demagogues that only wish to create problems for us, because traditional authority varies according to each individual's own tradition" (West and Kloeck-Jenson, 1999, p. 468). Even if the general population agrees on who "traditional authorities" are and on their right to hold authority, militias frequently displace traditional elites during the course of conflict, making it difficult for the former authorities to resume governance functions (see, for instance, Barfield, Nojumi, and Thier, 2006, p. 16; Harpviken, 1996).

Assessing Informal Institutions. Arising from everyday social relations, informal institutions are typically a strong, resilient, and inexpensive form of governance. Unsurprisingly, it is to these forms of governance—such as tribal militias, religious courts, and informal marketplaces—that societies turn when state institutions begin to collapse. Outside intervenors, however, must be careful when making use of them. Such institutions tend to provide services inefficiently and on a small scale, making them a poor basis for long-term economic development. They provide little "connective tissue" to link the communities of a deeply divided society emerging from a civil war. Relying on them may deepen divisions. Indeed, informal institutions may even have been the initial source of conflict or the channels through which conflict was directed. Restoring the status quo ante may then set the country up for renewed conflict. Finally, the option to use the informal institutions may only seem to exist: They may no longer be viable because of the war, although local actors may seek to use foreign intervenors to resurrect them.

Foreigners also encounter special difficulties in attempting to use informal institutions. The economist Ben D'Exelle (2009), for instance, finds that development specialists consistently misread the local political dynamics of Nicaraguan villages—reinforcing the precise patterns of behavior that they had sought to change, despite having had a sizable presence (accounting for 20 percent of gross national income) in

Nicaragua for years. Similarly, the anthropologist Harry West and his colleague Scott Kloeck-Jenson (1999) found that aid workers in Mozambique fundamentally misunderstood the nature of traditional authorities in that country, with the result that they unwittingly played parts in furthering the highly partisan agendas of local actors rather than promoting their intended peacebuilding visions. Similar stories abound. Local actors are aware of the foreigners' information disadvantage and skillful at exploiting it (Blunt and Turner, 2005; Fanthorpe, 2006, p. 40).

Military personnel operate at an even greater disadvantage. Self-studies by the U.S. armed forces have repeatedly found that available training time and career incentives simply do not permit acquiring the extensive local knowledge necessary to generate a future "Lawrence" (Burton, 2009). Even if additional training time were allotted, it is far from clear that the requisite knowledge can be gained without many years of in-country experience (Bennett, no date).

Numbers and time scale also matter. Highly decentralized clear-hold-build strategies are extraordinarily labor-intensive. Foreign intervenors will seldom have the troops and civilian experts needed for success (Dorronsoro, 2009). Similarly, developing bottom-up governance takes considerable time—time horizons inconsistent with modern-day foreign intervenors. The result is an emphasis on top-down strategies that conform poorly to the realities of civil society development (Belloni, 2008).

Finally, even if stabilization through informal governance is achieved, it may not meet the goals of intervenors. Tajikistan, for instance, was hailed by many as an example of "autonomous recovery" from civil war. The formal provisions of the 1997 power-sharing agreement that ended Tajikistan's civil war quickly failed, but the peace endured—largely because of an informal accommodation between the government and opposition, where the various warlords of Tajikistan effectively functioned autonomously. These warlords, however, rapidly expanded their narcotics trafficking in postwar Tajikistan (Paoli, Greenfield, and Reuter, 2009, Chapter 9), and Islamic extremist groups thrived (ICG, 2001). Over time, there has been a long-term decline in the country's economy, as well as renewed violence (ICG, 2009).

To make things worse, if the intervenor's objectives include achieving human rights, the prospect of a result with extreme versions of sharia law prohibiting the education of girls and encouraging practices such as stoning of women, amputation of hands, and the like, will not be palatable.

The strengths, weaknesses, and challenges of working with informal institutions as opposed to building strong, formal state structures are summarized in Table 4.2.

The conditions under which informal governance is most likely to work are precisely the conditions that are absent during periods of insurgency or their immediate aftermath. "Bridging" elements of civil society are most likely to function effectively prior to the polarization that accompanies descent into large-scale violence (Belloni, 2008, p. 188; Kaufmann, 1996). They are most likely to form around common material interests, such as mutually beneficial trading relationships (Varshney, 2002), but such shared interests are relatively few when the state and formal economy have collapsed. Informal governance may provide many important functions at the local level, but such functions are best performed in the presence of a central state capable of providing statewide public goods and regulating disputes between localities (Belloni, 2008, pp. 188, 204; Doherty, 2001; Wood-

Table 4.2
Utility of Working Through Informal Institutions of Governance

Strengths of Informal Institutions	Weaknesses of Informal Institutions	Challenges Faced by Foreigners
Adapted to local realities	Inefficiencies of scale	Variation between localities
Inexpensive, immediately available	Weaknesses in regulating inter-communal conflict	Visibility
Strong and resilient	Inequality	Training, experience of international personnel
Can be part of bottom-up legitimization of leaders and institutions	Degradation of traditional authority over years of fighting	Scale, personnel required for decentralized operations
		Potential incongruence with policy goals
		Potential incongruence with human rights standards

ward, 2002, pp. 29–30). Indeed, Belloni (2008, p. 208) goes so far as to proclaim that a "healthy civil society is the sign of a well-functioning state, not its cause."

Clearly, informal institutions of governance have an important role to play in stabilizing societies recovering from civil war and statelessness. Ideally, it would be possible to find ways of linking informal practices of governance with the central state so that each would strengthen the other in a mutually beneficial relationship that would evolve over time. Many have therefore called for gradualist strategies of stabilization. They, however, have their own problems, as discussed in the next section.

The Dilemma of Transition

Given the inclusion and state-capacity dilemmas, many critics of liberal democratic state-building have recommended alternatives that de-emphasize rapid transitions to elections and a strong central state. They argue that for sustainable peace and development to take root in post-conflict countries, strong political coalitions with a vested interest in a new political order must form. This, however, cannot happen overnight; a lengthy period is required in which new political relationships, norms, and loyalties are forged. Extended, incremental transitions seem to be a pragmatic response to the hubris of ambitious projects of political transformation.

Such evolutionary strategies pose their own challenges, however, resulting in the third dilemma of stabilization:

> **The Dilemma of Transition.** The transitional institutions and practices that may be necessary to secure an end to a civil war or insurgency are often very poor foundations for efficient and stable government in the long term. Once institutions are in place, however, power relationships tend to "crystallize" around them in a path-dependent manner, making them highly resistant to change through peaceful transition.[15]

Crises tend to shorten time horizons.[16] In stabilization missions, the focus on the short-term tends to produce peace settlements that satisfy the warring parties' immediate demands but may not provide an institutional framework that can be self-sustaining in the long run. The end result may be the commitment of enormous resources to a strategy that does not serve the country's long-term interests. Decisionmakers thus must consider both the short and longer terms (see also Chapter Six).

One of the central challenges in stabilization is to manage the gradual transition from war to a self-sustaining, peaceful political order. Each of the three primary approaches to stabilization—liberal democratic state-building, controlled state-building, and decentralized stability—has a different notion of how that evolution is likely to unfold. All are complicated by the transition dilemma.

Advocates of liberal democratic state-building recognize that stability operations will never be able to create "new Switzerlands," but they contend that gradual democratization (conditioned by formal mechanisms of power-sharing) is the "least bad" alternative. Proponents seek to erect more or less democratic institutions in countries hosting stability operations, accepting that they will function highly imperfectly at first. Over time, however, even imperfect democratic institutions can form a viable framework in which local actors can evolve. So long as the international community provides considerable assistance to buttress this process and prevent its collapse, then local actors will respond to the incentive structures provided by the democratic institutions and international aid. Even leaders with authoritarian inclinations will approximate the behavior of democrats if given sufficient incentives to do so; the longer such incentives remain in place, the more likely that politicians will eventually stop pretending and ultimately will actually become democrats (Rustow, 1970; Lindberg, 2006).

Proponents of controlled state-building also expect transitions to occur gradually. Indeed, much of the modernization literature of the 1960s was explicitly teleological, claiming that economic growth was a "precondition" for democracy, but that democracy would inevitably arise once economic fundamentals, such as a large middle class and widespread literacy, were in place. Similarly, Jeane Kirkpatrick (1979) claimed that authoritarianism may be inevitable in the short term in most of the developing world, but U.S. support for such regimes was ultimately justified because it provided the best long-term prospects for democracy.

Gradualist or evolutionary notions pervade thinking about decentralized S&R strategies. Many observers of stability operations have recommended building stability on the basis of informal institutions in the short term, while simultaneously seeking to link them to the central state and ultimately to transform them into more formalized mechanisms of governance in the long term (Mubarak, 1996; Samuels, 2006, p. 18). This view holds that formal government institutions, so long as they function well, will ultimately displace informal governance. A former U.S. civilian official in southern Afghanistan, Frank Ruggiero, recently predicted, "As you build up the strength of the formal functions of the state, the informal actors will see some of their powers fade away" (Trofimov, 2010).

Unfortunately, the institutions of governance put in place in the initial transition, whether formal or informal, tend to become highly resistant to change short of complete collapse and renewed fighting (Rothchild and Roeder, 2005). This "stickiness" is an example of path dependency—the tendency of initial actions to have durable and disproportionately large consequences over time.

The most powerful local actors in place at the end of a civil war are likely to manipulate the construction of new institutions to their own advantage. Even if institutions are imposed by international actors, local actors are likely to adapt, building alliances and networks around the opportunities and constraints presented. Once power relationships have "crystallized" around these institutional frameworks, local elites become highly resistant to any significant institutional changes, even if the institutions in place are dysfunctional for society as a whole. Perhaps the archetypal example is post-Dayton Bosnia, where many of the parties have fiercely resisted changes to the deadlock-prone institutions of the Dayton Accords. A similar story could be told about the Federally Administered Tribal Areas (FATA) of Pakistan, where systems of government put in place at the time of Pakistan's independence have proven highly durable, despite the significant obstacles to stability that they pose today (Markey, 2008, p. 8). Other examples abound, and analysts of post-conflict transitions repeatedly warn about the path dependency of early institutional choices (Kovacs, 2008, pp. 141–142; Lyons, 2004, pp. 260–261; Roeder and Rothchild, 2005; Samuels, 2006, p. 19; Woodward, 2002, p. 20), as do observers of institutional formation more generally (see especially Levitsky and Murillo, 2009, p. 123).

Not only do elites respond to the incentive structures created by institutions, but so too does the general population, making a gradual transition from less to more democratic structures (or from less formal to more formal governance) difficult. If citizens observe in the early post-conflict period that antidemocratic behaviors are not punished (either by the public through the ballot box or by external intervenors), then such behaviors become the popular expectation. The public is then unlikely to invest the time and effort (or take the risks) necessary to organize to demand greater accountability from elected officials (Diamond, 1999, Chapter 5). As undemocratic institutions persist, they thus become more deeply entrenched. Similarly, as corruption persists, individuals and businesses become less likely to pay their taxes, less likely to refer disputes to formal judicial institutions, more likely to pay bribes, and less likely to participate in the licit economy more generally (Hellman and Kaufmann, 2002), making it difficult to transition from weak governmental institutions to stronger ones. Related dynamics have been observed in the field of decentralization (Blunt and Turner, 2005, p. 85) and elsewhere.

Relying on incremental progress in reform agendas can thus be thwarted by path-dependent dynamics among elites and non-elites alike. Reforms can become frozen in what Joel Hellman (1998) has called "partial reform equilibria," where elites permit reforms to proceed only insofar as they can manipulate them to their own political and economic advantage. Such partial reform equilibria can be worse than the complete absence of reform. Although the implications are much broader, Hellman focuses on economic reforms in the former Soviet Union, where political elites in Russia and elsewhere introduced partial economic reforms that caused tremendous market distortions. These generated enormous rents—an economic term referring to the profits that can be earned in excess of the next-best investment opportunity:

> [R]ent-seeking activities have been ubiquitous in the postcommunist transitions. Rapid foreign trade liberalization with incomplete price liberalization has allowed state enterprise managers to

sell their highly subsidized natural resource inputs (for example, oil and gas) to foreign buyers at world market prices. Price liberalization without concomitant progress in opening market entry or breaking up monopolies has created opportunities for some producers to earn monopoly rents. Privatization without reform of the credit mechanism has allowed managers to divert subsidized state credits earmarked to uphold production into short-term money markets at high interest rates. In each case, these arbitrage opportunities have generated rents to those in a position to take advantage of these market distortions. (Hellman, 1998, p. 219)

Partial reforms, in other words, generated enormous rents for well-connected businessmen above the returns available in a properly regulated market economy. These oligarchs ensured that economic reforms would stall, thereby continuing to reap the profits available from the market distortions. They then were able to recycle a portion of their outsized profits back into the political realm, ensuring the reelection of politicians who would protect their rents. Similar partial reform equilibria are common in the countries in which stability operations take place.

Even if elites are not purposefully stalling reforms, the introduction of new institutions can disrupt existing, informal practices without providing an alternative that will be functional except in the long term (Haggard, MacIntyre, and Tiede, 2008, pp. 220–221; Messick, 1999, p. 2).

Expecting reforms to unfold gradually, over the course of many years or even decades, may seem like simple prudence. Unless the transition is managed carefully, however, the results can in fact be worse than no reform at all.

The dangers of gradual transition are all the greater when understood in the context of the ever-present possibility of a return to conflict. Unless a transition can quickly demonstrate either concrete results (Walter, 2004) or, at a very minimum, a real promise of significant change for the better, post-conflict states are at very high risk of descending back into violence. Such risks are particularly acute in the case of transitions to democracy.

Paths to Stabilization

The dilemmas of stabilization truly are dilemmas: They impose difficult trade-offs, and we should not assume that a sufficiently clever strategy will enable us to avoid the painful choices they imply. Ultimately, these dilemmas cannot be solved, only managed. Essential to managing these dilemmas is matching intervention strategies to the appropriate environments. Unfortunately, the social-science literature does not provide any hard-and-fast rules for formulating such strategies. This final section proposes a typology of stabilization environments and a few provisional rules of thumb for adapting to these different contexts.

Understanding Stabilization Environments

When the United States has intervened in the post–Cold War era, it has typically done so to achieve what might be called "inclusive stability," i.e., the absence of fighting and the political inclusion of major parties. External powers can encourage inclusive stability by manipulating the incentive structures of the opposed parties—the costs of fighting, the odds of winning, or the benefits of peace. This section will focus primarily on warfighting (the costs of fighting and odds of winning), since other chapters deal more extensively with the benefits of peace (e.g., humanitarian and development assistance and peacebuilding initiatives). In particular, this section focuses on two factors:

- the availability of resources
- the distribution of power among the warring parties.

Although both of these factors can be manipulated by external powers, achieving the desired outcomes is typically extremely difficult once a country has descended into large-scale violence. In more contested environments, there have only been a handful of cases in which the post-conflict state has achieved inclusive stability, at least in the short-to-medium term, without the assistance of a large external military intervention. These factors can, however, tell us much about the likelihood of success, the most likely dangers that a particular state will face in its war-to-peace transition, and the sorts of strategies that intervening states should adopt.

Availability of Resources. Drawing first on the statistical lessons from history, we note that a large proportion of the success stories of stability operations from the late 20th century are associated with the conjunction of two factors: the abrupt end of the Cold War and related funding of combatants by the superpowers, and the absence of alternative sources of financing for opposition factions. The end of the Cold War (and the end of apartheid in South Africa) deprived factions in numerous proxy wars of their sources of support. Where new external patrons for the warring parties did not exist, and where easily lootable resources did not provide an alternative source of finances and weapons, the conflicts burned out quickly. In these cases—including Namibia, Mozambique, Ethiopia, El Salvador, and Nicaragua—peace has endured, and most of the ensuing regimes have become relatively democratic. Where, however, easily lootable resources provided an alternative source of financing, as in Angola (diamonds) and Afghanistan (opiates), the conflicts that began as Cold War–era proxy wars metamorphosed and continued.[17]

Interestingly, the availability of resources has more explanatory power for understanding the historical cases than whether stability operations occurred. Stability operations in the form of UN peacekeeping missions were deployed to all of these countries except Afghanistan and Ethiopia; many were considered to be important peacekeeping successes. However, there were sizable stability operations that failed (Angola), tiny stability operations that succeeded (e.g., Nicaragua), and cases with no stability operations whatsoever that also turned out well (e.g., Ethiopia). In contrast to the mixed record of stability operations in these cases, results correlate well with the existence of resources (i.e., external patrons or lootable resources).

The importance of resources to the outcomes of recent war-to-peace transitions suggests that cutting off resources may be an important tool for the international community—and potentially much more inexpensive and risky than direct S&R missions. International actors have a number of instruments available to starve a conflict of resources. One mechanism involves buyers' cartels organized to ameliorate the conflict potential of the commodity (e.g., the Kimberly Process). Another is a "neotrusteeship" mechanism, such as that put in place for Chad (see Krasner, 2004, p. 114). Such mechanisms have their limitations (see especially Pegg, 2006), but they potentially offer a low-cost means of reducing the conflict potential of a target state.

Balances of Power. For purposes of simplification, we can distinguish among cases of low, medium, and high imbalances of power.

- *Low Imbalance:* Balanced distributions of power (i.e., low imbalance) exist when neither the government nor any opposition faction or coalition is able to emerge victorious in war, and both or all sides (government and opposition faction(s)) are able to maintain exclusive control over significant portions of the country's population or resources.[18] Iraq between 2003 and 2007, and especially during the period of intense civil war between 2006 and 2007, is one example.
- *Moderate Imbalance*: An intermediate imbalance of power exists when one side (usually the government) controls the majority of a country's population and territory but is constrained from seeking a complete monopoly of power by the opposition's residual strength and/or the high anticipated costs of trying to seek such a monopoly.[19,20] Iraq after the 2007 "Anbar Awakening" is an example.
- *High Imbalance*: A highly imbalanced distribution of power exists when one faction is able to decisively defeat all armed challengers to the state, and these challengers also lack nonmilitary means of constraining the victors. Iraq under Saddam Hussein is one clear example.

As the inclusion dilemma suggests, the balance of power is critical to the outcomes of transition processes. If the goal of most negotiated settlements is to substitute political competition for military competition, then we should expect the parties to a conflict to make political demands roughly in proportion to their military capabilities. The more evenly balanced the distribution of military capabilities, the more each party to a conflict is likely to make political demands that are inconsistent with the formation of a decisive, effective, and efficient government. Moreover, the more evenly balanced the parties' military capabilities, the more likely they are to return to violence if they are unable to secure their demands through negotiation, each party believing that it is likely to win in a renewed war. To the extent that external intervenors desire short-term stability, they may seek to tilt the balance of power decisively in favor of a favored faction. To the extent that would-be stabilizers value political inclusion or believe that political inclusion is the best guarantor of long-term stability, they may seek to more evenly balance power among the factions (much as the Dayton Accords did in Bosnia).

These two factors—the availability of resources for conflict and the balance of power between warring parties—can be used to distinguish different operational environments for stability operations. Drawing on both historical examples and the preceding discussion of the dilemmas of stabilization and particularly on the inclusion dilemma, we can discern different paths to inclusive stability in each of these environments. Figure 4.2 provides a summary of the six logical cases derived from the two factors with examples in each.[21] The following four subsections cover the most benign cases (cells 1–2), cases predisposed to political exclusion (cells 3–4), cases in which the balance of power may facilitate mutual accommodation even in unfavorable environments (cell 5), and what is perhaps the most challenging type of case (and the one most often faced by would-be stabilizers), instances of highly vulnerable balance (cell 6).

Structures Conducive to Inclusive Stability

The most benign structures (cells 1–2) for stability operations are those in which the environment inhibits renewed fighting and where the distribution of power is either balanced or only moderately imbalanced. Where the environment provides few of the raw materials for renewed fighting and the distribution of power is not tilted heavily, war-to-peace transitions are much more likely to succeed. As mentioned earlier, the end of the Cold War yielded a number of such examples. The peace settlements to nearly all such conflicts have proven stable, and most have proven fairly democratic as well. These cases were concentrated in

Figure 4.2
Typology of Power Distribution and Implementation Environments

		Distribution of Power		
		Balance	**Moderate Imbalance**	**High Imbalance**
Opposition's Resources for Fighting — **Favorable**		*Stability:* Very Low *Inclusiveness:* Medium Examples: • Angola, 1975–2002 • Sierra Leone, 1991–2003 • Afghanistan, 2001– • DRC, 1998–2003 • Iraq, 2003–2007 6	*Stability:* Medium *Inclusiveness:* Medium Examples: • DRC, 2003– • Iraq, 2007– • Tajikistan, 1997– • Sierra Leone, 2003–2007 5	*Stability:* Medium *Inclusiveness:* Low Examples: • Iraq, 1991–2003 • Kosovo, 1997–1999 • Kosovo, 1999– 4
Opposition's Resources for Fighting — **Unfavorable**		*Stability:* Medium-High *Inclusiveness:* High Examples: • Mozambique, 1992– • El Salvador, 1992– 1	*Stability:* High *Inclusiveness:* Medium Examples: • Cambodia, 1997– • Nicaragua, 1990– 2	*Stability:* High *Inclusiveness:* Medium-Low Examples: • Croatia, 1995– • Uganda, 1986– 3

RAND *MG1119-4.2*

the late Cold War hot spots of Central America and southern Africa.[22] Where the wars in question concluded with a relatively balanced distribution of power, the results have been both stable and increasingly democratic over time. Mozambique and El Salvador, for instance, have long rated in the top half of Freedom House's democracy index (Freedom House, 1972–2010), and El Salvador recently experienced its first democratic, peaceful alternation of executive power in the postwar period—a milestone for any post-conflict country.

Cambodia and Nicaragua provide a revealing contrast. In both, communist parties held power at the end of the Cold War. In Cambodia the former communist Hun Sen used his dominant position to oust winners of the 1993 elections, FUNCINPEC, in what has been described by many as a coup. In Nicaragua, in contrast, the Sandinistas acceded to their election defeat. The Cambodian example is consistent with the idea that imbalanced orders tend to be less politically inclusive than those characterized by balances of power. However, because the resources for the opposition to keep fighting in both Cambodia and Nicaragua declined precipitously with the end of the Cold War, what might have been highly destabilizing events—the 1997 coup in Cambodia and the 1990 electoral defeat of the ruling Sandinistas—both proceeded without reigniting war.

Highly Imbalanced Structures

Where one party can decisively defeat its rivals, short- and medium-term stability is likely to be relatively high, but purchased at the price of repression (cells 3 and 4 in Figure 4.2).

Cases in which the governing faction maintains a fully dominant position in a less threatening environment are more likely to be stable and may be somewhat more inclusive, but even in these relatively more favorable environments, broad political inclusion is rare. Uganda provides a telling example. Although it is frequently cited as an instance of "autonomous recovery," Uganda is a relatively "easy case"; it suffers neither from the "lootable-resource curse" of natural-resource wealth that might fuel conflict, nor from external parties arming insurgents. Nonetheless, Uganda under Yoweri Museveni has never scored in the upper half of the Freedom House index of democracy (Freedom House, 1972–2010).

Highly imbalanced political orders in more threatening environments are less stable, but they are also much more likely to be highly repressive. Saddam Hussein's Iraq in the wake of the 1991 Gulf War and Slobodan Milosevic's Kosovo are clear examples. In all of these cases, repression was able to maintain the regime in power and the territorial integrity of the state, but these regimes ultimately laid the foundations for their own downfall.

Stability operations that either oversee or create a highly imbalanced political order must provide effective protection for marginalized parties or else risk catastrophe. Stability operations can provide useful services in such environments, such as UNTAES (the United Nations Transitional Authority in Eastern Slavonia, Baranja and Western Sirmium) in Croatia. But the past two decades are full of examples of regimes that sought to take advantage of windows of opportunity to permanently subdue minority populations. Stability operations have often failed to protect minorities in such cases, whether it be the failure of UNAMIR (the United Nations Assistance Mission for Rwanda) when faced with Rwandan Hutu genocidaires in 1994, or (to a much lesser degree) the failure of UNMIK (the UN Interim Administration Mission in Kosovo) and KFOR (the NATO Kosovo Force) to protect Kosovar Serbs from ethnic Albanian extremists.

Vulnerable Dominance

Cell 5 corresponds to an unfavorable environment and moderate imbalance of power. Governments that hold a preponderance but not an absolute monopoly of power represent a middle ground. They are not as stable as when the power balance is extreme, nor so inclusive as with a balanced distribution of power. They are, however, somewhat more inclusive and somewhat more stable than the two extremes. Making dominant coalitions work requires a delicate balancing act. Often, such dominant coalitions are themselves highly fractious, as was the case in the Democratic Republic of Congo. Without constraints, the majority faction can attempt to exploit its initial advantage to secure a monopolistic position, as the Sierre Leone People's Party (SLPP) attempted in Sierra Leone. Despite their imperfections, however, these constrained-dominant governments proved superior to the alternatives in Sierra Leone, the Democratic Republic of Congo, and Tajikistan, and ultimately in Iraq after the Anbar Awakening.

Perhaps because of the fragility of balanced distributions of power, even ostensibly neutral external actors often act to strengthen favored parties during the course of stability operations. The European Union, for instance, was widely suspected of supporting Joseph Kabila against his rivals in the Democratic Republic of Congo (Englebert and Tull, 2008, p. 133), and Britain intervened decisively on behalf of the government of Sierra Leone against the Revolutionary United Front (RUF) and other militias.

Vulnerable Balances

The last case (cell 6 in Figure 4.2) involves relatively balanced power but with an unfavorable environment. This is perhaps the most common—

and the most difficult—situation for stability operations. Stabilizers are dispatched to such countries for the precise reason that the local parties themselves cannot bring the war to a conclusion. In such circumstances, it should come as little surprise that foreign powers also have difficulty in restoring peace, much less inclusive peace.

Recent history is littered with examples. In Angola, the UNAVEM (United Nations Angola Verification Mission II) peacekeeping mission was helpless to prevent the country's two primary antagonists, the MPLA (Popular Movement for the Liberation of Angola) and UNITA (Union for the Total Independence of Angola), from returning to civil war following the country's 1992 elections. Diamonds and oil provided the fuel for continued fighting, and Angola's civil war lasted until 2002, when government troops killed the rebel leader Jonas Savimbi and defeated the rebel UNITA forces. As social-science theory would predict, the peace that proved elusive in 1992 when the parties to the conflict had comparable capabilities has proven much more stable since the defeat of UNITA, despite the fact that no sizable stability operation facilitated the transition in 2002. Despite the advantages of peace and a booming economy based on oil revenues, Angola has remained autocratic, rating "not free" on Freedom House's democracy index (Freedom House, 1972–2010)—again, just as we would expect from the framework of Table 4.1.

Peace in Sierra Leone was similarly elusive so long as the parties' capabilities were balanced. Fighting was again fueled by so-called blood diamonds. The international community repeatedly attempted to broker power-sharing arrangements between the government and the rebel Revolutionary United Front under Foday Sankoh, buttressed by a Nigerian-led ECOMOG (Military Observer Group of the Economic Community of West African States) peace operation and later by UNAMSIL (the United Nations Mission in Sierra Leone). Sankoh, however, consistently believed he had more to gain from continued fighting than from power-sharing. Stability was only achieved when the balance of power tilted decisively in favor of the government, thanks to British forces and a British-brokered dominant coalition of anti-RUF forces (Richards, 2000).

Balanced distributions of power, in short, favor inclusive political orders, but such orders are extremely fragile in unfavorable environments, with or without the presence of a stability operation.

Paths Toward Stabilization: Tentative Prescriptions for Precarious Transitions

A number of policy suggestions follow from this analysis, although they have not been empirically tested in any detail and should therefore be seen as provisional conclusions rather than established guidance. The precise implementation of the suggestions would vary from one context to another, but as rules of thumb they can help to guide the formulation of strategy for stability operations.

1. **Reduce the vulnerability of the state by reducing the resources for conflict.**
   - Build regional security arrangements that reduce or eliminate foreign sponsorship of the warring parties.
   - If the parties are exploiting natural resources to support their fighting, then consider mechanisms such as buyers' cartels or "neotrusteeship" mechanisms.

2. **Balance the desirability of political inclusion with the need to create a functioning government.**
   - If a party to the conflict can be accommodated without sacrificing vital interests of the local government or the intervening powers, every effort should be made to facilitate political inclusion. In favorable intervention environments, the likelihood of success is high. In less favorable intervention environments, the risk of political paralysis in a powersharing arrangement is high, and would-be stabilizers will be required to stabilize the situation and facilitate the political process for an extended period of time.
   - If a party to the conflict cannot be accommodated without sacrificing vital interests, and if that party does not enjoy substantial popular support, then the balance of power should be altered in favor of the local ally. Such

an approach, however, will require considerable efforts to restrain the government from abusing its dominant position, especially when the potential for renewed conflict is high.

- If a party to the conflict cannot be accommodated without sacrificing vital interests, but that party enjoys substantial popular support, then would-be stabilizers face an extreme challenge. If possible, intervenors will have to take measures to reformulate the challenge into a more tractable one, ideally through "wedge strategies" designed to separate irreconcilable parties from those who are willing to join a power-sharing government under reasonable terms.

3. **Shape negotiations and the conduct of stability operations based on the reality of underlying power balances.**
   - Avoid peace negotiations divorced from underlying power balances, since doing so can undercut incentives to stop fighting, can lead to de jure implementation but with major de facto efforts contrary to the agreement, and can even cause efforts to preemptively create "facts on the ground" at the expense of civilian populations.[23]
   - If institutions are crafted that are inconsistent with the balance of power, then intervenors should prepare to "make up the difference" themselves, through an application of carrots and sticks over an extended period.

4. **Protect vulnerable groups.**
   - In seeking a dominant coalition, or if building political institutions that do not accord with the underlying balance of power, provide long-term protection for vulnerable groups through a combination of institutional protections and credible and sustainable carrots and sticks.
   - Regard providing such protections as both a moral imperative and as potentially necessary to prevent the radicalization of vulnerable groups (Kilcullen, 2009) or other destabilizing outcomes.

5. **Plan for evolution of the parties' bases of power.**

- Anticipate transitions over time in terms of which groups hold power, the basis of their power, and the way in which they exercise it. To the extent possible, avoid fashioning institutions (such as constitutions or electoral systems) in such a way as to prevent evolution toward more inclusive and responsive political orders.

- Recognize that organizations will frequently operate outside or on the fringes of law with networks that fuse the functions of political parties, patronage pyramids, gangs or militias, and illicit or semi-licit economic networks. Provide incentives to draw them into formal institutions and the rule of law.

Conclusions

The architects of stability operations are in an unenviable position. Ambitious projects of rapid democratization, as prescribed by the liberal democratic state-building orthodoxy common in the immediate post–Cold War period, have been viewed with increasing skepticism over the past several years. Many observers instead recommend strategies of controlled state-building or decentralized S&R, sacrificing either political inclusion or strong state institutions, at least in the short term, for the sake of more easily attainable goals. Yet the limitations of these alternative approaches should not be underestimated either. Controlled state-building too often yields autocracy, repression, and sometimes even genocide. In addition to the moral considerations, autocratic and violent processes of state-building generate their own "security externalities," such as refugee crises and radicalization, and American support for such strategies properly has proven difficult to sustain domestically. Decentralized S&R is also more easily achievable than democratic transformation, but it risks creating a perpetually weak state unable to foster long-term development and unable to police illicit transnational networks (such as those of narcotics traffickers or terrorists) operating within its own borders. Because of these limitations of controlled state-building and decentralized S&R, many proponents of such approaches see them as interim measures; the long-term goal remains the creation of a capable state responsive to its public through inclusive and participatory political institutions. Such gradual transitions, however, are hampered by path-dependent dynamics, and transitional institutions too often are ineffectual and fragile.

These dilemmas are daunting but not insurmountable. Even such highly challenging environments as wartime Bosnia or Iraq have been stabilized with sufficient investment of troops and resources. Many factors affecting the success of war-to-peace transitions—such as the country's level of development—are effectively beyond outside powers' ability to affect, at least in the short-to-medium term. The challenge faced by those who plan and conduct stability operations is to leverage those factors that are in intervenors' control—the scope and strategy of the stability operation—to best effect.

The tentative prescriptions outlined are not "recipes for success" so much as means of mitigating negative risk while also providing incentives for more positive outcomes. While such ambitions are modest, they are consistent with the trajectories of many successful war-to-peace transitions. Although these transitions are difficult, the historical record indicates that they are possible—indeed, perseverance and learning have led to successes where once they were thought impossible. Hopefully, the lessons of past operations and past transitions will reduce the costs endured while adapting to the next stabilization challenge.

Endnotes

[1]   Representative of this understanding is Boutros-Ghali (1996), in which he proclaims that

> Democratic institutions and processes channel competing interests into arenas of discourse and provide means of compromise which can be respected by all participants in debates, thereby minimizing the risk that differences or disputes will erupt into armed conflict or confrontation. Because democratic Governments are freely chosen by their citizens and held accountable through periodic and genuine elections and other mechanisms, they are more likely to

promote and respect the rule of law, respect individual and minority rights, cope effectively with social conflict, absorb migrant populations and respond to the needs of marginalized groups. They are therefore less likely to abuse their power against the peoples of their own State territories. Democracy within States thus fosters the evolution of the social contract upon which lasting peace can be built. In this way, a culture of democracy is fundamentally a culture of peace. (p. 6-6)

[2] The United States, of course, had intervened in numerous "small wars" for decades before the 1960s. Counterinsurgency in its modern form, however, did not become a central foreign policy preoccupation until later.

[3] Inglehart (1996) provides a more recent articulation of modernization theory.

[4] Samuel Huntington (1991) introduced the concept of "waves of democratization." The first, long wave of democratization had its roots in the American and French Revolutions, but the majority of countries in this wave democratized between 1828 and 1926. This wave included most of the countries of Europe and the British overseas dominions. The second wave occurred in the period immediately following World War II and lasted until the early 1960s, encompassing the former Axis powers of the war as well as many countries in Latin America. The third wave began in the 1960s. It was initially concentrated in southern Europe (Spain, Portugal, and Greece) and South America (Brazil, Argentina, Uruguay), but eventually it spread into Central America and Asia (Turkey, the Philippines, and South Korea), and ultimately it engulfed the Soviet bloc countries.

[5] The social-science literature on the resolution of civil wars is vast. On the contributions of democracy to peace-building, see especially Hegre et al., 2001. On the effectiveness of power-sharing, see Hartzell, 1999, and Hartzell, Hoddie, and Rothchild, 2001. On the role of external (especially UN) intervention, see especially Doyle and Sambanis, 2000 and 2006; Fortna, 2008; and Walter, 2002.

[6] Skeptical treatments of democracy motivated in part by the international experiences of the 1990s include Fearon and Laitin, 2003; Kaufmann, 1996; Mansfield and Snyder, 2002; Marten, 2004; Paris, 1996 and 2004; Snyder, 2000; and Weinstein, 2005. On the difficulties involved in "exporting" democracy, see, for instance, Bellamy and Williams, 2004; Carothers 2004, p. 232; and Whitehead, 1986, p. 5. These arguments will be explored at much greater length below.

[7] Former U.S. Ambassador to Afghanistan Ronald E. Neumann, for instance, recently commented,

> The lack of realism in the U.S. is leading to demands in Afghanistan that are not only unrealistic but may be dangerous. . . . To expect that the fourth-poorest nation on earth, with high illiteracy and an education system being rebuilt from near total destruction will produce an effective and efficient government in another year or two is wishful thinking. (Martin, 2010)

[8]   Examples include Freier, 2009; Gant, 2009; Jones, 2008; and Kilcullen, 2009.

[9]   Again, the list is too long to recount here, but recent examples include Ellis, 2005; Englebert and Tull, 2008; Etzioni, 2004; Herbst, 1996; Knaus and Martin, 2003; Marten, 2004; and Weinstein, 2005. Older research in this vein includes Packenham, 1963, and Shafer, 1988.

[10]   See also the discussion in Chapter Two, by Christopher Chivvis and Paul Davis, which sketches a conceptual model based largely in the literature, augmented by considerations that go beyond the commonly emphasized rational-choice model.

[11]   Researchers studying Latin America have found a positive relationship between preparations for external wars and state-building, but they have found a *negative* relationship between internal conflict and state-building. See, for instance, Thies, 2005, and Cardenas, 2010.

[12]   Another criticism is that Fortna's concept of "ties" combines negotiated settlements with ceasefires and informal truces.

[13]   At the end of the civil war in Sierra Leone, for instance, the country had only 125 lawyers for a population of approximately 5 million people (Decker, Sage, and Stefanova, 2005, p. 15); some 60 percent of the population had not seen an administrative representative of any sort in approximately two decades (Malan, Rakate, and McIntyre, 2002, Chapter 4). In Cambodia "only a handful of legal practitioners survived the Khmer Rouge regime and no student graduated from the Cambodian law school between 1965 and 1996" (Decker, Sage, and Stefanova, 2005, pp. 15–16). Even in many Latin American countries it is prohibitively expensive for much of the population to prosecute a case in state courts, even if reliable (noncorrupt) courts can be found (Van Cott, 2006, p. 253).

[14]   Perhaps the best study of such "bridging" civil society is that of Ashutosh Varshney (2002), but even Varshney warns that the same moderating dynamics he finds in India are not likely to be reproduced in societies rent by civil war (p. 11). See also Belloni, 2008.

[15]   Rothchild and Roeder (2005) make this argument powerfully in their critique of power-sharing such institutions as federalism, ethnic veto rights, and legislative seat set-asides. The argument, however, can be applied much more broadly.

[16]   Policymakers discount the future because immediate stakes are high and the time to make decisions is short. Such an approach is in many ways justifiable: The future is highly uncertain, and if the immediate crisis cannot be adequately addressed, then longer-term concerns may never become relevant.

[17]   Cambodia is an interesting "mixed" case. The end of Chinese and American support for the insurgent forces in Cambodia, combined with the end of Vietnamese and Soviet support for Phnom Penh, was a critical step toward peace. The Khmer Rouge was able to continue its operations, however, on the basis of illicit gem and

timber sales. The consolidation of the peace in Cambodia was not possible until the government was able to broker a deal with one of the leading Khmer Rouge commanders, in which it extended him control of a gem- and timber-rich region near the Thai border. See Ross, 2004, p. 54.

[18] Here, *control* refers to control by power rather than influence. The cases treated are different from, e.g., the power-balance issues in a working parliamentary democracy.

[19] The phrasing here allows for the possibility that the dominant side sees expense, difficulty, diversion, or even impropriety in seeking total control—even though it could be confident of success if it sought to destroy the opposition. That is, most of this chapter reflects a "realist" perspective emphasizing power, but other factors matter as well.

[20] Both Byman (2002) and Snyder (2000) advocate carefully controlled processes of political inclusion that somewhat resemble what is here called a dominant distribution of power.

[21] This breakdown is similar in spirit to the "ecologies of peace-building" discussed in Doyle and Sambanis (2005).

[22] It is possible that another reason for success is that the oppositions lost some of their zeal with the abject failure of the Soviet Union and its communist ideology. Since the struggles were only partially about political ideology, however, the more parsimonious assumption is that the drying up of external forces was crucial.

[23] If one party is clearly the dominant party in a conflict, for instance, then either that fact will have to be recognized at some level in the peace agreement, or the international community will have to provide the "muscle" necessary to enforce an agreement that requires major concessions by the dominant party. Either of these options is defensible. What is not defensible is demanding that a party accept peace terms far worse than what it believes it could achieve on the battlefield, then failing to back these demands up with credible threats of action. Such an approach likely prolonged the war in Bosnia, to name but one example.

References

Bakarat, Sultan, ed., *Reconstructing War-Torn Societies—Afghanistan*, New York: Palgrave Macmillan, 2004.

Bardhan, Pranab K., "Understanding Underdevelopment: Challenges for Institutional Economics from the Point of View of Poor Countries," *Journal of Institutional and Theoretical Economics*, Vol. 156, No. 1, 2000, pp. 216–235.

Barfield, Thomas, Neamat Nojumi, and Alexander J. Thier, "The Clash of Two Goods: State and Non-State Dispute Resolution in Afghanistan," Washington, D.C.: U.S. Institute of Peace, 2006.

Bates, Robert H., *Prosperity and Violence: The Political Economy of Development*, New York: W. W. Norton, 2001.

———, "State Failure," *Annual Review of Political Science*, Vol. 11, 2008, pp. 1–12.

Bellamy, Alex J., and Paul D. Williams, "Introduction: Thinking Anew About Peace Operations," *International Peacekeeping*, Vol. 11, Spring 2004, pp. 1–15.

Belloni, Roberto, "Civil Society in War-to-Democracy Transitions," in Anna K. Jarstad and Timothy D. Sisk, eds., *From War to Democracy: Dilemmas of Peacebuilding*, New York: Cambridge University Press, 2008, pp. 182–210.

Bennett, Huw, "The Reluctant Pupil? Britain's Army and Learning in Counter-Insurgency," no date. As of May 25, 2011:
http://www.rusi.org/analysis/commentary/ref:C4AD22F8DF284C/

Blaufarb, Douglas S., *The Counterinsurgency Era: U.S. Doctrine and Performance*, New York: Free Press, 1977.

Blunt, Peter, and Mark Turner, "Decentralization, Democracy, and Development in a Post-Conflict Society: Commune Councils in Cambodia," *Public Administration and Development*, Vol. 25, 2005, pp. 65–86.

Boix, Carles, "Civil Wars and Guerrilla Warfare," in Stathis N. Kalyvas, Ian Shapiro, and Tarek Masoud, eds., *Order, Conflict, and Violence*, New York: Cambridge University Press, 2008, pp. 196–218.

Boutros-Ghali, Boutros, "An Agenda for Peace: Preventive Diplomacy, Peacemaking, and Peace-Keeping," A/47/277–S/24111, New York: United Nations, 1992.

———, *An Agenda for Democratization*, New York: United Nations, 1996.

Bruton, Bronwyn E., "Somalia: A New Approach," Washington, D.C.: Council on Foreign Relations, 2010.

Burton, Janice, "Army Executive Irregular Warfare Conference Charts Army's Path," *Special Warfare*, Vol. 22, No. 6, 2009, pp. 16–19.

Byman, Daniel, *Keeping the Peace: Lasting Solutions to Ethnic Conflict*, Baltimore, Md.: Johns Hopkins University Press, 2000.

Cardenas, Mauricio, *State Capacity in Latin America*, Washington, D.C.: Brookings Institution, 2010.

Carothers, Thomas, "The End of the Transition Paradigm," *Journal of Democracy*, Vol. 13, No. 1, 2002, pp. 5–21.

————, *Critical Mission: Essays on Democracy Promotion*, Washington, D.C.: Carnegie Endowment for International Peace, 2004.

Cheema, G. Shabbirm, and Dennis A. Rondinelli, "From Government Decentralization to Decentralized Governance," in G. Shabbir Cheema and Dennis A. Rondinelli, eds., *Decentralizing Governance: Emerging Concepts and Practices*, Washington, D.C.: Ash Institute for Democratic Governance and Innovation of Harvard University and Brookings Institution Press, 2006.

Chesterman, Simon, *You, The People: The United Nations, Transitional Administration, and State-Building*, New York: Oxford University Press, 2004.

Clapham, Christopher, "Rwanda: the Perils of Peacemaking," *Journal of Peace Research,* Vol. 35, 1998, pp. 193–210.

————, "The Global-Local Politics of State Decay," in R. I. Rotberg, ed., *When States Fail: Causes and Consequences*, Princeton, N.J.: Princeton University Press, 2004.

Clunan, Anne L., and Harold Trinkunas, *Ungoverned Spaces: Alternative to State Authority in an Era of Softened Sovereignty*, Stanford, Calif.: Stanford University Press, 2010.

Collier, Paul, V. L. Elliott, Håvard Hegre, Anke Hoeffler, Marta Reynal-Querol, and Nicholas Sambanis, *Breaking the Conflict Trap: Civil War and Policy Development*, Washington, D.C.: The World Bank and Oxford University Press, 2003.

D'Exelle, Ben, "Excluded Again: Village Politics at the Aid Interface." *Journal of Development Studies*, Vol. 45, No. 9, 2009, pp. 1453–1471.

Decker, Klaus, Caroline Sage, and Milena Stefanova, *Law or Justice: Building Equitable Legal Institutions*, Washington, D.C.: World Bank, 2005.

Diamond, Larry, *Developing Democracy: Toward Consolidation*, Baltimore, Md.: Johns Hopkins University Press, 1999.

Dixit, Avinash K., *Lawlessness and Economics: Alternative Modes of Governance*, Princeton, N.J.: Princeton University Press, 2004.

Doherty, Ivan, "Democracy Out of Balance," *Policy Review*, Vol. 106, 2001.

Dorronsoro, Gilles, "Focus and Exit: An Alternative Strategy for the Afghan War," Washington, D.C.: Carnegie Endowment for International Peace, 2009.

Doyle, Michael W., and Nicholas Sambanis, "International Peacebuilding: A Theoretical and Quantitative Analysis," *American Political Science Review*, Vol. 94, No. 4, 2000, pp. 668–801.

————, *Making War and Building Peace*, Princeton, N.J.: Princeton University Press, 2006.

Dunning, Thad, "Conditioning the Effects of Aid: Cold War Politics, Donor Credibility, and Democracy in Africa," *International Organization*, Vol. 58, No. 2, Spring 2004, pp. 409–423.

Ellis, Stephen, "How to Rebuild Africa," *Foreign Affairs*, Vol. 84, No. 5, 2005, pp. 135–148.

Engerman, Stanley L., and Kenneth L. Sokoloff, "Debating the Role of Institutions in Political and Economic Development: Theory, History, and Findings," *Annual Review of Political Science*, Vol. 11, 2008, pp. 119–135.

Englebert, Pierre, and Denis M. Tull, "Postconflict Reconstruction in Africa: Flawed Ideas about Failed States," *International Security*, Vol. 32, No. 4, 2008, pp. 106–139.

Etzioni, Amitai, "A Self-Restrained Approach to Nation-Building by Foreign Powers," *International Affairs*, Vol. 80, No. 1, 2004, pp. 1–16.

European Stability Initiative, "After the Bonn Powers: Open Letter to Lord Ashdown," Berlin: European Stability Initiative, 2003.

Fanthorpe, Richard, "On the Limits of Liberal Peace: Chiefs and Democratic Decentralization in Post-War Sierra Leone," *African Affairs*, Vol. 105, No. 418, 2006, pp. 26–49.

Fearon, James D., "Ethnic Conflict as a Commitment Problem," in D. A. Lake and D. Rothchild, eds., *The International Spread of Ethnic Conflict*, Princeton, N.J.: Princeton University Press, 1998.

Fearon, James D., and David D. Laitin, "Ethnicity, Insurgency, and Civil War," *American Political Science Review*, Vol. 96, No. 1, 2003, pp. 65–90.

Filkins, Dexter, "Afghan Tribe, Vowing to Fight Taliban, to Get U.S. Aid in Return," *New York Times*, January 7, 2010.

Fortna, Virginia Page, "Does Peacekeeping Keep Peace? International Intervention and the Duration of Peace After Civil War," *International Studies Quarterly*, Vol. 48, 2004, pp. 269–292.

———, *Does Peacekeeping Work?* Princeton, N.J.: Princeton University Press, 2008.

Freedom House, *Freedom in the World* reports, Washington, D.C., published annually since 1972.

Freier, Nathan, *The New Balance: Limited Armed Stablization and the Future of U.S. Landpower*, Carlisle, Pa.: Peacekeeping and Stability Operations Institute and Strategic Studies Institute, Army War College, 2009.

Friedkin, Noah E., "Social Cohesion," *Annual Review of Sociology*, Vol. 30, 2004, pp. 409–425.

Fukuyama, Frances, *The End of History and the Last Man*, New York: Free Press, 1992.

———, *State-Building: Governance and World Order in the 21st Century*, Ithaca, N.Y.: Cornell University Press, 2004.

Gant, Jim, *One Tribe at a Time: A Strategy for Success in Afghanistan*, Los Angeles: Nine Sisters Imports, 2009. As of April 15, 2011:
http://www.stevenpressfield.com/wp-content/uploads/2009/10/one_tribe_at_a_time_ed2.pdf

Goldsmith, Arthur A., "Foreign Aid and Statehood in Africa," *International Organization*, Vol. 55, No. 1, 2001, pp. 123–148.

Goldstone, Jack, Robert Bates, Ted Gurr, and Monty Marshall, *A Global Forecasting Model of Political Instability*, State Failure Task Force, McLean, Va.: SAIC, 2005.

Greig, J. Michael, and Paul F. Diehl, "The Peacekeeping-Peacemaking Dilemma," *International Studies Quarterly*, Vol. 49, 2005, pp. 621–645.

Gurr, Ted Robert, *People versus States: Minorities at Risk in the New Century*, Washington, D.C.: U.S. Institute of Peace Press, 2000.

———, "Attaining Peace in Divided Societies: Five Principles of Emerging Doctrine," *International Journal of World Peace*, Vol. 19, No. 2, 2002, pp. 26–51.

Gurses, Mehmet, and T. David Mason, "Democracy out of Anarchy: Prospects for Post-Civil-War Democracy," *Social Science Quarterly*, Vol. 89, No. 2, 2008, pp. 315–336.

Habyarimana, James, Macarten Humphreys, Daniel Posner, and Jeremy M. Weinstein, "Why Does Ethnic Diversity Undermine Public Goods Provision?" *American Political Science Review*, Vol. 101, No. 4, 2007, pp. 709–725.

Haggard, Stephan, Andrew MacIntyre, and Lydia Tiede, "The Rule of Law and Economic Development," *Annual Review of Political Science*, Vol. 11, 2008, pp. 205–234.

Halperin, Morton H., Joseph T. Siegle, and Michael M. Weinstein, *The Democracy Advantage: How Democracies Promote Prosperity and Peace*, New York: Routledge, 2005.

Harff, Barbara, "No Lessons Learned from the Holocaust? Assessing Risks of Genocide and Political Mass Murder since 1955," *American Political Science Review*, Vol. 96, No. 1, 2003, pp. 56–63.

Harpviken, Kristian Berg, "Transcending Traditionalism: The Emergence of Non-State Military Formations in Afghanistan," *Journal of Peace Research*, Vol. 34, No. 3, 1996, pp. 261–286.

Hartzell, Caroline A., "Explaining the Stability of Negotiated Settlements to Intrastate Wars," *Journal of Conflict Resolution*, Vol. 43, No. 1, 1999, pp. 3–22.

Hartzell, Caroline A., Matthew Hoddie, and Donald Rothchild, "Stabilizing Peace After Civil War: An Investigation of Some Variables," *International Organization*, Vol. 55, No. 1, 2001, pp. 183–208.

Hechter, Michael, and Nika Kabiri, "Attaining Social Order in Iraq," in Stathis N. Kalyvas, Ian Shapiro, and Tarek Masoud, eds., *Order, Conflict, and Violence*, New York: Cambridge University Press, 2008.

Hegre, Håvard, Tanja Ellingsen, Scott Gates, and Nils Petter Gleditsch, "Toward a Democratic Civil Peace? Democracy, Political Change, and Civil War, 1816–1992," *American Political Science Review*, Vol. 95, No. 1, 2001, pp. 33–48.

Hellman, Joel S., "Winner Take All: The Politics of Partial Reform in Postcommunist Transitions," *World Politics*, Vol. 50, 1998, pp. 203–234.

Hellman, Joel S., and Daniel Kaufmann, "The Inequality of Influence," Washington, D.C.: World Bank, 2002.

Helmke, Gretchen, and Steven Levitsky, eds., *Informal Institutions & Democracy: Lessons from Latin America*, Baltimore, Md.: Johns Hopkins University Press, 2006.

Henderson, Willie, "Metaphors, Narrative and 'Truth': South Africa's Truth and Reconciliation Commission," *African Affairs*, Vol. 99, No. 396, 2000.

Herbst, Jeffrey, "Responding to State Failure in Africa," *International Security*, Vol. 21, No. 3, 1996, pp. 120–144.

———, *States and Power in Africa: Comparative Lessons in Authority and Control*, Princeton, N.J.: Princeton University Press, 2000.

Huntington, Samuel P., *Political Order in Changing Societies*, New Haven, Conn.: Yale University Press, 1968.

Huntington, Samuel, *The Third Wave: Democratization in the Late Twentieth Century*, Norman: University of Oklahoma Press, 1991.

ICG—*See* International Crisis Group.

International Crisis Group, *Sierra Leone: Time for a New Military and Political Strategy*, Brussels, 2001.

———, *Afghanistan: New U.S. Administration, New Directions*, Brussels, 2009.

Inglehart, Ronald, *Modernization and Postmodernization: Cultural, Economic, and Political Change in 43 Societies*, Princeton, N.J.: Princeton University Press, 1996.

Jones, Seth G., *Counterinsurgency in Afghanistan*, Santa Monica, Calif.: RAND Corporation, 2008. As of April 8, 2011: http://www.rand.org/pubs/monographs/MG595.html

———, *In the Graveyard of Empires: America's War in Afghanistan*, New York: W. W. Norton, 2009.

Kalyvas, Stathis N., "The Ontology of 'Political Violence': Action and Identity in Civil Wars," *Perspectives on Politics*, Vol. 1, No. 3, 2003, pp. 465–494.

———, *The Logic of Violence in Civil War*, New York: Cambridge University Press, 2006.

Kilcullen, David, *The Accidental Guerrilla: Fighting Small Wars in the Midst of a Big One*, New York: Oxford University Press, 2009.

Kaufmann, Chaim, "Possible and Impossible Solutions to Civil Wars," *International Security*, Vol. 20, No. 4, 1996, pp. 136–165.

Kirkpatrick, Jeane J., "Dictatorships & Double Standards," *Commentary*, Vol. 68, No. 5, 1979.

Knaus, Gerald, and Feliz Martin, "Travails of the European Raj," *Journal of Democracy*, Vol. 14, No. 3, 2003, pp. 60–64.

Kovacs, Mimmi Soderberg, "When Rebels Change Their Stripes: Armed Insurgents in Post-War Politics," in Anna K. Jarstad and Timothy D. Sisk, eds., *From War to Democracy: Dilemmas of Peacebuilding*, New York: Cambridge University Press, 2008.

Krasner, Stephen D., "Sharing Sovereignty: New Institutions for Collapsed and Failing States., *International Security*, Vol. 29, No. 2, 2004, pp. 85–120.

Levitsky, Steven, and Maria Victoria Murillo, "Variation in Institutional Strength," *Annual Review of Political Science*, Vol. 12, 2009, pp. 115–133.

Licklider, Roy, "The Consequences of Negotiated Settlements in Civil Wars, 1945–1993," *American Political Science Review*, Vol. 89, No. 3, 1995, pp. 681–690.

Lindberg, Staffan I., *Democracy and Elections in Africa*, Baltimore, Md.: Johns Hopkins University Press, 2006.

Luttwak, Edwards N., "Give War a Chance," *Foreign Affairs*, Vol. 68, No. 4, 1999, pp. 36–44.

Lyon, Fergus, and Gina Porter, "Market Institutions, Trust, and Norms: Exploring Moral Economies in Nigerian Food Systems," *Cambridge Journal of Economics*, Vol. 33, 2009, pp. 903–920.

Lyons, Terrence, "Transforming the Institutions of War: Postconflict Elections and the Reconstruction of Failed States," in Robert I. Rotberg, ed., *When States Fail: Causes and Consequences*, Princeton, N.J.: Princeton University Press, 2004.

Malan, Mark, Phenyo Rakate, and Angela McIntyre, *Peacekeeping in Sierra Leone: UNAMSIL Hits the Home Straight*, Pretoria, South Africa: Institute for Security Studies, 2002.

Mansfield, Edward D., and Jack Snyder, "Democratic Transitions, Insitutional Strength, and War," *International Organization*, Vol. 56, No. 2, 2002, pp. 296–336.

Markey, Daniel, "Securing Pakistan's Tribal Belt," Washington, D.C.: Council on Foreign Relations, 2008.

Marten, Kimberly Zisk, *Enforcing the Peace: Learning from the Imperial Past*, New York: Columbia University Press, 2004.

Martin, Susan Taylor, "Afghanistan Experts at USF Symposium Agree on One Thing: Things Don't Look Good," *St. Petersburg Times* (St. Petersburg, Fla.), 2010.

Messick, Richard E., "Judicial Reform and Economic Development: A Survey of the Issues," *World Bank Research Observer*, Vol. 14, No. 1, 1999, pp. 116–136.

Migdal, Joel S., "The State in Society: An Approach to Struggles for Domination," in Joel S. Migdal, Atul Kohli, and Vivienne Shue, eds., *State Power and Social Forces: Domination and Transformation in the Third World*, New York: Cambridge University Press, 1994, pp. 6–34.

Migdal, Joel S., Atul Kohli, and Vivienne Shue, "Introduction: Developing a State-in-Society Perspective," in Joel S. Migdal, Atul Kohli, and Vivienne Shue, eds., *State Power and Social Forces: Domination and Transformation in the Third World*, New York: Cambridge University Press, 1994, pp. 1–4.

Millen, Raymond, "Thinking Small: Applying Hobbes to Counterinsurgency," *Small Wars Journal*, 2008, p. 13.

Mubarak, Jamil A., "The 'Hidden Hand' Behind the Resilience of the Stateless Economy of Somalia," *World Development*, Vol. 25, No. 12, 1996, pp. 2026–2041.

North, Douglass C., *Structure and Change in Economic History*, New York: W. W. Norton, 1981.

Olson, Mancur, "Dictatorship, Democracy, and Development," *American Political Science Review*, Vol. 86, No. 3, 1993, pp. 567–576.

Ottaway, Marina, "Less Is Better: An Agenda for Africa," *Policy Brief*, Vol. 1, No. 2, Washington, D.C.: Carnegie Endowment for International Peace, 2000.

Packenham, Robert A., *Liberal America in the Third World*, Princeton, N.J.: Princeton University Press, 1963.

Paoli, Letizia, Victoria A. Greenfield, and Peter Reuter, *The World Heroin Market: Can Supply Be Cut?* New York: Oxford University Press, 2009.

Paris, Roland, "Peacebuilding and the Limits of Liberal Internationalism," *International Security*, Vol. 22, No. 2, 1996, pp. 54–89.

———, *At War's End: Building Peace After Civil Conflict*, New York: Cambridge University Press, 2004.

Peceny, Mark, "Two Paths to the Promotion of Democracy During U.S. Military Interventions," *International Studies Quarterly*, Vol. 39, 1995, pp. 361–401.

Pegg, Scott, "Can Policy Intervention Beat the Resource Curse? Evidence from the Chad-Cameroon Pipeline Project," *African Affairs*, Vol. 105, No. 418, 2006, pp. 1–25.

Pei, Minxin, and Sara Kasper, *Lessons from the Past: The American Record on Nation Building*, Washington, D.C.: Carnegie Endowment for International Peace, 2003.

Przeworski, Adam, *Democracy and the Market: Political and Economic Reforms in Eastern Europe and Latin America*, New York: Cambridge University Press, 1991.

Regan, Patrick M., "Conditions of Successful Third-Party Intervention in Intrastate Conflicts," *Journal of Conflict Resolution*, Vol. 40, No. 2, 1996, pp. 336–359.

Richards, Brigadier D. J.. "Operation Palliser." *Journal of the Royal Artillery CXXVII*, No. 2, 2000, pp. 10–15.

Ross, Michael L., "What Do We Know About Natural Resources and Civil War?" *Journal of Peace Research*, Vol. 41, No. 3, 2004, pp. 337–356.

Rostow, W. W., *The Stages of Economic Growth: A Non-Communist Manifesto*, New York: Cambridge University Press, 1960.

Rothchild, Donald, and Philip G. Roeder, "The Dilemma of Power Sharing After Civil Wars," in P. G. Roeder and D. Rothchild, eds., *Sustainable Peace: Democracy and Power-Dividing Institutions after Civil Wars*, Ithaca, N.Y.: Cornell University Press, 2005.

Rummel, R. J., "Democracy, Power, Genocide, and Mass Murder," *Journal of Conflict Resolution, Vol.* 39, No. 1, 1995, pp. 3–26.

Rustow, Dankwart, "Transitions to Democracy: Toward a Dynamic Model," *Comparative Politics*, Vol. 2, No. 3, 1970, pp. 337–363.

Samuels, Kirsti, "Rule of Law Reform in Post-Conflict Countries: Operational Initiatives and Lessons Learnt," Washington, D.C.: World Bank, Social Development Department, Conflict Prevention and Reconstruction, 2006, p. 64.

Schamis, Hector E., "Distributional Coalitions and the Politics of Economic Reform in Latin America," *World Politics, Vol.* 51, 1999, pp. 236–268.

Scott, James C., "Patron-Client Politics and Political Change in Southeast Asia," *American Political Science Review*, Vol. 66, No. 1, 1962, pp. 91–113.

———, "Corruption, Machine Politics, and Political Change," *American Political Science Review*, Vol. 63, No. 4, 1969, pp. 1142–1158.

———, *Seeing Like a State: How Certain Schemes to Improve the Human Condition Have Failed*, New Haven, Conn.: Yale University Press, 1998.

Shafer, D. Michael, *Deadly Paradigms: The Failure of U.S. Counterinsurgency Policy*, Princeton, N.J.: Princeton University Press, 1988.

Snyder, Jack, *From Voting to Violence: Democratization and Nationalist Conflict*, New York: W. W. Norton, 2000.

Stedman, Stephen John, "Spoiler Problems in Peace Processes," *International Security*, Vol. 22, No. 2, 1996, pp. 5–53.

Thies, Cameron G., "War, Rivalry, and State Building in Latin America," *American Journal of Political Science*, Vol. 49, No. 3, 2005, pp. 451–465.

Tilly, Charles, "War Making and State Making as Organized Crime," in Peter B. Evans, Dietrich Rueschemeyer, and Theda Skocpol, eds., *Bringing the State Back In*, New York: Cambridge University Press, 1999.

Toft, Monica Duffy, "Ending Civil Wars: A Case for Rebel Victory?" *International Security*, Vol. 34, No. 4, 2010, pp. 6–36.

Trofimov, Yaroslav, "Kandahar Offensive to Focus on Good Governance," *Wall Street Journal*, March 29, 2010.

UNDP—*See* United Nations Development Programme.

United Nations Development Programme, "Governance in Conflict Prevention and Recovery: A Guidance Note," New York, 2009.

Van Cott, Donna Lee, "Dispensing Justice at the Margins of Formality: The Informal Rule of Law in Latin America," in Gretchen Helmke and Steven Levitsky, eds., *Informal Institutions and Democracy: Lessons from Latin America*, Baltimore, Md.: Johns Hopkins University Press, 2006.

Van de Walle, Nicholas, "Overcoming Stagnation in Aid-Dependent Countries: Politics, Policies and Incentives for Poor Countries," Washington, D.C.: Center for Global Development, 2005.

Varshney, Ashutosh, *Ethnic Conflict and Civic Life: Hindus and Muslims in India*, New Haven, Conn.: Yale University Press, 2002.

Volkov, Vadim, "The Political Economy of Protection Rackets in the Past and Present," *Social Research*, Vol. 66, No. 3, 2000, pp. 609–644.

Walter, Barbara F., "Designing Transitions from Civil War: Demobilization, Democratization, and Commitments to Peace," *International Security*, Vol. 24, No. 1, 1999, pp. 126–155.

———, *Committing to Peace: The Successful Settlement of Civil War*, Princeton, N.J.: Princeton University Press, 2002.

———, "Does Conflict Beget Conflict? Explaining Recurring Civil War," *Journal of Peace Research*, Vol. 41, No. 3, 2004, pp. 361–388.

Watts, Stephen, *Enforcing Democracy? Assessing the Relationship Between Peace Operations and Post-Conflict Democratization*, New York: Columbia University International Politics Seminar, March 5, 2009.

Weinstein, Jeremy M., "Autonomous Recovery and International Intervention in Comparative Perspective," New York: Center for Global Development, 2005.

Werner, Suzanne, and Amy Yuen, "Making and Keeping Peace," *International Organization*, Vol. 59, No. 2, 2005, pp. 261–292.

West, Harry G., and Scott Kloeck-Jenson, "Betwixt and Between: 'Traditional Authority' and Democratic Decentralization in Post-War Mozambique," *African Affairs*, Vol. 98, No. 393, 1999, pp. 455–484.

Whitehead, Laurence, "International Aspects of Democratization," in Guillermo O'Donnell, Philippe. C. Schmitter, and Laurence Whitehead, eds., *Transitions from Authoritarian Rule*, Baltimore, Md.: Johns Hopkins University Press, 1986.

Widner, Jennifer, "Courts and Democracy in Postconflict Transitions: A Social Scientist's Perspective on the African Case," *American Journal of International Law*, Vol. 95, No. 1, 2001, pp. 64–65.

Woodward, Susan L., "Local Governance Approach to Social Reintegration and Economic Recovery in Post-Conflict Countries," in *A Local Governance Approach to Post-Conflict Recovery*, proceedings report on the workshop organized by the Institute of Public Administration, New York, October 8, 2002.

World Bank, *Fragile States: Good Practice in Country Assistance Strategies*, Washington, D.C., 2005.

Zakaria, Fareed, *The Future of Freedom: Illiberal Democracy at Home and Abroad*, New York: W. W. Norton, 2003.

Zuercher, Christoph, *Is More Better? Evaluating External-Led State Building After 1989*, Stanford, Calif.: Stanford University Center for Democracy, Development, and the Rule of Law, 2006.

CHAPTER FIVE
Establishing Social Conditions of Trust and Cooperation

Elizabeth Wilke, Paul K. Davis, and Christopher S. Chivvis

This chapter addresses certain social aspects of intervention, focusing on how sufficient cooperation among previously warring parties can be achieved so that stabilization and reconstruction (S&R) efforts can be successful. Though much depends on the context of the conflict—the composition of fighting parties, political aims, and economic and social backdrops, as well as international intervention—to facilitate long-term S&R, post-conflict interventions need to establish basic institutional structures that promote cooperation among groups in society, especially those prone to competition and conflict. Trust is a key enabler of cooperation, so the chapter's question becomes, How can useful degrees of trust and cooperation be created in a post-conflict environment?*

Introduction

Almost every study of social reconstruction and post-conflict stability calls for understanding conflict as the result of structural processes and institutions that sustain and promote the escalation of conflict (Botes, 2003; Jeong, 2003; Fisher, 2000; Widner, 2004; Donais, 2009; Rubenstein, 2003b). These structures can include corrupt or nepotis-

---

* Regrettably, due to inevitable resource limitations, we were unable in this study to address many other elements of the social component, such as the consequences of tribal relationships, corruption, organized crime, and ethnicity.

tic courts that unfairly enforce laws; laws that routinely favor certain groups over others; or economic growth that leaves behind certain groups or denies them access to resources, either de jure or de facto. *The successful cessation of conflict in the long run will require the restructuring of institutional structures to ensure fairness and access.* Disputes of fairness and equality arise daily in every society, and a successful resolution of intergroup conflict will require that mechanisms for assertively and cooperatively dealing with differences be built into decision- and policymaking processes.

Reestablishing peace and stability after conflict needs to include such social processes as changing attitudes, behaviors, expectations, social networks, and even culture. Post-conflict societies often have relationships characterized by distrust, exclusion of "outgroups," and unconstructive competitive behavior. People have witnessed, taken part in, or been victims of violence; groups across society have stereotyped and dehumanized others. Social relationships are strained further by a lack of physical security and economic opportunity. To have at least working relationships among stakeholder groups is vital to the success of reconstruction (Kelman, 2008; Bar-Tal and Bennik, 2004; Gaertner, Brewer, and Dovidio, 2005; Kaplan, 2009).

The psychological and social processes involved in post-conflict social reconstruction should ideally encourage emotional healing, positive contacts across groups, positive experiences with government, breaking down negative stereotypes, increasing respect and empathy, and positively adjusting cultural narratives. All of this is a tall order, and what is actually feasible may be far less. Nonetheless, the extent to which at least some of these occur can have a lasting impact on whether or not peace is sustained (Kelman, 2008; Bar-Tal and Bennik, 2004; Gaertner, Brewer, and Dovidio, 2005; Kaplan, 2009). It follows that those conducting S&R operations can benefit from the relevant social science. What follows draws selectively on extensive literatures in social psychology, sociology, cognitive psychology, anthropology, law, economics, criminology, business, political science, and peace research. Fortunately, these literatures reveal reason for optimism: Much *can* be done—but not easily and certainly not quickly.

The next section identifies key themes from the literature relevant to reconstructing society. The following section then applies them to common post-conflict challenges, addressing both promise and pitfalls. The last sections pull together approximate principles and conclude with a brief recapitulation.

Concepts, Literatures, and Themes

Concepts

It is useful at the outset to identify some important concepts and distinctions involving the terms *cooperation, trust, distrust, social capital, social reconciliation*, and *social reconstruction*.

Cooperation. Cooperation is the coordination of efforts or activities to produce a mutually beneficial outcome (Hardin, 1995). Some level of cooperation among parties previously engaged in violent conflict is essential if S&R is to succeed. Cooperation is not a zero-sum game, which makes it different from competitive behavior or violence. In fact, conflict scholars typically think of intergroup relationships as falling along a cooperative-to-competitive spectrum (Table 5.1).[1] Positive, cooperative group relations are characterized by trust and good feeling; negative or competitive relationships are characterized by distrust and negative social attitudes toward the other group(s).

Table 5.1
Characteristics of Competitive and Cooperative Relationships

Characteristic	Cooperative Relationships	Competitive Relationships
Parties' attitudes toward one another	Trusting, friendly, and helpful	Suspicious, hostile, and/or exploitative
Communication	Open, honest communication	Lack of or misleading communication
Similarities and differences	Maximization of similarities; minimization of differences	Maximization of differences; minimization of similarities
Outcomes	Partnership-oriented; win-win	Dominance-oriented; zero-sum

Cooperation, of course, can increase vulnerability: The willingness of groups to cooperate depends on their expectations of the other's likelihood of also cooperating, which is why trust plays such a powerful role in cooperation. Groups are more likely to be cooperative when there has been a history of cooperation, when structural conditions provide incentives for cooperation, or when positive attitudes exist about the trustworthiness of the other group. Because attitudes affect expectations, interventions to improve attitudes are important. In addition, if relationships are strained or competitive, monitoring and incentive structures may be needed to mitigate risks so that cooperation can continue (Powell, 1996). Outside intervenors can promote cooperation by contributing to environmental and institutional structures that promote cooperation.

Trust. Trust can be simply defined as *positive expectations about the actions of another party* (Deutsch, 2000a), or a belief in, and willingness to act on the basis of, the words and actions of another (Lewicki and Wiethoff, 2000; McAllister, 1998).[2] Trust is relevant to S&R because it affects cooperation, reducing uncertainty by providing expectations about the behaviors of people or groups (Axelrod, 1984). Trust across groups is key to facilitating conflict resolution, partly because it reduces the need for monitoring and punishment of parties in cooperation (Lewicki and Weithoff, 2000). Most scholars agree that while trust is not a *necessary* condition for peace (Ward et al., 2006; Axelrod, 1984; Deutsch, 1973), it *is* necessary if the peacemaking process is to take hold (Brune and Bossert, 2009; Gormley-Heenan and MacGinty, 2009).[3] Some important factors involved in enhancing trust and cooperation are depicted in Figure 5.1 and elaborated below. The concepts appearing in the tree will be discussed in what follows.

Types of Trust. Numerous scholars have identified types of trust, with their distinctions and terminology reflecting parent disciplines.[4] By and large, the biggest distinction in usage is between those coming from a rational-choice perspective (e.g., economics, business, or political science) and those coming from an emphasis on social constructions and shared values (e.g., sociology, psychology). Fortunately, good efforts have been made to relate and integrate the two perspectives (Rousseau et al., 1998; Lewicki, Tomlinson, and Gillespie, 2006;

Figure. 5.1
Factors Affecting Intergroup Trust and Cooperation

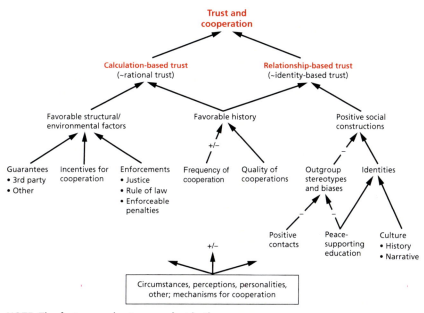

NOTE: The factors apply at a snapshot in time.

RAND *MG1119-5.1*

Saunders et al., 2010). Saunders et al. (2010) also specifically addresses cross-cultural issues, which is useful to the present chapter.

With some simplification, only two types of trust need be distinguished here: *calculation-based* and *relational trust.* This terminology has the advantage of intuitive labels and allowing for considerable generality. Calculation-based trust is a kind of trust that stems from assessing (whether correctly or not) that trust is justified—for a very concrete set of issues in a very concrete context—because it seems to be in the interest of the other party, or in his or her habit, to behave positively. This might be because it seems that different behavior will be deterred, because the desired behavior is incentivized, because it just "makes sense" (from the perceived perspective of the other), or because it is consistent with observed behavior of the other party.[5] Such trust is intendedly rational[6] and requires neither emotions nor affinity between parties, only that interests are best served by cooperation. As a result, efforts to increase rational trust should be concerned with, e.g., (1) incentive structures, (2) guarantees, and (3) building a history of repeated, positive interactions.[7] Such trust is usually "thin" in that, if the situation or issue changes, the trust may vanish quickly (i.e., it is not necessarily transferrable).

In contrast, relationship-based trust stems from positive expectations about another's behavior based on personal experience and ties. Relational ties may be made by group membership, if, for example, the other is part of the same family, group, tribe, community, people, or nation and is assumed, therefore, to be trustworthy (which might or might not be accurate). It may also be that the relationship has been strong enough in the past (e.g., with shared experiences) so as to create mutual empathy and the internalization of positive beliefs and good will. Relationship-based trust may be relatively thick. It *need* not be (people can drop their trust of even close family members or long-term neighbors, depending on events), but it can be. Emotions, including the sense of relationship itself, play a role. The key point is that relationships enjoying high levels of this "thick" trust typically require less monitoring to ensure compliance than relationships with thinner trust (Lewicki and Weithoff, 2000). It is this "thicker" trust that helps perpetuate longer-term stability.

Developing thicker forms of trust in post-conflict situations requires that group social identities become more inclusive and open (Lewicki and Weithoff, 2000; Dietz, Gillespie, and Chao, 2010). This means breaking down negative stereotypes that portray individuals from other groups as subhuman, untrustworthy, or incapable of honorable behavior. Wearing away negative attitudes and stereotypes about outgroup members makes it more likely that group members will be able to view each other as human beings with goals, aims, and motivations similar to their own. In addition, creating new and inclusive identities, such as a national identity, that include members of all groups may be a useful tool for creating cooperation and trust.

In most post-conflict situations, building calculation-based trust will be the immediate aim. That, however, opens the door to building relationship-based trust, which is the stronger and more enduring, over time. Table 5.2 compares these types of trust.

Trust and Distrust. The literature varies as to whether distrust is equivalent to a low level of trust or something else. The view taken here is that it is something else. Specifically, rather than being the absence of a positive expectation that an agent will behave positively, *distrust* is used here to mean a positive expectation that an agent will behave negatively. Not only do post-conflict societies lack trust, but they are deeply distrusting.[8] This does not change quickly, even if groups have enough trust to cooperate for specific narrow purposes. Figure 5.2 (adapted from Lewicki, Tomlinson, and Gillespie, 2006) distinguishes among four cases defined by low or high trust and low or high distrust. The bottom-right cell (low trust, high distrust) is all too characteristic of many post-conflict societies. It is not merely that the parties in question lack trust; rather, they are seriously worried about each other.

Table 5.2
Comparison of Calculation-Based and Relationship-Based Trust

	Calculation-Based Trust	Relationship-Based Trust
Source of trust	Intendedly rational calculations of others' self-interest[a]	Identification with others by relationship and association
	Experiential history of interactions	Some emotional attachment, perhaps including empathy or internalization of others' aims and goals
Actors' focus	Behavior control with incentives and enforcement mechanisms	Identifying common goals
	Information-gathering about motives and actions	Building positive familiarities
		Engaging in emotional reciprocity; encouraging empathy
Ways to develop	Education (e.g., about situational and historical facts)	Collaborative projects
	Clear, consistent communication	Building and/or emphasizing commonly held identities, values, and goals
	Credible commitments	Education about each others' histories, narratives, and travails (empathy-building)
	Repeated, equal-status interactions with appropriate incentive structures	

[a] Assessments will have limited rationality due to sometimes incorrect perceptions, difficulties in understanding the other's self interest, the effects of cognitive biases, and the effects of decisionmaker personalities (e.g., relative emphasis on risk reduction and opportunity creation).

Figure 5.2
Characteristics of Trust, Distrust, and Combinations

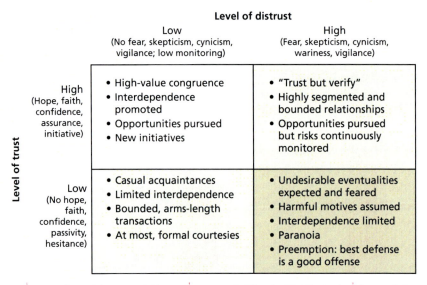

| | | Level of distrust | |
		Low (No fear, skepticism, cynicism, vigilance; low monitoring)	High (Fear, skepticism, cynicism, wariness, vigilance)
Level of trust	High (Hope, faith, confidence, assurance, initiative)	• High-value congruence • Interdependence promoted • Opportunities pursued • New initiatives	• "Trust but verify" • Highly segmented and bounded relationships • Opportunities pursued but risks continuously monitored
	Low (No hope, faith, confidence, passivity, hesitance)	• Casual acquaintances • Limited interdependence • Bounded, arms-length transactions • At most, formal courtesies	• Undesirable eventualities expected and feared • Harmful motives assumed • Interdependence limited • Paranoia • Preemption: best defense is a good offense

SOURCE: Adapted from Lewicki, Tomlinson, and Gillespie (2006). Used with permission.
RAND *MG1119-5.2*

Based on such considerations, Figure 5.3 suggests that even an optimistic projection for a post-conflict society might anticipate very high degrees of distrust for years, despite success in finding particular issues and actions on which trust and cooperation can be obtained. We might ponder history after World War II, noting that the nations of Western Europe cooperated rather well after the creation of NATO in 1949.[9] Elements of distrust remained strong for years, however, especially between Germany and its neighbors. Many decades later, today's Western Europeans see themselves collectively as Europeans, and cooperate extensively in most dimensions while retaining national identities. Thus, those involved in the social aspects of S&R should distinguish sharply between short, medium, and long-term goals—with the latter being dependent on developments long after intervenors are gone.

Horizontal and Vertical Trust. An important distinction also exists between "vertical" trust (that between state and society) and "horizon-

Figure 5.3
A Possible Optimistic Timeline for Building Trust and Reducing Distrust

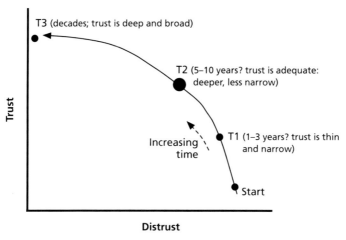

tal" trust, i.e., trust across groups within society, such as between ethnic groups. Reciprocal, self-sustaining processes have positive impacts for both types of trust. Horizontally, the provision of services decreases competitive behavior, and the consistent enforcement of rule of law and justice decreases information asymmetry and risk in personal and business interactions, increasing trusting and trustworthy behavior. Vertically, as states become more able to perform vital functions— equably and consistently—they build a history of positive interactions with society that affect perceptions of state legitimacy and encourage acceptance of state authority (Ghani and Lockhart, 2008). Wider processes of state-building and improving state capacity to deliver services equitably and uniformly, enforce justice and rule of law, and provide common security are all integral to building both types of trust. This chapter is largely about horizontal trust because of its importance in social reconstruction. Also, vertical trust is addressed Chapter Three's discussion of the political component of S&R.

Social Capital. The concept of social capital, much discussed in the literature, deserves mention here as a secondary layer of social

reconstruction that encompasses both trust and cooperation. Two definitions are worth mentioning:

> Social capital includes trust, as well as other social and cultural
> norms, values, and institutions that promote cooperation and col-
> lective action. (Fukuyama, 2002)

> Social capital includes the shared values and rules for social con-
> duct expressed in personal relationships, trust and a common
> sense of "civic" responsibility, which make a society more than
> just a collection of individuals. (World Bank, 2011)

As seen from the definitions above, social capital not only includes
trust and cooperation but also encompasses other social functions that
are beyond the scope of this chapter but enhance social and political
stability (Putnam, 1995). The World Bank provides a useful conceptu-
alization of these functions under five broad component categories, as
shown in Table 5.3.

While interventions should focus on cooperative behavior as an
outcome, building positive social capital is an important component
of post-conflict social reconstruction. Positive social capital enhances
both the frequency and quality of cooperative behavior by reducing
uncertainty about outcomes and interactions and providing mechanisms to accumulate goodwill between parties that facilitates politi-

Table 5.3
Five Dimensions of Social Capital

Dimension	Description
Groups and networks	Larger networks and cohesive groups provide opportunities for connecting people to ideas and information.
Trust and solidarity	High trust levels and social solidarity decreases the collective action problem.
Collective action and cooperation	Cooperation and collective action bring people to work together to address community needs or other public issues.
Social cohesion and inclusion	Inclusiveness mitigates conflict by promoting equal access to benefits of development and resources.
Information and communication	Information improves information asymmetries, as well as communicates intention and positive messages.

cal and economic cooperation (Putnam, 1993). Rebuilding depleted social capital is vital to reconstruction and is part and parcel of conflict resolution. Social capital also has economic and political payoffs that reinforce the reconstruction process over time (Glaeser, Laibson, and Sacerdote, 2002; Knack and Keefer, 1997; Fukuyama, 1995; Brune and Bossert, 2009).

Unfortunately, and despite the fact that academics and practitioners usually assume that higher levels of social capital are beneficial in society, it is not the case under the definitions above. Shared values and rules, for example, can exist within groups and be detrimental to society at large, e.g., the German Nazi party of the 1930s and 1940s or American Ku Klux Klan members in the 20th century. This type of social capital can have very negative effects. This said, in what follows we have in mind positive social capital across groups, which facilitates the social processes in Table 5.3, unless specified otherwise.

Social Reconciliation. At its heart, social reconciliation in the social psychology literature refers to the process of (re)building functioning, stable intergroup relationships that reinforce nonviolent means of interaction. *Social reconciliation* as a concept lacks a unified definition.[10] Some definitions focus on healing, reparations, justice, and truth; they do not presuppose much trust in the immediate or medium-term (Kumar, 1999; Gaertner, Brewer, and Dovidio, 2005). Indeed, many definitions of reconciliation see reconciliation as necessary *because* of the lack of trust (Kumar, 1999; Staub and Bar-Tal, 2003; Bloomfield, Barnes, and Huyse, 2003; Gaertner, Brewer and Dovidio, 2005). That is, social reconciliation processes are essential for rebuilding trusting relationships.

While social reconciliation may be beneficial for society at large, the term *reconciliation* is loaded and contentious. To many, the term means "forgetting" the past violence that they have witnessed or suffered. Many have deep feelings of hatred or fear toward their enemy groups, which leave them unable or unwilling to engage on any level with the other group. A major and more feasible goal of social reconciliation is to promote tolerance. Doing so is also essential to building even limited trust and cooperation; over time, with luck, it may also lead to healing, empathy, and acceptance.

With this background on major themes, the next four subsections touch briefly on several specific literature groups.

Identities, Stereotypes, and Narratives

The social psychology literature relevant to post-conflict processes deals with issues such as bias, prejudice and stereotypes, identities, social embeddedness, and the behavior of individuals in response to social cues. There are also useful discussions of cultural history, cultural narratives and the formation of social identities (Brubaker, 1996; Barth, 1966), and the sources and dimensions of ethnic conflict (Horowitz, 1985; Lake and Rothchild, 1996; Brubaker, 2009; Brubaker and Laitin, 2005). Topics in psychology include grievance and emotional healing, which provide insights for mechanisms of restorative justice and reconciliation. Psychology also has much to say about cognitive biases and the formation of individual attitudes, which can be juxtaposed with the literature on social attitudes. There are several key concepts from social psychology and sociology that are important for understanding social interactions relating to cooperation and trust.

Social Identities and Attitudes. Identities are lenses through which individuals perceive and make sense of the world (Brubaker, 2009). "Constructed" by learned and socialized attitudes, identities frame individuals' perceptions of social situations. Additionally, they may themselves situationally vary (e.g., depending on who interacts with whom or what cues define a situation).[11] In post-conflict situations, individual identities are often less context-dependent and linked to group identities. Though people commonly associate ethnicity, gender, and racial identity as being the main identity groups, the structure of identities to the individual is far more complex. Identities may conceivably be anything that serves to distinguish among people—fighter/civilian, socialist/capitalist, elite/poor, Northerner/Southerner. Similarly, certain identities are stronger than others to individuals; family and community identities may be stronger than national or regional identities. A good understanding of the "groups" in conflict will require an intimate knowledge of the make-up of identity groups in play.

Stereotypes, Prejudice, and Bias. Attitudes are formed from socialized and independent learning about the way groups in society interact. Attitudes influence expectations of cooperation and security, as well as adherence to and expectations about others adhering to norms of behavior (Gaertner, Brewer, and Dovidio, 2005). Attitudes are closely related to stereotypes and biases.

Stereotypes are oversimplified, inaccurate, or overstated beliefs about characteristics of an identity group. Groups in conflict tend to hold negative stereotypes of one another (Fisher, 2000). Negative stereotypes help ingroups to dehumanize outgroup members. Conversely, positive outgroup stereotypes lead to favorable treatment of the stereotyped group(s) and the positive interpretation of actions of group members.

Narratives. Narratives define the collective past of identity group members, creating a common origin and experience, which increases social cohesion among group members but can also create grievances or friction between groups with conflictive historical narratives.

Primacy of Group Attitudes. Some scholars have argued that because individual identities tend to be very closely intertwined with group identities, especially in post-conflict situations, attempts to change social attitudes at the individual level may be relatively ineffective.[12] Although programs exist to promote understanding between opposing group members and have had some anecdotal success, the effect of targeting individuals is not thoroughly tested. While strategies to affect group attitudes obviously need to have effects on large portions of the population, one idea would be to attempt to jump-start cooperation in "pockets" that might then "cascade" to the remainder of the group (Laitin, 1995; Kuran, 1998).[13]

The research on urban crime-reduction programs is worth brief mention as well here, since—although not directly related to post-conflict stability—it deals with cultural shifts resulting in violence reduction. Dramatic success has been achieved in reducing violence in a number of cities with programs that engage the small set of violent gang offenders. The best known of the efforts is the Ceasefire approach championed by David Kennedy (Braga et al., 2001a, 2001b).[14] One tack is deterrent in nature, making clear that failure to cease violence will bring authorities down on the entire groups (curfews, tough enforcement of parole conditions, hassling, etc). At the same time, intervenors urge the individuals to recognize that their violence is senseless and wrong with reinforcement from respected or feared individuals (mothers, clergy, leaders).[15] The effort is also made to weaken identity bonds by demonstrating the myths of close relationships ("brothers" consistently make deals with prosecutors to save themselves; they routinely step in with the girlfriends of those who go to prison; etc). No effort is made to achieve more general reform; the strategy has narrow objectives.

Contact Theory

Contact theory is a long-established model for attitude change. It is a reaction to the well-known observation that segregation or infrequent contact between groups helps maintain negative stereotypes and mutual ignorance (e.g., Ajdukovic, 2008). The essential idea of contact theory is that increased exposure, under certain conditions, gives each party the opportunity to gather more information about the other and adjust expectations and attitudes accordingly.[16] For interactions geared toward increasing contact and cooperation to be most effective in debunking stereotypes and improving relations, groups must have equal status in the situation, must have common goals identified, and must have the support of authority figures who condone and support cooperation (Allport, 1954). Through this kind of interaction, ingroups and outgroups establish affective, or emotional ties, which causes them to reappraise the negative stereotypes they hold and alter social attitudes toward outgroup members (Pettigrew, 1998). Contact can be direct, through physical interaction with opposing group members, or indirect, through secondary channels, such as media or knowing that one's friends interact with outgroup members. Both types of contact positively affect outgroup attitudes, reduce prejudice, and enhance intergroup trust in post-conflict situations (Pettigrew and Tropp, 2006).

Cautions. Clearly, merely putting people together is by no means sufficient. Indeed, as readers will understand, increased exposure or contact can worsen matters so as to encourage competition rather than cooperation (Deutsch, 1973; Saunders et al., 2010); also, behavior of the "other's" members may confirm rather than disconfirm negative outgroup stereotypes (Hewstone et al., 2008; McGuire 1998). To put it otherwise, contact theory is nothing at all like a panacea.

Post-Conflict Intervention

This section provides a general overview of the academic literature on specific types of post-conflict social interventions, while subsequent sections delve into greater detail.

Considerable literature exists on what makes post-conflict social intervention programs effective or ineffective. With the primary exception of the quasi-experimental literature investigating intergroup trust and forgiveness,[17] the literatures emphasize theory, best practices, and criticism, with an emphasis on practical applications. Intervention studies look at the *role(s) of civil society* (Posner, 2004; Pouligny, 2005; Paffenholz, 2009; Duthie, 2009; Pugh, 1998); *forms of justice* (Cobián and Reátegui, 2009; Avruch and Vejarano, 2001; Lie, Binningsbø, and Gates, 2006; De Greiff, 2009; Park, 2010); *media and propaganda* (Bloomfield, Barnes, and Huyse, 2003; Krabil, 2001; Howard, 2002, 2003); and *education* (Bekerman, Zembylas, and McGlynn, 2009; Bar-Tal, 2000; Danesh, 2006; Salomon, 2004).

All of these programs promote social reconciliation and build positive social capital—by increasing communication and information, encouraging direct contact, restructuring social values and norms of behavior, providing common goals, and improving civic activism. The roles and impacts of each are discussed in greater detail later in this chapter; they are only briefly overviewed here.

Justice. Transitional justice—post-conflict retributive and restorative justice—is the largest component of the social reconciliation literature and enjoys the most attention in the literature on post-conflict recovery.

The literature on post-conflict justice is divided mainly among overviews of transitional justice (Deutsch, 2000b; Elster, 2004; Lie, Binningsbø, and Gates, 2006); assessments of the value of retributive and restorative justice (Lundy and McGovern, 2008; Wilson, 2001; Park, 2010); and case-studies of specific transitional justice processes that discuss operational or tactical successes and shortcomings (Zorbas, 2004; Mitton, 2009; Megawalu and Loizides, 2010; Gibson, 2002).

However, there is little agreement about proper forms of justice or implementation for promoting stability.[18] There is some statistical evidence that formal justice mechanisms (as distinct from amnesty deals) are positively associated with longer peacetimes (Lie, Binningsbø, and Gates, 2006; Sikkink and Booth Walling, 2007). The relationships are not clear-cut, however, and there may be some optimal combination of transitional justice tools that includes both amnesty and tribunals.

The issue of justice is taken up in greater detail below.

Civil Society. Promoting engagement by building up "civil society" has been suggested as a new and beneficial strategy for post-conflict peacebuilding in situations where states lack capacity to provide services and maintain order (Parver and Wolf, 2008). Several studies have assessed the success or failure of specific programs or organizations related to civil society (e.g., Anckermann et al., 2005; Ager, Strang, and Abebe, 2005). A few empirical studies assess the effectiveness of these programs overall, as do a very few notable ones outside the narrow intergroup trust literature. Most of these studies use survey data to assess how community programs affect community cohesion among members of different groups (Widner, 2004; Ajukovic, 2008; Whitt, 2010; Brune and Bossert, 2009) Some empirical work has tested the effect of civil society on trust and general development, with mixed results (Newton, 2001; Knack and Keefer, 1997). This is discussed more in a later section.

Others. Overwhelmingly, the post-conflict intervention literatures have been devoted to transitional justice, and—more recently—to the potential for civil society to promote social capital and cohesion. However, there are small and growing bodies of knowledge about communication methods and education programs. The use of strategic media and public communication between groups has been shown to have potentially large effects on intergroup trust and cooperation (Deutsch, 1958; Kerr et al., 1997; Sally, 1995; Balliet, 2009). Indeed, meta-analyses have demonstrated this empirically (Sally, 1995; Balliet 2009). Education, also, has been shown to improve intergroup attitudes toward one another, and promote intergroup cooperation and trust (Bar-Tal, 2004; McGlynn, Niens, and Hewstone, 2004). These programs are also discussed in greater detail below.

A Composite Picture

There is still a great deal more to be done in theorizing and examining the process of social reconstruction in a post-conflict environment. However, based on the literature review, we see social reconstruction as involving both reconciliation and the buildup of positive social capital. Cooperation and trust, however, contribute to both reconciliation and social capital.

We next examine some of the main programs or interventions that have been identified in the theoretical and practitioner's literature as means of rebuilding trust, promoting positive social capital development, and promoting social reconciliation in post-conflict situations. Two subsections examine transitional retributive and restorative justice, respectively. The next subsection looks at the development of civil-society organizations as a means of enhancing state functions, improving civic participation, and encouraging local ownership of development projects. A subsection then deals with the use of media for improving social across-group attitudes, reinforcing cultural narratives, and disseminating information. That is followed by a subsection addressing the use of education to alter cultural tolerance for violence and modes of conflict and restructure cultural relationships to be inclusive and cohesive. Finally, a subsection describes ways in which these various interventions can interact with reinforcing feedbacks.

Policy Mechanisms for Social Reconstruction

Transitional Justice

Scholars and practitioners alike assert the need for justice to serve multiple purposes beyond its mandate in international law. Victims demand recognition and acknowledgement of their suffering, as well as moral condemnation of the perpetrators and retribution against them (Ajdukovic, 2008). Justice processes help establish a basis on which members of the group can interact as human equals, a necessity of trust-building encounters (Hofstede, 1991). Post-conflict justice, sometimes called "transitional" justice, has received much attention and is widely considered a necessary step in post-conflict reconciliation (Bloomfield, Barnes and Huyse, 2003; Gaertner et al., 2005; Rotberg, 2000).[19]

Appropriate and feasible forms of justice, however, are *very* context-dependent (Bloomfield, Barnes, and Huyse, 2003). Significantly, transitional justice can involve any or all of several very different types of process. These are sometimes called *retributive justice, restorative justice*, and *reconciliation* (Clark, 2008). On one end of the spectrum lies war crime trials, often international, for bringing major perpetrators of violence to justice. On the other end are such mechanisms as truth commissions, apology, and restitution. The relative merits of each are subject to debate.[20] It is certainly the case that the choice of transitional justice mechanisms in any context will require a serious examination of the politically and socially feasible options.

With this background, what follows draws on the literature relating to transitional justice mechanisms. The focus is on formal trials and truth commissions, as they are the common forms of transitional justice, but also includes other options, such as lustration, restitution, and hybrid courts; it goes beyond the experience of S&R operations.

Retributive Justice: Trials, Hybrid Courts, and Lustration. Prosecution of war criminals and perpetrators of human rights atrocities in the post-conflict setting has the potential to satisfy the societal demand for justice. A number of authors cite the need for retributive justice to stop potential instances of destabilizing vigilante or private justice (Elster, 2004; Bass, 2005). Indeed, failure to have such processes can cause difficulties. In Bosnia, for example, the failure of the Bosnian-Serbs to turn over war criminals wanted by the International Criminal Tribunal for the former Yugoslavia (ICTY) has tended to undercut trust between the ethnic groups. However, there is not universal agreement about the value of retributive justice, *as actually conducted*. Clark (2008), for example, uses empirical data gathered in the former Yugoslavia to argue that, while war-crime tribunals are an important part of the peacebuilding process, the retributive justice they deliver falls seriously short in promoting reconciliation—in significant part because alternative narratives exist and persist about what constitutes justice.

Well-managed retributive justice allows governments to blame individuals (rather than whole identity groups), purge threatening figureheads, and enhance state legitimacy and expectations of rule of law (Dobbins et al., 2007). Formal trials have been relatively scarce in the realm of post-conflict reconstruction; there have been only eight international war crimes tribunals since 1919. Compare this with truth commissions, of which there have been 27 since 1971. The scarcity of war tribunals suggests that there are far fewer situations in which they are appropriate and feasible. Retributive justice is most feasible (whether or not desirable) primarily when one side has had a decisive victory, or when intervenors have the ability and will to crush one or more of the contending parties. The Nuremberg Trials after World War II were an example. A more recent example is the work of the ICTY, created by the United Nations in 1993. And, of course, the Iraqi Special Tribunal (a construct of the Iraqi government, not the United Nations) had Saddam Hussein hanged in 2006.

Another emerging alternative has been the establishment of "hybrid" courts, or courts operating within the country and administered by local judicial authorities. Hybrid courts have a major advantage of being potentially much less costly than war-crimes trials.[21] In addition, they have the potential to support judicial capacity-building and to demonstrate rule of law and fairness at the local level (Dobbins et al., 2007). The Rwandan Gacaca courts, or "grass" courts, were established with the authority to mete out punishment and require those found guilty to make restitution. Based on a traditional system of justice, the courts were conducted quickly with few resources. Further, because they used a traditional system, they enjoyed relatively wide acceptance by Rwandans as legitimate and fair (Zorbas, 2004).

The level of retributive justice delivered in a post-conflict environment varies between the theoretical extremes of complete impunity or punishment for *all* perpetrators. A notable in-between is lustration, which deprives certain segments of the population access to power or privileges; it is designed to ensure that those previously in power do not regain access to the system (Dobbins et al., 2007). Notable examples are Democrats after the American Civil War, members of the Nazi party in post-World War II Germany, and members of the Ba'ath party in Iraq. Lustration is administratively easier than individual prosecution since it requires no proof of wrongdoing and the burden of proof for redress lies with the individual, not the government (Dobbins et al., 2007). Yet to ameliorate the effects of its necessarily arbitrary design, an apparatus capable of providing a path for reinstatement of the excluded population is necessary (Dobbins et al., 2007).

In the post-conflict situations most relevant to S&R, negotiations between opposing factions are taking place. In those situations, the primary objective is compromise and cooptation, not retribution. In this case, reconciliation measures such as apology and restitution—such as economic support to victims—may be more immediately implementable. Retribution may come decades later, as it did with Argentina and Chile belatedly facing up to their pasts, but it will seldom be the focus of S&R activities. Some will see a moral dilemma, as when negotiations are attempted between the Afghan government and selected elements of the Taliban, but putting aside retribution is perhaps necessary if complete victory is not in the cards. If negotiations are necessary between groups, then retributive justice mechanisms may be deferred, weakened, or narrowed in scope. [22]

Restorative Justice: Truth Commissions. Many scholars believe that *restorative* justice is the stronger and most generally feasible approach. Truth commissions generally act as complements rather than alternatives to retributive justice where the latter is feasible.[23] At root, truth commissions involve a cooperative effort to establish the facts of history to overcome competing group narratives of the war, narratives that often impede reconciliation and cooperation. Unlike criminal trials, they do not involve prosecution of individuals, but rather constitute an effort to set the record straight. Such programs are normally conceived as having four main objectives: reconciliation, accountability, truth-telling, and restitution for damage (Huyse and Salter, 2008). South Africa's Truth and Reconciliation Commission (TRC) is the most well known and is generally to be considered the largest success of historical truth commissions, but commissions have been implemented in many other situations with varying degrees of success—e.g., Rwanda, Peru, Liberia, El Salvador, and Nicaragua.

Truth commissions are officially empowered by the state to act over a set period, usually six months to two years, and investigate human rights abuses occurring over a predetermined period of time (Dobbins et al., 2007). The commissions systematically uncover and publicize the personal narratives of a country's past war period, generally culminating in a final report of findings. Truth commissions support social reconciliation and provide an avenue for direct participation by a large number of individuals (Dobbins et al., 2007). Truth-telling allows survivors, perpetrators, and victims alike to reenact past violence, wherein grudges, bitterness, and pain can be conveyed without the risk of inciting new cycles of violence (Huyse and Salter, 2008). Because the core of their mission is on fact-finding and not punishment, truth commissions are in a unique position to investigate collective guilt in a way that criminal trials or tribunals cannot (Bloomfield, Barnes, and Huyse, 2003).

Truth-telling, apology, and acceptance of blame together combat the tendency toward dehumanization of the other group and build a foundation on which each group can begin to see the other as humans rather than subhuman enemies. This helps establish a basis on which members of the group can interact as human equals, a necessity of trust-building. Establishing a valid historical narrative of past atrocities legitimizes the pain of individuals and entire societies and condemns the use of violence in the future. In the South African case, the truth commission centered its energies on collecting and publicizing personal testimonies of violence and war, to create an authoritative memory and to fight against a collective amnesia for the future (Henderson, 2000).

It is clear that thoughtful and strategic planning needs to be brought to bear on the organization of truth commissions and other restorative justice measures so that they have meaningful impact. A careful analysis of the cultural setting and other contextual factors will be a must, in addition to interacting transitional justice with other trust-building initiatives.

Other Mechanisms: Apology and Restitution. Truth-commission narratives sometimes also involve apology and announcements of remorse, although apologies and restitution to victims need not come via truth commissions. Apologies have powerful social import:

Although they cannot undo past wrongs, they can help to undo some of the damage of past wrongs by delegitimizing them (Tavuchis, 1991). Some authors argue that reconciliation efforts without any form of apology cannot hope to succeed (Smits, 2003). Public acts of contrition and apology can help build trust, especially when the act is costly, either socially, politically, or economically, for the contrite party (Pruitt and Olczak, 1995).[24] Apologies that are qualified, appear insincere, or are inconsistent with the apologizer's behavior will irritate conflict and reduce cooperative drives; unfelt apologies are better left unsaid.

Restitution for victims can also serve this function at the societal level as well as the individual level, while also promoting a more equal society in general (Huyse and Salter, 2008). Similar to procedural post-conflict justice, providing accountability and the equitable provision of restitution should also enhance the credibility of the justice-dispensing body, which increases vertical levels of trust in the new government.

Overall Cautions. All justice mechanisms—whether retributive or restorative—will be judged by the company they keep. While hybrid courts and national truth-finding commissions—for example, truth and reconciliation commissions in both South Africa and Sierra Leone—may gain legal authority to conduct their investigations via legislative or constitutional mandates, they do not necessarily gain legitimacy or credibility from these same sources. Tribunals and commissions supported or run by actors that took part in the atrocities, or actors who are seen as partial or weak, will hamper the impact of the commission's work. This was the case in Rwanda: Because the church took part in some of the wartime atrocities, its involvement with the Gacaca "grass" courts was an unwelcome signal that the impartiality of the courts might be compromised (Parver and Wolf, 2008).

Another operational caveat lies in offering amnesty or economic assistance in exchange for information, truth-telling, or laying down arms. While amnesty has been relatively successful in getting perpetrators to come forward for the purposes of truth commissions, it has not worked universally, and it is unclear whether more-violent perpetrators are more or less likely to step forward. On the one hand, amnesties may be the price of peace; on the other hand, they can deepen resentment among victims and society (Gibson, 2002; Wilson, 2001). Trade-offs between amnesty and trials and prosecutions—or, in the case of truth commissions, incomplete accounts of the past—will have to be made. Amnesty will promote reconstruction by incentivizing fighters to put down arms and come forward. Yet, amnesty undermines retributive justice goals and may lead to feelings in society that perpetrators got off scot-free.

An important conclusion from the literature is that *in all types of post-conflict justice, as in so many other areas, local ownership matters.* International and local norms of justice are not the same. A danger of putting justice in the hands of third parties is that outcomes will fail to fulfill culturally defined modes of justice and therefore be poorly accepted. Or, they may appear to be politically partial, fueling distrust and animosity toward the other side (Parver and Wolf, 2008). Linking justice mechanisms to traditional or indigenous forms of justice brings the process close to home for many and imparts a sense of local legitimacy. Moreover, locals are often better equipped than external agents to understand what their community needs to bury memories of past atrocities. However, international third parties need to ensure the safety of both victims and confessed perpetrators. If international actors enjoy perceptions of nonbias and credibility, they can also give their imprimatur process to help legitimize justice efforts.

In this view, international agents are best advised to be supporters of the local process, rather than administrators themselves. Giving room for local social and legal structures to enforce justice contributes to the legitimacy of the justice process and enhances indigenous governance structures, provided that the justice-implementing organizations are nonbiased and perceived to be so. They can help by providing manpower, resources, and facilities and advising on international legal requirements in the context of local justice. To be sure, local justice mechanisms are not always appropriate, or in accordance with international humanitarian standards. International third parties must make sure that humanitarian standards are upheld, and compromises may have to occur for both local justice and international requirements to be satisfied. Attempting to do so can raise dilemmas.

Overall, the forms of justice that occur in the post-conflict period are largely dependent on what is both acceptable by the population and feasible politically. If retributive justice is not an available option, then intervenors may depend on other reconciliation measures. This does not mean, however, that some form of reconciliation is not necessary for societies to move on in the longer term. Though Panama and Uruguay did not institute their own truth commissions until decades after the cessation of the conflicts they were mandated to investigate, the commissions were still needed to "bury the hatchet" on these conflicts. At the end of the day, the purpose of transitional justice is to help societies move on as a whole, rather than continue to hold onto the past conflict as a source of division.

Efforts to Develop Civil Society

The literature has substantial discussion of the value of civil society in post-conflict reconstruction, as reviewed by Paffenholz and Spurk (2006). The nature and functions of civil society in the literature include protecting citizen's rights, monitoring government, building community through engagement and socialization, delivering services, and mediating between citizens and the state (Paffenholz and Spurk, 2006; Parver and Wolf, 2008; World Bank, 2005). Civil society is often viewed as an alternative to weak, post-conflict states for the provision of public goods. Moreover, civil society can, in theory, build social capital and trust through civic engagement while forcing the government to become more transparent and accountable. To the extent that community organizations understand the needs of their communities, they can also help prioritize programs by providing contextual insights and adding legitimacy to both external and state partners.

Civil society organizations can promulgate social reconciliation in several ways. By providing services equitably they can satisfy needs and, in the process, reduce insecurity and competitiveness. As watchdogs and public-information providers, they can increase knowledge and reduce uncertainty. As organizers, they can stimulate intergroup cooperation and the accumulation of trust—for example, by bringing together adversarial groups and help identify common goals. Thus, they can help bolster nearly all of the dimensions of social capital identified by the World Bank (2006) and outlined in Table 5.3. Nor is such discussion purely speculative. Fearon, Humphreys, and

Weinstein (2009) have shown that the development of civil society in post-conflict communities alters patterns of social cooperation. Several case studies undertaken by the World Bank evaluating community-driven development in conflict areas suggest that, in certain contexts, joint-development programs improve civic participation (especially in youth), restore trust in mixed communities, and promote stability (World Bank, 2006).

Furthermore, besides building positive social capital, the sheer presence of community civil organizations acts as an integrative agent within the community, bringing people together outside of the home (Putnam, 1993, 1995)—perhaps across communities ("bridging" as well as "bonding"). As such, the sheer presence of civil society organizations can create a sense of community inclusiveness that promotes both direct and indirect contact. Although, to date, civil society organizations have been mainly talked about and evaluated in the context of development-assistance programs, the discussion here clearly suggests that they can be useful in promoting stabilization and reconstruction.

Cautions. There are also obvious problems and challenges involved with efforts to develop civil society.

1. *Limited Reach.* Efforts aimed specifically at promoting social harmony and attitudinal change often fail to reach large enough numbers of people to support social change (Paffenholz and Spurk, 2006).
2. *Lack of Sustainability.* International investments in civil society tend to be short-sighted and persist only as long as international engagement (World Bank, 2005; Donais, 2009). Thereafter, old patterns reemerge (Fearon, Humphreys, and Weinstein, 2009).
3. *Identifying Whom to Support.* Identifying the significant and appropriate actors to support can be problematic (Pouligny, 2005; World Bank, 2005), in part because a myriad of organizations may exist. Some may be politically motivated or marginalizing, such as organizations that operate exclusive programs along ethnic, gender, political or other lines; some will arise merely because of the prospect of donor funding; some deal with health, others with political advocacy, and still others

with education; even worse, some may seek to undermine the intervention itself by funneling money to insurgents, a problem in today's Afghanistan (Goodhand and Sedra, 2010).

4. *Capability of Civic Organizations.* The qualitative characteristics of organizations matter, not just their number. Many civil society organizations lack the absorptive capacity to collect and distribute aid in the same way that state bodies can (for the example of Sierra Leone, see Mitton, 2009).

5. *Undermining of Government.* In some cases, investments in civil society can undermine government authority or legitimacy, thereby contributing to long-run state weakness (World Bank, 2005). When the state is weak, civil society has the potential to overpower it (Burde, 2004) and to undercut intervenors' efforts to strengthen the state.

One lesson might seem to be that civil society organizations should provide services that are complementary rather than supplementary to state services, so as to avoid undermining state legitimacy. Thus, the organizations should be partnered with government rather than sidestepping or subverting it. That is not always possible, however, as discussed in Chapter Seven. Further, in the extreme it presupposes the desirability of a strong state system rather than one that is more decentralized.

Another lesson from the literature is that external actors must be and appear even-handed in their support for civic organizations, especially when it comes to those closely associated with particular groups that were once party to the conflict.

On the difficult issue of how to choose which groups to support, there is no simple formula for guidance. However, it would seem that external support should go to organizations whose core mission includes providing locally oriented, socially and economically inclusive programs that promote nonviolence.

Media and Communication

Communication can improve understanding of issues and relationships, enhance positive aspects of identity, and generate norms of cooperation (Kerr et al., 1997). It can frame the course of interpersonal interactions, analyze interests, diffuse mistrust, and provide safe emotional outlets (Howard, 2002, p. 4). It can be a form of contact between groups, which plays a role in breaking down negative stereotypes. A professionalized media can improve cooperation by correcting information asymmetries and mitigating distrust and competitiveness (Kumar, 1999). Recently, the strategic use of media as a stability tool in post-conflict states has moved from strict reporting to delivering a message of peace, choosing information that has the potential to transform conflict, and shifting identities and attitudes (Howard, 2002).

Communication can be either active—via speeches or declarations of intent directed at members of other groups—or passive, via subconscious priming of attitudes. For example, media programs in Rwanda have included ethnically integrated cast members to improve groups' attitudes toward the other (Levy Paluck, 2007). The forms of media are numerous and include traditional newspapers, radio, and television programming with, increasingly, less expensive alternatives, such as dialogue projects and social media.

Strategic development of an independent media can be a tool for social reconstruction in several ways. The media can be used to spread messages of peace, reconciliation, and solidarity that reinforce other trust-building programs. Media can be a form of indirect contact between groups, as well as a medium for subconsciously challenging social attitudes. Media can disseminate messages of reconciliation, peace, and apology from one group to another, which aids trust formation. There is evidence to suggest that integrated media encourages social reconciliation (Levy Paluck, 2007). For example, research in Rwanda finds that reconciliation media has potential to affect perceptions and social norms, as well as attitudes about trust, integration, and truth (Levy Paluck, 2007).

Sequencing. In developing professional media in post-conflict environments, sequencing appears to be important. One study (Howard, 2002) suggests that media development needs to start with basic skills training in reporting and objectivity. Focus should then transition to building norms of independence and professionalism, which enhance both quality and credibility. Only later in development should the media be used for disseminating messages seeking to change attitudes. In all of this, long-term commitment is necessary if self-sustaining results are desired (Howard 2002, 2003; Kumar, 1999). Bosnia is a case in point: The Organization for Security and Cooperation was successful in building a free and independent media. However, many media outlets later ran into difficulty financially, and in the struggle to survive were forced into the arms of partisan groups.

Cautions. Despite the potential for good, many issues, problems, and dilemmas exist.

1. *Sensationalism Sells.* A truly free and independent media in post-conflict states has the potential to negatively impact peace and trust. Excess attention to incidents of intergroup violence and the need for simple, easily packaged ideas that rob situations of their complexity can easily be detrimental (Howard, 2003). To make thing worse, examples of positive cooperation or peaceful negotiations are relatively less exciting and are therefore under-represented. This overreporting of negative events and under-reporting of positive ones can severely affect perceptions of the situation.

   It follows that to serve the functions of peace, media will require direction and guidance. Messages of peace must be actively disseminated, and journalists should be trained with an eye to emphasize peace-promoting media over sensationalist or conflict media (Lynch and McGoldrick, 2005). Accomplishing this is not straightforward, especially when such "direction" can undercut independence and credibility.

2. *Misunderstanding and Misappropriation.* Another problem is that communications can be misinterpreted, and the media can be used as a conduit for identity politicians to exploit. Unclear, vague, or antagonistic communication across groups can increase suspicion and distrust (Howard, 2003). An even worse outcome would be the use of a newly instantiated media network by identity politicians to fuel intergroup competition, spread malicious ethnic myths, and reinforce negative stereotypes. Political entrepreneurs often use sensational media to

reinforce negative stereotypes and enforce distrust between groups for their own political gain. Highly uncertain environments, such as those that characterize post-conflict situations, increase the willingness of individuals to accept such messages (Lake and Rothchild, 1996; Weingast, 1998).

It is clear, then, that while the media can have a potentially huge impact, it can be for good or bad. More research on such matters is needed so as to establish best practices for intervenors to work with.

Peace Education

The essential goal of peace education is to increase understanding and mutual respect between groups engaged in protracted conflict by acquiring "beliefs, attitudes, and behaviors that are in line with the ideas of coexistence" (Bar-Tal, 2004, p. 261). Through learning about and empathizing with other groups, people engage in a collective process of attitude change and belief restructuring. The intent is to change a group's narratives by (1) legitimizing the group's own narrative, (2) examining the group's own contribution to the conflict, (3) learning empathy for other groups' suffering, and (4) promoting intergroup engagement in nonviolent activities (Salomon, 2004). Overall, the concept of peace education centers on the process of de-essentialization of one's own group identity and humanization of the perception of other groups (Bekerman, Zembylas, and McGlynn, 2009).

How does peace education contribute to social reconstruction? Peace education contributes to intergroup trust by (1) establishing an arena for mutually respectful, equal-status contact between group members under the authority of an impartial third party (the teacher or administrator); (2) emphasizing the legitimacy of the cultural heritage of others and molding identity narratives; (3) building empathy for the suffering of the other groups in the conflict; (4) encouraging the acceptance of one's own role in the conflict. Peace education attempts to draw experiential parallels between the histories of the two groups, thus identifying the similarities between them. This builds a basis for empathy and cross-group identification.

Peace education programs can be centered around either the formal schooling system or the society at large. Recognizing that the school system is a major agent of socialization for youth, desegregated, school-based peace education approaches have been tried in Israel and in universities in Northern Ireland. The societal approach also includes political, social, and cultural institutions and both leaders and elites. The societal approach is tactically much more involved and requires credible institutional support, the cooperation of agents from all areas of society, and that new norms are developed conjointly between groups (Bar-Tal, 2004).

The efficacy of school-based peace education in altering youth orientations to problem-solving and conflict is generally positive. While schooling alone has surprisingly little impact on specific issues, it seems to have a large positive impact in influencing the general orientation to problems, such as open-mindedness or predisposition to make judgments (McGuire, 1998). In accordance with this, Salomon (2004) finds that peace education in Israel, despite the ongoing violence, yields positive effects regarding the willingness of Israeli-Jewish and Palestinian youngsters to view a problem from multiple angles and engage in contact with members of other groups, but does not generally affect their specific political views. Yet another study (McGlynn, Niens, and Hewstone, 2004) summarizes several studies on the impact of integrated education in Northern Ireland and elsewhere and concludes that integrated education positively impacts identity, attitudes toward the outgroup, forgiveness, and reconciliation. The authors argue that the Northern Ireland success provides hope for other attempts at co-education to assuage legacies of violent conflict.

The effectiveness of the broader, social approach has not been assessed. The social approach obviously calls for a massive level of coordinated effort and cooperation, and it is by no means clear that politically competitive or adversarial agents in government, civil society, and international parties will be able to effectively coordinate and manage priorities where states are too weak to manage the effort alone.

Cautions. A number of cautions also need to be expressed:

1. A unified, committed leadership that can agree on and coordinate the continual dissemination of messages seems to be nec-

essary. Achieving such a unified position among elites of a war-torn country may, however, be nigh impossible.

2. The state must be prepared to take on the role as the main source of socialization. This may also be difficult to achieve. In the past, families and communities have traditionally been the main socializers of children in many post-conflict environments—e.g., Sub-Saharan Africa, Indonesia, and Afghanistan. Families may be loathe to allow their children to attend a school where they believe their children will be taught to love people with whom they have been in such devastating conflict.

3. Although the literature to date is optimistic about the effects of peace education, most studies have dealt with relatively high-income countries that are either experiencing long-term pro-tracted conflict (Cyprus, Israel) or have had a relatively success-ful peace for more than a decade (Northern Ireland). Northern Ireland and Israel are unusually wealthy compared with other post-conflict countries. It is uncertain how viable peace educa-tion will be in post-conflict states where other more basic needs are lacking.

Linkages

The reciprocal, self-reinforcing nature of social reconciliation, coop-eration, trust, and social capital suggests "cocktail effects" in which the overall benefits to trust-building from several social programs can be significantly more than the sum of the programs' individual values. Also, the benefits to political and economic development can be improved by encouraging a variety of different interventions. For example, Mitton (2009) describes an instance in Sierra Leone in which the National Youth Council lobbied the government to establish a National Youth Commission, as part of the peace agreement. When the government was unresponsive, the council threatened to establish one independently, a move that received massive media attention and elicited a large public response. The Sierra Leonean government acqui-esced and established the commission. Here, the ability of civil society to improve government responsiveness was enhanced by media cover-age. Another example, given by Krabil (2001), is of the media coverage of the truth commission in South Africa. Media exposure of the truth commission spread the message of justice to a much larger number of people and brought the process of justice and reconciliation closer for many than would have been possible otherwise. Civil society organizations also helped contribute to the effectiveness of the commission by providing local information and support. Reciprocally, the truth commission improved perceptions of state legitimacy by providing legitimate local channels of conflict resolution and mediation.

There is, in general, a substantial potential for such synergies in S&R. For example, imagine a situation in which civil-society organizations that deliver health services increase trust and social capital, which in turn strengthens the ability of the local watchdog agency to monitor government responsiveness, whose findings are relayed via the local media, which moves government to act, which increases perceptions of government legitimacy, which increases security and decreases mistrust, which promotes more cooperation. Another example might be a situation in which peace education socializes young people to have more accepting attitudes and brings integrated media programs into the home, where they have an opportunity to affect parents and other adults. Figure 5.4 illustrates potential linkages among the social interventions discussed in this chapter.

Such reinforcing effects are not limited to processes within the social sphere. Social development can have positive effects on economic and political development and vice versa, a theme of the entire volume that will not be repeated here.[25]

Integrative Considerations and Discussion

Context-Specificity

Any successful cohesion-building program will benefit from an acute awareness of social dynamics, power structures, cultural narratives and identities, and local political economy—evidence again of the importance of local knowledge to successful post-conflict S&R. There is a great deal of variation in post-conflict situations. As examples, the challenges in Rwanda and Cambodia have been very different (e.g., with no groups to reconcile in Cambodia). Even understandings of trust

Figure 5.4
Illustrative Intervention-Program Linkages

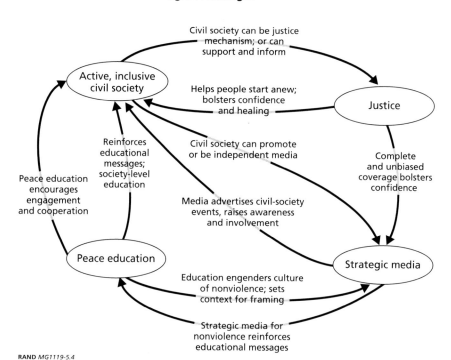

RAND *MG1119-5.4*

and trustworthiness are culturally rooted and context-specific (Brune and Bossert, 2009). All post-conflict situations are influenced by their own political-economic and socio-cultural histories, which is why local ownership is so important. Donors and external actors, of course, often have difficulty escaping their own cultural frames (Donais, 2009; Pouligny, 2005).

Context specificity, by definition, means that no specific policy recommendations will work for all, or perhaps more than any one, situation.

Therefore, there seems to be a great need for developing frameworks or approaches to developing programs that allow for the satisfaction of social development goals by context-appropriate means, rather than on the identification of specific programmatic forms for use in many situations.

Sequencing of Trust-and-Cooperation-Relevant Interventions

While there is no clear-cut timeline for implementing social interventions in the post-conflict period, some recommendations for sequencing of programs emerge from the literature.[26] Transitional justice, both retributive and restorative, cannot wait. Transitional justice mechanisms are consistently identified as paramount for post-conflict social reconciliation (Bloomfield, Barnes, and Huyse, 2003; Avruch and Vejarano, 2001; Cuevas, Rojas, and Baeza, 2002; Rotberg, 2000; Lundy and McGovern, 2008). Social reconciliation lays the foundation for the reconstruction of healthy social relationships characterized by cooperation. The details of violent experiences tend to fade fast (even if emotional memory remains strong), so getting individuals' stories into the record as quickly and accurately as possible is important. Retributive justice is logistically harder and takes more time due to the bureaucracy involved in trying prisoners, yet international actors should not hesitate to make clear steps toward implementing formal trials and tribunals. Victims demand retribution, and a delay in providing it will only increase dissatisfaction.

Public and frequent communication between groups in the immediate post-conflict period can also be an aid to developing initial levels of post-conflict cooperation (see earlier discussion of "thin" trust). A well-negotiated peace agreement can be a good jumping-off point for reiterating messages of cooperation, tolerance, and unity. Elites can have a very positive role in directing expectations via frequent, respectful communication.

Peace education programs, as previously noted, are clearly long-term prospects requiring unified leadership and infrastructure that may be very difficult to come by, and they divert resources away from more-effective interventions in the short term. Developing a professional media with a mission of promoting nonviolence and stability can be a good way to start moving toward a societal peace education program, by laying the foundation for the future dissemination of peace messages. Furthermore, the media can provide immediate benefits by increasing information in an insecure, information-scarce environment. A professional media that may be used as a tool for projecting information and positive messages can yield large and immediate benefits for S&R, as long as caution is taken to make sure that journalists are not seen as puppets of the intervenors.

Civil society is likely to be lacking in post-conflict situations. There is no clear recommendation for when and how to get involved with promoting civil society organizations. Benefits can be accrued in the short term if there are already some organizations that are capable of providing equal-access, inclusive, and stabilizing services that can partner with external agents. However, external agents should not be tempted to support weak or partisan organizations out of a need to do something; such efforts would be not only wasteful but also counterproductive, as discussed earlier.

Overall, some basic level of security needs to be established in order for social reconstruction to take place. In societies struggling with deep emotional turmoil and severely depleted social capital, the best intervenors can hope for at the beginning is cooperation motivated by "thin" trust. If intervenors cannot guarantee some security, including enforcement mechanisms, cooperation will be unlikely to occur at all, and social construction will be difficult to proceed with.

Local Ownership and Legitimacy

Local ownership of reconstruction processes has been routinely identified in the reconstruction literature as a necessity for successful peace (Donais, 2009; Goodhand and Sedra, 2010; Duthie, 2009). Local ownership of projects and processes builds endogenous social capital, establishes procedural legitimacy, aligns projects to needs more efficiently, and improves community cooperation and collective action. Additionally, local ownership can help build local capacity to run programs when intervenors leave. Local authority also often enjoys greater legitimacy and confidence with citizens than external actors. Yet, there is still a dichotomy between rhetoric and practice in international intervention in post-conflict states.

The very notion of ownership is contested in some places, and donors have to negotiate with and choose among multiple state and nonstate interlocutors (Goodhand and Sedra, 2010).

The ownership issue is only one example of how differences in norms can cause trouble, as expressed in the literature:

> This disjuncture between the local and the international does not only occur in relation to trust. . . . There is a danger that externally driven norms, practice, and expectations on trust are universalized, or assumed to have purchase in a wide range of societies. (Gormley-Heenan and MacGinty, 2009, p. 424)

The importation of external norms or institutions has a very short track record of success. When survivors do not have a stake in adjustments, they also lose incentives to perpetuate those changes (Pugh, 1998). In a space where debate on types of interventions, methods, and philosophy are still ongoing, there is overwhelming agreement that social capital cannot be developed externally; rather, processes of trust and social development must happen organically. Hence, it is argued that the best way for international actors to engage is in a supportive and/or consultative role rather than a directorial or leadership one (World Bank, 2005; Donais, 2009; Pugh, 1998).

Cautions. As noted in the discussions of justice, despite these broad conclusions, intervenors cannot leave everything in the hands of locals. A prime example is that of post-conflict justice. International humanitarian law demands that war crimes be prosecuted, yet local governments have sometimes sought to provide amnesty to leaders in order to guarantee a peace. Conversely, external actors may wish to guarantee that local justice complies with minimum standards of international justice. Some local definitions of justice are not only considered extremely harsh but are in violation of international humanitarian norms—such as those prohibiting cruel or unusual punishment and those providing for equal protection (e.g., for women).[27] External agents must walk a fine line between imposing external justice and making sure their legal and humanitarian obligations are met.

Another less obvious example is that of providing support to civil society organizations. While one goal of promoting the development of civil society is to bring members of different groups together under a common goal, imposing a standard of inclusion can be rejected by a traditionally segregated society. This is turn undermines social capital between the community and the peacekeepers, which makes maintaining order more difficult. Yet, encouraging "local ownership" by allowing civic organizations to deny access to membership or resources—such as providing funding to an organization that administers community health services only to members of certain groups, or that does not take measures to ensure that services are accessible to underprivileged groups—is antithetical to the goals of social reconstruction.

Yet it is important to remember that local ownership does not guarantee success. There is no shortage of cases where reconstruction efforts have failed to produce stability. As an example, the implementation of small government and conservative economic measures did not cause stable economic growth in East Timor but rather mass urbanization, which led to a resurgence of violence. While the idea of local ownership is highly supported in the literature, implementation that retains local autonomy while still achieving reconstruction aims and conforming to external parties' humanitarian obligations is often more difficult. In the end, trade-offs will have to be made depending on the situation and context of each case.

Role of Elites

Elites can play an important, even crucial role in post-conflict S&R. Popular leaders are highly visible symbols of the past, present, and future. Leaders act as symbolic representations of the group they represent; they are assumed to speak on behalf of the group and to represent the group's intentions and attitudes. *As such, elites and leaders have symbolic power to encourage (or enforce) acceptance of new norms of cooperation and promote reconciliation.* Turkey's Mustafa Kemal Ataturk is probably one of history's most remarkable positive examples for having created a modern nation and sense of nationality.[28]

As role models and ideologues for situations torn by conflict, leaders have the potential to dramatically affect the reconciliation process. Elite apologies for past injustices have a profound effect on healing as a collective apology from one group to another (Blatz, Schumann, and Ross, 2009). An apology or expression of empathy by the leaders of one group not only sets an example for others in the group itself, but also encourages trust and reconciliation in members of other groups via the social tendency for reciprocity. Additionally, with the power to speak with authority for the group, leaders have the power to commit group members to certain actions or behaviors, so long as they do not go so far as to alienate the group.

Conversely, situations that are characterized by high levels of insecurity, as post-conflict situations tend to be, are ripe for exploitation by ethno-nationalist politicians who would distort narratives and representations to mobilize groups along identity lines (Brubaker and Laitin, 2005). Identity politicians often create dividing lines that pair ethnic, social, or other identities with political ones, which increases competition and conflict among groups (d'Estree, 2003; Brubaker, 2009). The significance of the power-structure aspects and related exploitation of nationalism can be seen in a recent article (Wimmer and Feinstein, 2010).

Intervening third parties need to be especially mindful of the role of charismatic leaders who would use the cleavages between groups to mobilize political factions and take steps to mitigate their influence, by promoting social reconciliation and service delivery.

Conclusions

Trust and larger social capital-building processes in post-conflict situations are vital to the transition to social stability, but difficult to design and even more difficult to measure. They require long-term commitments and a finessed balance between top-down and bottom-up approaches; they can be undone by insufficient improvement(s) in the economic, political, or security arenas. The actual effectiveness of various types of interventions in the post-conflict setting is largely understudied. While much analysis has gone into understanding the tactical components of war, there has been much less rigor in approaching the tactical aspects of peace, perhaps partly due to the nontransferrable nature of reconstruction and recovery programs across space and time as well as to the relative nascence of modern, large-scale state-building efforts.

Unfortunately, there is no one-size-fits-all plan for determining what programs are appropriate or how to implement them for the best result. The success of cohesion-building interventions depends on technical implementation, program interactions, and such context-specific factors as the strength of internal and international commitments. Successful peacebuilding will depend on understanding interactions across systems and monitoring-and-feedback systems that allow adjustment of programs to meet evolving needs. Part of local ownership requires including local actors and groups and listening responsively to their counsel about needs and technical implementation.

Social reconciliation and cohesion-building programs can improve social relations in post-conflict situations, but their contribution will depend largely on resources, long-term strategy, process ownership, and the overall network of interactions of political and economic structures within the social system.

Endnotes

[1]   A large and well-established literature exists on the dynamics of conflict processes and factors that encourage cooperation over competition (Deutsch, 1958, 1973, 2000a; Lewicki and Weithoff, 2000; Hardin, 1995, Rubenstein, 2003a; d'Estree, 2003).

[2]   A longer definition is "a psychological state comprising the intention to accept vulnerability based upon positive expectations of the intentions or behavior of another," quoted in the recent review by Saunders et al. (2010, p. 10). However, in normal parlance, to trust someone does not necessarily imply a personal vulnerability. One more strongly dissenting view about definitions comes from constructionists who believe that trust should be seen strictly as a verb because it relates to continuously changing relationships for which no stable state exists (Wright and Ehnert, 2010).

[3]   Trust promotes cooperation, but cooperation then promotes future trust (Deutsch, 1973; Bloomfield, Barnes, and Huyse, 2003).

[4]   The types discussed have included, in particular, deterrence-based, competence-based, cognitive, calculus-based, knowledge-based, affective, identification-based, empathy-based, and relational trust.

[5]   Some individuals count on or appeal to the natural trusting character of people. That may be for either good or foul purposes. In post-conflict societies, however, "natural trust" is not especially conspicuous.

[6]   It would be better to refer to "limited rationality," since the judgments are affected by misperceptions, lack of information, cognitive biases, and the idiosyncrasies of

leaders who may, for example, weigh risk avoidance much more than opportunity creation, or vice versa. See also Chapter Two of this volume.

7   Such trust is enhanced when behavior on both sides is context-appropriate and consistent, stated deadlines are met, and tasks are performed and followed through as negotiated. Clear goals, expectations, timelines, and punishments for failure or defection are important. Expectations must be reasonable, and, to avoid confusion or misinterpretation, all expectations about behavior, measurement of goals, and punishment for failure need to be explicitly stated beforehand. It may even be necessary to explicitly negotiate expected behaviors. See Deutsch, 2000a, pp. 21–40, and Lewicki and Weithoff, 2000, pp. 86–107.

8   Making the distinction is both more descriptive generally and is important in discussing levels of trust and distrust simultaneously in the context of S&R. After all, a universal feature of post-conflict societies is "the pervasiveness of antagonism, mistrust, and hostility" (Kumar, 1999, p. v).

9   It is noteworthy that the elites in power after World War II were not the same, in Germany in particular, as before or during the war. If the same individuals as before are in power in a post-conflict period, there may be less likelihood of building trust and cooperation.

10   *Social reconciliation* generally refers to the healing that has to occur for former enemy groups to build healthy relationships. Kelman (2008) describes it as "changes in the ways in which former enemy populations think about each other, feel about each other, and act toward one another, as they learn to live together" (p. 16). These processes include arriving at a mutual group acceptance, healing, empathy, and discovering a common past (Bloomfield, Barnes, and Huyse, 2003; cf. Lederach, 1997). Staub and Bar-Tal (2003, p. 733) include programs designed to promote truth and justice, healing, forgiveness, and shared views of history. Kumar (1999) lays out the goals of a social reconciliation program as (1) preventing the recurrence of conflict by facilitating communication and developing peace structures, (2) reducing anger and prejudices vial reciprocal dialogue and cooperative action, and (3) establishing positive relationships among conflicting parties. Because this definition includes cooperative activities, it closely aligns with this chapter's use of the term *social reconstruction*.

11   The term *constructed* applies because the identities are often not objective realities, but rather distinctions that emerge from (i.e., are constructed from) social activities. Yes, an individual might objectively be from a particular ethnic origin, but whether and how that matters to him and other people is constructed.

12   It is said that "lessons will be smothered by the more embracing norms of his family, gang, or neighborhood" (Allport, 1954, p. 40).

13   It is not necessary that *all* members of the group change their personal attitudes to achieve a change in collective social attitudes (Axelrod, 1984: cf. Schelling, 1973). So, of course, the strength of social identities will vary; strong identities, such as

family and community identities, will exert a larger effect on personal attitudes and behaviors than weaker ones, such as nation or political party. Often the identities that matter most are those of family and friends. It follows logically that efforts to identify "pockets" in which to seed attitude changes may be most effective if they focus on points of authority, such as influential or charismatic leaders. Such cascade effects can create or exacerbate tensions (as when ethnic or nationalistic themes grow) or can improve relationships and cooperation (as, arguably, is now occurring in the United States with respect to gays in the military).

[14] David Kennedy is currently at the John Jay College of Criminal Justice. A good popular account of this program is Seabrook (2009).

[15] Remarkably, moral arguments have salience if coming from respected people.

[16] Contact theory enjoys widespread acceptance as an explanation for attitude change—the (trans)formation of prejudice and negative attitudes. It was first developed by Williams (1947) and elaborated on and expanded by Allport (1954), Cook (1978), Pettigrew (1998), Dovidio et al. (2003), Pettigrew and Tropp (2006), and others, For an overview with applications to prejudice, see Allport's seminal work (Allport, 1954). The mechanism through which contact works is simple. Contact between group members, given the right conditions, arouses cognitive dissonance in the individual (Cook, 1978), and this generates a desire to reconcile the conflict between their beliefs and their new information, in turn leading to a reassessment of the validity of the stereotype (Festinger, 1957).

[17] This refers to experiments that pass the usual tests for statistical experiments except that they lack the feature of random assignment. For example, an intervention may be made on one group while using a different but equivalent group as a control. There may be tests before and after the intervention in both cases, but statistical interpretation is more tentative than it would be if the subjects had been randomly assigned to the intervention or control group. Quasi-experimental designs are sometimes referred to as "natural experiments."

[18] Very few studies empirically test assertions or hypothesis. Notable exceptions are Mendelhoff (2009), Lie et al. (2006), Cuevas et al. (2002), and Başoğlu et al. (2005). The results from these empirical analyses are mixed. Lie et al. (2006), for example, find in favor of retributive justice, but find no support for truth-telling or peace commissions. Mendelhoff (2009) finds no support that restorative justice aids individual emotional recovery, but does not address recovery at the social level

[19] An extensive bibliography on transitional justice has been compiled by Brandon Hamber (2007).

[20] See also *The Beginner's Guide to Nation-Building*, which is heavily informed by practitioner experience and case histories (Dobbins et al., 2007, pp. 91–101). It discusses the practical benefits and perils of the implementation of several types of transitional justice, including trials and truth commissions.

[21] International war-crimes trials can be exceedingly time-consuming and costly. As an example, since 1993 the ICTY mentioned in the text has successfully prosecuted 161 individuals for war crimes, but has spent over $1.5 billion in the process (ICTY, no date).

[22] To illustrate, a quick analysis of the Uganda Survey of War Affected Youth revealed that amnesty was a major predictive factor of whether or not former abductees visited a reception center for assistance.

[23] For an excellent review on truth commissions, their effectiveness, and their historical implementation, see Avruch and Vejarano, 2001.

[24] A notable example of an effective public apology is Australian Prime Minister Kevin Rudd's apology for the Australian government's historical mistreatment of the Australian Aborigines, made in 2008. Although the apology was not accompanied by reparations, it was nevertheless very well received by Aborigines and white Australians. Even after long periods, apology can relieve tensions between groups (although not eliminate them).

[25] As examples, increased trust and social capital make economic interactions more likely. Higher levels of economic activity in turn increase incentives for entrepreneurs to form civil organizations to lobby for improved rule of law and property rights protections, which increase state legitimacy and improve the investment climate. The strength of the social contract and the power of the state to enforce the rule of law affect incentives for cooperative or conflictive behavior among individuals and groups (Jeong, 2003; Rubenstein, 2003b). Additionally, equitable and equally enforced rules and laws promote horizontal cooperation and trust by facilitating calculation-based trust. As a negative example, political corruption decreases trust in all levels of society (Mitton, 2009). Also, political structures that encourage nepotism or favoritism create disincentives to cooperation, which in turn decreases economic opportunity, which creates more competition, and so forth.

From the security perspective, trust and cooperation cannot be achieved without propitious conditions. As noted in Chapter Two, the high levels of risk or insecurity inherent in post-conflict situations impede trust and cooperation. Risky situations encourage reversion to the relative security of one's own group, increasing that group's cohesiveness but also its potential to threaten other groups (Brewer, 1999).

[26] See Chapter Three of this volume regarding the sequencing of political and social developments with elections.

[27] Several international agreements govern the treatment of people tried for crimes during periods of war: the Geneva Conventions and the two Additional Protocols, the International Declaration of Human Rights, and the International Covenant on Civil and Political Rights, to name the most relevant.

[28] The history of Turkey's emergence as a state was, however, severely marred by the tragedy that befell the Armenians. Some regard it to have been Turkish genocide; others interpret history differently, but President Obama noted the tragedy of when

"1.5 million Armenians were massacred or marched to their death in the final days of the Ottoman Empire" (Baker, 2010).

References

Ager, Alastair, A. Strang, and B. Abebe, "Conceptualising Community Development in War-Affected Populations: Illustrations from Tigray," *Community Development Journal*, Vol. 40, No. 2, 2005, pp. 158–168.

Ajdukovic, Dean, "Post-Conflict Socio-Emotional Obstacles to Reconciliation," paper presented at the Meeting of the International Congress of Psychology, Berlin, July 20–25, 2008.

Allport, Gordon W., *The Nature of Prejudice*, New York: Perseus Books, 1954.

Anckermann, Sonia, Manuel Dominguez, Norma Soto, Finn Kjaerulf, Peter Berliner, and Elizabeth Naima Mikkelsen, "Psycho-Social Support to Large Numbers of Traumatized People in Post-Conflict Societies: An Approach to Community Development in Guatemala," *Journal of Community and Applied Social Psychology*, Vol. 15, 2005, pp. 136–152.

Avruch, Kevin, and Beatriz Vejarano, "Truth and Reconciliation Commissions: A Review Essay and Annotated Bibliography," *Social Justice, Anthropology, Peace, and Human Rights*, Vol. 2, Nos. 1–2, 2001.

Axelrod, Robert, *The Evolution of Cooperation*, New York: BasicBooks, 1984.

Baker, Peter, "Obama Marks Genocide Without Using the Word," *New York Times*, April 24, 2010, p. A10.

Balliet, Daniel, "Communication and Cooperation in Social Dilemmas: A Meta-Analytic Review," *Journal of Conflict Resolution*, Vol. 20, No. 10, December 2009.

Bar-Tal, Daniel, "From Intractable Conflict Through Conflict Resolution to Reconciliation: Psychological Analysis," *Political Psychology*, Vol. 21, No. 2, 2000.

———, "Nature, Rationale, and Effectiveness for Education for Coexistence," *Journal of Social Issues*, Vol. 60, No. 2, 2004, pp. 253–271.

Bar-Tal, Daniel, and Gemma Bennik, "The Nature of Reconciliation as an Outcome and as a Process," in Yaacov Bar-Siman-Tov, ed., *From Conflict Resolution to Reconstruction*, New York: Oxford University Press, 2004.

Barth, Frederik, *Models of Social Organization*, London: Royal Anthropology Institute, 1966.

Başoğlu, Metin, Maria Livanou, Cvetana Crnobarić, Tanja Frančišković, Enra Suljić, Dijana Durić, and Melin Vranešić, "Psychiatric and Cognitive Effects of War in Former Yugoslavia: Association of Lack of Redress for Trauma and Posttraumatic Stress Reactions," *Journal of the American Medical Association*, Vol. 294, No. 5, 2005, pp. 580–590.

Bass, Gary, "Managing Amnesty," paper presented at the "Transitional Justice and Civil War Settlements" workshop in Bogotá, Colombia, October 18–19, 2005.

Bekerman, Zvi, Michalinos Zembylas, and Claire McGlynn, "Working Toward the De-Essentialization of Identity Categories in Conflict and Postconflict Societies: Israel, Cyprus, and Northern Ireland," *Comparative Education Review*, Vol. 55, No. 2, May 2009, pp. 213–234.

Blatz, Craig W., Karina Schumann, and Michael Ross, "Government Apologies for Historical Injustices," *Political Psychology*, Vol. 30, No. 2, 2009, pp. 219–241.

Bloomfield, David, Teresa Barnes, and Luc Huyse, eds., *Reconciliation After Violent Conflict: A Handbook*, Stockholm: International Institute for Democracy and Electoral Assistance, 2003.

Botes, Johannes M., "Structural Transformation," in Sandra Cheldelin, Daniel Druckman, and Larissa Fast, eds., *Conflict*, London: Continuum, 2003, pp. 269–290.

Braga, Anthony A., David M. Kennedy, Anne N. Piehl, and Elin J. Waring, "Problem-Oriented Policing, Deterrence, and Youth Violence, an Evaluation of Boston's Operation Ceasefire," *Journal of Research in Crime Delinquency*, Vol. 38, No. 3, 2001a, pp. 195–225.

———, *Reducing Gun Violence: The Boston Gun Project's Operation Ceasefire*, Washington, D.C.: National Institute of Justice, NCJ 188741, 2001b.

Brewer, Marilynn B., "The Psychology of Prejudice: Ingroup Love or Outgroup Hate?" *Journal of Social Issues*, Vol. 56, No. 3, 1999, pp. 429–444.

Brubaker, Rogers, *Nationalism Reframed: Nationhood and the National Question in the New Europe*, New York: Cambridge University Press, 1996.

———, "Ethnicity, Race, and Nationalism," *Annual Review of Sociology*, Vol. 35, 2009, pp. 21–42.

Brubaker, Rogers, and David Laitin, "Ethnic and Nationalist Violence," *Annual Review of Sociology*, Vol. 24, 2005, pp. 425–452.

Brune, Nancy, and Thomas Bossert, "Building Social Capital in Post-Conflict Communities: Evidence from Nicaragua," *Social Science and Medicine*, Vol. 68, 2009, pp. 885–893.

Burde, Dana, "Weak States, Strong Communities? Promoting Community Participation in Post-Conflict Countries," *Current Issues in Comparative Education*, Vol. 6, No. 2, 2004, pp. 73–87.

Clark, Janine Natalya, "The Three R's: Retributive Justice, Restorative Justice, and Reconciliation," *Contemporary Justice Review*, Vol. 11, No. 4, 2008, pp. 331–350.

Cobián, Rolando A., and Féliz Reátegui, *Toward Systematic Social Transformation: Truth Commissions and Development*, New York: International Center for Transitional Justice, July 2009.

Cook, Stuart W., "Interpersonal and Attitudinal Outcomes in Cooperation Interracial Groups," *Journal of Research and Development in Education*, Vol. 12, No. 1, 1978, pp. 97–113.

Cuevas, Victor E., Maria Luisa Ortiz Rojas, and Paz Rojas Baeza, *Truth Commissions: An Uncertain Path? Comparative Study of Truth Commissions in Argentina, Chile, El Salvador, Guatemala, and South Africa from the Perspective of Victims, Their Relatives, Human Rights Organisations, and Experts*, Geneva: Association for the Prevention of Torture, 2002.

Danesh, H. B., "Towards an Integrative Theory of Peace Education," *Journal of Peace Education*, Vol. 3, No. 1, March 2006, pp. 55–78.

d'Estree, Tamara P., "Dynamics," in Sandra Cheldelin, Daniel Druckman, and Larissa Fast, eds., *Conflict*, London: Continuum, 2003, pp. 68–90.

De Greiff, Pablo, *Articulating the Links Between Transitional Justice and Development; Justice and Social Integration*, New York: Research Unity, International Center for Transitional Justice, July 2009.

Deutsch, Morton, "Trust and Suspicion," *Journal of Conflict Resolution*, Vol. 2, 1958, pp. 256–279.

———, *The Resolution of Conflict: Constructive and Destructive Processes*, New Haven, Conn.: Yale University Press, 1973.

———, "Cooperation and Competition," in Morton Deutsch and James Coleman, eds., *The Handbook of Conflict Resolution*, San Francisco: Jossey-Bass, 2000a, pp. 21–40.

———, "Justice and Conflict," in Morton Deutsch and James Coleman, eds., *The Handbook of Conflict Resolution*, San Francisco: Jossey-Bass, 2000b, pp. 41–64.

Dietz, Graham, Nicole Gillespie, and Georgia T. Chao, "Unravelling the Complexities of Trust and Culture," in Mark N. K. Saunders, Denise Skinner, Graham Dietz, Nicole Gillespie, and Roy J. Lewicki, eds., *Organizational Trust: A Cultural Perspective*, New York: Cambridge University Press, 2010.

Dobbins, James, Seth G. Jones, Keith Crane, and Beth Cole DeGrasse, *The Beginner's Guide to Nation-Building*, Santa Monica, Calif.: RAND Corporation, 2007. As of April 7, 2011:
http://www.rand.org/pubs/monographs/MG557.html

Donais, Timothy, "Empowerment or Imposition? Dilemmas of Local Ownership in Post-Conflict Peacebuilding Processes," *Peace and Change*, Vol. 34, No. 1, January 2009, pp. 3–26.

Dovidio, Jack, Samuel Gaertner, and Kerry Kawakami, "Intergroup Contact: The Past Present and the Future," *Group Processes and Intergroup Relations*, Vol. 6, No. 1, 2003, pp. 5–21.

Duthie, Roger, *Building Trust and Capacity: Civil Society and Transitional Justice from a Development Perspective*, New York: International Center for Transitional Justice (ICTJ), November 2009.

Elster, Jon, *Closing the Books; Transitional Justice in Historical Perspective*, New York: Cambridge University Press, 2004.

Fearon, James D., Macartan Humphreys, and Jeremy M. Weinstein, "Can Development Aid Contribute to Social Cohesion After Civil War? Evidence from a Field Experiment in Post-Conflict Liberia," *American Economic Review*, Vol. 99, No. 2, 2009, pp. 287–291.

Festinger, Leon, *A Theory of Cognitive Dissonance*, Evanston, Ill.: Row, Peterson, 1957.

Fisher, Ronald, "Intergroup Conflict," in Morton Deutsch and James Coleman, eds., *The Handbook of Conflict Resolution*, San Francisco: Jossey-Bass, 2000, pp. 166–184.

Fukuyama, Francis, *Trust: The Social Virtues and the Creation of Prosperity*, New York: Free Press, 1995.

———, "Social Capital and Development: The Coming Agenda," *SAIS Review of International Affairs*, Vol. 22, No. 1, Winter–Spring, 2002, pp. 23–37.

Gaertner, Samuel, Marilynn Brewer, and John Dovidio, "Post-Conflict Reconstruction: A Social Psychological Analysis," in T. G. Garling, J. Backenroth-Ohsako, and B. Ekehammer, eds., *Diplomacy and Psychology: Prevention of Armed Conflicts After the Cold War*, Singapore: Marshall Cavendish Academic, 2005, pp. 275–300.

Ghani, Ashraf, and Clare Lockhart, *Fixing Failed States: A Framework for Rebuilding a Fractured World*, New York: Oxford University Press, 2008.

Gibson, James, "Truth, Justice, and Reconciliation: Judging the Fairness of Amnesty in South Africa," *American Journal of Political Science*, Vol. 46, No. 3, July 2002, pp. 540–556.

Glaeser, Edward L., David Laibson, and Bruce Sacerdote, "An Economic Approach to Social Capital," *Economic Journal*, Vol. 112, November 2002, pp. F437–F458.

Goodhand, Jonathan, and Mark Sedra, "Who Owns the Peace? Aid, Reconstruction and Peacebuilding in Afghanistan," *Disasters*, Vol. 34, No. 1, 2010, pp. S78–S102.

Gormley-Heenan, Cathy, and Roger MacGinty, "Introduction: Building and Breaking Trust," *Round Table*, Vol. 98, No. 403, August 2009, pp. 423–425.

Hamber, Brandon, "Transitional Justice Bibliography," March 2007. As of April 8, 2011:
http://www.brandonhamber.com/resources-tjbibliography.htm

Hardin, Russell, *One for All: The Logic of Group Conflict*, Princeton, N.J.: Princeton University Press, 1995.

Henderson, Willie, "Metaphors, Narrative and 'Truth': South Africa's Truth and Reconciliation Commission," *African Affairs*, Vol. 99, No. 396, 2000.

Hewstone, Miles, Jared Kenworthy, Ed Cairns, N. Tausch, J. Hughes, T. Tam, A. Voci, U. von Hecker, and C. Pinder, "Stepping Stones to Reconciliation in Northern Ireland: Intergroup Contact, Forgiveness, and Trust," in Arie Nadler, Thomas Malloy, and Jeffrey Fischer, eds., *The Social Psychology of Intergroup Reconciliation*, New York: Oxford University Press, 2008.

Hofstede, Geert, *Cultures and Organizations, Software of the Mind, Intercultural Cooperation and Its Importance for Survival*, New York: McGraw Hill, 1991.

Horowitz, Donald L., *Ethnic Groups in Conflict*, Los Angeles: University of California Press, 1985.

Howard, Ross, "An Operational Framework for Media and Peacebuilding," Vancouver, Canada: Institute for Media, Policy, and Civil Society, 2002.

———, "The Media's Role in War and Peacebuilding," paper presented at Conference on "The Role of Media in Public Scrutiny and Democratic Oversight of the Security Sector," Working Group on Civil Society of the Geneva Centre for the Democratic Control of Armed Forces, Budapest, February 6–9, 2003.

Huyse, Luc, and Mark Salter, *Transitional Justice and Reconciliation after Violent Conflict; Learning from African Experiences*, Stockholm: International Institute for Democracy and Electoral Assistance, 2008.

ICTY—*See* International Criminal Tribunal for the former Yugoslavia.

International Criminal Tribunal for the former Yugoslavia, "The Cost of Justice," no date. As of April 8, 2011:
http://www.icty.org/sid/325

Jeong, Ho-Won, "Peace-Building," in Sandra Cheldelin, Daniel Druckman, and Larissa Fast, eds., *Conflict*, London: Continuum, 2003, pp. 291–301.

Kaplan, Seth, "Fixing Fragile States," *Policy Review*, No. 152, December 2008–January 2009.

———, "Identity in Fragile States: Social Cohesion and State-Building," *Development*, Vol. 52, No. 4, December 2009, pp. 466–472.

Kelman, Herbert, "Reconciliation from a Social-Psychological Perspective," in Arie Nadler, Thomas Malloy, and Jeffrey Fischer, eds., *The Social Psychology of Intergroup Reconciliation*, New York: Oxford University Press, 2008.

Kerr, Norbert L., Jennifer Garst, Donna Lewandowski, and Susan Harris, "That Still, Small Voice: Commitment to Cooperation as an Internalized Versus a Social Norm," *Personality and Social Psychology Bulletin*, Vol. 23, 1997, pp. 1300–1311.

Knack, Stephen, and Phillip Keefer, "Does Social Capital Have an Economic Payoff? A Cross-Country Investigation," *Quarterly Journal of Economics*, November 1997, pp. 1252–1288.

Krabil, Ron, "Symbiosis: Mass Media and the Truth and Reconciliation Commission in South Africa," *Media, Culture, and Society*, Vol. 23, No. 5, 2001, pp. 567–585.

Kumar, Krishna, *Promoting Social Reconciliation in Postconflict Societies: Selected Lessons from USAID's Experience*, Washington, D.C.: U.S. Agency for International Development, January 1999.

Kuran, Timur, "Ethnic Norms and Their Transformation Through Reputational Cascades," *Journal of Legal Studies*, Vol. 27, 1998.

Laitin, David D., "National Revivals and Violence," *Archive of European Sociology*, Vol. 36, No. 1, 1995, pp. 3–43.

Lake, David A., and Donald Rothchild, "The Origins and Management of Ethnic Conflict," *International Security*, Vol. 21, No. 2, Autumn 1996, pp. 41–75.

Lederach, John Paul, *Building Peace: Sustainable Reconciliation in Divided Societies*, Washington, D.C.: U.S. Institute of Peace Press, 1997.

Levy Paluck, Elizabeth, "Reducing Intergroup Prejudice and Conflict with the Media: A Field Experiment in Rwanda," dissertation paper, Yale University, 2007.

Lewicki, Roy J., and Carolyn Wiethoff, "Trust, Trust Development, and Trust Repair," in Morton Deutsch and James Coleman, eds., *The Handbook of Conflict Resolution*, San Francisco: Jossey-Bass, 2000, pp. 86–107.

Lewicki, Roy J., Edward C. Tomlinson, and Nicole Gillespie, "Models of Interpersonal Trust Development: Theoretical Approaches, Empirical Evidence, and Future Directions," *Journal of Management*, Vol. 32, 2006, pp. 991–1022.

Lie, T. G., Helga Malmin Binningsbø, and Scott Gates, "Post-Conflict Justice and Sustainable Peace," paper presented at Polarization and Conflict Workshop, Nicosia, Cyprus, April 26–29, 2006.

Lundy, P., and Mark McGovern, "Whose Justice? Rethinking Transition Justice from the Bottom Up," *Journal of Law and Society*, Vol. 35, No. 2, May 2008, pp. 265–292.

Lynch J., and Annabel McGoldrick, *Peace Journalism*, Gloustershire, UK: Hawthorn Press, 2005.

McAllister, Daniel J., "Affect and Cognition-Based Trust as Foundations for Interpersonal Cooperation in Organizations," *Academy of Management Review*, 1998, pp. 473–490.

McGlynn, Claire, Ulrike Niens, and Miles Hewstone, "Moving Out of Conflict: The Contribution of Integrated Schools in Northern Ireland to Identity, Attitudes, Forgiveness, and Reconciliation," *Journal of Peace Education*, Vol. 1, No. 2, January 2004, pp. 147–163.

McGuire, William, "Attitudes and Attitude Change," in Lindzey Gardner and Elliot Aronson, eds., *The Handbook of Social Psychology*, 3rd ed., Vol. 2, Reading, Mass.: Addison-Wesley, 1998.

Megwalu, Amaka, and Neophytos Loizides, "Dilemmas of Justice and Reconciliation: Rwandans and the Gacaca Courts," *African Journal of International and Comparative Law*, Vol. 18, No. 1, 2010.

Mendelhoff, David, "Trauma and Vengeance: Assessing the Psychological and Emotional Effects of Post-Conflict Justice," *Human Rights Quarterly*, Vol. 31, 2009, pp. 592–623.

Mitton, Kieran, "Reconstructing Trust in Sierra Leone," *Round Table*, Vol. 98, No. 403, August 2009, pp. 461–471.

Newton, Kenneth, "Trust, Social Capital, Civil Society, and Democracy," *International Political Science Review*, Vol. 22, No. 2, April 2001, pp. 201–214.

Paffenholz, Thania, and Christopher Spurk, *Civil Society, Civic Engagement and Peacebuilding*, Washington, D.C.: World Bank, Social Development Papers, Conflict Prevention and Reconstruction, No. 36, October 2006.

————, "Civil Society and Peacebuilding," working paper, Centre on Conflict, Development and Peacebuilding, Graduate Institute of International and Development Studies, Geneva, 2009.

Park, Augustine S., "Community-Based Restorative Transitional Justice in Sierra Leone," *Contemporary Justice Review*, Vol. 13, No. 1, 2010, pp. 95–119.

Parver, Corinne, and Rebecca Wolf, "Civil Society's Involvement in Post-Conflict Peacebuilding," *International Journal of Legal Information*, Vol. 36, 2008, pp. 51–79.

Pettigrew, Thomas F., "Intergroup Contact Theory," *Annual Review of Psychology*, Vol. 49, February 1998, pp. 65–85.

Pettigrew, Thomas F., and Linda Tropp, "A Meta-Analytic Test of Intergroup Contact Theory, *Journal of Personality and Social Psychology*, Vol. 95, No. 5, May 2006, pp. 751–783.

Posner, Daniel N., "Civil Society and the Reconstruction of Failed States," in Robert Rotberg, ed., *When States Fail: Causes and Consequences*, Princeton, N.J.: Princeton University Press; Princeton, 2004.

Pouligny, Béatrice, "Civil Society and Post-Conflict Peacebuilding: Ambiguities of International Programmes Aimed at Building 'New' Societies," *Security Dialogue*, Vo. 36, No. 4, 2005, pp. 495–510.

Powell, Walter W., "Trust-Based Forms of Government," in Roderick Kramer and Tom Tyler, eds., *Trust in Organizations: Frontiers of Research and Theory*, Thousand Oaks, Calif.: Sage, 1996.

Pruitt, Dean, and Paul Olczak, "Beyond Hope: Approaches to Resolving Seemingly Intractable Conflict," in Barbara Benedict Bunker and Jeffery Rubin, eds., *Conflict, Cooperation, and Justice*, San Francisco: Jossey-Bass, 1995.

Pugh, Michael, "Post-Conflict Rehabilitation: Social and Civil Dimensions," *Online Journal of Humanitarian Assistance*, December 11, 1998.

Putnam, Robert D., "The Prosperous Community: Social Capital and Public Life," *American Prospect*, Vol. 13, Spring 1993.

———, "Bowling Alone: America's Declining Social Capital," *Journal of Democracy*, Vol. 6, No. 1, January 1995, pp. 65–78.

Rousseau, Denise R., Sim B. Sitkin, Ronald S. Burt, and Colin Camerer, "Not So Different After All: A Cross-Discipline View of Trust," *Academy of Management Review*, Vol. 23, 1998, pp. 393–404.

Rotberg, Robert I., "Truth Commissions and the Provision of Truth, Justice, and Reconciliation," in Robert Rotberg and Dennis Thompson, eds., *Truth v. Justice: The Morality of Truth Commissions*, Princeton, N.J.: Princeton University Press, 2000.

Rubenstein, Richard E., "Sources," in Sandra Cheldelin, Daniel Druckman, and Larissa Fast, eds., *Conflict*, London: Continuum, 2003a, pp. 55–67.

———, "Institutions," in Sandra Cheldelin, Daniel Druckman, and Larissa Fast, eds., *Conflict*, London: Continuum, 2003b, pp. 168–188.

Sally, David, "Conversation and Cooperation in Social Dilemmas: A Meta-Analysis of Experiments from 1958 to 1992," *Rationality and Society*, Vol. 7, 1995, pp. 58–92.

Salomon, Gavriel, "Does Peace Education Make a Difference in the Context of an Intractable Conflict?" *Peace and Conflict: Journal of Peace Psychology*, Vol. 10, No. 3, September 2004, pp. 275–274.

Saunders, Mark N. K., Denise Skinner, Graham Dietz, Nicole Gillesie, and Roy J. Lewicki, eds., *Organizational Trust: A Cultural Perspective*, New York: Cambridge University Press, 2010.

Schelling, Thomas, "Dynamic Models of Segregation," *Journal of Mathematical Sociology*, Vol. 1, 1973, pp. 143–186.

Seabrook, John, "Don't Shoot," *New Yorker*, Vol. 85, No. 18, June 22, 2009, pp. 32–41.

Sikkink, Kathryn, and Carrie Booth Walling, "The Impact of Human Rights Trial in Latin America," *Journal of Peace Research*, Vol. 44, No. 4, 2007, pp. 427–445.

Smits, Katherine, "Identity Politics Redux: Apologies for Historical Injustice and Deliberation about Race," paper presented at the annual meeting of the American Political Science Association, Philadelphia, August 27, 2003.

Staub, Ervin, and Daniel Bar-Tal, "Genocide, Mass Killing, and Intractable Conflict: Roots, Evolution, Prevention, and Reconciliation," in Davis O. Sears, Leonie Huddy, and Robert Jervis, eds., *Handbook of Political Philosophy*, New York: Oxford University Press, 2003, pp. 710–751.

Tavuchis, Nicholas, *Mea Culpa: A Sociology of Apology and Reconciliation*, Stanford, Calif.: Stanford University Press, 1991.

Ward, Michael D., John O'Loughlin, Kristin M. Bakke, and Xun Cao, "Cooperation Without Trust in Conflict-Ridden Societies: Survey Results from Bosnia and the North Caucasus," prepared for presentation at the 2006 Annual Meetings of the American Political Science Association, Philadelphia, August 31–September 3, 2006.

Weingast, Barry R., "Constructing Trust: the Politics and Economics of Ethnic and Regional Conflict," in V. Haufler, K. Soltan, and E. Ulsaner, eds., *Institutions and Social Order*, Ann Arbor: University of Michigan Press, 1998.

Whitt, Samuel L., "Institutions and Ethnic Trust: Evidence from Bosnia," *Europe-Asia Studies*, Vol. 62, No. 2, March 2010, pp. 271–292.

Widner, Jennifer, "Building Effective Trust in the Aftermath of Severe Conflict," in Robert Rotberg, ed., *When States Fail: Causes and Consequences*, Princeton, N.J.: Princeton University Press, 2004.

Williams Robin M., Jr., *The Reduction of Intergroup Tensions*, New York: Social Science Research Council, 1947.

Wilson, Stuart, "The Myth of Restorative Justice: Truth, Reconciliation, and the Ethics of Amnesty," *South African Journal of Human Rights*, Vol. 17, 2001.

Wimmer, Andreas, and Yuval Feinstein, "The Rise of the Nation-State Across the World, 1816–2001," *American Sociological Review*, Vol. 75, No. 5, 2010, pp. 764–790.

World Bank, *Engaging Civil Society Organization in Conflict-Affected and Fragile States*, Washington, D.C., 2005.

———, *Community-Driven Development in the Context of Conflict-Affected Countries: Opportunities and Challenges*, Washington, D.C., 2006.

————, "Measuring the Dimensions of Social Capital," 2011. As of April 8, 2011: http://go.worldbank.org/TC9QT67HG0

Wright, Alex, and Ina Ehnert, "Making Sense of Trust Across Cultural Contexts," in Mark N. K. Saunders, Denise Skinner, Graham Dietz, Nicole Gillespie, and Roy J. Lewicki, eds., *Organizational Trust: A Cultural Perspective*, New York: Cambridge University Press, 2010, pp. 107–126.

Zorbas, Eugenia, "Reconciliation and Post-Genocide Rwanda," *African Journal of Legal Studies*, Vol. 1, 2004, pp. 29–52.

CHAPTER SIX

Establishing Desirable Economic Conditions

Claude Berrebi and Sarah Olmstead

Introduction

This chapter discusses the economics of stabilization and reconstruction (S&R). First we suggest a generic system view of what is needed. We then discuss the differences between post-conflict and other development settings. These differences have major implications for economic objectives, goals, strategy, and metrics; what to an economist would normally be "optimal" in traditional development settings often becomes counterproductive when dealing with post-conflict settings. We then summarize what appear from the literature to be best practices for economic efforts. It is not accidental that much of the emphasis in this chapter is actually about establishing *political* conditions conducive to good economics. Ultimately, in the context of post-conflict desirable economic conditions, the primary economic challenges are political challenges.

To begin, then, Figure 6.1 is a general depiction (in the form of a factor tree)[1] of the pillars on which a healthy economy depends, as viewed by an economist. As indicated at the bottom, economic health also depends on adequate security, governance, and social considerations, which affect all of the factors in the tree itself. This factor tree could apply to either post-conflict or normal development settings, but with differences relating to the relative intensity of effort on different factors, the sequencing of those efforts, the type of aid employed, and the type of market system used. That is, the intent of Figure 6.1 is to be comprehensive, not to indicate priorities. For a given country, in a given situation, some of the branches will be much more problem-

Figure 6.1
Factors Contributing to Economic Health

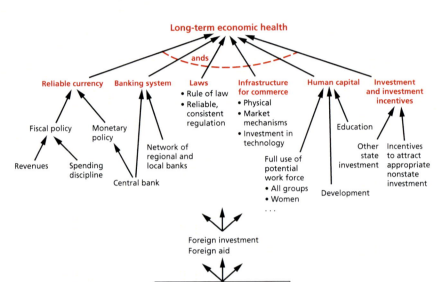

NOTE: The factors apply at a snapshot in time.

RAND *MG1119-6.1*

atic than others. Although we touch on all of the issues depicted in Figure 6.1 in what follows, we have organized the discussion around the particular issues and apparent dilemmas that arise in post-conflict situations.

Reorienting for Post-Conflict Environments

Post-Conflict Economics Versus "Business as Usual"

Generic Development Issues. Before addressing S&R, we should note that the literature reveals a heated, more general disagreement as to what developed countries can and should do for the poor of the world. Motives and practices are still being debated, but developed countries are certainly attempting, in various degrees, to help bring the poorest citizens of the world up to some minimum level of economic development. Members of the Organisation for Economic Co-operation and Development's (OECD's) Development Assistance Committee gave almost US$90 billion in economic development aid in 2008 (OECD, 2010)—a substantial sum, considering that the debate still rages as to whether aid actually helps countries, is simply wasted, or even makes countries worse (de Ree and Nillesen, 2009; Collier and Hoeffler, 2002, 2004; Fearon, Humphreys, and Weinstein, 2009; and Chapter Seven of this volume).

Economists Paul Collier and Jeffrey Sachs often argue that aid money, spent wisely, can help bring development to the poor of the world. Others, like William Easterly and Dambisa Moyo, suggest that the aid system is broken and that donor countries may actually be preventing growth in the countries they are trying to help. The debate is heated, with well-respected scholars landing on all sides of the matter. To date, there has been little empirical work that both sides can agree on, so the argument is somewhat deadlocked in the academic literature.

Part of the problem is that measuring the effects of aid is difficult. Further, organizations like the State Department and the U.S. Agency for International Development (USAID) have not traditionally set aside sufficient time and money for rigorous quantitative assessments. Recently, a parallel aid-giving organization, the Millennium Challenge Corporation (MCC), was formed by the U.S. government to try to implement aid programs in a way that is more accountable and based on empirical evidence and analysis. However, the MCC gives aid only to countries that reach a certain level of governance. Thus, it is not necessarily relevant for post-conflict settings characterized by relatively poor governance and weak institutions (see Chapter Seven).

Issues in Post-Conflict Settings. Many issues faced by developing countries are the same in normal and post-conflict circumstances, but exacerbated in the latter. There are also important differences. By most accounts, countries in post-conflict transition have roughly a 50 percent chance of reverting to war or chaos (Del Castillo, 2008; Collier, Hoeffler, and Söderbom, 2008). A basic goal of S&R, then, is to avoid relapse into conflict (see Chapters Two and Four of this volume). Beyond that, post-conflict states are "defined by inadequate human resources, weak institutions, lack of technology and industrialization, and low administrative and managerial capacity to use aid effectively" (Del Castillo, 2008). Ideally, S&R projects pave the way for economic development, but in these circumstances the challenge is enormous.

Table 6.1 lists some of the more dramatic differences between development in normal and post-conflict situations. *Economists seeking to advise in post-conflict circumstances must adjust their thinking substantially: The usual paradigms of "good economics" don't necessarily apply.* These differences are at the heart of bitter disagreements between some development economists and the World Bank and International Monetary Fund (IMF). The IMF's central policies include the desire to establish sustainable fiscal and monetary conditions and external balances, which often leads to the adoption of austerity measures. That clearly makes sense for the long term but can be the wrong prescription if the

Table 6.1
Economic Planning in Normal Versus Post-Conflict Development

Economic Planning in Normal Development	Economic Planning in Post-Conflict Circumstances
Focus is on medium- and long-term goals.	Focus must often be on short-term (potentially distortionary) emergency programs.
Choices are largely merit-based, without regard to group affiliations.	Choices must often include preferential efforts to assist groups affected by conflict and by social inclusion policies.
Foreign assistance is low and stable.	Foreign assistance spikes immediately after conflict, varying thereafter.
Government institutions establish and carry out rule of law.	Foreign troops support or possibly replace weak or nonexistent government institutions (e.g. police, army, judiciary) to promote rule of law.
International community need not involve itself in the country's politics.	International involvement in country politics is often intrusive and intense.

SOURCES: Adapted from Del Castillo (2008) and Demekas, McHugh, and Kosma (2002).

economy has completely collapsed, as in a post-conflict situation.* In the long term, such austerity measures as not printing money, cuts in public spending, high interest rates, and credit constraints are necessary to keep down inflation and decrease debt, but in the short term, intervenors in post-conflict settings must do somewhat the opposite so that people can start getting paid and money can start flowing through the system (Elbadawi and Schmidt-Hebbel, 2007; Adam, Collier, and Davies, 2008). Theory and data agree in this case. Empirically, the evidence from economists Barro and Lee (2005) implies that "a higher IMF loan-participation rate actually *reduces* economic growth" and "has small negative effects on democracy and rule of law." Even the World Bank and IMF have, in recent times (see previous footnote), shifted their stringent austerity policies in some post-conflict situations. In spite of continued disagreement over best practices in economic S&R, the field is working toward some consensus, at least, about the factors that intervenors should plan around.

Subsequent subsections deal with these special problems identified in Table 6.1; they address, respectively, economic aspects of problems related to insecurity; rule of law; corruption, poor governance, and weak institutions; foreign aid and foreign donations; macroeconomic problems; sovereignty issues; and fearing recurrence of conflict.

Insecurity

Insecurity strongly affects economic aspects of S&R. Most obviously, generalized insecurity (e.g., murders, kidnappings, rapes, the presence of landmines and unexploded ordinance) make it difficult to develop the economy beyond sustenance levels. Other security-related post-conflict problems include a lack of economic opportunity. Businesses that were closed during the war may not yet be hiring (and may be

---

* Interestingly, in Iraq, the IMF required the end of fuel-price subsidies and recommended an appreciation of the currency to tamp down inflation. Both policies had nearly immediate positive impacts and did not constitute radical austerity. The IMF also made the substantive case for immediate debt relief, which was cost-free for the Iraqis (costs were born by creditors). The IMF did not require the Iraqis to curtail the Public Distribution System, which provided a basic food basket to all Iraqis, with means testing.

damaged), while new-job creation is limited because investors and entrepreneurs are deterred.

It follows that the intervening powers, international financial institutions, and nongovernmental organizations seeking to get people back to work first need to restore the confidence of citizens, investors, and would-be builders.

Weak Rule of Law, or Bad Law

Economic development depends heavily on the so-called rule of law. To be sure, this phrase is often used so loosely as to be meaningless and is sometimes used in ways that beg the question of *whose* law rules. In the case of economic S&R, *rule of law* is used primarily as it reflects on the ability to do business. This involves not just physical security and freedom from crime but also the functioning of laws and regulations that allow for transparent and safe investment in an economy (Rose-Ackerman, 2008). Some crucial elements are

1. a clear and well-publicized legal code to which everyone is to adhere[2]
2. property rights (ideally both physical and intellectual property rights) and licensing, which must also prevent government appropriation
3. binding and enforceable legal agreements, which also requires a functioning and independent judiciary and clear rules on taxation of commercial activities and earned income (Cordesman, 2010).

Other elements include the assurance that laws will be *enforced* by the administrative and judicial systems, and sufficient checks and balances so that the systems will operate fairly.

Post-conflict conditions are often not ripe for investment—either because the institutions are too weak to engender trust or because potential investors fear recurrence of conflict and loss of their money (Hamre and Sullivan, 2002; Rose-Ackerman, 2008). A characteristic of post-conflict countries is the limited usage of banks, either because of a lack of understanding of what banks do, distrust of the banking system, or lack of banking infrastructure.

Corruption, Poor Governance, and Weak Institutions

Although institutions are fundamental to economic change and maintenance of economic equilibrium, there is little satisfying theory on the relationship between institutions and their economic effects (Chang and Evans, 2000; Acemoglu, Johnson, and Robinson, 2005; Rodrik, Subramanian, and Trebbi, 2004; Sachs, 2003). That said, it is easily observable that administrative weaknesses can lead to a dysfunctional government and dependence on foreign aid. Governments must raise money by taxing the citizenry. If they are unable to do so because of unchecked activities in the informal sectors or because they lack the infrastructure to enforce taxation, then they will be unable to be self-sufficient. This will lead either to state failure or ongoing dependence on foreign aid.

Depending on the quality of pre-conflict institutions and human capital, corruption may be high, expertise may be low, or both (Acemoglu, Johnson, and Robinson, 2003; Rose-Ackerman, 2008; Aron, 2003). Post-conflict countries may be missing a large part of their population, either due to economic migration or conflict. If large numbers of educated workers were killed or driven away—either prior to, during, or after conflict—the country may not have enough sufficiently educated people left to administer programs. This lack of human capital may make the society more dependent on foreign aid and technical assistance. However, if institutional structures of an underdeveloped country are not functioning, they may be unable to use donations effectively, cutting the potential benefits of the aid.

Institutions' ability to use aid effectively may also reflect their ability to use tax revenue effectively. There can be considerable resistance to paying taxes if it appears that the money is not being spent properly or that corrupt government officials are simply embezzling the money.[3] The poor capacity of the administrative infrastructure to extract revenue from the populace thus can lead to a cycle of aid.

Finally, weak institutions can foster corruption in the system, potentially exacerbating inequality, as the rich are generally better able to pay bribes and find their way in a corrupt system (Mauro, 2004; Rose-Ackerman, 2008). Even if the institutions are not in fact corrupt or especially corrupt, if they are not trusted by the citizenry, then they will be incapable of carrying out their missions. Anticorruption efforts must begin immediately in conjunction with other stability efforts, for there is evidence that the longer people live with corruption, the longer it takes to purge from the system (Mauro, 2004). Spending time and resources to get institutions right to begin with can save a lot of problems in the long run.

Foreign Aid and Foreign Donors

Aid takes diverse forms such as humanitarian aid, trade agreements, technical assistance, aid tied to specific projects or outcomes, and foreign financing, e.g., for credit institutions. Humanitarian assistance is necessary and important but mainly is for immediate consumption. For the most part, it does not contribute to sustainable investment and development, but it *does* buy time for other economic S&R projects to kick in. Unlike humanitarian assistance, foreign financing and technical assistance build capacity and are essential elements in post-conflict S&R programs. One of the biggest problems is the destruction of the human and physical infrastructure that occurred in conflict. Technical assistance and foreign financing can help redevelop or develop new local capacity allowing for sustainable development. Lastly, tied aid is also common. In a normal development setting, tied aid may be useful, but in a post-conflict context it often slows down and complicates reconstruction; also, it often leads to programs that the country does not need (Del Castillo, 2008).

A foreign donor can be involved in post-conflict S&R as a facilitator and coordinator or as the primary actor. In normal development scenarios, donors prefer not to implement aid programs themselves but rather to task foreign or local implementing partners (Ohiorhenuan and Stewart, 2008). So, for instance, if a foreign donor wants to support a program to foster better cooperation among farmers by developing water-user associations in Yemen, it would prefer to have local elements from the Yemeni civil society and perhaps Yemen's Ministry of Agriculture enact the actual program. The donor would then help along the way, but mainly it would just check that progress is being made in meeting the agreed-on goals. This method helps in getting program goals adopted because local workers perceive ownership, rather than having patronizing foreigners tell them what they are doing "wrong" and how they should be doing things "right." This approach may also mitigate the problem (Ghani and Lockhart, 2008) of having foreign assistance organizations outbidding the government in hiring scarce skilled staff, thereby weakening the state.

However, in cases where there is little local expertise on the ground, as is often the case in countries decimated by conflict or experiencing severe population flight, foreign-aid donors often play a more active role (see, for example, the case of East Timor in Dobbins et al., 2005). This may achieve satisfactory results in the short term, but in the long term, transition of implementation to the local administration is needed. Chapter Seven of this volume describes further details about the conditionality and effectiveness of aid, as well as the assorted uncertainties and dilemmas associated with its application (see also Roodman, 2007, for a survey of the aid-effectiveness literature).

Macroeconomic Problems

Deep macroeconomic challenges—often including high budget deficits, inflation, and debt burden—can strain even a well-functioning government. Stability and reconstruction projects must work even harder yet, however, if they must also deal with distorted economies, lack of transparency, poor governance, and corruption (Acemoglu, Johnson, and Robinson, 2003; Adam, Collier, and Davies, 2008). Nonetheless, these large-scale macroeconomic problems are initially second-order problems in that they mainly affect long-term economic growth and development, whereas rebuilding infrastructure, immediate job creation, confronting social inequities, etc., are short-to-intermediate-term necessities. Dealing with these challenges, then, requires thoughtful balancing of the short- and long-term needs.

Another immediate economic problem is the possible presence of a strong informal economy. Informal economies can be useful in employing people and allowing them to exchange goods and services. However, a thriving informal sector, or large black or gray markets, may also discourage participation in more-expensive licit transactions and investments and consequently limit economic development (Gerxhani, 2004). Additionally, since the informal economy is difficult to measure or control, it prevents the government from taxing or regulating these markets (Ohiorhenuan and Stewart, 2008).

Sovereignty Issues

Sovereignty is an issue in both underdeveloped countries and failed states, and it may challenge post-conflict S&R. Post-conflict governments may not have control over the full territory of the state, meaning both that they may not be able to provide goods and services and that they might not be able to police all areas of the country. Limited sovereignty can lead to strong criminal or terrorist networks and thriving black markets.

Sometimes, lack of sovereign control over territory is paired with a lack of control of important natural resources, which spells trouble for post-conflict governance (Collier, Hoeffler, and Söderbom, 2008). On the one hand, a government cannot afford to overextend its security services because of the risk of being unable to protect populated areas in the event of renewed insurgency. On the other hand, if the rebel insurgency during the conflict was fueled by extractive natural resources, it is important to cut off the funding for future insurgency groups by exerting firm control over those resources. Additionally, if governments have no control over the natural resources, they lose what would otherwise be related tax revenues from those resources, which also affects the extent to which they are able to fund and provide services to the nation (Easterlin, 1976; Ascher, 1999).

Control over natural resources in and of itself can be especially problematic if there is high corruption, opaque governance, or mismanagement. It is crucial that the government maintain control over access to these resources in a transparent fashion, regulate their exploitation, and use revenues derived from taxation or sales of the resources in a transparent way to further social welfare. Perceptions can be crucial, because if citizens observe that governments extract high-value commodities without providing any benefits in terms of service provision or other welfare-enhancing transfers, this can easily lead to discontent and possibly a recurrence of violence (Ascher, 1999; Sambanis, 2004).

Such state influence in managing resources is not so much to be thought of as a "socialistic" system, but one in which the government must maintain a common property regime, where "group size and behavioral rules are specified," but not an open access regime (a "free-for all") (Bromley and Cernea, 1989). As the World Bank asserts, "The establishment and strengthening of institutional arrangements can be essential for ensuring sustainable development and thus protecting the effectiveness of development investments and their stream of benefits" (Bromley and Cernea, 1989). In ensuring that resource markets are not a free-for-all, however, central and local governments must have a long-term plan for how to decrease the level of their activity in the resource market. There should be provisions set out at the beginning that dictate a schedule for opening markets and lay out some transition period from government control to a more ideal economic system for the particular cultural setting. A spectrum of possibilities exists between complete privatization and complete centralization.

Recurrence of Conflict

An overarching consideration is taking special note of the circumstances under which conflict first arose. Statistically, this is one of the most important factors in fostering economic recovery and preventing backsliding; it may also dictate the strategies that can be used to address the other challenges mentioned above. These will often be in conflict with narrowly construed economic efficiency but are necessary for the long-run success of economic reconstruction.

For instance, if the combatants in a conflict were divided by racial or religious lines, projects may need corrective inclusive policies (Fearon, Humphreys, and Weinstein, 2009). Policies that seen to benefit one group over another could lead back to conflict (Stewart, 2000; Brown, Stewart, and Langer, 2007). Projects therefore may need to ensure that beneficiaries, and local institutions implementing the programs, come from all the different combatant groups—or, alternatively, that enough separate programs exist for all groups to benefit from.

As a past example, we might consider Rwanda, which had a bloody 100-day ethnic conflict in 1994 between Hutus and Tutsi ethnic groups, leaving up to 1 million dead (mostly Tutsis and moderate Hutus). A Tutsi leader (Paul Kagame) regained control, ended the killing, and formed a government that sought to end the ethnic strife. In the name of reconciliation, a Hutu (Pasteur Bizimungu) was named President. Numerous issues arose that involved both economics and larger considerations. For example, if post-conflict banks only hired Tutsi loan officers, Hutus would have felt that the odds were stacked against them in getting a loan; that might have deterred them from applying, thereby stifling their full participation in economic reconstruction. Instead, a mix of loan officers was required. More generally, and despite expectations by some that the Tutsi-led government would adopt revenge-seeking policies, the government instead worked toward reconciliation—between Hutus and Tutsis, and also for other marginalized groups, such as women.

Pursuing the bank-loan example, economists might have balked at ensuring that Hutus and Tutsis gain equally (or perhaps proportionally) from bank loans, because such a division would not have been seen as maximizing marginal productivity. Bankers would have wanted to give loans to the technically best-qualified individuals, regardless of ethnicity. In post-conflict settings, however, such "optimal" economic policies could potentially lead to the recurrence of conflict, which is obviously not an optimal outcome, even if the policies that led there were "right" by standard economic thinking.

The post-conflict population might also need other types of distortionary aid, such as food aid or cash transfers. These types of aid, for which locals do not have to work or provide accountability, can create strong disincentives in the labor market; they would not be considered as viable options for economic development in nonemergency situations.

A Customized Approach

We have identified similarities and differences between normal and post-conflict development settings, but we need also to mention that each post-conflict setting comes with its own unique history, which affects greatly what is feasible and desirable.

Initial Conditions

Initial conditions, i.e., the reasons for the conflict and the method by which the conflict ended, can affect feasible reconstruction strategies. If the country had relatively high human capital prior to the conflict, it can be relatively easier to return to that point (Del Castillo, 2008). Some of the people will still remember a time when government was functional and what *normalcy* should mean. In that case, the focus might be physically rebuilding institutions that were destroyed, while simultaneously bringing human capital back from refugee camps or from abroad or renewing the educational processes that built that human capital in the first place. Table 6.2 lists some of the important characteristics.

Some post-conflict countries come from a level of relatively high development but also of high inequality. This is often the case in countries that are rich in natural resources—they may have high gross domestic product per capita, but the wealth and power is concentrated in the hands of a small elite. In such a case, S&R projects might want to focus on developing mechanisms for accountability, transparency, and profit sharing in the exploitation of the region's natural resources to avoid what might have been a contributor to the source of conflict in the first place. In the following paragraphs, we discuss how conflict began and ended, since those are two of the most important initial conditions, and then we discuss how initial conditions make a difference by comparing actual examples from post-conflict reconstruction projects.

How Conflict Began

The flashpoints and drivers of conflicts vary greatly depending on the setting and on who is involved in the conflict. Did one country invade

Table 6.2
Initial Conditions in Two Interventions

Condition	Somalia	Solomon Islands
Conflict Dates (from start to intervention)[a]	1991–1992	1998–2003
Population Size[b]	6,596,000	416,000
Number of deaths as a percentage of the population during conflict	6.00%	<1%
Displaced persons at intervention (per 1,000 inhabitants)[a]	126.3	0.1
Number of parties to conflict (factions and International)[c,d]	9	2
Peace treaty?[a]	No	Yes
Lack of prior experience with constitutional government?[e]	Yes	No
High levels of corruption prior to breakdown[a]	No	Yes
Proportion gross secondary school enrollment[e]	<7%	27%
Gross domestic product per capita in current US$ prior to breakdown[b]	137	1,021
Average annual assistance per capita over first two years of intervention[a]	137	181
Main donor/aid channel[a]	United States	Australia
Average gross domestic product per capita growth five years after intervention[a]	—	2.9%

[a] Dobbins et al., 2008a.
[b] United Nations, 2008.
[c] Project Ploughshares, 2007.
[d] ABC Radio Australia, 2005.
[e] World Bank, 2009.

another? Did a region attempt to secede? Did one element of society turn against the other? Was there a coup? Was there some other trigger, such as the death of a leader or other sudden event? All of these factors will affect how post-conflict reconstruction should take shape.

How a conflict began will have ramifications for which economic factors to emphasize. For instance, if a country's leader died and that instigated a violent scramble for power between two parties, it may be important to work with both parties on the economic and reconstruction plans and involve each of them in the post-conflict political process, lest the loser take on an obstructionist stance. However, as discussed in other chapters of this volume, the problems of power-sharing are severe, and some scholars argue that post-conflict prospects are best if there is a decisive victor.

How Conflict Ended

Conflicts can end in any number of ways: with one side or the other surrendering, through negotiated peace, through militarized international intervention, or through one side retreating to regroup and recover its strength in order to fight anew at some later date. The manner of a conflict's ending greatly affects both the possibilities of reconstruction and the methods that should be used. For instance, in the case of East Timor, the peacekeeping forces made specific efforts to include the pro-Indonesian groups in the pre-independence referenda and public education campaigns and in the post-independence transition activities. If there is an armed group contesting the legitimacy of the post-conflict government, this could seriously damage the progress of S&R programs and prevent citizens and businesses from wanting to invest in what might well be a short-lived peace. Thus, making sure that potential spoilers are included in the process at all stages, even if it would be easier or faster to exclude them, may be crucial to successfully transitioning to peace. As mentioned above, difficulties of this sort are absent if there was a more decisive victory.

There is suggestive evidence that if peacekeeping and aid donations start flowing too early in a conflict, the conflict might actually continue longer than it otherwise might have (Elbadawi and Sambanis, 2000). This kind of counterproductive outcome could be a matter of combatants believing that a foreign nation-builder is taking a partisan position, which may give their cause a convenient rallying point. Alternatively, it could be that the government overestimates its abilities to confront rebellions and engage in what would otherwise be deemed premature actions (such as offensive actions against a stronger or better armed foe) because they now enjoy the support of peacekeeping forces on their side (Elbadawi and Sambanis, 2000).

There are also important reasons not to let conflict continue and reach a state in which chances of a recovery process succeeding are significantly reduced. Civil war and other conflicts have far-reaching regional, and even global, effects. The longer a conflict continues, the more economic and social misery it spreads to neighboring states and elsewhere and the harder it is for the entire region to recover (Collier, 2003; Sambanis, 2004).

How a conflict ended will also likely decide what kind of government the postwar society will have. If the conflict ended by peace treaty, there may be a transitional authority that will run the country for a short time until a permanent government is elected. This could also be the point at which a country decides how much power it wants to give the central government versus regional governing authorities. These decisions will have ramifications for how intervenors should plan to work with local and national government.

Somalia and the Solomon Islands: A Comparison

To illustrate these distinctions, let us look at the examples of post-conflict reconstruction in Somalia and the Solomon Islands. The intervention efforts in both countries had similar approaches but vastly different outcomes. Somalia and the Solomon Islands saw $137 and $181, respectively, in average annual assistance per capita over the first two years of intervention operations (Dobbins et al., 2008a, p. 221). Somalia and the Solomon Islands had, respectively, 6.7 and 3.96 foreign troops and 0.01 and 0.66 police per 1,000 people at the intervention's peak (Dobbins et al., 2008a, pp. 211–212). Despite similar S&R strategies, the Solomon Islands recovered well, while Somalia is still in shambles two decades later. Part of the reason is that the countries started out from very different sets of initial conditions, but also, the Australians intervening in the Solomon Islands were able to learn from mistakes made in Somalia and elsewhere and managed to adjust their policies to achieve greater results with the same basic resources.

Somalia fell into conflict in 1991 following the overthrow of Major General Muhammad Siad Barre, and the entire country quickly fragmented into warring factions. The UN intervened in 1992 to provide humanitarian assistance and monitor a ceasefire in the capital,

Mogadishu. This initial intervention was fought by General Mohamed Farah Aideed, one of those fighting for control over Mogadishu. His forces attacked UN forces and forced the UN Security Council to send in U.S.-led troops to safeguard the humanitarian mission (Dobbins et al., 2003). This is in contrast to the case of the Solomon Islands, where the transitional Prime Minister (appointed as part of a peace treaty) officially requested that the Australians come in and help provide security to mediate in the conflict that had been going on for several years between the residents of the country's two largest islands, Guadalcanal and Malaita (Dobbins et al., 2008a). The difference in situations here points to the importance of understanding how a war has ended—whether there has been a mutually adopted peace treaty or whether some factions are ready to continue the violence.

Both countries had limited and weak institutional structures before conflict. The Solomon Islands had serious corruption problems prior to their conflict, while in Somalia it was less an issue of corruption as an absence of any functioning systems of government. The fact that the government in the Solomon Islands had not *completely* collapsed was one of the key reasons Australia agreed to get involved in the situation (Dobbins et al., 2008a). In the end, the failure in Somalia was in large part due to a failure to get the security situation under control and a peacekeeping force that was too small to take on security while simultaneously dealing with trying to build a new government. This comparison demonstrates that similar S&R efforts in different settings can and will likely yield differing outcomes.

What Can We Learn from History?

Intervenors can glean much from studying the combinations of what has and has not worked historically. Expectations must be tempered, however. Unfortunately, there is little quantitative analytical research (as distinct from higher-level observational research) regarding such reconstruction efforts in the post–Cold War period. Numerous papers look at post–World War II economic reconstruction, but that is not very relevant to today's situations. The world wars involved industrialized economies with well-educated labor forces and highly developed socioeconomic and political institutions that could be adapted to economic reconstruction. This century has most commonly seen conflicts in more pre-industrial settings. Also, analysts of post–world war reconstruction focused on the impact of economic reparations, which are not a major issue in recent post-conflict situations. Yet another shortcoming of the empirical literature as a basis for current thinking is that many of the past studies have looked at transitions from communism or socialism to democratic regimes. In recent conflicts, the issue is less one of previously closed markets as perhaps a lack of access to international markets due to poor infrastructure in existing institutions or combative international relationships.

Goals and Measurements for Economic Reconstruction

Given the many variables and challenges faced in a post-conflict reconstruction setting, it is not a simple matter to identify what goals nation-builders should realistically try to set. Most broadly, the aims should be to rehabilitate basic services and infrastructure and to lay a framework for recovery growth. This includes creating a macroeconomic agenda for the "reactivation of licit investment and sustainable and equitable growth" (Del Castillo, 2008). The second main goal, as previously stated, is to consolidate and maintain peace.

How can these broad goals be measured?[*] It is helpful to break the goals down into smaller, more-concrete goals with associated metrics. Many of these relate to creating an administrative system that is strong, transparent, and able to manage the program of economic reforms (Acemoglu, Johnson, and Robinson, 2003; Rodrik, Subramanian, and Trebbi, 2004; Sachs, 2003). The metrics should be useful, relevant, and timely to decisionmakers and credible to the public (Barton, 2008). Measures should be realistically gatherable, which is a challenge. For instance, getting accurate estimates of an informal economy can

---

[*] For some purposes, it can be argued that the key metrics for monitoring progress are relatively simple: (1) Are jobs increasing or decreasing? (2) Are prices stable or inflating? (3) Is the banking system working or failing? (4) Is corruption moderate or outrageous? (5) Are jobs and economic gains concentrated or widely dispersed? In what follows, we found it necessary to go into more depth.

be very difficult. Thus, it is often necessary to find reasonable proxies for values of interest, proxies that can be measured fairly often so that they can be used to inform potential mid-course corrections of policy (Barton, 2008). Proxies are imperfect, however, and can also be "gamed." Changes may then be necessary, which may sacrifice the flow of consistently defined data.

Ultimately, intervenors wish to know whether their efforts had a positive impact. For that, they need to collect a lot of information, particularly reliable before-and-after data, and preferably data from similar places, only some of which benefited from S&R programs (to permit a so-called quasi-experimental design). Unfortunately, it is not always possible to collect such extensive data (see also Chapter Seven of this volume).

Given that evaluation of progress is so important, intervenors should plan an evaluation strategy from the beginning of the project. To do this, researchers must decide on which metrics best capture the qualities they are trying to promote adequately and are also testable and measurable. For instance, if an international financial organization wants to support the improvement of the rule of law, it should not just count how many judges have been trained on rule-of-law issues. Instead, measures of output and outcomes should be sought, such as the number of relevant court decisions and the quality of these decisions. The U.S. State Department has developed a list of indicators for evaluating their foreign assistance programs (Department of State, 2008). Selected metrics are displayed in Table 6.3. These relate to the S&R themes discussed later in this chapter.

Providing Conditions for Economic Improvements

Economic growth depends on the strength of a country's macroeconomic foundations and administrative institutions. Intervenors will want to emphasize the creation of corresponding bodies dealing with, notably, sound fiscal and monetary policy, management of external debt, identification of needed structural reforms, trade policy, the Foreign Exchange regime, rule-based governance (including property and intellectual property rights), the development of markets, and environmental policies and regulations.

Table 6.3
Selected Indicators Developed by the State Department

Factor	Less-Specific Indicators	More-Specific Indicators
Security and maintaining peace	Number of public information campaigns completed by USG programs Number of municipalities strengthened by USG programs Number of monitors deployed with USG assistance Number of communities in USG-assisted areas using community policing methods Number of nongovernmental constituencies built or strengthened with USG assistance	Percentage of illicit small arms and light weapons in circulation or at risk of circulation addressed by USG programs Square kilometers of de-mined land returned to productive use with USG assistance Increased sales of licit farm and nonfarm products in USG-assisted areas over previous year Hectares of drug crops under cultivation in USG-assisted areas
Governance and rule of law	Improved rule of law and individual rights Number of judges trained with USG assistance Number of consensus-building processes assisted by USG Number of government officials receiving USG-supported anti-corruption training Constitution incorporating fundamental freedoms drafted with USG assistance	Number of policies that have been influenced by civil society organizations Mean case disposition time in courts assisted by USG in the area of case management Number of positive modifications to enabling legislation/regulation for civil society accomplished with USG assistance Number of prosecutions and ratio of convictions to prosecutions for corruption-related crimes
Public sector and social assistance	Public expenditure on health Number of social protection policy reforms drafted, adopted, or implemented with USG support Number of nationwide poverty/vulnerability mapping efforts being supported	Cumulative number of HIV-positive individuals treated with USG assistance Net enrollment rate for primary, secondary, and tertiary Percentage of war victims, poor, and vulnerable people receiving targeted social assistance or services

Table 6.3—Continued

Factor	Less-Specific Indicators	More-Specific Indicators
Economic recovery and growth	Regulatory Quality Index	Cost of starting a business
	Land Rights and Access Index	Days to start a business
	Growth in per capita income	Share of women in wage employment in nonagricultural sector
	Infrastructure investment as percentage of GDP	
	Percentage change in per capita food production index	Number of days necessary to comply with all procedures required to import/export goods
	Percentage change in growth in agriculture value added	Credit to the private sector as a percentage of GDP
	Number of analysts trained in off-site surveillance with USG assistance	Value of the USG-supported special funds loans issued this year

SOURCE: Adapted from Department of State, 2008.

NOTE: USG = U.S. government; GDP = gross domestic product.

Two types of measurement metrics are possible in this case—measurements of the institutions built and measurements of the outcomes of their policies:

1. *Measurements of Institutions.* The first set of measurements addresses whether the appropriate institutions are in place and functioning; for example, are they transparent, do they have actual decisionmaking authority or are they beholden to political powers, and are checks and balances in place?

2. *Measurement of Outcomes.* The second set of questions relates to actual economic changes, such as the rate of growth of GDP, poverty and inequality, distributional considerations (across regions, factions, ethnic groups, etc.), estimated activity in licit and illicit markets, food and commodity prices, exchange rates, foreign investment, investment in human capital (education, health), and other common measures of economic health.

The measurements of institutional quality are often a mix of perception-based indicators (control of corruption, regulatory quality, transparency and rule of law from the World Bank's World Development Indicators, Transparency International, and other NGOs) and theoretical assessment of the legal architecture (Are there assurances in the constitution that give institutions power? Are there clear checks and balances?) (Kaufmann and Kraay, 2002; Rodrik, Subramanian, and Trebbi, 2004). The reality of whether institutions are functioning properly is more difficult. One can measure whether people are being tried and convicted on corruption charges, or the length of time it takes to apply for a business license, but these measurements may be more time-consuming and costly than gathering opinions or noting the existence of policies (whether or not they are actually enforced) (North, 1990).

The second set of indicators may require special effort by the intervenor to get thorough and reliable data. For instance, while prices, exchange rates, and other measures may be readily observable, other measures are not so (black/gray market activity, measures of equality, etc.). Furthermore, some of the measures that are typically used, like GDP growth rate or poverty, are troublesome. Observing simple GDP growth rates, for instance, may obscure distributional issues or temporary distortions due to the influx of foreign funds (Citro and Michael, 1996; Deaton, 2005; Firebaugh, 2006). Also, several measures of poverty exist, with different usefulness. For example, the percentage of the population earning less than $2 a day in purchasing power parity (PPP) may be less explanatory than measures of consumption, which may better measure participation in informal markets (Citro and Michael, 1996; Elbadawi, 1999; Deaton, 2005; Firebaugh, 2006).

The following subsections discuss generating employment, tackling horizontal inequities, and public-sector management in more detail.

Generating Employment

Restoring economic health will help with employment generation, but special steps may need to be taken to achieve sufficient job creation and other economic opportunities, especially for youth and especially in the short term. Employment opportunities can also give displaced people a reason to return to their homes and give people who were considering criminality a viable alternative. Depending on the level of infrastructural damage, it may take a while for businesses to return to full capacity. Some temporary work may be generated directly by the renovation efforts—roads and buildings will need to be rebuilt in the short run—but if these short-term hires do not see better, longer-term job prospects coming down the road, resentment and unhappiness may build. It is therefore especially important to focus on high-risk groups, such as young men, ex-militants, and disaffected or traditionally marginalized social groups, such as ethnic minorities or women.

Incomes have been shown to correlate negatively with conflict, which has been interpreted to mean that those with higher incomes have higher opportunity costs if they stay out of the licit economic system and rather engage in rebel movements (Collier and Hoeffler, 2002). This theory represents the traditional economic approach, though in the face of some empirical data that show that high incomes are sometimes positively correlated with militant activity, the idea is still being debated (Easterlin, 1995, 2001; Berrebi, 2007). However, even if incomes are not directly correlated with conflict, it is still necessary to generate good employment outcomes to achieve economic stability and well-being.

One of the serious threats to security, especially after a conflict, is disparity between expectations and reality. If the conflict or post-conflict period started off with promises of a bright new future and that is not what transpires, frustration could easily build. This kind of disparity often contributes to the outbreak of war to begin with (Easterlin, 1976)—when people are overeducated relative to existing market opportunities or have been told that there would be great economic opportunities waiting for them after school, and they find a different reality. This is especially troublesome with youth (Cincotta, Engelman, and Anastasion, 2003).

There is some dispute, however, over how much unemployment levels influence conflict. Berman, Felter, and Shapiro (2009) assert the surprising result that "high unemployment is associated with a difficult operating environment for insurgents, either because unemployment is an inadvertent side-effect of effective security pressure (greater state security precautions might restrict travel and thus increase unemployment), or because the price of information about insurgent activity is lower in a depressed economy" (it could be that, when unemployment rises, the price of leaking information to the authorities declines). They find evidence that when unemployment is high, insurgents switch to tactics that are less directly targeted at international forces.

Whether or not unemployment is directly related to higher levels of conflict, it is certainly a crucial indicator of the health of an economy. Where possible, immediate, low-skill work should be created that would, at minimum, contribute to other reconstruction projects, such as rebuilding infrastructure. Those involved in S&R should make sure, however, to minimize the distortion of the job market. In East Timor, the UN peacekeeping mission was responsible for 12–20 percent of all formal employment, and wages were out of keeping with local standards (that is, those working for the UN were paid significantly higher rates than those employed in the locally supported economy) (U.S. Joint Forces Command, 2009). Such an overactive role may be avoided if intervenors work through local partners. Prior to launching S&R operations, it is necessary to assess the country's levels of human capital and the state of its physical infrastructure, level of functioning domestic enterprise, the population's entrepreneurial abilities, the availability of raw materials, accessibility to markets, and other business-related factors, all of which will determine the best approach strategy of how to develop long-term employment growth.

Measuring job creation can be done effectively to the extent that most jobs are in the formal sector, but if there is significant informal labor force, more effort will be needed and estimates will remain only approximate. Additionally, if there is a large diaspora population, households could be relying heavily on remittances from family members abroad, which could confound implication of the unemployment figures.

Tackling Horizontal Inequalities (Distributional Issues)

Horizontal inequalities are systematic inequalities that tend to fall along ethnic, religious, or geographic lines. Frances Stewart has argued that because people of similar groups tend to clump geographically, regional data can often be a proxy for other differences, such as ethnicity and religion (Stewart, 2000; Brown, Stewart, and Langer, 2007). In supporting recovery, external assistance should seek to reduce tension points, such as group-based inequality. To do this, those involved with S&R operations, with the help of local knowledge, must assess the extent and nature of inequalities and adopt appropriate policies to address them. Inequalities can be addressed through indirect policies (building infrastructure in underserved areas, for instance) or through progressive taxation and expenditure that favor the poor (Ohiorhenuan and Stewart, 2008).

Other socially inclusive policies might include special programs for poverty monitoring and analysis or "pro-poor" programs. These also might include rebuilding the social safety net. Collier and Hoeffler have found evidence that "the post-conflict society should pay more attention to improvements in social policy and less attention to improvements in macro policy" (2004, p. 11). One of the policies that could foster social inclusion is using aid to subsidize domestic enterprise, particularly to hire and train particular target groups, and provide investment through micro- and small-size lending. This type of policy can spur job growth and give natives a stake in the economic outcomes of the country (Del Castillo, 2008). It also builds on local knowledge of domestic needs and supports entrepreneurial creativity, which can be a very valuable tool for engaging natives in the reconstruction process.

Agricultural subsidies and special "reconstruction" or "free-trade" zones that target the production of exports could be another way to improve social inclusion. Agricultural subsidies can help lower food prices, which are a significant indicator of quality of life, and the dual strategy of agricultural and industrial support helps support people in all parts of the economy (one should, however, evaluate carefully the distortionary losses caused by subsidies against potential welfare gains in each case separately). Economic growth and S&R does not guarantee social inclusion, but policies that provide access to economic opportunities for all parts of society will help in tackling horizontal inequalities and contribute to stability.

Public-Sector Management

If a post-conflict country has lost significant infrastructure and specific local institutional "know-how," this can have serious repercussions for its ability to provide basic services to people. Public-sector management issues include the efficiency and equity of public expenditures, revenue collecting, the accountability of public services, and the managing of natural resources and distributing related revenues in a transparent and equitable way. Equitable sharing of resources, natural and economic, is very important in a post-conflict zone, especially if there was a class, race, religious, or other sectarian rivalry that contributed to the violence (Brinkerhoff, 2005; Brown, Stewart, and Langer, 2007). Measures and metrics associated with public-sector management again should relate to transparency of institutions, particularly the ones taxing residents and deciding how to spend that money (Rodrik, 2000, 2004; Rose-Ackerman, 2008).

Proper public-sector management is a longer-term end and is extremely important for a sustainable pattern of growth. When the foreign assistance fades away, post-conflict countries must be left with a functional apparatus that allows the state to collect revenue and spend it on its citizens (Rodrik, 2003). However, metrics used in measuring the effectiveness and progress of new infrastructure should not be content with simply measuring the number or size of projects that allows for delivering of public services (roads, utilities, etc.), but rather must also include the context in which each project was built and other less tangible characteristics, such as where it was built, which communities it serves, etc.

Other Post-Conflict Development Issues

As discussed throughout this volume, economic reconstruction does not occur in a vacuum; it is one element of S&R. The literature makes it clear that several interconnected facets need to be taken into account when undertaking S&R projects, including security, politics, prior planning, timing, coordination, and foreign aid. All of these work together and interact, and if one element is lacking in the overall S&R plan, it can jeopardize the rest. We discuss this briefly in what follows.

Security First

As mentioned previously, security is one of the most important first steps to building economic recovery. If people are afraid to go out on the street and get to work, then all other recovery measures are unlikely to succeed. Of course, the economic situation will also have feedback effects on the level of security in a post-conflict country. Economic reconstruction projects can contribute to resolving conflicts by giving people some desirable end to act toward, an end that frequently requires and enables cooperation across social groups (Stewart, 2002). However, it is important that foreign peacekeepers understand what is possible in terms of security. The process by which stable states form is a slow one. Foreign donors should not be under the impression that they can quickly or easily enforce security regardless of traditional culture and other societal variables (Krause and Jutersonke, 2005). In the end, building trust and cooperation is what improves security, and the trust-building process is naturally a long one.

How security relates to S&R programs is the subject of Chapter Two of this volume.

Keep Politics in Mind

If the political agreement and economic program are not integrated, the country risks plunging back into conflict. There are several factors that influence this relationship. First is that the government receiving the aid must feel engaged in the process of using that aid and developing the reconstruction plans. If domestic political partners are not on board with the reconstruction agenda, then they are not likely to get much support anywhere in the rest of the country. The situation may become politically sensitive if it is perceived that there is a foreign body moving autonomously within a country, enacting policies and building infrastructure, etc. Without political support, S&R programs can be undermined or dismissed by the local stakeholders from which support is necessary (Barton, 2008). It is essential for foreign actors to assess the political state of the post-conflict country and work with local leaders to determine the types of reconstruction efforts that are politically viable (Pouligny, 2000; Rose-Ackerman, 2008).

The political aspect of S&R programs is the subject of Chapter Three of this volume.

Timing and Prior Planning

There is a tension between, on the one hand, planning S&R programs out thoroughly before initiating a strategy that might not be appropriate, and, on the other hand, establishing a reconstruction presence early on in the process. The literature debates the most appropriate and effective point at which S&R projects should be implemented in a conflict timeline. Should donors wait until the fighting has completely stopped to begin economic recovery programs, or can these operations work even before every last bit of insurgency is quelled? The evidence is not clear on this matter, and often donor governments feel that they cannot wait too long to intervene, if only due to humanitarian concerns. However, Elbadawi and Sambanis (2000) have found macroeconomic evidence that interventions too early in a conflict can actually prolong it.

The timing and level of prior planning is also related to the magnitude of the reconstruction efforts. Comprehensive reforms require longer planning, but there is theoretical evidence that suggests that gradual reforms are less likely to work than ambitious, comprehensive reforms (Mauro, 2004). The idea is that when reforms are gradual, individuals in the post-conflict society have more time to grow accustomed to the "bad" way of doing things.

Some actions must be taken immediately before economic reconstruction can occur. First, humanitarian crises must be addressed; additionally, policymakers must focus immediately on such problems as job creation, infrastructure-rebuilding, and institution-building. These are first-order issues that are essential for S&R and to avoid the loss of whatever political and social stability may still be present after the conflict concludes. Also, some S&R projects must be undertaken quickly to take advantage of the spike in donor aid that usually accompanies the end of a war; there may be only a short window of opportunity for these kinds of aid and structural changes to work (Demekas, McHugh, and Kosma, 2002; Collier and Hoeffler, 2004; see also Figure 6.2).

Figure 6.2
Levels of Development Aid Over Time

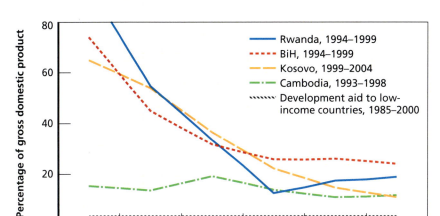

SOURCE: International Bank for Reconstruction and Development/The World Bank
(Demekas, McHugh, and Kosma, 2002). Used with permission.
NOTE: BiH = Bosnia and Herzegovina.
RAND *MG1119-6.2*

While these short-term projects are being implemented, the foreign intervenors can take the opportunity to think and carefully plan
the mid- and long-term strategies. These plans must take into account
the specific conflict's context, including the needs of the country as
well as their capacity to enact reforms and S&R strategies. It is crucial
in the planning phase to identify the critical factors that need to be
addressed in light of the particular circumstances (Ohiorhenuan and
Stewart, 2008).

In the longer term, those implementing S&R projects must also
help develop the strong microeconomic foundations that will continue
the growth into the future. This second-order work should include
the development of "legal and institutional frameworks, a functioning financial sector and an effective public sector to create an adequate
business climate, and promote policies to alleviate poverty and support
human development" (Del Castillo, 2008).

Coordination

Coordination of activities with all relevant actors—all the institutions of government, civil society, the UN, international financial institutions, other foreign actors, etc.—is critical to the success of S&R efforts. Institutions in many countries, from developed to post-conflict, suffer from ill effects of compartmentalization, both between and within institutions. Within aid-giving agencies, as well, compartmentalization has been a perennial problem. Even though many agencies have made statements and commitments to promoting "harmonization and alignment" of activities and priorities, little has come of it (Burke, 2008). One approach the international community has taken to combat this problem is to introduce the idea of a multidonor trust fund (MDTF), in which all donors contribute money to a single fund that is then centrally distributed to make sure that each agency is not working at odds or reinventing the wheel (though critics also suggest that MDTFs may charge excessive overhead and prioritize their own projects rather than local initiatives) (Ohiorhenuan and Stewart, 2008, p. 91).

If communication and coordination is lacking, those involved in S&R programs cannot know what kind of capacity exists to carry out their agenda. Even worse, it could be that activities are not only poorly coordinated or duplicated but actually contradict each other. One practitioner gave an example in an interview: "You might have a situation where the UN is trying to build capacity of a local government by setting up a trust fund to pay civil servants' salaries, and at the same time the government is under fiscal austerity measures from the IMF" (Herrhausen, 2007, p. 34). Such inconsistencies erode both the credibility and the effectiveness of reconstruction activities. Further, if there is poor coordination, implementers are forced to be reactive rather than proactive—they are left cleaning up messes rather than planning successful operations. There are three basic groups of actors among which the intervenor must coordinate: state institutions, civil society, and other aid donors.

First and foremost, there must be coordination between those involved in S&R programs and all the state governmental institutions. Intervenors should make sure not just that there is transparency between themselves and the government, but that all the governmental ministries are also transparent and cooperative with each other. Next, there needs to be coordination between those involved in S&R programs and civil society. In an inclusive government, civil society should serve a great role in implementing policies, training locals, and garnering support for reconstruction initiatives (Herrhausen, 2007). Finally, there needs to be coordination and cooperation among aid donors. Part of the challenge here is that aid agencies themselves may be very compartmentalized, leaving very little room for them to coordinate with other groups. Additionally, there may be some level of proprietary feeling over activities that makes actors less willing to cooperate and coordinate; good planning should make sure to put these aside and enforce cooperation.

Foreign Aid

As discussed earlier, the utility of foreign aid has been debated extensively, with no clear conclusions. That debate has occurred mostly in the context of normal development situations, rather than specifically about post-conflict settings. However, aid may contribute to the recurrence of violence, and, if post-conflict countries are not supported in their initial transition phases, resources and investments can be lost and conflict perpetuated. Post-conflict countries will likely also need some kind of aid, both in the short and longer term, for S&R operations to be successful.

For more on foreign aid and its use in S&R programs, see Chapter Seven of this volume.

Best Practices

General

The transition to peace from a post-conflict setting is a difficult path with many pitfalls. Economic development is difficult enough; in an insecure and potentially unstable setting, it is even more difficult. To make the process of planning economic S&R programs more simple, we have gathered below a set of best practices from the literature. When considering these practices, planners still need to take into account the individual circumstances of the target country, such as the origins and ending of the conflict, amount of conflict damage, and resources and capacities. Keeping these caveats in mind, we lay out the basic rules of thumb for economic reconstruction below.

Three overarching themes to keep in mind in this are the need for

1. realistic expectations
2. clear measures of success (including simple measures sometimes referred to as metrics)
3. simplicity and flexibility.

Expectations are a problem. Too often, those involved in stability and reconstruction programs have unreasonable expectations about what is possible—or, at least, about how quickly progress can be made. If nominal expectations are set too high, then "failures" will occur, undercutting political support for continued efforts that are, in fact, paying off (Barton, 2008). Given objectives and expectations, the measures employed may or may not be the same as those in a normal development setting. One reason has been described as follows:

> Even the phrase "state building" is grandiose. A more realistic description would be "jump starting"—helping a people, society and government to get going. Foolish overstatements of grand objectives and temporary improvements breed "gotcha" news stories and investigations. What must be established is a "get it started and establish responsible local ownership" attitude. (Barton, 2008)

The goals and objectives might reflect purely declaratory expectations of success, but once these goals are declared publicly, they become the actual expectations of the people at the receiving end of the aid, whether or not those goals are actually achievable. This is not to suggest that expectations should be set so low as to always be obtainable—but it might point to the benefit of having a range of goals from minimum acceptable objectives to optimal outcomes. Additionally, it is here where having good and comprehensive data matters. Even if the outcomes do not appear to be successful on their own, it is always important to look at them in the context of the outcomes in similar places that did not benefit from S&R projects.

The need for "simplicity" is often mentioned, almost as a cliché. We have in mind that strategy should not have too many components and, certainly, should not be sensitive to intricate interconnections and subordinate controls. "Moving in the right direction" along several lines of effort, and "doing essential coordination" conveys the idea. Imagining complex orchestration, as might be common in a modern commercial setting, is the opposite. Simplicity has other virtues as well, of course: It can improve transparency and increase buy-in and support by local stakeholders.

Finally, plans need to be flexible, especially if it becomes clear that components or the entirety of ongoing plans are not working. That is, it is important to plan for adaptation because it will usually be necessary. Measures to identify failure and enable smooth changes of course need to be planned and agreed on in advance. Although planners will never be able to foresee all possible outcomes, it is important to recognize warning signs along the way that would signal the need for a change of course. To the extent that plans are simple, they will also be easier to change along the way.

Role of International Organizations Versus Role of the State

We have discussed extensively the need for international intervenors to interact with the state and other organizations, but it is useful to lay out the best-practices role of each of these actors in a post-conflict setting.

Role of the United Nations, Nongovernmental Organizations, and International Financial Institutions. Ideally, the role of the UN, international financial institutions, and other aid donors would be to supervise while the post-crisis governmental institutions implement the actual reconstruction projects. This "backseat" approach is easiest to implement in cases where the necessary infrastructure and human capital existed before the conflict and institutional knowledge has not been completely destroyed in the conflict. International organizations must, wherever feasible, work with the state to develop plans for S&R operations, ensuring that the state is involved and has a clear say on whether a plan makes sense given the context. The state will likely have better knowledge of the situation on the ground, including possible pit-falls, than will foreign planners (Del Castillo, 2008; Ohiorhenuan and Stewart, 2008). Further, to the extent that the government is associated with operations that are providing jobs and accomplishing something, it strengthens the state itself. Although that might seem obvious, it is in practice all too easy for outsiders to plunge into S&R projects inde-pendently, which undercuts the political aspects of S&R.

Some S&R missions reflect an alternative, more intrusive role for international agencies than has previously been common. In partic-ular, the United Nations Transitional Administration in East Timor (UNTAET) and the United Nations Interim Administration Mission in Kosovo (UNMIK) assumed some or all of the sovereign powers during their operations. While these worked out in the end (for the most part) in terms of a sustained peace and stability, they had other drawbacks. For instance, Kosovo, which experienced $577 annual assistance per capita over the first two years of operations (Dobbins et al., 2005), is still heavily dependent on international aid, in part because it grew accustomed to the role of the international agency as dominant.

East Timor, which saw $240 in annual assistance per capita over the first two years of operations (Dobbins et al., 2008b), did relatively well after the UN intervention, aside from some renewed riots in 2002 and 2003. While it is best to minimize the role of international inter-venors to avoid later dependencies, it may not be possible to cut them out completely. For instance, upon the independence vote in East Timor, 8,000 Indonesian civil servants promptly left the country, leav-ing a vacuum in the civil administration that the UN was forced to fill (Dobbins et al., 2005). In situations like this, there may be no escaping a heavy role for the intervenor.

To the extent feasible, then, the UN system, nongovernmental organizations, and other international financial institutions should take on the role of facilitating, coordinating, and monitoring the inter-national community's technical and financial support (Del Castillo, 2008). The greatest help to a transitioning power is in training the civil servants and politicians who will run the social services, banks, and other governmental institutions after the international forces leave.

Additionally, intervenors should monitor the use of aid money and help resolve and overcome barriers that prevent the money from going where and doing what it should.

Another tool gaining popularity in helping donors coordinate their activities are multidonor trust funds, which (despite criticisms mentioned earlier) allow all donors to a certain region to compile their money and use the common fund to support needed programs. This allows money to flow where and when it is most needed and prevents some of the problems of coordination mentioned earlier (Ohiorhenuan and Stewart, 2008).

Role of the Post-Conflict State and Local Government. Perhaps the first and primary role of the state in the post-conflict period is to establish security and to promote the rule of law (although this may depend on substantial assistance for intervening forces). The challenge of establishing security is described in Chapter Two of this volume. Here, let it suffice for us to mention that some combination of state and local governments are in the best position to assume the role of protector and that doing so bolsters citizens' trust of the government and its intentions.

Turning now to the state's role in economic matters, even if the post-conflict state is largely nonfunctional in terms of human and physical capital, it may be either taking the lead or preparing to take the lead in implementing S&R programs with the help of outside intervenors. If unable to take complete control, it should at least take ownership of the programs in name and participate to the extent possible. The state (to include *local* government!) should play a large part in determining what is or is not appropriate to the particular post-conflict setting and should express this to donors. By implementing local knowledge, S&R programs gain acceptance by the beneficiaries and are less likely to make culturally based mistakes.

Employing inclusionary processes should not be limited to the make-up of the security forces. The state should seek to work with all parties of the prior conflict. This includes the establishment of a "social contract" that clearly lays out "the reciprocation between the state's provision of security, justice and economic opportunity and citizens' acceptance of the authority of the state" (Ohiorhenuan and Stewart,

2008). This contract, as well as all policies that the government adopts, should be laid out in plain language and presented publicly. The state might want to invite civil-society partners to help disseminate this information to the public through education campaigns.

Another essential component of a state's role in reconstruction is to build its core capacities. The state should focus on providing the basic needs and necessities of the public, which include having an effective and responsive civil service. A strong civil service bureaucracy is what will allow the state to continue its functions seamlessly as leaders change and as intervenors pull their experts out (Elbadawi, 2008). The civil service, as the name implies, exists to serve the civilian population, and the public should perceive that it deserves its name: The public should see that it is getting the services from their government that justify the associated taxation, which is economically essential. The civilian population, then, needs to understand what the government does with the people's tax dollars, why and how it is doing it, and how the people are benefiting (Aron, 2003). This openness and transparency of the government and willingness to involve the public can produce the "peace dividend" required to maintain stability (Collier, 2000). If the state is not seen to be acting in the best interest of the people, they may be less inclined to join the formal economy and support the rebuilding of the post-conflict state.

Finally, the state should work toward building economic opportunities by establishing clear and stable property rights, strengthening opportunities for lending and borrowing, and controlling corruption, all of which are basic requirements for economic activity to evolve in any given setting, and even more so in post-conflict environments.

Basic Institutional Framework

Functions. It is crucial to the long-term health of the post-conflict nation—or, indeed, any nation—to build a solid institutional framework that can carry on functioning as time passes and leaders change.

For this to happen, there needs to be solid physical infrastructure and physical security as well as a good supply of human capital, financial resources, and an institutional network that covers the country. It is through these assets that goods and services can be distributed and revenue can be collected, and these activities are crucial both for near-term recovery and long-term sustainability.

A step in building this framework can be massive public-works projects* that build on what is left of a country's infrastructure. If communities within a country are physically or otherwise disconnected, it is very difficult to support domestic markets, provide services to those who are farther afield, and collect revenues from the entire territory. A lack of infrastructure and services also has political implications, as it casts doubt on the level of governance and sovereignty over a country's entire area. Additionally, conflicts could emerge where some communities are isolated and neglected. Such was the case in Darfur, where the Sudan Liberation Army and Justice and Equality Movement's rebels began attacking government military and police outposts in the remote western Sudan. Their officially stated reason was that the central government was not providing for the region's well-being (Reuters, 2010). That conflict displaced hundreds of thousands of civilians, causing numerous deaths and deteriorating health conditions along the way and in refugee camps in neighboring Chad.

Building infrastructure that reaches all parts of a country is not easy, especially where some countries have vast deserts or densely forested jungles. Nevertheless, the central government must find a way to serve all of these areas. When the government does not have control over an area, parallel mechanisms arise to provide the most essential goods and services that the government is meant to provide. This undermines a government's legitimacy, and so reliance on such parallel mechanisms should be avoided in the mid to long term, although during the period in which the government is building capacity from

---

* These should usually be left to the international financial institutions mentioned earlier and accomplished with loans rather than, e.g., bilateral U.S. grant aid (exceptions may be necessary for roads). They should include provisions for maintenance.

a low base, it may have no choice but to rely on parallel mechanisms (Ohiorhenuan and Stewart, 2008).

It is important to address early on the mechanisms by which the state will operate in a post-conflict situation. This could include designing a system from scratch or drawing on prewar structures and practices, provided that they were not overly problematic or the cause for the conflict in the first place (Ohiorhenuan and Stewart, 2008). As discussed in Chapter Three, a country will want to plan what kind of government it will have (presidential, parliamentary, or other) and then what cabinet ministries it will need (Security, Foreign Relations, Economy, Finance, etc.). It is critical to plan how these ministries will interact with each other and how and whether they will be a part of the post-conflict S&R projects. One idea, for example, is to have a temporary cabinet ministry that deals solely with reconstruction (Del Castillo, 2008). This could allow for a single point of contact between the donors and the government, which would handle aid coordination and communication, limiting potential duplication of effort and preventing aid projects from working at cross purposes to one another. All effort should be made to ensure that ease of knowledge transfer among these different agencies or ministries is smooth and transparent, both to people within the system and to the public (Rodrik, Subramanian, and Trebbi, 2004; Rose-Ackerman, 2008). The planning and training stage is the point at which it would be optimal to avoid potential compartmentalization, as discussed earlier.

Once the state framework is developed, human capital is needed to organize and direct the institutions of the state. Again, if the necessary educated workforce that existed prior to the conflict survived and has not fled the country, it will be faster to ramp up to full capacity. However, if the remaining available human capital is too low, the next step the state must take is to build an educated civil service that can run the day-to-day operations in the ministries. Building this kind of competent workforce will be time-consuming, and this is exactly where technical assistance and training would be a very appropriate form of aid.

Macroeconomic Policymaking

In a chapter on economic issues, the most basic question to ask early in a post-conflict situation is, How should the state be involved in the economy? Post-conflict markets are generally not going to be efficient markets; it takes time for markets to reach an equilibrium, and, as discussed earlier, distortionary measures may be unavoidable (those for jump-starting). Thus the question remains, To what extent should a government interfere with the markets? For instance, to what extent should the government privatize or liberalize for the sake of economic efficiency? This should be decided by the state, while considering recommendations from the international community and the national context and taking into account the situation prior to the conflict.

Whatever the state decides, the first step is to establish solid rule-of-law policies so that any regulation can be enforceable (Del Castillo, 2008). If regulation is not in place, liberalization or privatization has the possibility of going very wrong. The rule of law, as discussed earlier, should be interpreted to mean the presence of sound and enforceable contract law and acceptance by the state of long-term international obligations that transcend leadership, in addition to achieving security and having the bulk of the economy follow legitimate paths rather than those of the black market or crime. Unless the government can show that it has control over the economy and that investors will be able to enter into contracts knowing that their rights will be upheld, then economic S&R cannot succeed (Hamre and Sullivan, 2002; Rose-Ackerman, 2008).

The most important institution that will deal with macroeconomic policymaking is the central bank. Such a bank's role includes the following (see, among many others, Addison, Le Billon, and Murshed, 2001; Clarida, Galí, and Gertler, 2000; Ohiorhenuan and Stewart, 2008):

1. establishing a currency
2. protecting the integrity of that currency
3. rebuilding the domestic financial and banking sector to permit and protect investments

4. helping to ensure sustainable systems of intermediation to distribute money from lenders to borrowers.

These activities are central to economic recovery and a vital role of a central bank. Poorly resourced or undertrained central banks provide only weak regulation and are therefore a dangerous liability to stability, investment, and sustainability (Addison et al., 2001; Adam, Collier, and Davies, 2008). Given its key importance to economic recovery, intervenors and their government partners should quickly reopen banks, if they are closed, but then take the time to thoroughly plan and implement banking reforms and recapitalization (Addison et al., 2001).

Another role of the central bank should be to attain or restore trust and credibility to the monetary system. The "fight against inflation" is a long-term fight and it requires a long-term framework for success, but a credible monetary policy must also balance price stability concerns with the need for liquidity jump-start development and attenuate employment concerns (Del Castillo, 2008; Ohiorhenuan and Stewart, 2008). Post-conflict settings are different than in a normal development context where there is less of a need to "jump-start" development as much as to just continue with the development process. It is important to note that dealing with monetary policy is, as stated, a long-term fight, and states should consider this as a second-order priority, to be dealt with after basic economic activity has been restored.

Finally, a sound fiscal policy is important in creating a sustainable state. Allocating the national budget is a difficult political process that takes serious planning and practice. Fiscal prudence is also a long-term effort. It can be difficult to even gauge the levels of revenue and expenditures that are needed or available when a new government is first taking over. It may be necessary to create shorter-term budgets to begin with, because in the first few years of a transition, needs might be changing rapidly (Del Castillo, 2008). Starting out with relatively crude but frequent (quarterly or semiannual) budgets might be useful. Also, post-conflict countries will often have a significant amount of debt (Barro and Lee, 2005). Timely payment of these debts will help maintain good donor relations and will extend the likelihood of further aid in the future. Cooperation and guidance from international financial institutions, such as the International Monetary Fund, should be sought in cases of significant external-debt-to-gross-domestic-product ratio.

Microeconomic Policymaking

Employment and private-sector development are necessary for sustained economic recovery. To achieve them, states and intervenors must engender trust from the business community, remove obstacles to economic activity, provide incentives for business activity, and provide direct support to businesses or individuals if needed (Ohiorhenuan and Stewart, 2008). Policies promoting employment and private-sector development are tied to the institutional factors and macroeconomic factors.

A good business climate is characterized by a number of factors (Porter, 2003):

1. clearly explicated rules and regulations that are transparently and consistently enforced
2. low amounts of government bureaucracy
3. strong judicial systems and strong rule of law
4. flexible and productive labor markets and available human capital
5. good physical infrastructure
6. investment in innovation and technological infrastructure
7. fair competition (lack of monopolies, informal markets, etc.).

All of these factors relate to the ease of doing business and are necessary to support and encourage local investment and entrepreneurship along with international commercial investment. In previous sections, we have discussed how rule of law affects the economy: Without a strong rule of law, businesses might be hesitant to invest in a country, as it is not clear to what extent regulations are enforceable. Business also needs resources, both physical and human capital, in order to function. These may not be available in the short term, depending on the amount of destruction and migration, but efforts to start building or rebuilding the human capital should begin immediately. Markets require all these factors in order to function and provide the trade opportunities that are required to stabilize and reconstruct post-conflict economies (Dollar and Kraay, 2003).

Alternative Funding Mechanisms. Aside from business investment, another way to boost domestic markets is to use microfinance and remittances. Microfinance has been shown to directly produce economic activities, though most microcredit schemes are still highly subsidized. There has been some complaint that "designers and sponsors of new initiatives have abandoned innovation, and 'replication' is leading to a growing uniformity in financial interventions" (Morduch, 2000), but this method of getting small loans to entrepreneurs and small business owners has nevertheless been shown to have great promise.

Remittances can also help finance economic recovery. Somaliland over the past 17 years has managed to establish a degree of security and effective governance in a conflict-riddled region that was mainly due to remittances from the diaspora population (Figure 6.3). In this time, Somaliland's health provision and primary school enrollment have risen,

Figure 6.3
Illustrative Economic Flows Versus Time

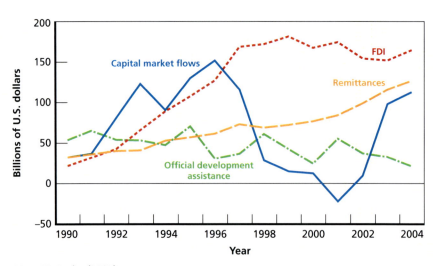

SOURCE: Ratha (2005).
NOTE: FDI = foreign direct investment.
RAND MG1119-6.3

poverty levels have fallen, and these indicators are on par with regional neighbors that have not experienced similar conflict (Ohiorhenuan and Stewart, 2008). Research suggests that part of the reason for Somaliland's growth is due to regional, clan-based credit systems, which help protect assets and settle disputes. Additionally, remittances have helped not just with household consumption but also financing small business development (Ohiorhenuan and Stewart, 2008). On a global scale, remittances run in the tens of billions of dollars annually (though currently the top recipients of remittances are *not* the poorest countries) and have a significant impact on income and consumption in many developing nations (Addison, Mavrotas, and McGillivray, 2005; Ratha, 2005). The Somali example shows how a relatively simple tool such as remittances can operate in concert with local traditions and experiences to help economic growth and reconstruction.

Though local actors and resources are critical for the success of economic reconstruction, local efforts are not always sufficient on their own and should be used in concert with valuable external assistance. These various tools, actors, and resources should work in complementary ways to provide a whole range of policy options with which to tackle the difficult problems associated with transitioning to peace.

Conclusions

We have discussed the different factors that contribute to economic stability and reconstruction at length. These factors can be put into a system of relationships that are shown in Figure 6.1. However, the factor tree in Figure 6.1 could be true for either post-conflict or normal development settings. There are four main differences between these two situations that affect how Figure 6.1 should be viewed:

1. *Intensity.* In post-conflict settings, there is urgent and imminent need to get control of the security situation, build/rebuild human capital, and establish the rule of law.
2. *Timing.* Some factors must be tended to before success on the others will be possible. Security must be assured before markets

can function properly. It is also important to attract back highly skilled refugees and establish rule of law, whereas more general human capital development is a longer-term goal. Other factors, such as investment, fiscal policy adjustment, and rebuilding infrastructure, must also come immediately, whereas reconstruction of monetary policy might be more mid- to near-term factors.

3. *Type of Aid.* Post-conflict settings are targets for security aid in addition to the usual development aid. Security aid will come in quickly and in high volumes; it requires immediate use before the wells of international interest dry up. A low, steady flow of development aid may continue, but the window for high levels of security aid will be narrower.

4. *Appropriate Market Systems.* Short-term measures that economists usually do not favor may be necessary. These include distortionary policies (such as subsidies and direct transfers of cash or food) and government nationalization of services (such as utilities) or production of natural resources. Countries and intervenors must have a solid plan, from the inception, for the transition to more economically optimal strategies.

Figure 6.4
Summary of Priorities Over Time

		Timing		
		Early	Mid-Term	Later
Intensity	High	Security Good use of post-conflict security aid	Human-capital development Revenue collection	Incentives to attract investment
	Medium	Physical infrastructure Education Rule of law	Rebuilding central bank	Network of regional banks
	Low	Full assessment of available workforce	Fiscal policy	Monetary policy

RAND MG1119-6.4

As emphasized throughout this chapter, some outcomes must be achieved before others are achievable; security, for instance, is the precursor to almost everything else. The timing of the factors and levels of intensity that they require in a post-conflict situation will be roughly what is shown in Figure 6.4. This differs from a normal development context in a number of ways: Security will likely be a higher-intensity priority for a post-conflict country, which may still be experiencing the aftershocks of the conflict, whereas fiscal policy might be more urgent in a normal development context, as budgetary discipline in a post-conflict setting will be put off to the mid term. These are general priorities, of course, because every post-conflict reconstruction setting will be different, depending on the history of the conflict and other factors.

Endnotes

[1]   The factor-tree methodology is discussed succinctly in Davis (2009) and at more length in Chapter 11 of Davis and Cragin (2009). Briefly, an arrow from factor A to factor B means that an increase in the former tends to increase the latter, although the actual effect will depend on other factors that also influence B.

[2]   The degree and nature of adherence is never perfect, of course.

[3]   Corruption is a matter of degree. In some states it is common to have multiple payments in the course of business, payments that may be considered as either bribes (corruption) or informal transaction fees of a less troublesome nature. However, when the extent and magnitude of these payments becomes excessive and the resulting processes inefficient, and when a significant portion of the money goes into the foreign accounts of leaders, corruption severely affects the state's economy. Corruption indexes have been constructed to characterize degree on a country-by-country basis (see, e.g., the website of Transparency International).

References

ABC Radio Australia, "Places: Solomon Islands," 2005. As of April 11, 2011: http://www.abc.net.au/ra/pacific/places/country/solomon_islands.htm

Acemoglu, Duane, Simon Johnson, and James A. Robinson, "Institutional Causes, Macroeconomic Symptoms: Volatility, Crises and Growth," *Journal of Monetary Economics*, Vol. 50, No. 1, 2003, pp. 49–123.

————, "Institutions as the Fundamental Cause of Long-Run Economic Growth," in Philippe Aghion and Steve Durlaf, eds., *Handbook of Economic Growth*, New York: Elsevier, 2005, pp. 385–472.

Adam, Christopher, Paul Collier, and Victor A. B. Davies, "Post-Conflict Monetary Reconstruction," *World Bank Economic Review*, Vol. 22, No. 1, 2008, pp. 87–122,

Addison, Tony, Alemayehu Geda, Philippe Le Billon, and S. Mansoob Murshed, "Financial Reconstruction in Conflict and 'Post-Conflict' Economies," Discussion Paper No. 2001/90, United Nations University–World Institute for Development Economics Research, Helsinki, 2001.

Addison, Tony, Philippe Le Billon, and S. Mansoob Murshed, "Finance in Conflict and Reconstruction," *Journal of International Development*, Vol. 13, 2001, pp. 951–964.

Addison, Tony, George Mavrotas, and Mark McGillivray, "Aid, Debt Relief and New Sources of Finance for Meeting the Millennium Development Goals," *Journal of International Affairs*, Vol. 58, No. 2, 2005, pp. 113–127.

Aron, Janine, "Building Institutions in Post-Conflict African Economies," *Journal of International Development*, Vol. 15, No. 4, 2003, pp. 471–486.

Ascher, William, *Why Governments Waste Natural Resources: Policy Failures in Developing Countries*, Baltimore, Md.: Johns Hopkins University Press, 1999.

Barro, Robert J., and Jong-Wha Lee, "IMF programs: Who Is Chosen and What Are the Effects?" *Journal of Monetary Economics*, Vol. 52, No. 7, 2005, pp. 1245–1269.

Barton, Frederick. D., "Measuring Progress in International State Building and Reconstruction," Aspen European Strategy Forum, August 20, 2008. As of April 11, 2011:
http://csis.org/files/publication/080820_barton_mop.pdf

Berman, Eli, Joseph Felter, and Jacob N. Shapiro, "Do Working Men Rebel? Insurgency and Unemployment in Iraq and the Philippines," National Bureau of Economic Research, Cambridge, Mass., NBER Working Paper 15547, 2009.

Berrebi, Claude, "Evidence About the Link Between Education, Poverty and Terrorism Among Palestinians," *Peace Economics, Peace Science and Public Policy*, Vol. 13, No. 1, 2007.

Brinkerhoff, Derick W., "Rebuilding Governance in Failed States and Post-Conflict Societies: Core Concepts and Cross-Cutting Themes," *Public Administration and Development*, Vol. 25, No. 1, 2005, pp. 3–14.

Bromley, Daniel W., and Michael M. Cernea, *The Management of Common Property Natural Resources: Some Conceptual and Operational Fallacies*, Washington, D.C.: World Bank Publications, 1989.

Brown, Graham, Frances Stewart, and Arnim Langer, "The Implications of Horizontal Inequality for Aid," United Nations University–World Institute for Development Economics Research, Helsinki, Research Paper 2007/51, 2007.

Burke, Adam, "Peacebuilding and Rebuilding at Ground Level: Practical Constraints and Policy Objectives in Aceh," *Conflict, Security, and Development*, Vol. 8, No. 1, 2008, pp. 47–69.

Chang, Ha-Joon, and Peter Evans, "The Role of Institutions in Economic Change," paper for meeting of the "Other Canon" group, Venice, Italy, January 13–14, 2000.

Cincotta, R. P., R. Engelman, and Daniele Anastasion, *The Security Demographic: Population and Civil Conflict After the Cold War*, Washington, D.C.: Population Action International, 2003.

Citro, Constance F., and Robert. T. Michael, *Measuring Poverty: A New Approach*, Washington, D.C.: National Academies Press, 1996.

Clarida, Richard, Jordi Galí, and Mark Gertler, "Monetary Policy Rules and Macroeconomic Stability: Evidence and Some Theory," *Quarterly Journal of Economics*, Vol. 115, No. 1, 2000, pp. 147–180.

Collier, Paul, *Economic Causes of Civil Conflict and Their Implications for Policy*, Washington, D.C.: World Bank, 2000.

———, *Breaking the Conflict Trap: Civil War and Development Policy*, Washington, D.C.: World Bank, 2003.

Collier, Paul, and Anke Hoeffler, "Aid, Policy and Peace: Reducing the Risks of Civil Conflict," *Defence and Peace Economics*, Vol. 13, No. 6, 2002, pp. 435–450.

———, "Greed and Grievance in Civil War," *Oxford Economic Papers*, Vol. 6, No. 4, 2004, pp. 563–595 (see also earlier CSAE Working Paper 2002-01, Oxford University).

———, "Aid, Policy and Growth in Post-Conflict Societies," *European Economic Review*, Vol. 48, No. 5, 2004, pp. 1125–1146.

Collier, Paul, Anke Hoeffler, and Måns Söderbom, "Post-Conflict Risks," *Journal of Peace Research*, Vol. 45, No. 4, 2008, p. 461.

Cordesman, Anthony E., *Economic Challenges in Post-Conflict Iraq*, Washington, D.C.: Center for Strategic and International Studies, 2010.

Davis, Paul K., *Specifying the Content of Humble Social-Science Models*, Santa Monica, Calif.: RAND Corporation (reprint of an article from Proceedings of the Summer Computer Simulation Conference, Istanbul, Turkey, 2009), 2009. As of April 8, 2011:
http://www.rand.org/pubs/reprints/RP1408-1.html

Davis, Paul K., and Kim Cragin, eds., *Social Science for Counterterrorism: Putting the Pieces Together*, Santa Monica, Calif.: RAND Corporation, 2009. As of April 7, 2011:
http://www.rand.org/pubs/monographs/MG849.html

de Ree, Joppe, and Eleonora Nillesen, "Aiding Violence or Peace? The Impact of Foreign Aid on the Risk of Civil Conflict in Sub-Saharan Africa," *Journal of Development Economics*, Vol. 88, 2009, pp. 301–313.

Deaton, Angus, "Measuring Poverty in a Growing World (or Measuring Growth in a Poor World)," *Review of Economics and Statistics*, Vol. 87, No. 1, 2005, pp. 1–19.

Del Castillo, Graciana, *Rebuilding War-Torn States: The Challenge of Post-Conflict Economic Reconstruction*, New York: Oxford University Press, 2008.

Demekas, Dimitri G., Jimmy McHugh, and Theodora Kosma, "The Economics of Post Conflict Aid," International Monetary Fund, Washington, D.C., IMF Working Paper WP 02/198, 2002.

Department of State, *Master List of Standard Indicators*, Washington, D.C., 2008.

Dobbins, James, Seth G. Jones, Keith Crane, Christopher S. Chivvis, Andrew Radin, F. Stephen Larrabee, Nora Bensahel, Brooke Stearns Lawson, and Benjamin W. Goldsmith, *Europe's Role in Nation-Building: From the Balkans to the Congo*, Santa Monica: RAND Corporation, 2008a. As of April 7, 2011:
http://www.rand.org/pubs/monographs/MG722.html

Dobbins, James, Seth G. Jones, Keith Crane, Andrew Rathmell, Brett Steele, Richard Teltschik, and Anga R. Timilsina, *The UN's Role in Nation-Building: From the Congo to Iraq*, Santa Monica, Calif.: RAND Corporation, 2005. As of April 7, 2011:
http://www.rand.org/pubs/monographs/MG304.html

Dobbins, James, John G. McGinn, Keith Crane, Seth G. Jones, Rollie Lal, Andrew Rathmell, Rachel M. Swanger, and Anga R. Timilsina, *America's Role in Nation-Building: From Germany to Iraq*, Santa Monica, Calif.: RAND Corporation, 2003. As of April 7, 2011:
http://www.rand.org/pubs/monograph_reports/MR1753.html

Dobbins, James, Michele A. Poole, Austin Long, and Benjamin Runkle, *After the War: Nation-Building from FDR to George W. Bush*, Santa Monica, Calif.: RAND Corporation, 2008b. As of April 7, 2011:
http://www.rand.org/pubs/monographs/MG716.html

Dollar, David, and Aart Kraay, "Institutions, Trade, and Growth," *Journal of Monetary Economics*, Vol. 50, No. 1, 2003, pp. 133–162.

Easterlin, Richard A., "The Conflict Between Aspirations and Resources," *Population and Development Review*, 1976, pp. 417–426.

———, "Will Raising the Incomes of All Increase the Happiness of All?" *Journal of Economic Behavior and Organization*, Vol. 27, No. 1, 1995, pp. 35–47.

———, "Income and Happiness: Towards a Unified Theory," *Economic Journal*, Vol. 111, No. 473, 2001, pp. 465–484.

Elbadawi, Ibrahim A., "Civil Wars and Poverty: The Role of External Interventions, Political Rights and Economic Growth," paper presented at the World Bank's Conference on "Civil Conflicts, Crime and Violence," Washington, D.C., February 1999.

———, "Postconflict Transitions: An Overview," *World Bank Economic Review*, Vol. 22, No. 1, 2008, pp. 1–7.

Elbadawi, Ibrahim A., and Nicholas Sambanis, "External Interventions and the Duration of Civil Wars," World Bank, Washington, D.C., Policy Research Working Paper 2433, 2000.

Elbadawi, Ibrahim A., and K. Schmidt-Hebbel, "The Demand for Money Around the End of Civil Wars," World Bank, Washington, D.C., Policy Research Working Paper, 2007.

Fearon, James D., Macartan Humphreys, and Jeremy M. Weinstein, "Can Development Aid Contribute to Social Cohesion after Civil War? Evidence from a Field Experiment in Post-Conflict Liberia," *American Economic Review*, Vol. 99, No. 2, 2009, pp. 287–291.

Firebaugh, Glenn, *The New Geography of Global Inequality*, Cambridge, Mass.: Harvard University Press, 2006.

Gerxhani, Klariat, "The Informal Sector in Developed and Less Developed Countries: A Literature Survey," *Public Choice*, Vol. 120, No. 3, 2004, pp. 267–300.

Ghani, Ashraf, and Claire Lockhart, *Fixing Failed States: A Framework for Rebuilding a Fractured World*, New York: Oxford University Press, 2008.

Hamre, John J., and Gordon R. Sullivan, "Toward Postconflict Reconstruction," *Washington Quarterly*, Vol. 25, No. 4, 2002, pp. 85–96.

Herrhausen, Anna, "Coordination in United Nations Peacebuilding—A Theory-Guided Approach," WZB (Social Science Research Center Berlin), discussion paper 301, 2007.

Kaufmann, Daniel, A., and Art Kraay, "Growth Without Governance [with Comments]," *Economia*, Vol. 3, No. 1, 2002, pp. 169–229.

Krause, Keith, and Oliver Jutersonke, "Peace, Security and Development in Post-Conflict Environments," *Security Dialogue*, Vol. 36, No. 4, 2005, pp. 447–462.

Mauro, Paolo, "The Persistence of Corruption and Slow Economic Growth," International Monetary Fund, Washington, D.C., IMF Staff Papers, Vol. 51, No. 1, 2004, pp. 1–18.

Morduch, Jonathan, "The Microfinance Schism," *World Development*, Vol. 28, No. 4, 2000, pp. 617–629.

North, Douglass C., *Institutions, Institutional Change and Economic Performance*, New York: Cambridge University Press, 1990.

OECD—*See* Organisation for Economic Co-operation and Development.

Ohiorhenuan, John F. E., and Frances Stewart, *Post-Conflict Economic Recovery: Enabling Local Ingenuity*, New York: United Nations Development Programme, 2008.

Organisation for Economic Co-operation and Development, "DAC Aid Statistics," 2010. As of April 11, 2011:
http://www.oecd.org/dac/stats

Porter, Michael E., "Building the Microeconomic Foundations of Prosperity: Findings from the Microeconomic Competitiveness Index," in World Economic Forum, *The Global Competitiveness Report 2002–2003*, New York: Oxford University Press, 2003. As of April 11, 2011:
http://www.isc.hbs.edu/pdf/GCR_0203_mci.pdf

Pouligny, Beatrice, "Promoting Democratic Institutions in Post-Conflict Societies: Giving Diversity a Chance," *International Peacekeeping*, Vol. 7, No. 3, 2000, pp. 17–36.

Project Ploughshares, "Armed Conflicts Report: Serbia and Montenegro (ex-Yugoslavia)—Kosovo," January 2007. As of April 11, 2011:
http://www.ploughshares.ca/libraries/ACRText/ACR-Yugoslavia.html

Ratha, Dilip, "Workers' Remittances: An Important and Stable Source of External Development Finance," in Samuel M. Maimbo and Dilip Ratha, eds., *Remittances: Development Impact and Future Prospects*, New York: World Bank Publications, 2005, pp. 19–51.

Reuters, "Timeline—Darfur Rebels to Sign Peace Agreement with Sudan," February 23, 2010. As of April 11, 2011:
http://www.reuters.com/article/idUSTRE61M2ST20100223

Rodrik, Dani, "Institutions for High-Quality Growth: What They Are and How to Acquire Them," National Bureau of Economic Research, Cambridge, Mass., NBER Working Paper 7540, 2000.

———, "Institutions, Integration, and Geography: In Search of the Deep Determinants of Economic Growth," in Dani Rodrick, ed., *In Search of Prosperity: Analytic Narratives on Economic Growth*, Princeton, N.J.: Princeton University Press, 2003.

———, "Getting Institutions Right," CESifo DICE Report, Ifo Institute for Economic Research at Munich University, Vol. 2, No. 2, 2004, pp. 10–16.

Rodrik, Dani, A. Subramanian, and Francesco Trebbi, "Institutions Rule: The Primacy of Institutions over Geography and Integration in Economic Development," *Journal of Economic Growth*, Vol. 9, No. 2, 2004, pp. 131–166.

Roodman, D. "The Anarchy of Numbers: Aid, Development, and Cross-Country Empirics," *World Bank Economic Review*, Vol. 21, No. 2, 2007, pp. 255–277.

Rose-Ackerman, S., "Corruption and Government," *International Peacekeeping*, Vol. 15, No. 3, 2008, pp. 328–343.

Sachs, Jeffrey D., "Institutions Don't Rule: Direct Effects of Geography on Per Capita Income," National Bureau of Economic Research, Cambridge, Mass., NBER Working Paper No. 9490, 2003.

Sambanis, Nichoas, "Using Case Studies to Expand Economic Models of Civil War," *Perspectives on Politics*, Vol. 2, No. 2, 2004, pp. 259–279.

Stewart, Frances, "Crisis Prevention: Tackling Horizontal Inequalities," *Oxford Development Studies*, Vol. 28, No. 3, 2000, pp. 245–262.

———, *Horizontal Inequalities: A Neglected Dimension of Development*, QEH Working Paper Number 81, University of Oxford, 2002.

Transparency International, homepage, no date. As of April 18, 2011: http://www.transparency.org/

United Nations, *World Population Prospects: The 2008 Revision*, 2008.

U.S. Joint Forces Command, *Military Support to Economic Normalization*, Joint Forces Commanders Handbook, Suffolk, Va., 2009.

World Bank, *World Development Indicators Database*, 2009.

CHAPTER SEVEN

Dilemmas of Foreign Aid in Post-Conflict Areas

*Claude Berrebi and Véronique Thelen**

Introduction

One of the primary whole-of-government instruments for stability and reconstruction (S&R) operations is foreign assistance. However, social-science research reveals serious uncertainties and disagreements about the role and effectiveness of aid; it also raises what can be seen as recurring dilemmas, or at least tensions. This chapter attempts to synthesize the related literature and clarify selected issues, primarily for the purpose of informing government officials concerned with S&R. The chapter is organized as follows:

1. Background on Foreign Assistance and Its Effectiveness
2. Using Conditionalities to Improve Effectiveness
3. Reconciling Short- and Long-Term Objectives
4. Improving Effectiveness by Using More Objective Criteria for Aid
5. Whether to Provide Aid Through the Government or Around It.

We then end with brief conclusions, including some cautions about using aggregated quantitative methods when assessing options for specific countries.

---

* Toulouse School of Economics (ARQADE), Université of Toulouse I, France.

Background on Foreign Assistance and Its Effectiveness

Types of Aid

Foreign aid can be categorized by a number of methods. The U.S. Congress refers to five types: bilateral development assistance, economic aid supporting U.S. security objectives, humanitarian assistance, multilateral assistance, and military assistance (Tarnoff and Nowels, 2004). The names used for these categories can be confusing; Table 7.1 is our attempt to clarify distinctions. The number of bullets indicates the relative degree to which aid in one of these categories affects the functions shown in the top row. The composition of foreign aid varies over time, of course; Figure 7.1 illustrates the breakdown for 2008 (Tarnoff and Lawson, 2009).

Within *post-conflict* environments (a subset of the total aid in Figure 7.1), the United States employs all five types of aid, but bilateral

Table 7.1
Relationships Among Types of U.S. Foreign Assistance

	Function				
Category of Aid	Immediate Humanitarian Assistance	Mid-and Long-Term Development	Specific and Functional Military Aid	Incentives or Quid Pro Quos, Often for Specific Efforts	Examples
Bilateral development		•••			USAID, Peace Corps
Economic aid supporting U.S. security objectives		•		•••	Support of Middle East peace process; counternarcotics (Latin America)
Humanitarian assistance	•••				Haiti
Multilateral assistance	••	•••			World Bank, regional development banks
Military assistance			•••	•••	Israel, Egypt

NOTES: Number of bullets indicates weight of emphasis. USAID = U.S. Agency for International Development.

Figure 7.1
Composition of Foreign Aid

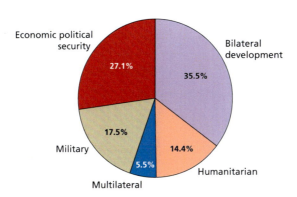

SOURCE: Department of State, Summary and Highlights, International Affairs, Function 150, FY2009, House and Senate Appropriations Committees, and Congressional Research Service calculations.
RAND *MG1119-7.1*

development assistance and economic security aid are primary. The coexistence of normal economic-development aid and S&R-related aid is unique to post-conflict states and presents a hazard: The functions associated with the two types of aid may be in contradiction.

The level of foreign aid varies tremendously across states, with such states as Iraq, Afghanistan, Bosnia, and East Timor receiving large quantities of aid while others receive relatively scant funding (Collier and Hoeffler, 2004).

Other distinctions are also important when performing evaluations. Suhrke and Buckmaster (2005) distinguish among types of aid, between commitments and disbursements, and among different levels and timings of aid.

Normal development aid and post-conflict (S&R) aid are frequently implemented by different institutions and with contrasting mechanisms. S&R aid aims to diminish the likelihood of renewed violence and to enhance the legitimacy and operation of the central government. It frequently seeks results as soon as possible. The physical projects that receive funding are often related (especially in early periods) to the needs of military and police forces.[1] Countries with the greatest relevance to the donor's geopolitical interests and security can expect the greatest amount of aid. The U.S. Departments of State and Defense implement most S&R aid (Tarnoff and Nowels, 2004).

Normal development aid operates on a longer timeline, which can be a decade or more. The aid investments are often in projects that target economic growth and poverty and frequently involve state infrastructure improvements and agricultural advancement. In principle, development aid allocation is linked with liberal political and economic policies of the recipient country. Major U.S. agencies that specialize in development aid are the Millennium Challenge Corporation (MCC) (discussed in a later section) and the U.S. Agency for International Development (USAID) (Tarnoff, 2009).

Motivations and Objectives

The objectives of aid and the reasons for its allocation are many, and they are not solely, or even particularly, those of poverty alleviation or promotion of economic development.

Empirical analysis is one way to understand de facto objectives. Kang and Meernick (2004) use historical data and statistical methods to infer the determinants of foreign assistance by the nations of the Organisation for Economic Co-operation and Development (OECD) to nations involved in conflicts. As expected, humanitarian needs and economic conditions affect the level of aid. Also, OECD assistance is significantly greater in post-conflict years, particularly where OECD members have intervened militarily. Donor actions are also guided by donor assessments of the immediate economic and human needs, a sense of responsibility, and possible long-term benefits or interests for the region. Broadly speaking, then, objectives seem to be benign and even altruistic. However, deeper analysis reveals additional motives, which can undercut some aspects of S&R and affect judgments about the rationality of how aid has been allocated. These motives include supporting governments that are under political threat where stability is a matter of U.S. concern, pursuing commercial interests, subsidizing counterterrorism, and rewarding nations for international cooperation.[2,3] Overall, the literature suggests that allocation of foreign aid responds primarily to certain national-strategic motivations, rather than to the likely performance of recipient countries in combating poverty and furthering growth.

Some authors draw ethical conclusions from this, while others regard these correlations as natural. Why wouldn't a nation's foreign aid move preferentially to countries with which there are historical ties (e.g., a former colony)? Why shouldn't a nation be more charitable if it perceives the likelihood of future commerce with the recipient state? We (the present authors) are not concerned here with assessing the ethical merits of de facto aid policies, but rather with noting that they are sometimes at odds with the economic effectiveness in S&R narrowly. Thus, assessments of "effectiveness" are more complicated that some authors have suggested.

Studies of the effectiveness of combined U.S. foreign aid reach varied conclusions. Matters become even more complicated for post-conflict settings, in which humanitarian and development aid is integrated with stabilization and military aid. The threat of violence shortly after war frequently requires using military personnel to deliver or accompany delivery of humanitarian aid. In Iraq and Afghanistan, Provincial Reconstruction Teams (PRT) have both military personnel and civilians from the State Department, USAID, and the Department of Agriculture. The teams have a hybrid mission consisting of reconciliation promotion, counterinsurgency, and fostering economic growth and development (Clawson, 2010a).

With this background, let us now discuss the long-standing issue of aid's effectiveness.

Controversy About Effectiveness and Efficiency

The "aid-ineffectiveness literature" has accumulated evidence that foreign aid does *not* consistently or efficiently reduce poverty or enhance education in the recipient countries.

Easterly (2007) presents a synthesis of this literature and argues that the failure of aid to reduce poverty is due to (1) specific economic constraints and conditions and (2) incentive systems that are either inappropriate or lacking entirely. He argues that corruption, lack of property rights and contract enforcement, and the ineffectiveness of aid-recipient governments in providing services strongly contribute to aid's ineffectiveness. These economic conditions are even more important in the case of fragile-state or post-conflict reconstruction. Security, stability, and the quality of institutions are at least as important.

Beyond ineffectiveness, another issue is the risk that foreign aid will be downright counterproductive, with conflict renewing if the population does not perceive a "peace dividend" (Del Castillo, 2008) or if aid creates a "moral hazard," i.e., generating disincentives for stability by reducing the costs to participants of renewed war (Benmelech, Berrebi, and Klor, 2010). Even worse, aid can become an asset for people to fight over (Zoellick, 2008).

This aid-ineffectiveness literature also raises the question of why the international community consistently gives away billions of dollars if such a flow of aid is ineffective. A possible answer is that—as discussed in the previous section—the objectives of aid are many, and are not solely, or even particularly, those of poverty alleviation or promotion of economic development.

In any case, considerable effort has been made to assess the effects of development aid on conflict and post-conflict S&R. In this connection, de Ree and Nillesen (2009) explore the effect on state conflicts, specifically sub-Saharan civil wars. According to their study, development aid is negatively correlated to the duration of civil war. More precisely, a 10 percent increase in aid is correlated with an 8 percent smaller probability of war continuation (they did not find a correlation between the onset of civil conflict and development aid).

Conflicting Results. Statistical studies of the impact of foreign aid at the micro and macro levels have often contradicted one another. For example, Hansen and Tarp (2001) look at the relation between aid and growth using the measure of real gross domestic product per capita. Their results show that the impact of aid on growth is highly sensitive to the empirical approach of the analysis and can lead to opposing conclusions on the effectiveness of foreign aid, depending on the estimation technique used and the set of control variables included (e.g., the level of domestic investment, human capital, or foreign direct investment). Easterly (2003) explains these contradictory results by showing that the impact of aid on economic growth is sensitive to reasonable variations in the definitions of the variable used and to the period considered. His work calls into question the considerable econometric analysis that does not adequately address such sensitivities.

These different results on the impact of foreign aid on stability, growth, and poverty are not surprising given the heterogeneous nature of aid, motives, and timeframes—as well as limitations of tools being used. Sound quantitative analysis of the effects of aid targeted toward state-building requires aid data at the locality or project level, as well as measures of institutional quality and state capacity, both of which are rarely available. Moreover, the complex causality chain linking the allocation of foreign aid to final outcomes has been often ignored.

As another example of how tensions arise among studies, Azam and Delacroix (2006) and Azam and Thelen (2008, 2010) look at measures to curb the flow of terrorist attacks by intervening directly in the perpetrators' countries of origin. Their theoretical framework views aid, in part, as a way of defraying the cost of the recipient government of protecting the donor's interests by fighting terrorist organizations that would otherwise target the interests of the donor country. They found, using both the official development assistance (ODA) measure per capita and as a percentage of gross domestic product, that foreign aid can be efficient for fighting terrorism. In contrast, they found that military intervention has ambiguous impact. One of their key findings (again, hardly a surprise) was that donor countries are using foreign aid as a tool to fight terrorism. The donor community is preferentially allocating aid to governments facing more militant groups likely to use terrorism in the first place.

As shown by Azam and Delacroix, however, by not using proper specification and controls, they could find the spurious result that more foreign aid led statistically to *more* terrorist attacks. These papers highlight the importance of having a theoretical foundation and of using sound empirical methods. Unfortunately, the literature sometimes falls short, particularly by using highly aggregated data. One must be aware of conclusions of narrowly sound statistical analysis that can be translated into seriously incorrect policy implications.[4] Better methods are available and should be used.

Given these caveats about understanding "normal" aid effectiveness, care should be taken when assessing options for post-conflict aid using so-called common knowledge, especially knowledge derived from the over-aggregated analysis mentioned above. To be blunt, analysis needs to address the specific goals and circumstances of the country in question for it to be useful as a basis for assessing policy options.

Using Conditionalities to Improve Effectiveness

Drawing on the ineffectiveness-of-aid literature, a natural conclusion is that aid should be tied to explicit or implicit past performance criteria or to the expected future performance of the recipient governments. Conditionality is increasingly used to support medium-term reforms (World Bank, 2005). Such conditionality refers to conditions attached to the disbursements of policy-based lending or budget support. Conditionality along these lines is particularly relevant for post-conflict countries and may also help control corruption.

The International Monetary Fund and the World Bank often use the conditionality of aid for short-term stabilization purposes and for longer-term structural adjustment. Bilateral donors also use various kinds of conditionalities to pursue rather commercial or geopolitical objectives, such as agreement to purchase goods and services produced by the donor country.

In the context of S&R, one aim of imposing conditionality is that it may force the recipient government to make decisions in the broader public interest, which in turn may help prevent another conflict. Unfortunately, the social science tells us that doing so has many problems and dilemmas.

Del Castillo (2008) points out possible downsides of conditionalities, such as detrimental effects on immediate humanitarian assistance. The question is, When and what types of conditions on foreign aid are useful in post-conflict countries? For example, should conditionality be on the institutional efforts of the government, on its economic and reconstruction efforts made, or both?

Adding to the complexity, a World Bank (2003b) study suggested that it takes about three years before assistance starts having any kind of impact. Also, in post-conflict situations, the time needed for institutional reforms to take effect is often longer than the time required for the flow of reconstruction aid to begin implementation. Therefore, any conditionality on foreign aid assistance that is linked to institutional reforms (e.g., those promoting rule of law, an equalitarian and functional electoral system, or proper civil rights) needs to be using reasonable time scales and metrics of performance that reflect expected delays. As discussed in Chapter One of this volume, such considerations argue strongly for at least high-level depiction of system dynamics when developing measures of effectiveness and performance. Otherwise, interim monitoring will lead to misleading conclusions.

Boyce (2007) also addresses conditionality, noting again that peace and stability are not always the sole or even the dominant objectives of the donor community. A donor may be concerned, for example, with geopolitical, economic, and commercial interests, or may be responding to other concerns of domestic public opinion (e.g., the prevalence of HIV/AIDS or a natural disaster). In this context Boyce explains the roles of economic assistance and conditionality in improving the peacebuilding process. One of his ideas is to impose conditionality on types of aid that are most valued by political leaders while least damaging to the overall population. He maintains that such conditionality should only be applied to nonhumanitarian aid, although he recognizes the difficulties in making the distinctions.

Since conditionalities are developed on a case-by-case basis, flexibility exists. There are, however, potential additional problems that have attracted attention. Dreher (2002) shows that the number of conditionality criteria of the World Bank and the International Monetary Fund has increased over time. These apply primarily to monetary and fiscal policy, reduction in relative price distortions, reductions in public-sector budget deficits, reduction of current account deficits through import substitution and export promotion, and privatizations. Many of these conditionalities can be quite inappropriate economically to post-conflict settings (see also Chapter Six), quite aside from the exceptional monitoring difficulties that also exist (World Bank, 2003a). Another major criticism of conditionality approaches is that, while they add complexity and delays, noncompliance has not always been rigorously punished, resulting in costs but few benefits. This imperfect control of implementation and imperfect knowledge of the local environment raise serious doubts about the wisdom of imposing aid conditionality in the first place. The tactic may be the least bad of numerous bad options, so long as it does not impede humanitarian efforts or other short-term S&R objectives, but better methods need to be used in defining conditions, monitoring developments, and interpreting information.

Reconciling Short-Term and Longer-Term Objectives

Sources of Tension

A United Nations Development Programme (UNDP) report on post-conflict economic recovery (2007) gives a good overview of the interconnected cyclical conditions for rebuilding and sustaining peace. The report sensibly argues that economic recovery can lead to reconstruction, income generation, and improved public services, which in turn will enhance economic recovery. The report also discusses the importance of local institutions and infrastructures, especially for the health and education sectors, since these can substantially benefit from foreign aid. The report finds a correlation between countries' income and wealth inequalities and their predisposition to conflict. It accordingly suggests that post-conflict aid policies should aim to reduce such inequalities and tension. Foreign aid and debt relief are viewed as ways to provide a "breathing space" for governments to use in building political consensus and restoring institutional capacities. *The report, however, does not emphasize the practical tensions between the long-term economic recovery and the immediate needs faced by post-conflict economies.* Such tensions can aggravate inequalities and renew conflict.

Trade-offs exist between the short-run and long-run objectives of post-conflict foreign aid. To be sure, foreign assistance may pursue short-run objectives, mainly humanitarian and reconstruction-oriented in nature, but also long-run objectives focused on development and peacebuilding. However, in a budget-constrained environment, one objective comes at the expense of the other. Moreover, policies required for short-term objectives are often detrimental to achieving long-term goals (e.g., providing free food and shelter to relieve humanitarian crises will reduce incentives to commercial providers of food and shelter, as well as diminish the urgency of finding employment). Similarly, policies required for achieving long-term objectives are often in conflict with the short-term needs (e.g., fiscal and monetary constraints to establish economic credibility and control inflation conflict with the provision of immediate government services to the population). Ambiguity of strategy and mission objectives can lead to development teams favoring quick action over long-term impact aid projects, as was well documented in a report on the integration of development and security assistance (Morrison and Hicks, 2008).

Failures of "Political Markets" Affecting Short- and Long-Term Prospects

Keefer (2008) argues that, in post-conflict countries, prospects for peace and development depend sensitively on the political institutions and "political-market imperfections." These have effects in both the short and longer terms, as well as in the transitions between them. Keefer and Khemani (2005) and Keefer (2008) study the impact of four political-market imperfections on the incentives of politicians to provide public goods:

1. *Asymmetries of Information:* Citizens cannot easily observe the specific contributions of politicians to public policy and the quality of public goods. Nor can they easily assess the quality of public goods. As a result, politicians have less incentive to provide what they have promised or to assure quality.
2. *Social Polarization:* Ethnic, linguistic, religious, and economic heterogeneity can affect political behavior inappropriately.
3. *The Noncredibility of Political Promises*: Politicians may simply be unable to make credible promises, leading to insurgency.
4. *Coercion in Elections:* The continued use of violence to gain electoral support or to undermine the opponents distorts political functioning.

These political-market imperfections distort development prospects and decrease political incentives to pursue the broad public interest, including peace and development.

What can be done to reduce such political-market imperfections? Drawing on Keefer's discussion, a number of possibilities can be listed. Donors can target the imperfections by increasing information and credibility. Aid conditions can encourage concrete and observable actions to reduce political-market imperfections. When the government is unable to serve and protect the interests of its citizens, the more effective way to improve the welfare of the citizens is humanitarian assistance provided directly by the donors. With less political imperfection, donors can rely on the government to channel aid, if the policy instruments are observable and if they do not require high government capacity. In this case, aside from funneling money and aid to the government for immediate purposes, donors can focus their strategies on long-run development and peacebuilding objectives. Table 7.2 summarizes our appreciation of these distinctions. Each row is a different case, with a preferred relative emphasis on either short- or long-term emphasis, and with different prescriptions for going through or around the government. The first row corresponds to a case with low levels of governance and capacity. In this case, the aid strategy should be tilted toward the short term, i.e., toward jump-starting. Much of it will need to go directly to the population, as when military and other international organizations pass out food and water, establish sanitation, and generally attend to the most fundamental necessities while also seeking to build governance capacities for the longer term. In contrast, when governance is relatively higher (row 4), the emphasis should be on the longer term, and aid should be funneled through the government, in part to improve its perceived effectiveness and legitimacy and in part to lay the basis for sustained development without foreign assistance.

The two objectives of building peace and fostering economic recovery may be seen as complementary. Economic recovery and reconstruction without a peacebuilding or peacekeeping process is unlikely to succeed, and vice versa. Collier and Hoeffler (2004) examined the relationship between aid, economic growth, and economic-policy variables in countries that have emerged from civil war. Their objective

Table 7.2
Relating Donor Strategy to Quality and Capacity of Governance

	Circumstances		Response		
			Donor Strategy's Relative Emphasis		Nature of Donor Actions
Case	Governance Quality	Governance Capacity	Short-Term	Long-Term	
1	Low	Low	•••	•	Direct to people
2	High	Low	••	••	Direct to people; but government presence and guidance
3	Low	High	••	••	Through government if possible; direct if necessary
4	High	High	•	•••	Through government

NOTE: Number of bullets indicates weight of emphasis.

was to identify the optimal timing and magnitude of aid in relation to economic growth. They argue that aid reduces the risk of conflict recurrence, although this result is still debated in the literature. Suhrke, Villanger, and Woodward (2005) demonstrate that the result is not "robust to specification changes" (i.e., it depends on details of methodology, such as selection and coding of data, the form of the assumed regression model, and aggregations). For example, using the same statistical methods while varying specifications, they find, in contrast to Collier and Hoeffler (2004), that aid has an impact on growth during the fifth to eight years after peace but not during the first four years. Furthermore, they show that variation in the timeframe of the data sample used can lead to large variation in the possible effect of extra aid on growth, down to no effect at all.

Demekas, McHugh, and Kosma (2002) use a theoretical model to understand the impact of different types of aid on capital accumulation, growth, welfare, and resource allocation. The model assumes that post-conflict aid differs from conventional development aid with respect to goal, circumstances, and both the size and duration of aid. They show that post-conflict humanitarian aid is welfare-enhancing in the short run but does not help capital accumulation and growth in the long run. Conversely, the allocation of resources to reconstruction aid encourages capital stock but does not address the recipient country's immediate needs. This work shows, theoretically, the value of distinguishing between the types of post-conflict aid to fully understand impacts.

Mlambo, Kamara, and Nyende (2009) found that countries emerging from conflict require the collaboration of aid agencies with specialties in economic development, security, and policy advice. They conclude that for development tools to resolve the tension between short- and longer-term objectives in post-conflict states, and to break conflict cycles, they must be paired with peace and security operations (a conclusion consistent with the overall system perspective of this volume, as discussed in Chapter One). A qualitative study of aid in failed states (François and Sud, 2006) concludes that donors ought to deliver aid only after conflict has subsided and security conditions have improved, since delivering aid to corrupt and weak national governments has been largely ineffective. McGillivray and Feeny (2008) support these findings and empirically demonstrate that "fragile" states, or those currently engulfed in conflict and instability, use aid less effectively and absorb less aid than other similar, but more secure, states. Here again, following Table 7.2, providing aid directly to the population and working around the potentially corrupt government may be more efficient and result in better response to the urgent needs. Oxfam America (2008) calls for a grand national foreign aid strategy so that greater coherency is brought to the wide variety of U.S. aid operations. Such a strategy would bring equal consideration to both long-term development needs and immediate security requirements. The broad perception that development aid and security aid needs enhanced coordination and integration reflects the underlying belief that the different types of aid operate ineffectively or counterproductively when they exist independent of each other, in part because the timeframe they address is so different (Clawson, 2010a).

Making Aid More Effective by Allocating It More Objectively

One way to improve the effectiveness of S&R aid may be to give it a more rational basis that considers not only need, but also prospects for the aid being used well. This suggests looking to the experience of the Millennium Challenge Corporation (MCC) for lessons learned. Although the MCC itself may not play a role in post-conflict situations, and thus might be regarded as tangential to the S&R theme of this chapter, the MCC experience illustrates how aid practices can in fact change. Further, some of the lessons emerging will likely be relevant to post-conflict S&R.

The proposal to create the Millennium Challenge Corporation marked a stark departure from traditional U.S. bilateral foreign aid practices (Radelet, 2003). Established in 2004, MCC's core philosophy is that effective foreign aid relies on recipient governments that embrace free-market principles, transparent democracy, and social investment. Accordingly, MCC's aid allocation process vigorously seeks to objectively identify countries that not only demonstrate a need for aid but also have the promise of dramatic improvement with targeted MCC investment. The selection process makes use of performance indicators that provide scores on countries' political, social, and economic progress. The countries chosen are then provided with a program of three to five years funding, which includes detailed investment projects targeting growth and development (Tarnoff, 2009).

The MCC allocation of aid seeks to realize three principal objectives:

- Select recipient countries irrespective of U.S. strategic foreign policy objectives.
- Invest in economic development projects as a means to relieve poverty.
- Promote democratic government, social investment, and economic openness.

Taking these in order, the MCC attempts to avoid placing undue value on countries that the United States finds strategically important; it instead seeks to select recipients based on the countries' need for aid and likelihood of success (Radelet, 2003). The MCC attempts to do so by preferentially investing in countries with liberal economic and political ideals (e.g. fee markets and democracy), rather than countries with the greatest poverty.

By awarding aid based on a variety of liberal values, the MCC hopes to incentivize positive governance and influence supporting behavior. This objective, whose outcome is sometimes known as the "MCC effect," is intended to affect not only the countries that receive aid, but all candidate countries (Radelet, 2003).

Because of the relatively short history of this program, it is difficult to evaluate whether or not MCC has been successful in achieving its objectives. Although outcomes are still being debated, it is already clear that the MCC's selection reduces significantly the potential for politicization. The initial pool of candidate countries to be evaluated by the MCC is assembled in an objective manner based on countries' per capita income as determined by the World Bank. To determine eligibility, each candidate country then receives scores within the categories of "ruling justly," "investing in people," and "economic freedom." The scores are based on 17 performance indicators produced by the World Bank, the International Monetary Fund, and Freedom House. It is only after eligible countries submit applications that the MCC's board of directors decides whether a country receives aid. There is a potential risk that the board's subjective opinion at the last stage will politicize the process, but evidence suggests that the MCC is acting in accordance with its mission and is largely delivering aid solely on a basis of need and the criteria mentioned above (Clawson, 2010b).[5,6]

Unbiased selection is merely a means to an end. The ultimate question (not yet answerable) remains whether MCC programs will be successful at alleviating poverty. The MCC's approach to development and poverty relies on long-advocated economic principles and is therefore attractive. Nonetheless, there have been criticisms and cautions.

Criticisms and Cautions

Mawdsley (2007) argues that the MCC's neoliberal approaches to development can actually exacerbate overall poverty and inequality, often assisting only small segments of the poor population. Similarly, Carbone (2004) notes that the selection process overlooks some of the poorest countries in the world, many of which have made great positive strides, such as Kenya, Uganda, and Ethiopia, since they fail one or more of the MCC's performance indicators. Johnson and Zajonc (2007) concluded that it is probably too early to evaluate the MCC's effect on poverty, since the benefits of the MCC's investment projects are likely not to be evident for years after completion.

Another concern with MCC was that, instead of increasing the pool of aid resources, it would merely substitute aid from one agency to another or from one donor to another (Brown, Siddiqi, and Sessions, 2007). However, empirical analysis by Dreher, Nunnenkamp, and Öhler (2010) finds that the amount of aid received increased across all eligible countries (i.e., including countries that have not (yet) signed binding agreements on aid programs with MCC). Also, Dreher, Nunnenkamp, and Öhler (2010) conclude that MCC countries not only benefited in comparison with non-MCC countries but also received higher aid in absolute terms from all U.S. donors taken together. These new findings, then, contradict earlier findings of Brown, Siddiqi, and Sessions (2007).

Finally, it is important to know whether the MCC program has influenced governments' behavior by incentivizing democracy, social progress, and economic openness. The idea was that the MCC would not only spur meaningful development through direct investment but also impact the broader developing world through the competition for aid (MCC, 2007). Johnson and Zajonc (2007) provided the first empirical evidence of such an effect, and the 2008 MCC report provided an abundance of additional anecdotal evidence to support an effect on countries competing for aid (Clawson, 2010b). However, once countries enter an aid agreement with the MCC, the positive effect seems to diminish, as countries appear to frequently suffer declines in their performance indicators and do not necessarily continue to improve once aid programs have been accorded (Gootnick, 2008).

MCC's future remains unclear. It has remained true to its mission, but the ambiguity of its effects on poverty alleviation and economic development, as well as the political, social, and economic reforms made by candidate countries in order to become eligible, may not be sufficient to maintain support for the program. In particular, MCC's ability to take investment risks and to use innovative approaches may be compromised by skeptical politicians more interested in traditional aid practices (Hewko, 2010). This said, the MCC (an initiative of the administration of George W. Bush) has been publicly applauded by Secretary of State Hillary Clinton in the Obama administration. She recently asked for a 15 percent increase in its funding (Clinton, 2010). As mentioned above, the MCC is not likely to be used for post-conflict S&R, but the lessons learned from its experiences will be. The MCC experience demonstrates that aid practices *can* be reformed. Further, its approach has structural elements that could more objectively determine distributions of post-conflict S&R aid in accordance with the specific goals of the case. Finally, we observe that the MCC is using better and more reliable econometric tools than those we criticized above (e.g., for over-aggregation and the ignoring of endogeneity problems).

When Aid-Giving Should or Should Not Go Through the Recipient Government

The last topic we deal with has to do with how donors should operate with respect to the recipient government (a topic presaged by Table 7.2). The donor can deliver assistance to the government or can bypass the government and fund nongovernmental organizations and other private actors. Decisions on the matter can involve dilemmas, because there are distinct pros and cons and likely side effects of any choice.

The previous sections suggest that whether or not foreign aid should be directly given to the population or delivered through the government depends on the short-term and long-term objectives and on the capacity and quality of the governance. However, when the needs of the population are urgent, they often cannot await the development of government capacity and institutions, as indicated above;

this is particularly the case in instances of severe political imperfection, such as weak governance capacity.

That said, by bypassing the government, the donor community denies government an opportunity to build its capacity and its legitimacy. The increase of the legitimacy and credibility of the government, as well as the feeling of ownership over the recovery process by local stakeholders, can also be a way of curbing support for potential insurgency and by itself contribute to the peaceful alternative.

According to Myerson (2009, 2011), while recent interventions have had other priorities when the goal is state-building, the primary focus of all military and economic operations should be on supporting broad development of political networks under the leadership of the state. Hence, the essential measure of success for a reconstruction project may be not in how many bridges or schools it repairs, but in how it enhances the reputations of political leaders who spend the project's funds. Interestingly, related points were made decades ago when Galula (1964) emphasized, as an essential goal of any stabilization operation, building a political machine from the population upward; he also observed that political machines are generally built on patronage. This perspective suggests that successful S&R will depend on the new regime developing a political network that distributes power and patronage throughout the nation (Myerson, 2009).

Myerson argues that to compete for power in any political system, a leader must build a base of active supporters, and that the key to motivating this base is the leader's reputation for distributing patronage benefits to loyal supporters. The idea is that real political strength of the regime must be found in the leaders who have stakes in the regime and in their ability to mobilize active support. When such leaders are too few or too weak, the regime can be sustained only with the help of foreign intervention. If there are communities where the regime lacks any local supporters, then these communities can become a fertile ground for insurgents to begin building a rival system of power, with encouragement from disaffected local leaders. If a new regime is endorsed by an overwhelming majority of local leaders throughout the nation, then the others will feel compelled to follow suit. Accordingly, in this view, foreign aid must be directly channeled toward the creation and support of patronage benefits to the supporters of local leaders.

If the idea is to build a stable political system, the leaders of the nation (including the leaders of the insurgency) should thus be recognized as political forces, and aid should be allocated with respect to an appropriate balance between national, provincial, and local leaderships. The improvement of the relationships between national and local power is vital for the development of the state, and for this, the donors must take responsibility in influencing the distribution of power across different levels of government through the balanced allocation of aid.

It is important to note, however, that the resulting network might not be democratic, which in turn suggests that the results of economic aid would benefit if accompanied by a constitutional structure broadly supported by regional powers that are committed to democratic principles.

As an example of misguided balancing of foreign aid, Myerson discusses the case of occupied Iraq. He argues that the Coalition Provisional Authority could have begun in 2003 to cultivate local democratic leadership by holding local elections throughout Iraq and then giving the elected leaders responsibility for spending local reconstruction budgets. Even if much of this money had been wasted (from a development perspective), the local leaders who spent it well would have gained good reputations that could have made them serious contenders for higher office after national sovereignty was restored. Instead, priority was put on drafting a national constitution before any introduction of local democracy in occupied Iraq, and while local leadership was not cultivated, insurgencies took root.

A related matter was discussed earlier in this chapter. Keefer and Khemani (2005) discussed the ability of the government to make credible commitments to pursue broader public policies. The credibility of the government depends on the information of the citizens. The lack of information about the performance of politicians and the decisions of the government that have a direct impact on the welfare of the citizens influences the credibility of the government and thus the peacebuilding process.[7] Myerson (2009) specifies that to develop the credibility of government, transparent accounting for public funds is essential, especially to the local population. The local population should be able to observe how the funds are used by the recipient government and what the government has accomplished with them. Indeed, donors must insist on accountability to the local population.

Aid can and should be used to build up the credibility of the government or its legitimacy. The idea is to give the government an opportunity to show that it is delivering what it is promising. In this way, the government can gather the political support from the citizens and in turn be less vulnerable to insurgency. The government will also have greater incentives to pursue a policy protecting the broader public interests. Once the government has acquired initial credibility and legitimacy through concrete and observable actions and by increasing spending transparency, it remains for the government to maintain its credibility and sustain peace with reduced levels of continued international assistance.

An important side note here is that the mechanisms for administering aid can severely undercut the government. As discussed by Ghani and Lockhart (2008), among others, foreign-assistance organizations can outbid the government in hiring scarce skilled staff, thereby weakening the government, which desperately needs such expertise.

Azam (1995) describes how redistribution of the resources controlled by the government and military expenditure can be combined for buying peace. Peace depends entirely, he argues, on the ability of the government to commit credibly to such redistribution as public expenditures in health and education sectors or giving away some "gifts" to the opponents. The study illustrates the suggested framework with reference to various African countries, including post-conflict countries such as Ethiopia and Uganda in the 1990s. Azam (2001) developed this idea further and provides a discussion of the various means used by African governments to gain credibility based on promises made. He presents a formal game theoretic model to understand the impact of the ability of the government to commit credibly to its expenditure policy and of redistribution on rebellious activity. Using the model, he shows that a credible, strong government will rely more on redistribution than on repressive actions. However, according to this study, maintaining credibility in the long run requires that the institutional framework be more important than the government's reputation, since the latter is liable to disappear once the government changes. This has important implications for aid policy in the case of post-conflict countries and in particular with respect to the most-appropriate conditionality. It suggests that *for a peaceful environment, and for maintaining the government's credibility in the long run, political conditionality on aid should focus on institutional solutions and restrictions.*

Similarly, Azam (2008) presents a theoretical framework to understand the role of deterrence and redistribution in peacekeeping and suggests that the government must balance its expenditure between redistribution and deterrence in order to establish a peaceful equilibrium. According to this model, high enough levels of institutional and military efficiencies are required to make peace credible. In particular, with respect to the role of foreign aid, the model suggests that the cost of peace can be reduced and peace can be reached more efficiently by combining institutional reconstruction with a concomitant effort at improving the military capabilities of the government to deter rebellion. This study illustrates how the donor community can help the post-conflict country create a peaceful environment for attracting investors and, over time, reduce its reliance on international assistance. Specifically, according to the model, foreign aid must be used to increase the level of effective deterrence—for example, to increase the professionalism of its armed forces as well as to increase the efficiency of public funds management and all kinds of policies aimed at improving public service delivery to the population. This approach illustrates ways in which continued though limited foreign aid might help to prevent conflict recurrence while emphasizing again the importance and the role of the recipient government.

The institutions that implement development aid are still gaining experience and learning how to operate in countries recovering from war. For aid to be effective in post-conflict environments, states may need to adapt and adjust for their specific needs and circumstances along the lines discussed above. However, it is important to recognize that, at the moment, most development-aid agencies have limited experience in post-conflict areas and are not particularly sensitive to the special circumstances of each post-conflict case. Staff members and personnel on location have claimed to have learned tremendously from their individual experiences, but they struggle in attempting to draw lessons that are widely applicable (Collier and Hoeffler, 2004). Recent literature suggests that one major, but rarely addressed, challenge is how to improve the collaboration of development aid with security and stabilization aid, both within and outside of post-conflict states (Epstein, 2010).

Conclusions

We began this chapter with a lengthy discussion of dilemmas associated with foreign aid in post-conflict situations. These relate to conflicts between (1) short-term versus longer-term objectives; (2) traditional versus more-specific S&R objectives; (3) strengthening government by funneling aid through it versus improving the efficiency of aid by direct delivery to the population; (4) strengthening central government and improving some kinds of efficiency by working through the government, versus emphasizing bottom-up developments at local and province levels through the buildup of a decentralized patronage system; (5) imposing conditionalities to improve national performance, versus attending quickly to urgent needs.

Table 7.3 summarizes our attempt to reconcile these tensions.

Further empirical and theoretical work is needed to understand the role and the impact of foreign aid in S&R, which conditionalities are most efficient in post conflict settings, and how they should be enforced. However, as discussed also in Chapter One, care should be exercised in drawing policy conclusions from statistical-empirical studies in this domain. As discussed above, the better literature shows that results of the existing studies often depend sensitively on such methodological details as the assumed form of regression models, the coding of historical points, aggregation (e.g., length of time periods), and other matters. Careful studies that include sound empirical approaches and design have to overcome the inherent "endogeneity problem"[8] and possible omitted-variables bias. Careful studies will restrict conclusions to the specific set of countries and cases studied in the analysis, because

Table 7.3
Reconciling Tensions

Tension	Resolution
Short term versus long term	Base relative emphasis on starting conditions as suggested in Table 7.2.
Traditional versus S&R-unique objectives	Improve the collaboration and the integration of the different development aid agencies.
Working through or around governments	Base strategy on circumstances, i.e., the governance quality and the governance capacity, as suggested in Table 7.2.
Strengthening government by building up patronage systems (bottom-up approach) versus strengthening central government (top-down approach)	In whichever approach is taken, build the credibility and the legitimacy of the government—e.g., encourage concrete actions observable by the population, balance aid between national and local powers, and promote accountability to the local population.
Imposing conditionalities or not; doing so in the interest of speed	Focus conditionalities on matters important to leaders rather than the population at large—e.g., exclude conditionality on humanitarian activities. Include institution-building in the conditions. Use conditionalities to improve the credibility of the government by improving information flows to local populations and increasing the transparency of government action.

generalizability is limited in a domain with such heterogeneity of circumstances. Sound empirical analysis also needs to be informed by understandable theoretical arguments, needs to include alternative perspectives, and would benefit from other forms of empirical information, such as detailed case studies and even the more anecdotal experiences of practitioners, to begin with. Without an adequate econometric design and such cross-methodology work and presentation of competing analyses, efforts to infer causal relationships and suggest strategies for policymakers should be regarded with suspicion.

Endnotes

[1]   In Iraq, funding for such physical projects has come from both the Department of Defense and the Department of State. The Economic Stabilization Fund (ESF) was used for both short-term stabilization and longer-term development programs at a rate of roughly $500 million–$1 billion per year.

[2]   Lancaster (2008) has studied patterns of U.S. bilateral aid in recent years and concludes that it has sometimes been used as a pure instrument of U.S. foreign policy—i.e., as an instrument for furthering perceived U.S. interests (hardly surprising or troubling). There is a good deal of additional literature that attempts to infer the effective agenda of the donor community and to note incongruities. Svensson (1999), for example, explains that historically the statistical impact of aid on growth has depended on the degree of civil and political liberties, but that aid is not allocated accordingly (i.e., to countries where success would be most likely). Chauvet (2002) looks at the relationship between aid allocation and "sociopolitical instabilities." Her findings suggest that elite instability (including coup d'etat, revolutions and major government crises) and violent instability (including political assassinations, guerilla warfare and civil wars) are correlated with increased aid—i.e., that aid flow is directed at governments that are under political threat. In contrast, social instability (including strikes, demonstrations and riots) is correlated with reduced aid, indicating that aid shies away from threats directed instead at the economy. Alesina and Dollar (2000) explain that political and strategic considerations play a much more important role than the economic conditions and policy performance of the recipient countries in the allocation of foreign aid. They conclude that history (e.g., ties from the colonial period) and strategic alliances are the main statistical determinants of the amount of aid received by poor countries. Fleck and Kilby (2006a) show that commercial relationships play an important part in determining the allocation of U.S. bilateral aid across countries. Fleck and Kilby (2006a, 2006b) extend their analysis and show that U.S. trading and political interests significantly influence the aid allocation of the World Bank, but caution that reverse causation between aid and trade may influence these findings—i.e. rather than trade interests causing aid, the provision of aid (or expectations of assistance) influences the level of trade between the recipient and donor country. Dreher, Sturm, and Vreeland (2009) also show with a panel study of 157 countries over the period 1970–2004 that a two-year membership in the UN Security Council correlates positively with the number of World Bank projects a country receives. They find these results to be robust even after controlling for the economic, political, and regional country characteristics.

[3]   Statistical tests have been conducted on many other factors that might be thought to be determinants of foreign-aid allocation. These have included supporting democracy (Svensson, 1999; Alesina and Dollar, 2000), fighting corruption (Alesina and Weder, 2002), and reducing undesirable immigration (Azam and Berlinschi, 2009). Arguably, such analysis to understand the de facto motivations of donor countries in foreign-aid allocation, whether for normal development aid or S&R, is needed to understanding the potential value of aid under different policies.

[4]   For more on this issue, see Easterly (2003).

[5]   Some exceptions include the board's decision to accord aid for Jordan, a critical country for U.S. interests in the Middle East, which failed many of the performance indicator tests and was opposed for approval by Freedom House and independent analysts. Another example is Bolivia, which qualified as eligible by all performance indicators but was denied eligibility due to deteriorating political relations with the United States (Tarnoff, 2009).

[6]   Some have raised concerns about the criteria used in the scoring process, such as the "ruling justly" category, which is based largely on opinion surveys (Jafari and Sud, 2004). Others have been concerned about the speed in which MCC operates. For example, Lancaster (2008) notes that the MCC has been extraordinarily slow in disbursing the sizable amount of funding appropriated to it, raising questions about the efficacy of this new model.

[7]   The inherent asymmetric information is due to the fact that it takes a significant amount of time to build the infrastructure needed for the provision of services and for those to have an effect on the citizen's welfare while in the meantime citizens are left with no reliable information as to the quality performance of the government.

[8]   The "problem of endogeneity" arises when the factors that are supposed to affect a particular outcome depend themselves on that outcome.

References

Alesina, Alberto, and David Dollar, "Who Gives Aid to Whom and Why?" *Journal of Economic Growth*, Vol. 5, No. 1, March 2000, pp. 33–63.

Alesina, Alberto, and Beatrice Weder, "Do Corrupt Governments Receive Less Foreign Aid?" *American Economic Review (Papers & Proceedings)*, Vol. 92, No. 4, 2002, pp. 1126–1137.

Azam, Jean-Paul, "How to Pay for the Peace? A Theoretical Framework with References to African Countries," *Public Choice*, Vol. 83, Nos. 1–2, 1995, pp. 173–184.

———, "The Redistributive State and Conflicts in Africa," *Journal of Peace Research*, Vol. 38, No. 4, 2001, pp. 429–444.

———, "Macroeconomic Agenda for Fiscal Policy and Aid Effectiveness in Post-Conflict," Institut d'Économie Industrielle, Toulouse, France, IDEI Working Paper No. 539, 2008.

Azam, Jean-Paul, and Ruxanda Berlinschi, "The Aid Migration Trade-Off," Toulouse School of Economics, Toulouse, France, Working Paper No. 77, 2009.

Azam, Jean-Paul, and Alexandra Delacroix, "Aid and the Delegated Fight Against Terrorism," *Review of Development Economics*, Vol. 10, No. 2, 2006, pp. 330–344.

Azam, Jean-Paul, and Véronique Thelen, "The Roles of Foreign Aid and Education in the War on Terror," *Public Choice*, Vol. 135, Nos. 3–4, 2008, pp. 375–397.

———, "Foreign Aid vs. Military Intervention in the War on Terror," *Journal of Conflict Resolution*, Vol. 54, No. 2, 2010, pp. 237–261.

Benmelech, Efraim, Claude Berrebi, and Esteban F. Klor, "The Economic Cost of Harboring Terrorism," *Journal of Conflict Resolution*, Vol. 54, No. 2, 2010, pp. 331–353.

Boyce, James, "Post-Conflict Recovery: Resource Mobilization and Peacebuilding," University of Massachusetts, Amherst, Political Economy Research Institute Working Paper 159, February 2007.

Brown, K., B. Siddiqi, and M. Sessions, *US Development Aid and the Millennium Challenge Account: Emerging Trends in Appropriations*, Washington, D.C., Center for Global Development, 2007. As of April 11, 2011: http://www.cgdev.org/doc/MCA/USDev_Aid_MCA.pdf

Carbone, M. "The Millennium Challenge Account: A Marginal Revolution in US Foreign Aid Policy?" *Review of African Political Economy*, Vol. 31, No. 101, September 2004, pp. 536–542.

Chauvet, Lisa, "Socio-Political Instability and the Allocation of International Aid by Donors," *European Journal of Political Economy*, Vol. 19, 2002, pp. 33–59.

Clawson, Matthew M., "Economic Development Aid and Stabilization Aid in Post Conflict States: Contradicting or Reinforcing?" unpublished manuscript, UCLA, 2010a.

———, "The Millennium Challenge Corporation: Realizing Its Mission or Achieving Unintended Results?" unpublished manuscript, UCLA, 2010b.

Clinton, Hillary, testimony before the Senate Appropriations Subcommittee on State, Foreign Operations, and Related Programs, Washington, D.C., February 24, 2010. As of April 7, 2011: http://www.state.gov/secretary/rm/2010/02/137227.htm

Collier, Paul, and Anke Hoeffler, "Aid, Policy and Growth in Post-Conflict Societies," *European Economic Review*, Vol. 48, No. 5, 2004, pp. 1125–1145.

de Ree, Joppe D., and Eleonora Nillesen, "Aiding Violence or Peace? The Impact of Foreign Aid on Civil Conflict in Sub-Sahara Africa," *Journal of Development Economics*, Vol. 88, 2009, pp. 301–313.

Del Castillo, Graciana, *Rebuilding War-Torn States: The Challenge of Postconflict Economic Reconstruction*, New York: Oxford University Press, 2008.

Demekas, Dimitri G., Jimmy McHugh, and Theodora Kosma, "The Economics of Post Conflict Aid," International Monetary Fund, Washington, D.C., working paper, November 2002.

Dreher, Axel, "The Development and Implementation of IMF and World Bank Conditionality," Hamburg Institute of International Economics, discussion paper, 2002.

Dreher Axel, Jan-Egbert Sturm, and James Raymond Vreeland, "Development Aid and International Politics: Does Membership on the UN Security Council Influence World Bank Decisions?" *Journal of Development Economics*, Vol. 88, No. 1, 2009, pp. 1–17.

Dreher, Axel, Peter Nunnenkamp, and Hannes Öhler, "Why It Pays for Aid Recipients to Take Note of the Millennium Challenge Corporation: Other Donors Do!" Kiel Institute for the World Economy, Germany, IFW-Kiel Working Paper 1609, 2010.

Easterly, William, "Can Aid Buy Growth?" *Journal of Economic Perspectives*, Vol. 17, No. 3, 2003.

———, *The White Man's Burden. Why the West's Effort to Aid the Rest Have Done So Much Ill and So Little Good*, New York: Penguin Press, 2007.

Epstein, S. B., *Foreign Aid, National Strategy, and the Quadrennial Review*, Washington, D.C.: Congressional Research Service, 2010.

Fleck, Robert K., and Christopher Kilby, "How Do Political Changes Influence U.S. Bilateral Aid Allocation? Evidence from Panel Data," *Review of Development Economics*, Vol. 10. No. 2, 2006a, pp. 210–223.

———, "World Bank Independence: A Model and Statistical Analysis of U.S. Influence," *Review of Development Economics*, Vol. 10, No. 2, 2006b, pp. 224–240.

Françios, Monika, and Inder Sud, "Promoting Stability and Development in Fragile and Failed States," *Development Policy Review*, Vol. 24, No. 2, 2006, pp. 141–160.

Galula, David, *Counterinsurgency Warfare: Theory and Practice*, Westport, Conn.: Praeger, 1964.

Ghani, Ashraf, and Claire Lockhart, *Fixing Failed States: A Framework for Rebuilding a Fractured World*, New York: Oxford University Press, 2008.

Gootnick, David, *Millennium Challenge Corporation: Summary Fact Sheet for 11 Compacts Entered into Force*, Washington, D.C.: Government Accountability Office, GAO-08-1145R, 2008.

Hansen, Henrik, and Tarp, Finn, "Aid and Growth Regressions," *Journal of Development Economics*, Vol. 64, No. 2, 2001, pp. 547–570.

Hewko, John, *Millennium Challenge Corporation: Can the Experiment Survive?* Washington, D.C.: The Carnegie Institute, 2010.

Jafari, Sheherazade, and Inder K. Sud, "Performance-Based Foreign Assistance Through the Millennium Challenge Account: Sustained Economic Growth as the Objective Qualifying Criterion," *International Public Management Journal*, Vol. 7, No. 2, 2004, pp. 249–270.

Johnson, Doug, and Trustan Zajonc, "Can Foreign Aid Create an Incentive for Good Governance? Evidence from the Millennium Challenge Corporation," working paper, 2007.

Kang, Seonjou, and James Meernik, "Determinants of Post-Conflict Economic Assistance," *Peace Research*, Vol. 41, No. 2, 2004, pp. 149–167.

Keefer, Philip, *Foreign Assistance and the Political Economy of Post-Conflict Countries*, New York, World Bank, 2008.

Keefer, Philip, and Stuti Khemani, "Democracy, Public Expenditures, and the Poor: Understanding Political Incentives for Providing Public Services," *World Bank Research Observer*, Vol. 20, No. 1, 2005, pp. 1–27.

Lancaster, Carol, *George Bush's Foreign Aid: Transformation or Chaos?* Washington, D.C.: Center for Global Development, 2008.

Mawdsley, Emma, "The Millennium Challenge Account: Neo-Liberalism, Poverty, and Security," *Review of International Political Economy*, Vol. 14, No. 3, August 2007, pp. 487–509.

MCC—*See* Millennium Challenge Corporation.

McGillivray, Mark, and Simon Feeny, "Aid and Growth in Fragile States," United Nations University–World Institute for Development Economics Research, Helsinki, Research Paper No. 2008/3, 2008.

Millennium Challenge Corporation, *The "MCC Effect": Creating Incentives for Policy Reform; Promoting an Environment for Poverty Reduction*, Washington, D.C.: The Millennium Challenge Corporation, 2007.

Mlambo, M. K., A. B. Kamara, and M. Nyende, "Financing Post-Conflict Recovery in Africa: The Role of International Development Assistance," *Journal of African Economies*. Vol. 18, 2009, pp. i53-i76.

Morrison, J. Stephen, and Kathleen Hicks, *Integrating 21st Century Development and Security Assistance*, Washington, D.C.: Center for Strategic and International Studies, 2008.

Myerson, Roger B., "A Short Overview of the Fundamentals of State-Building," Center of Capitalism and Society, Columbia University, New York, Working Paper No. 44, 2009.

———, "Rethinking the Fundamentals of State-Building," *PRISM*, Vol. 2, No. 2, March 2011, pp. 91–100.

Oxfam America, *Smart Development: Why US Foreign Aid Demands Major Reform*, Boston, 2008.

Radelet, S., *Challenging Foreign Aid: A Policymaker's Guide to the Millennium Challenge Account*, Washington, D.C.: Center for Global Development, May 2003, pp. 1–3.

Suhrke, Astri, and Julia Buckmaster, "Post-War Aid: Patterns and Purposes," *Development in Practice*, Vol. 15, No. 6, 2005, pp. 737–747.

Suhrke, Astri, Espen Villanger, and Susan L. Woodward, "Economic Aid to Post-Conflict Countries: A Methodological Critique of Collier and Hoeffler," Chr. Michelsen Institute, Bergen, Norway, Working Paper 2005:4, 2005.

Svensson, J., "Aid, Growth and Democracy," *Economics and Politics*, Vol. 11, No. 3, 1999, pp. 275–297.

Tarnoff, Curt, *Millennium Challenge Corporation,* Washington, D.C.: Congressional Research Service, June 2009.

Tarnoff, Curt, and Larry Nowels, *Foreign Aid: An Introductory Overview of U.S. Programs and Policy*, Washington, D.C.: Congressional Research Service, 2004.

Tarnoff, Curt, and Marion Leonardo Lawson, *Foreign Aid: An Introduction to U.S. Programs and Policy*, Washington, D.C.: Congressional Research Service, 2009.

United Nations Development Programme, *Post-Conflict Economic Recovery: Enabling Local Ingenuity*, New York, 2007.

World Bank, *Breaking the Conflict Trap: Civil War and Development Policy*, Washington, D.C., 2003a.

———, "Social Development Notes, Conflict Prevention and Reconstruction," No. 14, December 2003b.

———, *Conditionality Revised: Concepts, Experiences and Lessons*, New York, 2005.

Zoellick, B. Robert, "Fragile States Securing Development," *Global Politics and Strategy*, Vol. 50, No. 6, 2008, pp. 67–84.

CHAPTER EIGHT

Final Observations

Paul K. Davis

The starting point for any student of stabilization and reconstruction (S&R) should be humility, since history tells us that many civil wars have come to a halt only to be reignited later (not necessarily with the same actors). Avoiding the resumption of hostilities is a considerable challenge; maintaining peace and achieving a good measure of nation-building is all the more so. That said, the challenge is by no means hopeless, and degrees of success have been achieved historically. This short, concluding chapter comments briefly on some of the contributions that we sought to make in the study, some higher-level cross-cutting conclusions, some conclusions about analytic methods, and suggestions for future research and analysis. The monograph's executive summary is a more comprehensive review of the whole document.

What We Have Tried to Do

Our study was a step toward using the social-science base to work toward a humble *system theory* for S&R: a theory intended to assist understanding, diagnosis, discussion, and strategy-setting under uncertainty. Accurate, precise, and reliable predictions are not in the cards for most S&R situations, but informed and structured reasoning can be.

As discussed in Chapter One, at the top level of our description we identify security, political, social, and economic components. We discussed each of these separately, which is certainly feasible and fruitful, but we also consistently discussed their interactions, including the idea that the failure of any of these components can doom S&R as a whole. Analytically, this approach was different from treating factors as though they were independent (as, e.g., in linear modeling) and from versions of systems modeling in which such interactions as feedback loops are so heavily emphasized as to depict everything as constantly connected to everything else, with the result being difficult to comprehend and discuss.[1] We have instead summarized social-science constructs using a combination of both static "snapshots" in the form of factor trees and other influence diagrams depicting dynamic interactions over time.

A theme of our study turned out to be the ubiquitous presence of both uncertainties and dilemmas—some of them real and some of them merely apparent. We sought, with varying success, to suggest how the dilemmas can either be resolved (e.g., with more discriminating situational assessment and recognition of different time scales) or at least be better understood and discussed when developing strategy.

Another unsettling aspect of S&R is that the challenge often involves what theorists call "wicked problems"[2] For these, the problem itself is not tightly defined, and, thus, there is no straightforward solution to be found by logic alone. The *process* of addressing the issues with the multiple stakeholders may allow a solution to "emerge" in that, at some point, stakeholders may find themselves adequately satisfied with a set of arrangements. However, those arrangements may not have been preordained but rather the result of events, personalities, compromises, and opportunities along the way. Students of political and social history will not find this surprising, but it has deep implications for strategy and supporting analysis, as discussed below.

In confronting the dilemmas, we addressed a number of sensitive issues candidly, such as issues relating to the potentially contradictory influences of increased security efforts (Chapter Two); regime type, partitioning, and centralization (Chapters Three and Four); and "political" considerations in S&R economics (Chapters Six and Seven). Rather than attempting to identify the "best" among contending "mini-theories," we have sought unifying depictions within which the different mini-theories can be seen as playing roles.

While conveying the literature's emphasis on context dependence, we attempted to give that concept more concrete meaning by identifying different "cases." In some instances (as in the economics chapters), this helped to resolve what may seem to be dilemmas but are better described as tensions to be dealt with by mixed strategies recognizing multiple simultaneous objectives. In some cases, the tension can be resolved by accepting an uncomfortable reality, such as that postwar economics is fundamentally different from normal development economics and is appropriately tied closely to politics.[3]

Another unusual facet of our study was devoting an entire chapter to the social component of S&R (Chapter Five), a subject often given short shrift because the issues are inherently "soft and squishy" and not amenable to technical solutions. We focused on the trust-and-cooperation aspects of S&R because those appear to be critical to its success. Fortunately, much is known about how to foster at least modest degrees of trust and cooperation.

As discussed below, our study had a number of broad observations mirroring those of an earlier RAND study (Dobbins et al., 2007) and more-specific conclusions related to strategy formulation, decision support, and analytic methods.

Broad Observations

The social science on which we drew is not yet mature. From a historical perspective, it is in some ways still in its infancy. No one should expect to find clear-cut laws and formulas, whether for forecasting, diagnosing situations, or prescribing details of strategy. Nonetheless, there are some broad observations.

First, failures in S&R are most commonly associated with resource-objective mismatches: Intervenors may set objectives that exceed the resources they are willing to allocate and sustain. Objectives, then, should be set realistically. One appropriately restrained suggestion on this matter is as follows:

The objective of S&R should be to leave behind a society likely to remain at peace with itself and its neighbors once external security forces are removed and full sovereignty is restored . . . and to expect that the nation will do at least as well as others "in the neighborhood."*

Second, foreign forces can help stabilize a situation but can also become destabilizing as resentment to their presence grows. The identity and character of the forces matters greatly. There is good evidence that, despite unevenness in quality, UN efforts have had the best combination of low cost, success rate, and internal legitimacy (Doyle and Sambanis, 2006). They are not, of course, suitable for large-scale efforts, much less for invasions to achieve regime change.

Third, success is very difficult if neighboring states are committed to frustrating the S&R effort. Thus, such states must be engaged diplomatically, hopefully to become part of the solution.

Fourth, "seizing the moment" early is often important: Steps taken early in S&R operations can not only be effective in initial stabilization, but also set patterns and attitudes affecting subsequent possibilities (Dobbins et al., 2007).

As another broad observation, it is commonly asserted that S&R activities should be increasingly taken over by civilian agencies and operations. However, when a long view is taken historically, military forces have usually done the lion's share of work in past activities of this nature. It is important to distinguish between having civilian expertise and guidance in political, social, and economic domains and having the manpower to accomplish the related tasks. Military forces can and have provided much of the manpower. Further, if the environment remains dangerous, the bulk of activities may need to be conducted by military forces (Moore, 2010).

---

* Paraphrased from comments of Ambassador James Dobbins in a project conference with academic experts, September 2008.

Strategies and Decision Support for Strategy-Making

A recurrent theme in our study was recognizing that, because of uncertainties, dilemmas, and wicked problems, S&R strategies often need to be tentative, well hedged, and adaptive. Such characteristics are arguably features of good strategy generally, but they are especially important in S&R. This said, adaptations are often difficult to make unless the need to do so has been anticipated and preparations laid, and unless higher authorities (and even the public) understand the philosophy of "experimenting" with approaches, monitoring progress, and shifting course as necessary. Although not much discussed in our monograph, a good deal is known from the planning literature about how to prepare for adaptiveness. This includes, during strategy formulation and implementation,

- applying the methods of uncertainty-sensitivity planning, which includes planning "branches and sequels" and also providing capabilities to permit at-the-time adaptation in response to shocks (Davis, 2002, 2003a, 2003b).
- identifying critical assumptions that underlie the strategy but may prove to be invalid (Dewar, 2003).
- identifying "signposts" of failure of those assumptions, so that the need for adaptations can be flagged when they appear.
- implementing associated monitoring, with related data collection and analysis, even if there is resistance to doing so (as there may be for fear that some of the inevitable failures will be criticized).
- defining metrics and analysis methods that reflect a system view (Davis et al., 2010) and dynamics, such as lag times, so as not to misdiagnose developments. At least rudimentary dynamic models are needed, as has long been taught in business planning (Sterman, 2000) and practiced in capabilities-based planning (Davis et al., 2010).

All of this also has implications for decision support and related analysis. Such analysis should, for example, (1) develop options that hedge in various ways, (2) show option assessments against multiple criteria so that tensions and dilemmas are visible, (3) include as criteria risks and the feasibility of subsequent adaptations, and (4) promote and facilitate hedging and anticipation of possible adaptation. This approach is very different from, e.g., seeking to inform the decision-maker as to what option is "optimal" by a dominant criterion and a set of best-estimate assumptions.

Analytic Methods

Although fragmented, the theoretical literature suggests numerous "risk factors," influences, and structures for thinking seriously about S&R. We have sought to reflect those in the current study.* Although the empirical literature has not converged in assessing the diverse hypotheses, the competing studies and debates have greatly sharpened the issues, as when noting that a previously identified risk factor was too aggregated and failed to distinguish between importantly different kinds of situations. The "risk-factor" nature of much empirical work also provides important cautionaries for planners (e.g., the often-cited observation that success in stabilization has usually required large numbers of "boots on the ground" and that success is strongly associated with a population-centric approach).

Some critical observations about analytic methods are appropriate, especially because misunderstandings exist about what should be expected from social-science research and what constitutes more and less "rigorous" evidence. The term *evidence-based research*, which has recently been advocated for S&R related issues, has a connotation associated with statistical analysis of controlled trials, as in large-scale tests

---

*Although the literature we reviewed largely emphasizes risk factors, recent work by the State Department's Office of the Coordinator for Reconstruction and Stabilization (S/CRS) has importantly emphasized looking for resiliency factors and processes. We strongly endorse that view, which is well supported by segments of the social-science literature. See the Interagency Conflict Assessment Framework (ICAF) framework (United States Institute of Peace and United States Army Peacekeeping and Stability Operations Institute, 2009) and the State Department's list of web links to relevant current reports (Department of State, no date).

of medicines. That type of evidence, however, has little to do with evidence to inform S&R strategy and policy.[4]

Empirical evidence comes in many forms, including anecdotal accounts, somewhat more structured testimony of practitioners, case histories, and quantitative data analysis. It is sometimes assumed that the latter is more "rigorous" and "scientific," but the reality for S&R is different. As discussed in earlier chapters, very few findings have held up well across studies. This is due largely to fundamental problems in data. Researchers have depended on historical data from civil wars. Problems have also arisen from overly simple models (e.g., linear models rather than system models), over-aggregation, failures to test routinely for robustness, and shortcomings of the data itself. The data are not in any sense the result of controlled experiments, but rather usually the result of pooling data from the diverse wars that have occurred (mostly in the last half of the 20th century); there is no particular reason to believe that the aggregate statistics from such heterogeneous cases inform us about what will happen in the next case—especially given the repeated insistence by researchers doing in-depth work that context-specific factors and events have been crucial in individual cases.

Excellent and constructive critiques have arisen within the social-science community itself (Sambanis, 2004; Kalyvas, Shapiro, and Masoud, 2008). Kalvyas, Shapiro, and Masoud state:

> the problems of econometric studies are well known: their main findings are incredibly sensitive to coding and measurement procedures (Hegre and Sambanis, 2006…); they entail a considerable distance between theoretical constructs and proxies . . . as well as multiple observationally equivalent pathways; they suffer from endogeneity . . . ; they lack clear microfoundations or are based on erroneous ones . . . ; and, finally, they are subject to narrow (and untheorized) scope conditions.

The Sambanis study cited above is a convincing, in-depth but accessible discussion of both the problems and ways to address them, one urging research that draws heavily on case-study research to supplement the more usual aggregate-level historical data.

Sambanis (2004), Kalyvas, Shapiro, and Masoud (2008), and others recommend more "micro" studies in which individual countries are studied at higher resolution, perhaps distinguishing among multiple phases and areas of conflict and accounting for special influences known to be important in the cases studied. As an example of what this entails, a recent paper examines empirical evidence on the second Chechen war, drawing conclusions about the relative effectiveness of Russian-only and Russian-Chechen operations in counterinsurgency (Lyall, 2010).

Another very positive development, one illustrating how science proceeds with competitive studies, debate, and responses, is that recent quantitative research on civil wars has included more robustness analysis (Collier, Hoeffler, and Rohner, 2009; Goldstone et al., 2010). Perhaps that will become routine as the field develops.

Although we did not discuss the subject except in passing in the current study, another fruitful area of analytic modeling needs to be mentioned: forecasting models that combine aspects of agent-based rational-choice decisionmaking. In circumstances in which a number of political factions are competing for influence, the factions change their positions along various dimensions as they seek allies to improve their relative power. A substantial amount of research has gone into studying the related dynamics, which have been shown to have considerable predictive power. They can be employed with "moderate" data requirements (a good deal of expert judgment).[*] Further, substantial advances have been made in very recent times, including work by RAND colleague Ben Wise (unpublished) that extends the range of circumstances for which the models can be used.

---

[*] The seminal work in this field was done by Bruce Bueno de Mesquita (see Bueno de Mesquita 1981, 2009). Variants of the approach are embedded in related models, such as the Sentia Group's Senturion (see Abdollahian et al., 2006). See Larson et al., 2009, for discussion of the class of such models.

Future Research

A great deal of additional research is needed on S&R, at all levels of detail. As suggested by the above discussion, however, we see special value in case histories and "micro dynamics" analysis that draws on contextually rich information as well as the methods of econometrics. We also urge an increased emphasis on theory-informed analysis in which, e.g., known interactions are built in from the beginning (as suggested in Chapter One) rather than added piecemeal and grudgingly, as is common in statistical analysis dominated by data-driven philosophies.

Especially important, we see the need to develop new methods of analysis and strategic decision support for S&R, methods aligned with the concepts of multiple objectives, tensions, dilemmas, hedging, and adaptations. To be most useful, these should depend on *simple* models and data that can actually be obtained or estimated. As discussed in Chapter Two, subjectively based estimates are appropriate in some cases, but they need to be elicited within a sound structure so that experts understand the implications of questions and are assisted in making distinctions known to be important.

Finally, we believe that a fresh approach is needed in defining S&R measures and approximate metrics,[5] one that (1) reflects the results of this study and future research that also takes a causal system-model perspective rather than a correlational perspective and (2) incorporates both static and dynamic views of the S&R process. Such work should be approached from a whole-of-government perspective and, indeed, should be approached with the assumption that multiple governments are involved. Use of metrics has a long history, much of it dismal because of organizations having used metrics that lacked grounding in sound theory and that led, as a result, to misleading assessments and counterproductive incentives. Something much better is needed for S&R because the stakes are high.

Endnotes

[1] One can be a strong supporter of basic precepts in *System Dynamics*, as promulgated a half-century ago by the Massachusetts Institute of Technology's Jay Forrester (1961) and described in a more recent textbook by John Sterman (2000), while also recognizing that complex systems are usually "nearly decomposable" in the sense discussed by Herbert Simon (1981): The components of such systems can be distinguished and studied more or less separately to great benefit, but a full understanding of the system requires treating the interactions as well. These, however, may be separable by recognizing, e.g., that some interactions are weak, that some operate over longer time scales, and that still others can be described in low-resolution terms. Recognizing that is also important in multiresolution modeling, which has myriad benefits for analysis (Davis, 2003b; Davis and Bigelow, 2003) and strategic planning (Davis, 2002).

[2] See also a recent paper (Menkhaus, 2010); a somewhat older paper by Horst Rittel, who introduced the concept (Rittel and Noble, 1988); and Roberts (2009).

[3] See especially Chapter Five and the work of Roger Myerson (2008).

[4] Such matters were discussed at USAID's "Evidence Summit," September 7–9, 2010.

[5] Substantial interagency work has already been accomplished on S&R-related metrics, much of which appears to be quite useful (Agoglia, Dziedzic, and Sotirin, 2010). However, the approach we suggest would be different in important respects.

References

Abdollahian, Mark, Michael Baranick, Brian Efird, and Jackek Kugler, *Senturion: A Predictive Political Simulation Model*, Washington, D.C.: National Defense University, 2006.

Agoglia, John, Michael Dziedzic, and Barbara Sotirin, eds., *Measuring Progress in Conflict Environments (MPICE): A Metrics Framework*, Washington, D.C.: U.S. Institute of Peace Press, 2010.

Bueno de Mesquita, Bruce, *The War Trap*, New Haven, Conn.: Yale University Press, 1981.

———, *The Predictioneer's Game*, New York: Random House, 2009.

Collier, Paul, Anke Hoeffler, and Dominic Rohner, "Beyond Greed and Grievance: Feasibility and Civil War," *Oxford Economic Papers*, Vol. 61, 2009, pp. 1–27.

Davis, Paul K., *Analytic Architecture for Capabilities-Based Planning, Mission-System Analysis, and Transformation*, Santa Monica, Calif.: RAND Corporation, 2002. As of April 11, 2011:
http://www.rand.org/pubs/monograph_reports/MR1513.html

———, "Uncertainty-Sensitive Planning," in Stuart Johnson, Martin Libicki, and Gregory Treverton, eds., *New Challenges, New Tools for Defense Decisionmaking*, Santa Monica, Calif.: RAND Corporation, 2003a, pp. 131–155. As of April 11, 2011:
http://www.rand.org/pubs/monograph_reports/MR1576.html

———, "Exploratory Analysis and Implications for Modeling," in *New Challenges, New Tools for Defense Decisionmaking*, in Stuart Johnson, Martin Libicki, and Gregory Treverton, eds., Santa Monica, Calif.: RAND Corporation, 2003b, pp. 255–283. As of April 11, 2011:
http://www.rand.org/pubs/monograph_reports/MR1576.html

Davis, Paul K, and James H. Bigelow, *Motivated Metamodels: Synthesis of Cause-Effect Reasoning and Statistical Metamodeling*, Santa Monica, Calif.: RAND Corporation, 2003. As of April 11, 2011:
http://www.rand.org/pubs/monograph_reports/MR1570.html

Davis, Paul K., Stuart E. Johnson, Duncan Long, and David C. Gompert, *Developing Resource-Informed Strategic Assessments and Recommendations*, Santa Monica, Calif.: RAND Corporation, 2008. As of April 11, 2011:
http://www.rand.org/pubs/monographs/MG703.html

Davis, Paul K., Richard Hillestad, Duncan Long, Paul Dreyer, and Brandon Dues, *Reflecting Warfighter Needs in Air Force Programs: A Prototype Analysis*, Santa Monica, Calif.: RAND Corporation, 2010. As of April 11, 2011:
http://www.rand.org/pubs/technical_reports/TR754.html

Department of State, "What We Do," web page, no date. As of April 19, 2011:
http://www.state.gov/s/crs/what/index.htm

Dewar, James, *Assumption-Based Planning: A Tool for Reducing Avoidable Surprises*, New York: Cambridge University Press, 2003.

Dobbins, James, Seth G. Jones, Keith Crane, and Beth Cole DeGrasse, *The Beginner's Guide to Nation-Building*, Santa Monica, Calif.: RAND Corporation, 2007. As of April 7, 2011:
http://www.rand.org/pubs/monographs/MG557.html

Doyle, Michael W., and Nicholas Sambanis, *Making War and Building Peace: United Nations Peace Operations*, Princeton, N.J.: Princeton University Press, 2006.

Forrester, Jay W., *Industrial Dynamics*, New York: Productivity Press, 1961.

Goldstone, Jack A., Robert H. Bates, David L. Epstein, Ted Robert Gurr, Michael B. Lustik, Monty G. Marshall, Jay Ulfelder, and Mark Woodward, "A Global Model for Forcasting Political Instability," *American Journal of Political Science*, Vol. 54, No. 1, January 2010, pp. 190–208.

Hegre, Håvard, and Nicholas Sambanis, "Sensitivity Analysis of Empirical Results on Civil War Onset," *Journal of Conflict Resolution*, Vol. 50, 2006, pp. 508–535.

Kalyvas, Stathis N., Ian Shapiro, and Rakek Masoud, eds., *Promises and Pitfalls of an Emerging Research Program: The Microdynamics of Civil War*, New York: Cambridge University Press, 2008.

Larson, Eric V., Richard E. Darilek, Daniel Gibran, Brian Nichiporuk, Amy Richardson, Lowell H. Schwartz, and Cathryn Quantic Thurston, *Foundations of Effective Influence Operations: A Framework for Enhancing Army Capabilities*, Santa Monica, Calif.: RAND Corporation, 2009. As of April 8, 2011: http://www.rand.org/pubs/monographs/MG654.html

Lyall, Jason, "Are Coethnics More Effective Counterinsurgents? Evidence from the Second Chechen War," *American Political Science Review*, Vol. 104, 2010.

Menkhaus, Kenneth J., "State Fragility as a Wicked Problem," *PRISM*, Vol. 1, 2010, 85–100.

Moore, R. Scott, "Complex Operations: The Civ-Mil Dilemma," National Defense University, Center for Complex Operations, Washington, D.C., 2010.

Myerson, Roger B., "A Short Overview of the Fundamentals of State-Building," Columbia University, Center on Capitalism and Society, New York, Working Paper No. 44, 2008.

Rittel, Horst, and Douglas Noble, "Issue-Based Information Systems for Design," Institute of Urban and Regional Development, University of California, Berkeley, Working Paper 492, 1988.

Roberts, Nancy C., "Coping with Wicked Problems: The Case of Afghanistan," in Lawrence R. Jones, J. Guthrie, and P. Steane, eds., *Learning from International Public Management Reform, Vol. II*, Amsterdam: JAI Press, 2009, pp. 353–375.

Sambanis, Nicholas, "Using Case Studies to Expand Economic Models of Civil War," *Perspectives on Politics*, Vol. 2, 2004, pp. 259–278.

Simon, Herbert, *Sciences of the Artificial, 2nd Edition*, Cambridge, Mass.: MIT Press, 1981.

Sterman, John D., *Business Dynamics: Systems Thinking and Modeling for a Complex World*, Boston: McGraw-Hill/Irwin, 2000.

United States Institute of Peace and United States Army Peacekeeping and Stability Operations Institute, *Guiding Principles for Stabilization and Reconstruction*, Washington, D.C., 2009.

Wise, Ben P., "A Generalization of the Median Voter Theorem, with Applications," unpublished RAND research (2011 documentation of the RAND Compass model).

MR 3 0 '12